ACCIDENTAL TYRANT

FYODOR TERTITSKIY

Accidental Tyrant

The Life of Kim Il-sung

OXFORD
UNIVERSITY PRESS

OXFORD
UNIVERSITY PRESS

Oxford University Press is a department of the
University of Oxford. It furthers the University's objective
of excellence in research, scholarship, and education
by publishing worldwide.

Oxford New York

Auckland   Cape Town   Dar es Salaam   Hong Kong   Karachi
Kuala Lumpur   Madrid   Melbourne   Mexico City   Nairobi
New Delhi   Shanghai   Taipei   Toronto

With offices in

Argentina   Austria   Brazil   Chile   Czech Republic   France   Greece
Guatemala   Hungary   Italy   Japan   Poland   Portugal   Singapore
South Korea   Switzerland   Thailand   Turkey   Ukraine   Vietnam

Oxford is a registered trade mark of Oxford University Press
in the UK and certain other countries.

Published in the United States of America by
Oxford University Press
198 Madison Avenue, New York, NY 10016

Library of Congress Cataloging-in-Publication Data is available

ISBN: 9780197800881

Printed in the United Kingdom
by Bell and Bain Ltd, Glasgow

CONTENTS

PART III
UNDER THE RED SUN

ACKNOWLEDGEMENTS

I would first like to thank my father, Konstantin Tertitski, on whose help and advice I could always rely during my research on North Korea, as well as my mother Marina Filipenko and sister Anna Tertitskaya. Special thanks go to my colleague Natalia Matveeva, who inspired me to write this book; her remarkable insight into North Korean economic history was most helpful. Andrei Lankov's writings were what brought me to North Korean studies, and he has always provided his kind assistance, help and advice, both with this book and many other projects. Peter Ward has remained my closest friend for more than a decade, and his recommendations greatly improved the manuscript. Peter's continuous support was instrumental in the writing of this book. The Korean author of the blog botw.egloos. com provided immense help, especially with the first part of the book; he has asked not to be identified by his real name, and I honour this request. His skill in finding historical sources is truly unparalleled.

Chapter 6—the one dealing with the Korean War—greatly benefitted from the advice of Sheila Miyoshi Jager, one of the world's leading specialists on the conflict, and her husband Jiyul Kim, a historian and retired colonel of the US Army. Pak

ACKNOWLEDGEMENTS

Haeng-ung kindly read the entire manuscript; his advice was most valuable.

Peter Sylvestre was the first editor of my draft, meticulously correcting my non-native writing. He was a far better copy-editor than I could ever hope for. All the remaining mistakes, are, of course, my sole responsibility.

I would like to extend my heartfelt gratitude to Ed Pulford for his invaluable recommendation that I submit this manuscript to Hurst. I am also deeply appreciative of Hurst's managing director, Michael Dwyer, for graciously accepting my submission. Their support and guidance have been instrumental in bringing this book to fruition. I would like to express my special thanks to Alice Clarke, the book's managing editor, for all the days she spent working on the manuscript and her diligent and meticulous work. I would also like to thank Niamh Drennan, Daisy Leitch, Kathleen May, Tim Page, Lara Weisweiller-Wu and Jess Winstanley. Without the dedication and expertise of the Hurst team, the book you are holding in your hands would never have come to be.

Those who provided unique testimonies about the North include Yuriy Kang, who lived close to Kim Il-sung's house in North Korea in the 1940s; Dmitriy Kapustin, who served in the Soviet embassy in the North in the late 1960s; Adrian Buzo, whose diplomatic tenure in the Australian embassy in North Korea came a decade later; Anton Bebler, who was a member of the team preparing Kim Il-sung's visit to Yugoslavia in 1975; An Chan-il, who fled North Korea in 1979; and Kim Yong-hwan, who met Kim Il-sung in 1991. I am deeply grateful to them for their valuable interviews.

I also would like to express my deep gratitude to Rose Adams, Cheong Seong-chang, Choe Hyon-jun, Vladimir Dorohov, Tatyana Fyodorova, Anastasiia Goi, Christopher Green, Nick Holt, Boris Kantorovich, Ki Kwang-so, Kim Son-yong, Anastasiya

ACKNOWLEDGEMENTS

Korolyova, Taisiya Lapteva, Lee Dong-hun, Lee Mi-yon, Owen Miller, Brian Myers, Oliver Hotham, Pak Chang-phyo, Igor Selivanov, Elizaveta Semyonova, Alek Sigley, Balázs Szalontai, Yeo Hyunjun and Aida Zujo.

Of the archives I visited while writing this book, the archive of the National Institute of Korean History and the Russian State Archive for Contemporary History were by far the most pleasant places to do research, and I would like to thank their staff for their assistance.

A NOTE ON ROMANISATION

Unlike, say, Japanese studies, where the Hepburn transliteration system is universally accepted, or Chinese, where Hanyu Pinyin is the predominant system of transliteration, there is no consensus on Romanisation in Korean studies. The two dominant systems are McCune–Reischauer transliteration, invented by American scholars George McCune and Edwin Reischauer in 1937, and the Revised Romanisation, which has been promoted by the South Korean government since 2000.

There are issues with both systems. The McCune–Reischauer system is useful in reflecting the actual pronunciation of Korean words, but it uses an abundance of diacritical marks, leading to spellings like Ch'ŏngju. Revised Romanisation does not use diacritical marks, but the way it prescribes writing words strays too far from the original. The Korean name for the famous Turtle ship invented in the sixteenth century, for example, is spelt *geobukseon*, while the Korean pronunciation is [kʌbuksən].

I have opted for a compromise occasionally resorted to by other academics. In the main text of the book, the simplified version of McCune–Reischauer without diacritical marks is used. As the references will probably be of interest to readers who are either academics or take a particularly deep interest in

Korea, I use the original McCune–Reischauer with diacritics in the endnotes. Names of well-known Koreans, such as the main character of the book and South Korean presidents, are given according to common usage.

There are two rival approaches in the English-language academic tradition when it comes to foreign terms. One is to transliterate them—for example, the People's Commissariat for Internal Affairs, the Soviet secret police, is far more frequently abbreviated from its Russian name as NKVD rather than 'PCIA', but Mao's Red Guards are very rarely called *hongweibing*.

I believe the second approach—translating foreign terms—is more helpful. Translating foreign terms not only allows their meaning to be explained; it actually conveys the same feeling people in these nations have when they see them in their own languages. Thus, in this book, North Korean terms will be translated, not transliterated—i.e., it is 'origins', not *chulsin-songbun*, 're-education centre', not *kyohwaso*, 'Heavenly Way', not Chondogyo. The exception to this is the name of the state ideology—Juche—since, as you will learn from the book, this term is now as meaningless in Korean as it is in English.

There are two terms for which I have chosen a different translation from the traditional one. The first is a title for Kim Il-sung's son, Kim Jong-il. The traditional translation is 'Party Centre', which I instead translate as 'Party Central'. This expression was an abbreviated form of the sobriquet 'Party Central Committee', and the revised translation allows for a more accurate reflection of this nuance.

The second is the name for Kim Il-sung's version of totalitarianism, which he proclaimed in 1967. This term—*yuil sasang chegye* in Korean—is usually translated as 'Monolithic Ideological System'. This is a mistranslation, as the Korean word *yuil* does not mean 'monolithic' but rather 'one and only', and the word *sasang* has a broader meaning than just 'ideology'.

To reflect this, I have instead translated the term as 'Singular Thought System'.

Finally, unless specifically stated otherwise, the author has preserved the original name order of Asian individuals—surname first, given name second.

LIST OF ILLUSTRATIONS

1. South Pyongan province, where Kim Il-sung was born, in the 1910s.

2. Shang Yue, Kim Il-sung's middle school teacher.

3. Major-General Nozoe Masanori, commander of the anti-partisan liquidation unit.

4. Han Song-hui, an anti-Japanese partisan and Kim Il-sung's first wife.

5. Anti-Japanese partisans in Manchuria, 1939.

6. Former partisans in the Soviet Union.

7. General Iosif Apanasenko, commander of the Soviet Far Eastern Front.

8. Captain Kim Il-sung in the Eighty-Eighth Brigade.

9. The *Emelian Pugachev*, the ship that brought Kim Il-sung back to Korea after World War Two.

10. Demonstration in Pyongyang in honour of the Red Army, 14 October 1945.

LIST OF ILLUSTRATIONS

INTRODUCTION

THE IMPROBABLE DYNASTY

North Korea is a nation so closed it defies comprehension. The country possesses its own heavily censored version of the Internet, and the count of all North Koreans who have ever accessed the genuine World Wide Web is so minuscule they would likely fit inside a train carriage. Most information, including basic economic statistics, is classified. Watching a foreign soap opera or listening to a K-pop song is considered a criminal offence, subject to punishment by years of forced labour.

You are holding a book about the man who constructed that nation and established its system—his name is Kim Il-sung, the founding figure of a family dynasty that has maintained control over North Korea ever since. Kim Il-sung ascended to power in 1945, shortly after the end of the Second World War. He was succeeded by his son, Kim Jong-il, in 1994; he, in turn, was succeeded by his son, Kim Jong-un, in 2011. No other family has managed to govern a country for three successive generations without formally being a monarchy.

Many readers are likely to have at least some familiarity with North Korea. The regime has excelled in advancing its weapons technology—if it so desires, it reportedly possesses the capability to launch a nuclear strike on cities as distant as Los Angeles and Melbourne. The regime's nuclear and missile programmes are frequently discussed in international media, and all efforts to dissuade Pyongyang from advancing these programmes have, thus far, yielded no tangible results.

Although the nuclear threat to the Western world remains hypothetical, the suffering of the population living under the Kim family's rule is an undeniable reality. This fate was moulded by the dynasty's progenitor, Kim Il-sung, whose impact continues to cast a shadow over the nation long since his demise.

In certain respects, North Korea has changed since 1994, the year of Kim's death—the country's economy, for instance, has shifted considerably closer to a market-oriented system than during the Kim Il-sung era. However, in most other areas, North Korea remains essentially unchanged.

If you are a North Korean citizen, you are strictly prohibited from reading any book that hasn't received state approval, and accessing the World Wide Web is only possible with authorisation from the Leader himself. Engaging in a phone conversation with a foreign friend can lead to punishments more severe than those for armed robbery. Within your residence, portraits of the Leaders will be prominently displayed as a constant reminder of their authority; defacing them is punishable by death. At best, you might be able to venture to the Chinese border to catch a glimpse of a markedly different style of life on the other side. This entire system was constructed by Kim Il-sung.

Several generations have come and gone since the start of Kim Il-sung's rise to power in 1945. But the overwhelming majority of North Koreans possess no memory of any existence apart from life under a Kim.

Only a few individuals have exerted as dramatic and enduring an influence on the history of their countries as Kim Il-sung. He, to a large extent, fulfilled Louis XIV's famous dictum: 'L'état, c'est moi'—'I am the state.'

Was this inevitable? Was North Korea's strategic, economic and social context bound to give rise to such an inhumane system? This book contends that it most certainly was not; nor was Kim Il-sung's ascension to power preordained. Only a sequence of improbable coincidences allowed him to leverage his political acumen and become and remain the unopposed leader of North Korea.

At the time of writing this book, North Korea remains closed, and there will undoubtedly be more to be said about Kim Il-sung when the regime reforms or collapses. However, no one knows when either will happen. For now, I have tried to combine the information about Kim Il-sung available from sources across the world—Korean, Soviet, Chinese, Japanese and others—and to sift through the unverified and frequently erroneous data that saturates the information landscape concerning this nation.

I hope this work will be an asset to the current generation of scholars and the general public alike, as well as being of some value to future historians as well. Whether this will ultimately be the case is for its readers to judge.

PART I

VICTORY IN DEFEAT

1

FROM KOREA TO MANCHURIA

At the beginning of the twentieth century, Korea was a backward and underdeveloped country. The main reason for its sorry state was Neo-Confucianism, a doctrine proclaiming that the ideal social order was that of China in the early first millennium BCE. This ideology was nearly Luddite in its rejection of technological and social progress; any country following it was doomed to stagnate and fail.

In 1910, the Japanese Empire formally annexed the Korean Peninsula. Ruled by Terauchi Masatake, the first governor-general to be appointed from Tokyo, what used to be a country had become a colony.

Japan and the governor-general saw the colony as many colonisers did at the time: a backward, uncivilised land that needed to be brought into the light of Japanese civilisation, as Japan was the only Eastern country that had been welcomed into the club of the great powers.

And this is what they did. After a few months of settling in, the new governor-general started to impose 'civilisation' with an iron hand, ignoring all protests. It should, however, be noted that many of the changes he implemented were eventually accepted by Korean society. Terauchi abolished the old Confucian education system, replacing it with a modern one. He also introduced and enforced public hygiene in Korean cities and villages; life expectancy started to rise.

On Monday, 15 April 1912, a year and a half since the annexation and the day forever remembered as the date the *Titanic* sank, another subject of the Japanese emperor was born. The child was called Kim Song-ju. His home was the small settlement of Chilgol,[1] literally, 'seventh valley'.[2] Although administratively part of Pyongyang, Korea's second largest city, Chilgol was just a small village of thatched roof houses.

Song-ju was the second oldest of four sons. His younger brother Chol-ju was reportedly born in 1916, and Yong-ju, the youngest, in 1920. The fourth and eldest brother, Ryong-ho, was de facto adopted by the Kims after he lost his parents. He was a year older than Song-ju.[3]

The family was quite successful. Kim Song-ju's father, Kim Hyong-jik, was a teacher affiliated with a Protestant church.[4] He was eighteen when Song-ju was born.

Not many details are known about the family. In later years, North Korea produced an enormous number of publications about them, but, naturally, each and every one of them was heavily edited for political reasons. The only information that can be considered trustworthy, if only because there was little to be gained from changing it, is the name of Kim Song-ju's mother—Kang Ban-sok.

A rare source on Kim Song-ju's childhood is the memoirs of his fellow villager, Kim Hyong-sok, who later became a professor in South Korea's Yonsei University. Born in the same area as Song-ju, Kim Hyong-sok is eight years younger than the future Great Leader and met him in person in the mid-1940s. When Kim Hyong-sok was a child, he heard stories about

Kim Hyong-jik and his children. According to him, Song-ju was remembered as a sporty, active and cocky kid; when local children played football, he was chosen to lead the team. Yet it should be remembered that Professor Kim was about 100 years old when he was talking about these events, and human memory is not the most reliable thing.[5]

Yet, we can certainly learn something from Kim being born into a Protestant family. By the 1910s, Christianity in Korea—both its Catholic and Protestant denominations—was firmly associated with the West and Western progress. The religion was originally brought to Korea by Western missionaries. Most missionaries and converts did not welcome Korea's annexation by Japan, a non-Christian power, and thus, at the time, Christianity had strong connotations with political opposition to the colonial government.

One could expect a child brought up in such a family to be sent to a good school, to hold little to no sympathy for the colonial government and to be open to Western influence, and all of this indeed proved true with Song-ju.

Based on multiple testimonies, the house in Mangyongdae village, near Chilgol, which North Korea claims as Song-ju's own, was not actually the one in which he was born.[6] The house, which received the nickname 'cradle of the revolution' and is shown to foreign visitors, belonged to his father's parents and was located in a neighbouring district. It is more likely that Song-ju's mother would have given birth in her own parents' house in Chilgol. This house had probably been destroyed by the end of the Second World War, as by that time his mother and maternal grandparents were already dead.

The Korean uprising and flight to Manchuria

In 1916, when Song-ju was four, a new governor-general of Korea, Hasegawa Yoshimichi, was appointed. Previously a commander of a Japanese garrison in Korea under Resident-General Ito Hirobumi, Hasegawa was notorious for persistently, if usually unsuccessfully, asking his superior for permission to conduct punitive raids on Korean villages.[7] Unlike his predecessor, Hasegawa did not implement any meaningful reforms in Korea. His sole policy was to maintain control and order through the governor-general's paramilitary force, the gendarmerie, which was always ready to crush dissent.[8]

Even those who had been able to respect or at least tolerate Terauchi had no warm feelings for the brutish administrator now in charge of the peninsula. His policy resulted in a massive uprising against the colonial authorities in March 1919, greatly alarming even the governor-general himself. Fearful of Japan's international reputation, the colonial authorities' official publications explained that 'the average Korean is a great liar' and that Koreans were not to be trusted.[9]

The uprising was eventually named after the day the demonstrations reached their peak: 'the 1 March movement'. Kim Hyong-jik was an active participant in this movement, as verified by contemporary Japanese records.[10] Governor Hasegawa responded to the rebellion in the only way he knew: by calling up the gendarmerie and cracking down on the protestors, forcing the Kim family to flee. In May of the same year, Kim Hyong-jik took his wife and sons and fled to China, settling in Badaogou, near the border of colonial Korea.[11]

'China' at the time was more of an abstract concept. The country had two competing governments—the northern government, located in Beiping (now Beijing), and one to the south. Most of 'China' was under the control of warlords—the chiefs of local juntas, who, while not formally proclaiming their independence, were running independent states in all but name. Manchuria was one of these semi-independent fiefdoms. The primary figure was Zhang Zuolin, a former bandit chief who seized power in 1916, at a time of political instability.[12]

Zhang's Manchuria did not have a concept of citizenship or immigration control in the modern sense, and the border with the Japanese Empire was a de facto open one. Those who behaved themselves, paid taxes to Zhang and caused the authorities no trouble could openly live and work in Manchuria.

This is what Kim Hyong-jik did. Contrary to what North Korean propaganda has since implied, the family continued to be quite prosperous, as Japanese estimates of 1925 assessed the Kims' assets as 1,000 yen[13]—slightly more than the average two-year income in Manchuria at the time.[14]

The uprising in Korea came just a few months after the end of the First World War. The end of the Great War saw many people across the world, including the Japanese, call for a better and more equal world order, and that such a big part of the empire as Korea was completely subjugated to the whims of the colonial viceroy met with criticism from mainland Japan. Hasegawa was given a choice: resign or be removed from office. The governor-general chose the former option, and his reign of terror finally came to an end.

The new man to rule Korea was a retired admiral, Saito Makoto.[15] Saito started to move Korea in an increasingly liberal direction: he ended segregation in schools; provided religious freedoms to Christians; eased censorship, thereby allowing criticism of the colonial authorities; encouraged local enterprises; and, despite some doubts in Tokyo, opened the first university in Korea.

Many Koreans, still remembering their life in poverty under the *ancien régime*, were swayed by his blandishments. That the economy of Korea grew steadily under Japanese rule, and the fact that under Saito Koreans were treated with much more respect than under Hasegawa, made colonial rule more acceptable for many Koreans.

Yet Kim Hyong-jik was adamant that Korea should be an independent state. He, along with a significant number of Korean intellectuals, thought that Japan was not to be trusted. The family stayed in Manchuria, and this was where Song-ju received his education. Official North Korean records claim he attended primary school in Badaogou, moved back to Korea and attended Changdok Primary School in Pyongyang before finally returning to Manchuria, where he attended Fusong Primary School and Hwasong Middle School.[16]

There is no way to prove or disprove those claims. Thus the focus should perhaps be directed to his next and last school, on which both the North Korean state narrative and historical sources agree. Yuwen Middle School—whose name literally means 'nurturing culture'—is located in Jilin City in the Chinese province of the same name. Kim Song-ju became a student in the first grade.[17] Little did the school realise then that he would become the most consequential figure in Yuwen's history.

As readers can see, little is known about our main character's childhood other than that his upbringing was quite unusual for a Korean boy at the time. Born into a well-to-do family of a political activist, Kim Song-ju received at least some of his education in a foreign school—and being an outsider teaches one to adapt. He was exposed to a foreign culture and its values during his childhood, and he grew up in a highly politicised environment among people generally open to Western ideas. As we will see, all of this had an impact on his personality and his future destiny.

2

FROM MANCHURIA TO THE SOVIET UNION

Manchuria of the late 1920s was a rather peculiar place. Zhang Zuolin had seized power in the region over ten years ago. In the 1910s, he and his Fengtian Army had brought Manchuria the stability it desperately needed, and in the early 1920s the region saw substantial economic growth. Located between the Soviet Union and the Japanese Empire, the region became a shelter for Japanese and Soviet dissidents.

Manchuria's Korean community grew significantly in the 1920s. Since a substantial number of these Koreans were political emigrants, this milieu was bound to produce various associations seeking to restore Korea's independence. A significant number were also attracted to the relatively new left-wing ideology: communism.

Only a few years had passed since the Red Army's victory in the Russian Civil War and the creation of the Soviet Union, and communism's call for the independence of colonies and equality of nations and people proved attractive to many Koreans.

Another factor that contributed to communism's popularity among local Koreans was the beginning of a crisis in Manchuria itself. Zhang's attempts to conquer 'inner' China resulted in the collapse of the Manchurian economy. Moreover, the very future of the region's independence was uncertain: most of inner China had been unified under the Nanjing government of Chiang Kai-shek, which had plans to conquer the north-east as well.

On 4 June 1928, Zhang was assassinated by the Japanese, who wanted to install someone more compliant to rule Manchuria. However, these plans failed when Zuolin's son, Zhang Xueliang, quickly solidified his control over Manchuria after his father's death.

Young communist

It was during this time of rapid change that Kim Song-ju enrolled in the Yuwen Middle School. By the age of seventeen, he appeared to be a typical boy for an upper middle-class ethnic minority family in Manchuria. The very fact that he attended a middle school put him among the few educated people in China, as by the late 1920s most Chinese citizens were still illiterate.[1] That he had been educated in a foreign language—Chinese— was also quite impressive. Yuwen Middle School was of course no Eton College, but its graduates could have realistically expected to become somewhat successful.

Song-ju became interested in communism in his late teens. It is quite possible that he was influenced by one of his teachers, Shang Yue, who taught at the school in early 1929. Judging by Shang's reminiscences, the communist ideology Song-ju received was rather crude: Shang confessed that he had based his teachings on one small brochure containing an English translation of Vladimir Lenin's work *Imperialism, the Highest Stage of Capitalism* (1917).[2] Shang remembered Song-ju as a 'Korean student with a round face, big eyes, who was not talkative, but precise',[3] and that he had strong feelings against the Japanese Empire and rich Korean landlords.[4]

Lenin had written *Imperialism* while in Switzerland in 1916. In it, he argued that capitalism was bound to create large monopolies that would eventually start to control governments and expand their influence outside, looking for colonies to be exploited. Korea's fate was explicitly mentioned in the work. Lenin stated that if a Japanese person opposes the landgrabs of other empires, then this opposition should only be considered genuine if they also oppose their own nation behaving in the same way. Lenin later stated that he had to choose this example instead of speaking about the Russian Empire and its many colonies in order to have his book published in Russia,[5] but it is very much possible that this support for Korea's independence is what made Song-ju receptive to Lenin's views.

That Kim Song-ju's initial communist education was limited to a single work of Lenin's is one of the reasons why in his later years many people noticed he had a very simplistic understanding of Marxism and Leninism[6]—it was not the theories about 'primitive accumulation' or 'base and superstructure' that attracted his interest; instead, he was impressed by a theory that could be used to bring down the regime he hated—the Japanese Empire—and by an image of a society where the state would provide necessities for all.

Official North Korean records say that Kim Hyong-jik died in 1926. This seems to be a truthful statement, as it was at the time when the Kim brothers parted ways. Ryong-ho's fate remains unknown. Chol-ju, as previously mentioned, was subsequently apprehended by the Japanese and vanished. Yong-ju's trajectory is very intriguing: he was the sole family member to outwardly align, if not collaborate, with the Japanese colonial regime. Taking the name Il-son (literally 'Japan and Korea'),[7] he worked as an interpreter for the Japanese Army—his fluency in Chinese,

Japanese[8] and Korean was a great asset to him. He later claimed he had done so in order to protect himself, as both Song-ju and Chol-ju had joined the resistance, and being a younger brother of two anti-Japanese partisans was downright dangerous. Thus Yong-ju allegedly decided to hide in plain sight.[9]

As for Song-ju, in 1929 he joined an organisation called the Communist Society of the Korean Youth. This was not a school group but rather an unofficial club of local Korean communists. It seems that Song-ju was the organisation's youngest member. Song-ju was appointed a member of the children's section and, together with another comrade, given the responsibility of conducting surveys among schoolchildren. The survey was not supposed to be political—he merely had to ask the children's names, origins and age.

The surveys were to be conducted within a month and reported to the head of the organisation, a Korean named Ho So, on a weekly basis. Yet Kim Song-ju did not even submit his first report. In less than a week, he, along with other members of the organisation, was arrested by the authorities.[10] By Kim's later testimony, he was in the seventh grade at the time.[11]

Song-ju served a five-month prison sentence. In 1941, he testified that some people had vouched for him, and he was released, although the identities of his guarantors remain unknown.[12] The authorities may have thought that five months would be sufficient to make the young man reconsider his commitment to communist ideology. Yet it had the opposite effect. Song-ju's faith in communism became even stronger.

It was about this time that Kim Song-ju started to use different characters for his name. As readers may know, East Asian names are composed of graphic Chinese characters, each of which has a special meaning. Many are homonymous, so a change of spelling would not necessarily be reflected in pronunciation and transliteration.

This was exactly the case with Song-ju. At least until 1929, the young Kim spelt his given name, Song-ju, as 'foundation of the holy ones'.[13] This name was probably influenced by his family's Christian background and did not befit a communist. By 1930, Song-ju started to use characters meaning 'becoming the foundation' instead.[14]

The anti-Japanese movement in Manchuria

The late 1920s saw an attempt to unify the Korean anti-Japanese movement in Manchuria with the formation of the National Chamber, an umbrella organisation of Korean independence activists. The organisation had its own militant wing, the Korean Revolutionary Army (KRA),[15] and united people of various beliefs—from rightists to communists. Kim Song-ju was one of the many that joined. By 1930, his position was listed as 'a member of the organisation committee for Fusong and Antu of the Korean Farmers' General Union in Eastern Provinces'.[16] Such a long name reflected the National Chamber's complex and somewhat chaotic structure. There are also testimonies that Lee Jong-nak, one of the National Chamber's cadres, sent Song-ju to study at a private educational institute, a lyceum in South Manchuria.[17]

Lee Jong-nak and leftist members of the National Chamber eventually left the organisation and established their own, called the Army of the World Fire; Kim Song-ju was a member of its Military Political Council.[18]

Then came the year 1931, when Japan conquered Manchuria and everything changed.

Without Tokyo's blessing, the Kwantung Army, stationed in Japanese-leased Liaodong peninsula, organised a false-flag attack on the Japanese-owned South Manchurian railroad. Blaming the Chinese for the attack, the army used it as a pretext to conquer the whole of Manchuria. In the following March, the Japanese proclaimed that the region had become a new state, called Manchukuo. The last emperor of Qing China, Aisin-gioro Puyi, was installed as a figurehead, while the Japanese ambassador to Manchukuo became the real ruler of the new-born country. All commanding generals of the Kwantung Army stationed in Manchuria were automatically appointed ambassadors, effectively making the country the army's protectorate.[19]

Japan was swept up in a wave of patriotic euphoria following its rapid and relatively bloodless conquest, which appeared to establish Japan as the uncontested regional hegemon. However, this triumph was short-lived, as the League of Nations sided with China and refused to recognise Manchukuo. This setback paved the way for a power shift towards the military, which portrayed itself as the defender of Japan against a hostile world. Japanese democracy rapidly eroded, and by the mid-1930s the nation found itself firmly under the control of militaristic forces.

One can only imagine how Kim Song-ju perceived this conquest. His family had not had any loyalty towards Tokyo, and neither had he. They had fled from their homeland of Korea to avoid being persecuted due to their participation in the independence movement. And now the enemy, which had already annexed their native land, had come to their adopted home of Manchuria and conquered that too. Naturally, Kim Song-ju had a great resolve to fight the Japanese, whom he considered nothing more than evil conquerors.

He was not alone. Japan's conquest of Manchuria galvanised the Communist Party in the territory. Fighting Zhang Zuolin and his son was one thing, but having a very real foreign enemy was a good reason to push many waverers to join the resistance.

By that time, Kim Song-ju had met a Korean named Lee Chong-san. Little is known about Lee other than that he was a communist, was born in 1900 or 1901 and lived in Antu in

Fengtian province.[20] But as Song-ju himself testified in 1941, it was Lee Chong-san who recommended him to the Communist Party of China (CPC).[21] As the party's Constitution of 1928 prescribed, the only necessary requirement for 'intellectuals'—and Kim Song-ju definitely qualified as such—to join was one recommendation[22] from a party member. Once Lee Chong-san provided it, Kim joined the Party. As of 1932, Kim Song-ju was already a full member.

Not everyone in the anti-Japanese movement was a communist, though, as many pledged loyalty to the central government of China in Nanjing. Yet the Party tried to make the best of the situation.

The assignment the CPC gave to Song-ju was to join the resistance army organised by Wang Delin, a former battalion commander in the Chinese Army.[23] Created in February 1932, this Chinese People's National Salvation Army was affiliated with Nanjing and Chiang Kai-shek. Song-ju was a propagandist there, and his task was to convince as many people as possible that the best way to fight Japan would be under the banner of the Communist Party.[24]

Initially, this task appeared not to be that challenging, since Wang decided to pursue extensive cooperation with the CPC. He appointed two prominent communists as his deputies: Li Yanlu[25] became his chief of staff and Zhou Baozhong[26] his chief of the general staff in the high command. This situation met with disapproval from Nanjing, as the Chinese government had ordered a purge of communists from the army. Acting on the government's orders, Wang expelled many communists from the army's ranks,[27] including the entire unit of propagandists where Kim Song-ju had served.

The communists went on to create their own resistance units. These were initially very small, comprising around ten people. Song-ju entered the Antu partisan unit, named after the county in which it was based. People who served with him remembered that he was dressed as a student and was working as a teacher at a primary school.[28] Teaching was Song-ju's last civilian occupation before he became the leader of North Korea.

Many partisans assumed aliases to render them and their friends and family members more difficult to apprehend, and Kim Song-ju was no exception. From then on, he was no longer Kim Song-ju but Kim Il-song, or, using a more colloquial spelling, Kim Il-sung. It seems he initially spelt this new name—Il-sung—with characters meaning 'one star', or 'becoming the only one', before later changing it to 'becoming the sun' (the Korean reading of the characters remained the same).

Kim Song-ju was not the first man to use the alias 'Kim Il-sung', as several other anti-Japanese activists had used the name before him. The first Kim Il-sung was born in 1888, seemingly with this as his original name. Born in Korea's Tanchon county, he became a prominent partisan commander operating in the vicinity of Paektu Mountain near the border with China fighting against the Japanese Empire, which had established a protectorate over Korea in 1905. He died in 1926.[29]

The second and more famous Kim Il-sung was originally named Kim Hyon-chung, and 'Kim Il-sung' was just one of his multiple aliases.[30] His father was an officer in the Korean Imperial Army,[31] and his brother Kim Song-un was a graduate of the Military Academy of the Imperial Army of Japan. Given such a background, it should be of no surprise that Kim Hyon-chung also enrolled in the same academy in 1909, one year before Japan formally annexed Korea. The young cadet was an exemplary student, graduating at the top of his class in 1911. He was commissioned second lieutenant of cavalry.[32] However, by 1919 Kim Hyon-chung had ceased being loyal to Japan. After the 1 March movement, he fled to Russia, at the time engulfed in civil war, joined the communist cause and stayed in the country after the Bolsheviks triumphed.[33]

Along with many Soviet Koreans, Kim Hyon-chung was deported to Central Asia in the 1930s. He worked as a farming unit foreman until 1939, when he became another victim of Stalin's purges. On 5 April 1939, he was arrested by the Soviet police and sentenced to eight years' imprisonment for alleged espionage.[34] Kim Hyon-chung, the second Kim Il-sung, died in a Soviet concentration camp.[35]

The activities of both men created an image of 'Kim Il-sung' as a famous and semi-legendary figure in the anti-Japanese movement. Kim Song-ju may have adopted the new spelling deliberately, as the name of 'Kim Il-sung' from the urban legend was spelt 'becoming the sun', especially given that Song-ju's father Kim Hyong-jik had reportedly told him stories about 'Kim Il-sung'.[36] The subsequent actions of Kim Song-ju—or, as he should be called from now on, Kim Il-sung—further contributed to the survival and expansion of this legend.

The Antu unit, where Kim was serving, did not last long. In short order, the Communist Party merged it with two others, creating the Wangqing Anti-Japanese Partisan Unit;[37] Kim Il-sung became the unit's commissar following the death of his predecessor, Kim Un-sik. Thus, Kim's first position as a cadre was that of a political officer. In other words, he was trusted more for his loyalty to the CPC than for his military skills. Given that he had no military background, this seemed to be a logical decision, although a later assessment of him by his superiors stated that Kim 'does not know much about political issues'.[38]

He was later promoted to chief of staff and political commissar of a regiment. The official name of the unit was the Third Regiment of the Independent Division of the Second Army of the North East People's Revolutionary Army. However, despite these grandiose names, these regiments and divisions were significantly smaller than their regular army counterparts.

In February 1936, the CPC proclaimed that armed resistance would be unified under the name North East Anti-Japanese United Army (NAJUA). Yet this was a 'united' army in name only, as it did not have a single commanding officer or even staff. All that unified it was a common goal—expelling the Japanese from Manchuria—and the general allegiance of its fighters to the CPC.

Dark years

In August 1936, the situation in Korea deteriorated dramatically when the calm, moderate Governor-General Ugaki Kazushige was replaced by a militarist, Minami Jiro. As the army had effectively seized control of the government in Tokyo, such a change was bound to happen sooner or later. However, the man Korea got as its ruler was one of the worst. Previously commander of the Kwantung Army and, as such, the ambassador to Manchukuo, the governor-general immediately cancelled the freedoms granted by his predecessors.

Minami's rule generally resembled the age of Hasegawa, the main difference being that his cruelty was less haphazard. The new governor-general had a goal: erase the separate identity of Koreans and make them Japanese. Tokyo had launched a policy of empire-wide mandatory attendance at Shinto shrines even before Minami was appointed. The governor-general supplemented this policy with a reduction in the number of hours of Korean-language education, eventually banning it altogether, and reducing the number of Korean-language newspapers to one—the newspaper published by the colonial government itself. He imposed mandatory pledges of loyalty to the state and used a carrot-and-stick policy to actively encourage Koreans to adopt

Japanese names.[39] Finally, the governor-general discouraged the use of the word 'Korea', suggesting that the former country be called 'the peninsula' instead. Minami Jiro also instituted what was perhaps the most sickening aspect of Japanese colonial rule: the mass recruitment of women to serve as prostitutes for the military. At the time of writing, this topic is highly politicised in Japan and South Korea, and while estimates vary from study to study, historians agree that a significant number of these women were recruited against their will.[40]

As the regime became much less popular, it also became more intimidating. As the army solidified its grip over Japan, resistance to its rule—be it in the homeland or in Korea—started to disappear. By that time, an entire generation of Koreans had been born under Japanese rule and could not really see any alternative.

Meanwhile, the partisan movement in Manchuria faced its own crisis, as its leadership was swept up in paranoia and started looking for traitors within its ranks. Word spread that many partisans were secret members of the Group for the People's Welfare (GPW), a small organisation of loyalist Koreans that existed in 1931–2. However, the CPC was convinced that it continued to exist covertly and that many people in the resistance were secret members. Those who were accused but denied being a member of the GPW were often shot on the spot,[41] so it was safer to confess to having been a member while simultaneously renouncing the organisation. Kim Il-sung was among those who had to confess alleged membership in the GPW multiple times despite having nothing to do with the organisation.[42]

As the CPC's regional leaders realised the scale of the campaign and its potentially disastrous consequences, the purges ceased, and the partisans were at least spared from being persecuted by their own.[43] Kim was promoted further—to the commander of the Sixth Division of the Second Army of the NAJUA.[44] It was while holding this position that Kim conducted his most famous attack—the 1937 raid on Pochonbo.[45]

Pochonbo, or Fort of the Wide Sky, was the name of a hamlet near the Japanese–Manchurian border in Korea. Located near Paektu Mountain, the tallest in Korea, the hamlet was surrounded by a national park.[46] This ill-protected place was where Kim and his partisans launched their attack.

On the night of 4 June 1937, a group of about 200 guerrillas crossed the border and launched a surprise attack on the hamlet's police station and its surroundings. The garrison, which was unprepared for such a surprise assault either from Manchukuo or Korea, immediately raised the alarm and called for reinforcements.[47] Many partisans managed to retreat, but some were captured by the Japanese authorities. They testified that one of the leading figures in the raid was Kim Il-sung and revealed his real name—Kim Song-ju.[48] By that time, Kim was well known to the Japanese.[49]

The raid was reported by major Korean newspapers,[50] one of which even published a special issue on the attack.[51] Later the same year, some Korean newspapers reported a rumour that Kim Il-sung had been killed[52]—although Kim was in fact very much alive.

A few months after the raid, the partisans tried to create their own network of agents inside Korea. This network, which operated under an umbrella name, 'The Society of Koreans for the Restoration of the Motherland', had agents in various cities, but it did not survive for long, as it was soon discovered and crushed by the Japanese police.[53]

With the empire's territory brought fully into the fold, Japan decided to finally cleanse its oldest client state—Manchukuo—of any partisans. The Kwantung Army, de facto rulers of Manchukuo, appointed Major-General Nozoe Masanori[54] head of a taskforce, the Second Independent Guard Unit, with the specific task of dealing with the partisans. This was the partisan movement's darkest hour, as Nozoe was an ideal man for such a task. He took more pleasure in risk and field work than in planning operations for large units and formations. For some time, Nozoe Masanori even operated as a spy in the Chinese city of Tianjin.[55]

Assisted by his trusted aide Kitabe Kunio,[56] Nozoe employed a carrot-and-stick policy: those who surrendered, renounced communism and assisted the general in hunting down the remaining partisans were spared prosecution and paid monetary compensation.[57] The campaign was a success—many partisans, losing all faith that their cause would ever triumph, surrendered to Nozoe.

Apart from the efforts of Nozoe and Kitabe, there was one more reason for the failure of the partisan movement: the efforts of the guerrillas failed to yield any significant results. Manchukuo was not going to disappear, and there was no prospect of any assistance from inner China. A full-scale Sino-Japanese war broke out in 1937, and the Republic of China was steadily pushed back.

Thus, the empire appeared invincible, and the Manchurians could not see any real alternative to submitting to Japanese rule. Given that the Republic of China was a dictatorship, it did not have the appeal of a free country over Manchukuo, which had been flooded with Japanese investment; moreover, since Manchukuo was not formally part of Japan, Tokyo did not try to assimilate the locals. Some Manchurians consequently concluded that the Japanese were not so objectionable after all.

It was at this time that Kim Il-sung reached the peak of his partisan career in the NAJUA, becoming commander of the Second Area Army of the First Route Army.[58] That this was a high-ranking position was little consolation given that the movement was collapsing, and ever more partisans, including prominent commanders, were being killed by the Japanese. Kim's superior, the commander of the First Route Army, Yang Jingyu, was killed on 23 February 1940.[59] Kim's second-in-command, Chief of Staff Lim U-song, switched sides and defected to the Japanese.[60] As the partisan movement was crumbling, the CPC issued a command to restructure large partisan formations into 'small units', tacitly acknowledging their cause was nearing defeat.[61]

Fleeing Manchuria

The crackdown also had grim consequences for Kim's personal life. We do not know whether Kim dated any girls back when he was in Yuwen Middle School; however, in the 1930s, he met his first spouse, Han Song-hui, in the partisan unit.[62] Han was commander of the unit's female guerrillas, a duty she had been fulfilling before she was arrested in 1940. The report of her arrest in the colonial Korean press mentioned her fake name, 'Kim Hye-sun', which she had taken to protect the secrets of the partisan movement. However, the report also mentioned her pledging loyalty to the empire.[63] The militarist regime of Japan was more lenient to its enemies than, say, Hitler or Stalin, and Han Song-hui was released after she had yielded. But her husband had no way of knowing about her fate.

Losing his wife to the enemy would undoubtedly have come as a shock to Kim Il-sung. Nevertheless, he soon found a new wife for himself: Kim Jong-suk, one of Han Song-hui's subordinates, who looked so similar to Han Song-hui that some thought Kim Jong-suk was her little sister.[64] This might have been one of the reasons why Il-sung and Jong-suk became close: he might have seen her as a substitute for Song-hui. Born in the small border town of Hoeryong in 1919,[65] Kim Jong-suk was a dressmaker in the partisan unit.[66] They seemingly married in 1940, when she was only twenty-one.

As General Nozoe's campaign intensified, the partisans had no other choice but to retreat. The only place they could go was the Soviet Union, and 1940 was a time of massive exodus.[67] Chinese sources state that Kim Il-sung crossed the Manchukuo–USSR border on 23 October 1940,[68] whereupon he was detained by the Soviets and given a thorough check—along with his comrades. The officials conducting this check were a team of four officials from the Communist International (Comintern), at least one of whom, Aleksandr Kogan, spoke Chinese. Kim had to complete a questionnaire in Chinese, which was then translated into Russian by the Comintern officials.[69] He and his comrades also compiled a report for the Comintern in which they humbly asked to be put in touch with the Central Committee of the CPC, so that they could receive guidance and instructions.[70]

The Comintern team was overseen by none other than Georgy Dimitrov, the most senior official in the entire Communist International. Upon receiving reports[71] and assessing the status of the partisans in Manchuria, including Kim Il-sung, Dimitrov's diary entry for 17 March read simply 'this is very bad'.[72] His pessimism was justified, as the partisan movement had been defeated. Many of the movement's most prominent leaders were dead, having succumbed to disease or Japanese bullets. The NAJUA effectively ceased to exist.

Kim had one more reason to flee to the USSR. By the time he crossed the Manchurian–Soviet border, his wife, Kim Jong-suk, was pregnant. On 16 February 1941, she gave birth to their first son. He received a Russian name, Yura, which is actually a diminutive form, suggesting that his full name was either Yuriy or Georgiy.[73] Reportedly, the name was coined by the Soviet doctor who delivered him;[74] according to other testimony, this doctor was Nikolay Nikitenko,[75] who later served in the same unit as Kim Il-sung.[76] According to the story, he gave the boy the name of a famous Soviet military commander.[77] If true—and

27

it very likely is—then Yura was probably named after Georgiy Zhukov.

The choice was quite natural, as General Zhukov was a well-known figure in the East. He was a commander of one of the Red Army's two skirmishes with the Japanese in 1938–9—while both skirmishes ended in Soviet victory, the second Soviet commander, Vasiliy Blyuher, was later purged, making Zhukov the only available choice of the two. After Yura was born, Kim Jong-suk had difficulty breastfeeding, and he was instead nursed by another female partisan, Li Zaide,[78] as the latter personally testified.[79] In the decades to come, Yura would eventually succeed his father in the North. He is better known under the Korean name he later adopted—Kim Jong-il.

The surviving partisans were settled in two camps. One of them, the 'northern camp' or camp A, was located near the Vyatskoye village several dozen miles to the north-east of Khabarovsk. Another, the 'southern camp' or camp V, was probably located in the area of the Okeanskaya settlement near Vladivostok.[80] 'A' stood for the neighbouring Amur River[81] and 'V', perhaps surprisingly, not for Vladivostok but rather for another adjacent city, Voroshilov (Ussuriysk), despite the camp actually being closer to Vladivostok.[82] The former guerrillas were to be trained in intelligence and sabotage work, as the Soviet government had not abandoned the plan to continue using them in Manchukuo.[83]

The Comintern officials were especially disappointed by the revelation that Wei Zhengming, one of the highest-ranking survivors among the guerrillas, was nowhere to be found. Eventually, they decided to form two teams—one under Kim Il-sung's command and another under Kim's friend, An Kil—and sent them back to Manchuria to look for Wei and other partisans.

The teams departed from camp V on 9 April 1941 and crossed the border into Manchukuo.[84] A few months later, on

28 August, part of Kim Il-sung's team, including Kim himself, returned to a Soviet training camp, while the others remained in Manchuria.[85] Kim reported on the mission's lack of success: they failed to find Wei Zhengming, as the latter had reportedly died after contracting a disease.[86] On 14 September, Kim went back to Manchuria for a second time, where he met the rest of the unit and, with them, re-entered the USSR, returning on 12 November 1941.[87]

Finally, after years of guerrilla life, Kim could settle down and find some stability and peace.[88] For the next few years, the Soviet Union became Kim's home.

3

IN THE USSR

The early 1940s were an odd period for the Soviet military in the Russian Far East. In April 1941, the Soviet Union, not yet at war with Germany, and the Japanese Empire signed the Neutrality Pact, pledging mutual recognition of their borders and those of their counterpart's satellite states—Manchukuo and Mongolia—and, more importantly, staying neutral in the event either became involved in a war. Thus Japan was no longer an enemy of the USSR. Yet Tokyo remained a member of the Axis pact, and in June 1941, the leading Axis power—Hitler's Germany—attacked the USSR, launching the war that took tens of millions of Soviet lives.

When Germany invaded the Soviet Union, the Far Eastern Front command, stationed in Khabarovsk, and its commanding officer, General Iosif Apanasenko, realised they were by no means a priority for the Supreme Command.[1] As the German Army advanced ever eastward, more and more units were recalled from the Far East to the Western Front in Moscow's desperate attempt to halt the deadly advance.

Under such conditions, an ordinary general would have simply followed the orders given, especially in light of the terrifying atmosphere pervading the country. The Red Army had just experienced the Great Purge of 1937–8, which had led to most of its high-ranking commanders being liquidated on farfetched accusations of conspiracy and high treason.[2] Stalin, caught up in his paranoia, believed the country was infiltrated with foreign intelligence agents from top to bottom, many of whom also presumably sympathised with his major rival, Leon Trotsky, whom Stalin had exiled in 1929. If anything, the fate of Apanasenko's immediate predecessor, General Grigoriy Shtern, who was shot after being falsely accused of membership of a Trotskyist conspiracy, was an instructive example of what could happen to anyone suspected of disobedience.[3]

But Apanasenko was not an ordinary man. He felt responsible for the eastern border he was entrusted to defend. What if Japan—especially seeing Germany's successes—decided to violate the Neutrality Pact and attack the USSR? The Eastern Front needed to be prepared lest it be overrun by the Japanese.

Apart from developing the military infrastructure, Apanasenko had to deal with the question of personnel. As ever more units were ordered westward, he summoned his top aides and set them a task: for each division recalled to the west, the Far Eastern Front would create a new one.[4]

Accomplishing such a feat required considerable manpower, and one of the few available options was to arrange a mass amnesty. There were quite a few concentration camps in the Soviet Far East, and, on Apanasenko's orders, one of his men, Colonel Pyotr Grigorenko, visited them and demanded that certain able-bodied men be released and conscripted. The Gulag authorities, naturally, saw this as an outrageous violation of their autonomy and resisted. But Grigorenko asserted that his orders came from the top, and the camp administration ultimately capitulated, albeit grudgingly so: the camp's commandant tried to have Grigorenko arrested and executed, and the colonel was only saved by General Apanasenko's personal intervention.[5]

Joining the Eighty-Eighth Separate Infantry Brigade

Another source of manpower on the Far Eastern Front was the Manchurian partisans. Never before or since were foreigners admitted to the Red Army. However, allowing the partisans to join the army made a lot of sense. In peacetime, these fighters were useful for intelligence gathering, and, in the event of war with Japan, they could also be used as provisional administrators of any occupied territories.

By July 1942, more divisions were being transported to fight the Germans at Stalingrad. Apanasenko had to reconsider his option of replacing the departing troops. It was no longer 'division for division'—the general instead had to settle for at least one brigade to replace each departing division.[6] A brigade was supposed to be more than twice as small as a division,[7] but even that proved to be a challenging task. And here, the Manchurian guerrillas proved to be of use. Their camps A and V were reorganised into the Eighty-Eighth Separate Infantry Brigade, which effectively became the Red Army's Foreign Legion.

The number eighty-eight did not have any special meaning. Previously, the Red Army had had another Eighty-Eighth Separate Infantry Brigade, but that unit, which had been formed mostly of Turkmen personnel, had been disbanded, so the newly created brigade simply took its number. The 'Separate' part meant that it reported directly to the command of the Far Eastern Front and not to a division, like a normal brigade should. Finally, it can be argued that, of all the military branches, infantry required the least training and was the closest to the partisans' actual combat experience.

Experienced partisans were appointed officers even though they had not received any proper military education.[8] Their ranks reflected their position in the now defunct NAJUA. Zhou Baozhong, a Bai[9] Chinese and arguably the most prominent surviving member of the guerrilla movement, was commissioned lieutenant-colonel and appointed the brigade's commanding officer. His de facto second-in-command was Li Zhaolin, the brigade's political officer, who was given the rank of major.

Kim Il-sung—or, as the Soviets then called him, Jin Richeng, based on the Chinese reading of the characters that composed his name—was commissioned as captain and appointed to command the first of the four battalions that formed the core of the brigade. The second and third battalions were led by Chinese officers, while command of the fourth was a little more complicated. Initially, its commander was the Chinese partisan Chai Shirong;[10] however, in August 1943 he was transferred to a position on the brigade's staff. Chai was replaced by a Korean partisan, Kang Shin-thae, who is better known under his alias, Kang Gon.[11]

The brigade was also unique since it had two Communist Party organisations in it. One was, naturally, Soviet, and the other, that of the CPC. The CPC's committee was led by another Korean partisan, Choe Yong-gon. Thus, together with Kang Gon and Choe Yong-gon, Kim Il-sung was one of the top three ranking Korean partisans in this unusual unit.

Eventually, they all became core figures in the North Korean elite. Kang Gon became the first chief of staff of the Korean People's Army (KPA), and Choe Yong-gon was elevated to first minister of national defence. And, of course, battalion commander Kim became the Great Leader of North Korea.

They were not the only ones. Virtually every Korean who was in the Eighty-Eighth Brigade and lived long enough to see Kim Il-sung's rise to power received an influential position in North Korea. Company commander Choe Yong-jin became a deputy premier. Platoon commander Choe Hyon became a minister of the people's armed forces. Squad commander Pak Song-chol rose to be a vice-president.

The full list of Eighty-Eighth Brigade personnel with a spectacular career in the North would include more than two dozen names. However, it should be noted that this related only to men who served in the brigade. Kim's general attitude towards women was remarkably misogynistic even by the rather patriarchal standards of his time.

There were some Soviet Koreans in the brigade as well. The fate of two of them deserves special note. The first was Mun Il. A radio instructor in the brigade, he became a close friend of Kim Il-sung and later played a crucial role in his rise to power. Another was Kim Bong-nyul, a former director of a collective farm who had been arrested and spared the rest of his term in a concentration camp due to Apanasenko's amnesty.[12] Kim Bong-nyul subsequently went to the North and became one of the very few to survive the purge of Soviet Koreans initiated by Kim Il-sung in the 1950s as the latter sought to establish his political independence from Moscow. Kim Bong-nyul, known in the brigade mostly for his tractor-driving skills,[13] died in Pyongyang in 1995 as a Vice-Marshal.[14]

Finally, a number of Soviet officers and soldiers served in the brigade as well. Most of them were not ethnic Russians but hailed from many of the smaller ethnic groups in the Far East. The reason for this was racial: the brigade was doing intelligence work, and it was important to look Asian in order to blend in while infiltrating Manchuria or Korea.

The brigade inherited the structure of the former camps and was stationed in two villages in the Soviet Far East. The main base was near the village of Vyatskoye to the north-east of Khabarovsk, like camp A before it. This was where the unit's members lived together with their families. The secondary base was near Vladivostok at the site of camp V, and quite far away from Vyatskoye. This was the base from where the servicemen were sent into Manchukuo and Korea to collect information about the situation there and gather intelligence about Japan's plans.

Kim Il-sung never participated in these raids.[15] After returning to the Soviet Union from his search for Wei Zhengming, he spent several months in camp V.[16] In late March 1942, as many partisans were relocated to camp A, Kim was appointed to a position of political and military leadership among those guerrillas who were still stationed in camp V.[17] In July 1942, Kim was summoned to Khabarovsk, where he, Zhou Baozhong and Li Zhaolin were given a forty-minute briefing by General Apanasenko on the purpose of the newly created Eighty-Eighth Brigade.[18] After the briefing, Kim relocated to Vyatskoye.[19]

Life on the Far Eastern Front

In the same year, 1942, Zhou Baozhong tasked Kim Il-sung with writing a history of the First Route Army of the NAJUA, in which Kim had served. Most of the NAJUA's other commanders were dead. In fact, Kim may have been the only high-ranking survivor, and hence the task fell on his shoulders.[20] Many years later, in 1987, this report was published in China.[21] The publication did not say who its author was, but a few years later the book's editor Jin Yuzhong[22] confirmed that it was written by Kim Il-sung himself.[23]

Written in a rather dry style, the report repeatedly mentions that it was difficult for the Chinese and Koreans to work together. Mutual distrust was not uncommon, which was further fuelled by Japanese propaganda. Kim was particularly forceful in his criticism of the purge of Koreans associated with the GPW in the mid-1930s—by his estimates, 500 innocent people were shot during the purge.[24]

The brigade members were trained as reconnaissance and shock troops. As well as being used for intelligence gathering,[25] the command also entertained rather futile dreams of reinvigorating the partisan movement in Manchuria and was hoping that the brigade's members would persuade some people in Manchuria to join the resistance.[26] The training course was highly diverse: soldiers were schooled in assassination techniques, shooting, grenade throwing, chemical defence training, anti-tank operations, reconnaissance, marching, skiing[27] and even parachuting.[28]

Another part of the training involved learning Russian—and Captain Kim Il-sung was one of those who excelled at this task.[29] His determination and successes in language studies earned him a commendation from the command,[30] while some of the Chinese members thought that he was studying too hard—they were hoping they would soon leave the USSR, and thus Russian skills would not be that useful for them.[31] Importantly, mastering Russian meant that Kim could communicate with the Soviets with greater ease than other Korean officers could, and this was undoubtedly an important factor in his future ascension.[32]

By 1944, some of the brigade's members had been captured and interrogated by the Japanese, and the Okeanskaya base became known to Japanese intelligence.[33] The brigade members working undercover in Korea and Manchuria reported on a rather grim situation. In Korea, Japanification was in full motion, and in both Korea and Manchuria any opposition was completely eradicated by Tokyo.[34]

In Vyatskoye, life was relatively calm,[35] at least by the standards of a country at war. The brigade lived in total isolation from the outside world, with its personnel being overseen by the Soviet secret police. Those who elicited suspicion were sent even further north to the camps near Evoron Lake, never to be seen again. Yet the majority did ultimately pass the course.[36]

Since the Eighty-Eighth Brigade was a rear unit, its provisioning was not a priority for Moscow.[37] The brigade had farms attached to it, where cows and pigs were reared, and was expected to be self-supporting. Judging by the typical Russian names of the animals, like Zorka, Krasulya and Ryabusha,[38] and through the testimonies of the brigade members' descendants,[39] Soviet soldiers took care of both the cattle and the brigade's supplies.

Thus, although Kim Il-sung did not himself participate in this rather unusual 'military farming', he perceived it as the norm. Later, in 1945, he saw Japan surrender merely a week after the Soviet Army entered the war, which he saw as definitive proof of the Red Army's superiority. Since the only part of the Red Army he knew was the Eighty-Eighth Brigade, it was quite natural that Kim would later model the KPA after it. Even decades later, at the time this book is being written, many KPA units are required to maintain their own small farms for self-supply.[40]

During Kim's service in the brigade, there was one episode that could have ended badly for his career. In July 1944, another meeting of CPC members in the brigade took place. Among the usual loud atmosphere with speakers yelling their speeches instead of merely articulating them, one of the battalion-level political officers from China rose up and started accusing Captain Kim Il-sung of murdering civilians and communists back in the 1930s, during his partisan unit's raid into Jilin province, and that the unit itself had been closely linked to two gangs of bandits and robbers that had terrorised the locals.

The participants were furious. If they truly had killed communists, then Kim would be guilty of having betrayed their cause. After Zhou Baozhong and Li Zhaolin managed to restore some order, everyone demanded an explanation from Kim, who did not deny that the events had happened. However, he said that the people he had murdered—and he confessed to having shot them himself—were Trotskyists and thus not real communists. This explanation did not gain him much support, and the conference decided to ask the Soviets for advice. Kim was very depressed, waiting for severe sanctions, but they never came, as the brigade's superiors chose not to pursue the matter.[41]

Some of the other members of the Eighty-Eighth Brigade were less fortunate. The former commander of the Fourth Battalion,[42] Chai Shirong, and his deputy for political affairs, Ji Qing, were arrested by Soviet military counterintelligence.[43] Given that the records of the Japanese intelligence show that they were only aware of the Okeanskaya camp, and not the one near Vyatskoye or even of the Eighty-Eighth Brigade's existence,[44] it appears that the espionage charges were completely unfounded, and Chai and Ji—both of whom were sentenced to long periods of hard labour—were yet more victims of Stalin's terror. Kim was lucky not to share their fate.

End of the Neutrality Pact

In 1944, the Kims had another son. He was also given a Russian name: Shura, a diminutive for 'Aleksandr'. This name was also reportedly given by the same Soviet doctor after a Soviet commander.[45] The only famous Aleksandr in the Red Army's high command at the time was Marshal Aleksandr Vasilevskiy—perhaps the doctor had been impressed by his successes in

Stalingrad, for which Vasilevskiy had been promoted to marshal less than a month after becoming the first Soviet officer to be promoted to full general since the beginning of the war with Germany.

Meanwhile, the war in Europe was approaching its conclusion. In February 1945, during the Yalta Conference, Stalin agreed that the USSR would enter the war with Japan within three months of Germany being defeated in Europe. This meant that the USSR would share the spoils of the war in Asia as well.

On 4 April of the same year, Vyacheslav Molotov, the head of the People's Commissariat for Foreign Affairs, summoned the Japanese ambassador Sato Naotake and informed him that the USSR was renouncing the Neutrality Pact. The agreement stated that it would remain in effect for one year should one side decide to nullify it. Sato asked Molotov if this was the case and received the commissar's assurances that it was.

Yet both sides understood that this was unlikely, and preparations for war began. The Far Eastern Front was split in two: the First and Second Fronts, with the Eighty-Eighth Brigade reporting to the Second. Both Far Eastern Fronts, as well as the neighbouring Transbaikal Front, were to report to the high command of the Soviet Forces in the Far East, headed by Marshal Vasilevskiy, the very individual after whom Kim Il-sung's second son appears to have been named.

By early May, it had become clear that Nazi Germany was about to surrender. Around that time, Zhou Baozhong started to prepare the brigade for future conflict with Japan. The Chinese and Korean personnel were to formally organise into groups, which would then be dispatched to Manchuria and Korea respectively. Kim Il-sung was appointed head of the Korean group; Choe Yong-gon, the representative of the CPC, was assigned to the same group.[46]

On 6 August 1945, the world was forever changed when the United States dropped an atomic bomb on Hiroshima. Two days later, Ambassador Sato received the proclamation stating that the USSR had declared war on Japan, effective at midnight. It was 17:00 in Moscow but 23:00 in Tokyo. Sato had to inform the government, which in turn had to contact the frontlines. However, by the time the message reached its intended recipients, the invasion had already begun.

The day the Red Army started its advance, 9 August, was also the day when Nagasaki was obliterated by the second atomic strike. It was becoming clear that Japan's surrender was both inevitable and imminent, and the United States was concerned the USSR would occupy the entirety of Korea unless some sort of agreement was reached.

It was Friday, 10 August 1945. On this day, a minor decision by two American colonels—Charles Bonesteel and Dean Rusk—set up the order that would define Korea for the next seven decades and counting. Although Bonesteel later went on to become a four-star general and Rusk was destined to become secretary of state, this August day witnessed their greatest impact on history.

Bonesteel and Rusk's superiors had tasked them with outlining a plan to divide Korea into two occupation zones. As the USSR was advancing from the north while the US Army at the time was conducting landings at Okinawa to the south of Korea, it was becoming clear that the US zone would be in the south and the Soviet zone would be in the north of the peninsula.

The only map of Korea available to the colonels was the National Geographic Society's 'Asia and Adjacent Areas', published in 1942.[47] There were no provinces marked there, only cities, towns, meridians and parallels. The colonels, reasonably enough, thought that the zones should be more or less equal; otherwise, Stalin would have been unlikely to accept the deal.

They also wanted Korea's administrative capital—the city now called Seoul—to fall into the American zone.[48]

They first suggested drawing the demarcation line between Pyongyang and Wonsan. However, since such a line would have cut the cities in half and the colonels had no detailed map of either of them, the second plan—dividing the peninsula at the 38th parallel—was put in motion instead.[49] The division was intended to be temporary, yet it has led Korea to be divided for decades, and thus the country's 1,000-year history as a single, unified nation came to an end in August 1945.

The colonels' plan was approved by their superiors and formally presented to Stalin by President Truman. Since it was part of the general occupation plan of the entire Japanese Empire, the Soviet dictator approved the Korean part without raising an eyebrow. Of greater concern to him was the Soviets' possible participation in the occupation of the Japanese island of Hokkaido, which, in the event, Truman failed to allow.[50]

The war continued for a few more days while the Japanese government's more fanatical elements launched a coup in an effort to prevent the inevitable capitulation. On 15 August, after this attempt had failed, Emperor Hirohito addressed the nation, announcing that Japan accepted the provisions set by the Allies and would now surrender.

The face of Asia was thus changed irrevocably in the space of a week, between 8 August and 15 August. For Japan, the post-war settlement meant the country would permanently lose all its colonies and even parts of its core territory—notably the Kuril Islands—and that it would be placed under foreign occupation. But it also meant that the cruel military regime was finally gone. In China, the settlement preceded eight years of war that culminated in a surprising victory; however, Manchuria now also came under the control of the USSR, with the spectre of civil war in the near future. And for Korea, the settlement meant both independence from Japan and division into Soviet and American zones.

After the war

As for the Eighty-Eighth Brigade, the unit did not participate in the war at all. In fact, the brigade was all but forgotten. Its commanding officer, Zhou Baozhong, was frustrated that he and his men had been left behind. He had wanted to fight Japan. Moreover, had he been in Manchuria, rather than in a camp near a remote Soviet village, in the middle of nowhere, he would have had an opportunity to launch a spectacular career after the Japanese capitulation, as the Soviets would need Chinese to administer the occupied territories. After several of his requests to be relocated went unanswered, Zhou sent a request to the very top—to Marshal Vasilevskiy himself.

Zhou requested that the Chinese personnel be relocated to Changchun, the former capital of Manchukuo, where they would assist the Soviets and become 'the core' of the 'People's Army in Manchuria' and 'unite all the members of the Communist Party of China in Manchuria': 'We will wage struggle against all reactionary elements and movements. We will conduct daily work among the masses and educate the Chinese people in the spirit of friendship and love towards the great neighbour—the Soviet Union, towards the nations of the Soviet Union, towards the Great Stalin', read the letter.[51]

Zhou was granted a personal audience on 2 October,[52] but his plan had in fact been put in motion earlier. Though no Manchurian People's Republic was ever created, Zhou and many others managed to enter the elite of the CPC. Some of them later suffered during the Sino-Soviet split of the 1960s and '70s, not least due to their wartime Soviet connections.[53] The Korean members were to be returned to Korea, and the Soviet Koreans were to go with them.[54] Captain Kim, naturally, was the first on the list of his battalion.[55]

There was one more matter to attend to before the Koreans and the Chinese departed. The war was over, and the USSR was giving decorations to the veterans. Although the Eighty-Eighth Separate Infantry Brigade had not participated in the war, the command of the Second Far Eastern Front, to which it reported, considered its members worthy of decorations too. On 30 August, the front commander, General Maksim Purkayev, signed an order giving awards and medals to its personnel. Captain Kim Il-sung, who was fifth on the list, was presented with the Order of the Red Banner.[56]

Finally, it was time to go home. The initial plan was to go by land through Manchuria, but the railway bridge between Korea's Shinuiju and Manchuria's Andong had been destroyed by bombing. The group consequently headed to Vladivostok, where they boarded the ship *Emelian Pugachev*, a Liberty-class ship that had originally been built in the United States before being given to the Soviet Union as part of the lend-lease programme.[57]

With the ship's speed of 11.5 knots, they needed slightly less than a day and a half to arrive at Wonsan.[58] On 19 September, the ship anchored in Wonsan port, and Kim stepped on to Korean soil for the first time since the Pochonbo raid. He and his comrades were welcomed by Soviet colonel Vladimir Kuchumov, the commandant of Kangwon province.[59] Kim's wife and both of his sons were still in Vyatskoye and came to Korea later, reportedly on 16 November.[60]

It was an emotional moment: 'It feels like the entire universe is in my grasp', uttered one of the group, Choe Yong-jin.[61] Yet Kim was still cautious. Who knew how he would be welcomed in Korea? He instructed his unit not to talk about him; if they were asked directly, they were to say he would be arriving later with a bigger team.[62]

Still dressed in his captain's uniform,[63] Kim soon took a car to Pyongyang, where he had been dispatched by the local Soviet command.[64] Fittingly, the next day, 20 September, was the beginning of the three-day Autumn Eve, the Korean holiday during which people visit their homeland and meet their families. One can only wonder how Kim Il-sung felt at the time. His country was no longer a colony, a goal he had sought to achieve for most of his life, and yet he could not be credited for this in any way, as Korea's independence had been brought about by foreign powers.

4

THE ASCENSION

The autumn of 1945 was undoubtedly the most crucial period in Kim Il-sung's life, one in which fate would propel him from simple battalion commander to the leader of an embryonic nation.

The Soviet sphere of influence expanded dramatically in 1945. Before the Second World War, the USSR had only two satellite states: Mongolia and the Tuvan People's Republic just to the north of that country. By the end of the war, in addition to the Kuril archipelago, the USSR had annexed the Japanese part of Sakhalin Island as well as the northern half of East Prussia. The Soviet Army also occupied Hungarian, Romanian, Bulgarian, Polish and Czechoslovakian lands, had overrun Manchuria and controlled occupation zones in Germany, Austria and, of course, Korea. It was a world-altering change, and northern Korea was merely a small part of Stalin's new acquisitions.

By that time, Moscow had already made a strategic decision that the new countries were not to be formally incorporated into the USSR, but it had not yet outlined a strategic line on what was to be done with them. Thus, the Twenty-Fifth Army, which was put in charge of northern Korea, had to improvise. Late August witnessed the establishment of an order that evolved into the regime that would define North Korea in the coming decades.

The very first item on the agenda was the location of the army's headquarters in Korea. As Seoul, the capital of the peninsula, was in the American zone, the Red Army command initially considered the city of Hamhung on the eastern coast of Korea as the location from which the Twenty-Fifth Army would administer the North.[1]

On 25 August, the commanding officer of the Twenty-Fifth Army, Colonel-General[2] Ivan Chistyakov, was summoned by his superior, Marshal Kirill Meretskov, who ordered him to relocate the command to Korea and offered two options: Hamhung or Pyongyang. The general chose the latter.[3]

This may be why Pyongyang eventually became the North Korean capital. In the years to come, North Korea went a long way to extol the virtues of its capital city. Northern propagandists would go on to claim that the Taedong River culture, named after the river flowing through the city, was one of the world's most ancient. It is, the North asserts, equal only to Thebes of Egypt, Babylon of Mesopotamia, Mohenjo-daro of the Indus Valley and Shang of China.

On 25 August, a team of Soviet officers arrived to inspect Pyongyang.[4] Chistyakov came to the city the next day. On that same day, 26 August, the commander of the local defence district, Lieutenant-General Takeshita Yoshiharu, formally surrendered to Chistyakov, thus ending Japanese rule in northern Korea.

Political movements in Soviet-occupied Korea

For about a month, the future was quite unclear, and local Koreans took the initiative in their own hands. A few days before Emperor Hirohito announced Japan's surrender, the last governor-general of Korea, Abe Nobuyuki, called Pyongyang and instructed the local provincial governor, Furukawa Kanehide, to create local self-governing organisations made up of local Koreans. Abe—a moderate, intelligent man appointed to Korea partly because the more militaristic elements in Japan wanted to keep him away from political developments in Tokyo—sought to make the transfer of power as bloodless as possible.

These self-governing organisations—People's Committees—were thus stuffed with a strange hybrid consisting of members of the former elite, independence fighters and affluent locals.[5] In Pyongyang, the chairman was a former educator and independence activist, Cho Man-sik,[6] whose appointment had been approved by Furukawa.[7] Thus, it should be of no surprise that the People's Committees were not exactly trusted by the Soviets.

Outside the People's Committees, the political activists in North Korea could be roughly divided into three groups: right-wing nationalists, social democrats and communists.

The National Party of Korea was formed on 31 August. As the Soviet military administration solidified itself, its members seemingly decided to appease the new authorities by renaming the Party as 'National Socialist'.[8] It occurred to no one that the new name bore a strong resemblance to that of the Nazi Party, even though it had been less than a year since the Nazi regime had fallen. Naturally, the National Socialist Party was soon dissolved by the Soviets, who perceived it as a hostile organisation.

Next was the Social Democratic Party, which was formed not in Pyongyang but in the city of Shinuiju near the Chinese border. Shinuiju was home to many active, courageous and entrepreneurial North Koreans. The social democrats assessed the situation in the country correctly: the Soviets were in control, but the decision to create a separate communist regime in the North had not yet been made. Thus the best course of action was to strive for an independent, left-wing country that would be friendly to the USSR but not actually controlled by Moscow.

The party's programme stated that it endorsed the democratic order in Korea, and while it was 'thankful to America and the USSR for the liberation', it stood 'against the influence of foreign states in the internal and foreign policy of Korea'.[9]

At the time, the idea of a neutral social-democratic nation with a constructive relationship with Moscow looked like something the Kremlin may have endorsed. Austria was in nearly the same position: its independence had been restored in 1945, with part of the country being placed under a Soviet occupation zone. Yet, the efforts of the left-wing Austrian social democrat Karl Renner prevented this division from becoming permanent, and Austria was unified as a neutral democracy in 1955.[10]

Finally, there were communists. Those sympathetic to Soviet ideology were overjoyed at the Red Army's arrival. They started publishing newspapers with names such as *Pravda* and *Izvestiya*, mimicking the Soviet ones.[11] Many people later joined the communists out of opportunism, but at this point, most of those coming forward were genuine supporters.

On 20 September, the Twenty-Fifth Army finally received instructions from Stalin on its course of action. Stalin commanded them to start building a 'bourgeois-democratic' order in North Korea based on a 'wide coalition of all anti-Japanese parties and organisations'. This new order was explicitly not to be a Soviet one, and freedom of religion was not to be infringed in any way.[12]

Judging by later events in both North Korea and Eastern Europe, it seems that Stalin initially envisioned his satellite states becoming hybrid regimes: somewhat democratic but generally loyal to Moscow. Eventually, however, he realised that democracy and unconditional loyalty to the Kremlin were mutually exclusive, so Moscow began installing local communists in positions of power. As readers will see, for multiple reasons, this process happened faster in North Korea than in Eastern Europe.

Thus, as early as September 1945, Moscow was already instructing the army to create a separate government in the North rather than entering into talks with the Americans on a unified administration for the peninsula. During the subsequent talks with the Americans in 1946, the Soviets genuinely considered agreeing to a unified government on the peninsula, if the Americans would yield and allow it to be dominated by leftists. However, a separate government for the North was already the preferred option.

Finding a leader for the North Korean client state

There are reports that one of the first people to suggest Kim Il-sung's candidacy to the Soviet-controlled leadership was Mun Il, a Soviet Korean who knew Kim from his service in the Eighty-Eighth Brigade. Reportedly, when Moscow was first considering a future war with Japan and the possibility of occupying Korea in the spring of 1945, Mun mentioned to a representative of the Central Committee that an individual named Kim—a former partisan who was serving near Khabarovsk—may be of use to them.[13]

However, as of late August 1945, the question of who would lead North Korea was still completely open. Moscow instructed the intelligence section of the Twenty-Fifth Army to identify Koreans qualified to lead the nation. Political officers were to train them. There was a list of criteria attached: the candidates were to have suitable origins, education, political views and even personal habits.

The intelligence section did their work and submitted a list that does not appear to have included Kim Il-sung. However, the political officers concluded that no-one on the list fully met the criteria. Not willing to quarrel with the intelligence officers, the political officers instead decided to lower their standards and began training the candidates, with seven instructors assigned to each person on the list. The list itself was sent to Moscow.[14]

The first option presented on the list was to take someone from the former Communist International. Before the Comintern was formally dissolved in 1943, its worldwide network of agents had included some individuals who had worked in colonial Korea. Kim Yong-bom and Pak Chong-ae were first on the list. They were a couple: two Comintern agents who married each other after having originally been sent to Korea solely to pose as husband and wife.[15] Ms Pak was one of the first to greet Chistyakov when he arrived in Pyongyang and was present when General Takeshita surrendered to the Soviet Army. They made a good impression on Chistyakov, and thus both she and her husband ended up on the list of candidates.

Other Comintern candidates included Chang Shi-u, future minister of commerce of North Korea; Kim Gwang-jin and Pak Chong-ho, two Comintern agents working in colonial Korea; and Yang Yong-sun, a former member of the intelligence bureau of the Pacific Fleet who had been on assignment in Korea since 1937.

The next in the list after the Comintern members was Kim Du-bong. An old linguist and an independence activist, he had spent many years working with the CPC in China.

Another candidate was Cho Man-sik, whom the Japanese had appointed to head the local self-government organisation in Pyongyang at the end of the war. Several Soviet Koreans were also on the list. Aleksei Hegay was a Communist Party bureaucrat. Yu Song-chol was one of the Soviet Koreans in the Eighty-Eighth Brigade. Pavel Kim (aka Kim Chan) was an accountant in the Uzbek Soviet Republic. Another was Pak Pyong-yul, a low-level Soviet bureaucrat and a native of the town of Suchan (Partizansk) in the Russian Far East.[16]

Finally, some of the Soviet officers had reportedly considered Major Mikhail Kan, a Soviet interpreter, for this position, but he did not end up on the list of candidates.[17]

All of those on the list later became prominent in the North:[18] Hegay became one of the Central Committee's vice-chairmen;[19] Yu Song-chol became a two-star general;[20] Pak Pyong-yul was placed in charge of the North's military industry;[21] Yang Yong-sun embarked on a diplomatic career, becoming ambassador to Czechoslovakia in 1954;[22] and Kim Chan became the first president of the Central Bank.[23]

Yet, none of these individuals was chosen to lead the North. As Major-General Nikolay Lebedev, the senior political officer of the Twenty-Fifth Army, later discovered, the most likely reason for this was the interservice rivalry between the Soviet police and military intelligence. The head of the police, Lavrentiy Beria, wanted to limit the influence of military intelligence, and the best way to do that was to show that the police could do things better. Thus, he started searching for a more suitable candidate in the USSR.[24]

The rise of Kim Il-sung

One of those who ultimately ended up contributing to Kim Il-sung's rise was Lieutenant-Colonel Grigoriy Mekler. By 1945, Mekler was in charge of the Seventh Section of the political department of the First Far Eastern Front. 'Seventh' was a codename for sections and departments in the Red Army responsible for working with people in enemy territories overrun by the army.[25]

In late August 1945, by order of the front's commanding officer, Marshal Meretskov, Mekler visited the Eighty-Eighth Brigade together with the marshal. Meretskov talked to the

Chinese servicemen, while Mekler's job was to write an assessment of Kim Il-sung.

Mekler liked Captain Kim: 'He seemed to me a demanding and attentive person, respected and even loved by his men.' Mekler talked to Kim's subordinates and to Kim himself, noticing that Kim spoke fluent Chinese and some Russian—accented but sufficient for communication. 'When he was talking to me, I saw that his thoughts, his assessments of events were mature', remembered Mekler. He attended one of the training sessions Kim organised for his men and ultimately wrote a highly positive assessment letter on the battalion commander Kim Il-sung.[26]

Kim was then summoned to talk to Purkayev, commander of the Second Far Eastern Front, and Iosif Shikin, the political officer of the entire command of the Soviet Armed Forces in the Far East. Shikin asked him to confirm whether he was indeed a Korean born to the south of Pyongyang and enquired about his party membership and family status. The general then asked him: 'What would you say if we were to send you to North Korea?' Kim replied enthusiastically: 'I am always ready, if it will help the World Revolution.' Shikin was pleased to hear such an answer.[27]

The position Kim was interviewed for was not that of the country's leader. Rather, he was supposed to become deputy commandant of Pyongyang city,[28] assisting its commandant, Colonel Vasiliy Korolyov.

After Kim returned to Korea and moved to Pyongyang, the man who introduced him personally to the Soviet generals there was the same Mun Il who thus, willingly or unwillingly, played the role of North Korean kingmaker. The generals took a liking to Kim. After arriving in Pyongyang, Kim and some of his men intended to start their own businesses, but General Lebedev recommended that he be more proactive.[29]

The biggest factor contributing to Kim Il-sung's eventual success was the absence of an obvious candidate for leader among the others, making North Korea distinct from the rest of the newly acquired Soviet satellites. Bulgaria, for example, had the former chief of the Comintern, Dimitrov—the very one who had overseen Kim's interrogation in 1941—and the communist movement in Czechoslovakia had Klement Gottwald, who had been the head of the Party about as long as Stalin had been in the USSR.

Yet things were different in Korea. The major problem was the absence of an established Communist Party. The Communist Party of Korea had not existed since 1928, when it was dissolved by the Comintern, which had become exasperated at the Korean communists' constant internal squabbling. The Party was reborn only in August 1945 in the American zone, and it seems that the list of candidates had already been sent to Moscow by the time its leader, Pak Hon-yong, had established contact with the Soviets.

The second factor was that, of all the candidates, only Kim Il-sung was sufficiently native and sufficiently Soviet. Unlike the Soviet Koreans, he had been born in Korea and would thus be more likely to be perceived as an indigenous ruler rather than a foreign viceroy. At the same time, he was a Soviet officer and thus considered by the Red Army as one of their own.

Finally, there was a more peculiar reason for the decision. As observant readers may remember, Kim Il-sung was not the first man to carry this alias. This led to confusion in the minds of many in Korea, as the image of 'Kim Il-sung' was a fusion of several people, including the future Great Leader. Thus, in October 1945, for example, one leftist newspaper in the American zone referred to 'Kim Il-sung' as 'hating the idea of becoming an officer in the age of imperialism'[30] as part of the biography of another man, Kim Hyon-chung, who also used this *nom de guerre* (as readers may recall, Kim Hyon-chung was once a promising officer in the Japanese Army). Thus, among those who welcomed independence, 'Kim Il-sung' was bound to become a popular figure, further strengthening the positive impression Kim made on the Soviet generals.

In late October, Kim Il-sung was explicitly recommended for leadership in a report to the deputy head of the Soviet government, Georgiy Malenkov, as well as the Deputy Commissar of Defence Nikolay Bulganin and General Shikin, who by that time had become the chief of the Red Army's Main Political Directorate. The report stated that Kim had been a Manchurian guerrilla for ten years and had served as a battalion commander 'from 1941'— actually, from 1942—to 1945. It stated that 'his name is widely known among many Korean people', he 'is known as a fighter and a hero of the Korean people against Japanese imperialism' and the 'Korean people made many legends about him.'[31]

It is at this point that Beria seems to have learned of Kim's existence and took his candidacy to Stalin. Beria stated that the people suggested by the military were problematic as they did not fully meet the original criteria, while Kim Il-sung was not. The Twenty-Fifth Army was thus instructed to dismiss the other candidates and focus on Kim Il-sung.[32] As General Lebedev later remembered, Stalin's final decision was passed to Politburo member Andrei Zhdanov, then to General Terentiy Shtykov and then to the Twenty-Fifth Army.[33]

Kim's promotion was intended to be temporary. The Soviets still entertained some possibility of creating a unified government in Korea, and should that have transpired, Kim Il-sung would not have remained in charge. Yet, during this period Kim started to prove himself a true master of political scheming, which ensured he would remain in his chair and rule North Korea until his death in 1994.

PART II

THE PUPPET KING

5

THE NEW BEGINNING

Soviet control over North Korea was solidified on 11 October 1945, when Chistyakov issued a widely publicised executive order to the Korean people.[1] The order to a large extent mirrored Stalin's directive from 20 September.[2] All paramilitary units were to be dissolved, and all political organisations were to be registered with the Soviet administration. The period of initial chaos, hopes and fears was over, having lasted for around two months, and a new age had begun.

The first order of business was to reorganise the Communist Party. But as the headquarters of the re-founded Communist Party of Korea were in American-controlled Seoul, and the Soviets still hoped that the two halves of Korea would one day be reunified under a friendly government, establishing a separate party for North Korea was not an option.

The solution was the creation of the North Korean Branch Office of the Communist Party. Its ruling council, the Organisation Bureau, was formed on 13 October 1945. Interestingly, while Kim Il-sung was appointed to the bureau, he was not its first secretary. That honour went to Kim Yong-bom instead.[3] As one Soviet officer explained in a report, the reason for this decision was that Kim Il-sung was scheduled to be appointed to an even higher position: the one at the top of the North Korean proto-government. In communist nations, the Party was normally considered to be above the government; however, this document showed that the order envisioned by the Soviets at the time was different in that regard.[4]

Kim Il-sung's grand debut

With the Organisation Bureau established, the Soviets continued the preparations for Kim Il-sung's first public appearance, scheduled for the following day, Sunday, 14 October. From 1 October, it had been planned that Kim would make his debut appearance at a mass demonstration scheduled for 14 October. Pyongyang Radio had aired regular broadcasts about the upcoming event, saying that 'the national hero Kim Il-sung may be present there as well'.[5] Soviet aeroplanes blanketed the city with leaflets containing similar content.[6]

For his grand appearance, Kim needed suitable attire, and, obviously, a Soviet captain's uniform with the Order of the Red Banner attached to its breast, which was what he was wearing, was not befitting a supposed Korean national hero. Finding suitable attire proved a formidable task, as Kim was taller than most Koreans.[7] After several failed attempts, the Soviets eventually found a dark suit with a white shirt and striped tie in Kim's size.[8] Despite General Lebedev's ardent efforts, Kim refused to remove his Order of the Red Banner from the suit. It was his only decoration, and he was very proud of it.[9]

On that sunny Sunday day, a huge crowd assembled near Moran Hill in the centre of Pyongyang. There was a podium and lectern for the speakers, which the Soviets had assembled just before the event. Three Soviet generals and several prominent

Koreans were in attendance; Major Kan was tasked with interpretation. A huge portrait of Stalin dominated the tribune, with a slogan—'Long live Stalin! Long live the Workers' and Farmers' Red Army!'—written underneath. But Kim Il-sung was nowhere to be seen. In fact, the future Great Leader was hidden under the podium—in a special cavity covered with a wooden lid.

Then Major Kan announced that Kim Il-sung would give a speech. The lid opened, and Kim emerged in front of the Korean people for the first time. Perhaps Kim himself never learnt about this, but one of the men in the crowd was Paik Sun-yup, who, in a few years, would become one of South Korea's most famous generals. Less than five years remained until the North and the South would enter into the most destructive war in Korea's history.[10]

Kim started speaking. For the first time, the Pyongyangites heard his unusually hoarse voice. He read his short speech hailing Stalin and the Red Army and calling for national unity.[11] This speech had been written for him by the Soviets and then translated into Korean. At the time, Kim was not fluent in Korean—since his youth, he had mostly spoken in Chinese and later in Russian and could not communicate in Korean as a native speaker.[12]

The public was puzzled. The young man they saw was not the semi-legendary 'Kim Il-sung' many had expected to see. To some, he looked more Chinese than Korean. As one eyewitness later remembered, 'he looked like a waiter in a Chinese restaurant'.[13] This mix-up gave birth to an urban legend that there was some other 'real Kim Il-sung'—the true national hero—and that the man everyone saw on 14 October was an impostor. This remained a popular belief in South Korea until the 1960s.[14]

To counter this rumour, the Soviet authorities organised a public trip to Kim Il-sung's home village. However, the one they selected was not the village of Chilgol, where Kim had been born, but neighbouring Mangyongdae, where he had spent his childhood (see Chapter 1). Kim himself reportedly considered Mangyongdae his home, and most of his surviving relatives, including his paternal grandparents Kim Bo-hyon and Lee Bo-ik, lived in Mangyongdae, not Chilgol.[15]

The Soviets intimidated the locals into testifying that Kim was born in this village and had lived there throughout his childhood. General Lebedev later testified that the Soviets went so far as to threaten to execute anyone who dared disagree, including their relatives.[16] The threat worked perfectly: the visit went as planned,[17] and from then on Mangyongdae was Kim Il-sung's official home village.[18] Kim, however, did not settle there but lived in the former building of the Oriental Development Company in Pyongyang, one of the largest Japanese companies in Korea, which had been partly owned by the colonial government.[19] His house was located near the residences of important Soviet officials: Colonel-General Shtykov, Colonel Aleksandr Ignatyev and Counsellor Grigoriy Tunkin.[20] Tunkin played tennis with Kim, delighted to find a skilled partner. Sometimes, Kim's son Yura also came to watch his father playing.[21]

In the late 1940s, an entire government district was built in Pyongyang, with Kim Il-sung occupying the most expansive house. Located on the top of a small mountain,[22] it had two floors and more than a dozen rooms.[23] Kim's second son Shura was too young to go down the mountain on his own, but his brother Yura did go there to play with Soviet kids. The future Leader's son was often dressed in a uniform resembling that of a general, sparking envy among many of the local children. Yura once took away a toy submachine gun from his namesake, a son of Soviet officer Kang Sang-ho. The victim's mother then went directly to Kim Il-sung's house, took the stolen possession away and returned it to its proper owner.[24]

This was not the only episode showing how close the Kims were to the Soviet diaspora in the late 1940s. For example, Kim Il-sung himself suggested that students from the Soviet school in Pyongyang should be allowed to use his personal swimming pool.[25] In merely a few years, such familiarity would be completely unthinkable.

In 1945, Kim Il-sung was reunited with his brother Yong-ju, who had previously been an interpreter in the Japanese Army. He moved to Seoul after Japan surrendered. Yong-ju heard reports about 'Commander Kim Il-sung' appearing before the people on 14 October and was overjoyed to learn his brother was still alive.[26] While he was afraid that Kim Il-sung would be less than welcoming due to his having served the Japanese, he still departed for Pyongyang to meet his brother, and the reunion was a happy one.[27] In the years to come, Yong-ju would rise to political prominence in North Korea and, for a time, was even considered Kim's second-in-command.

The new order

Meanwhile, the moderate opposition to the new order took advantage of Chistyakov's permission to create political parties and established the Democratic Party, which held its founding ceremony on 3 November. Cho Man-sik, whom the Japanese had appointed to facilitate the transition of power in the August of that year, was elected as its standard-bearer. One of its two vice-chairmen was Choe Yong-gon—Kim's confidant and former comrade in the Eighty-Eighth Brigade.[28] The flags of all the major Allies were flown during the ceremony: the Red Banner of the USSR, the Union Jack of the UK, the Stars and Stripes of the United States and the White Sun Flag of the Republic of China.[29]

ACCIDENTAL TYRANT

It was one of the last events in North Korea in which these flags were hoisted together, as the beginning of the Cold War made it not only impossible but also doomed the nascent Democratic Party. Indeed, apart from the founding ceremony, this party never did anything of note.

In late November, the existence of another major force of peaceful opposition in North Korea, the Social Democratic Party, also came to an end. Fearful of Soviet intervention following a skirmish in Shinuiju between local young activists and communists,[30] the party's leadership fled to the South, and, with that, the Social Democratic Party effectively ceased to exist. The new order was rapidly taking shape, as the opposition to it was vanishing.

From November, the Branch Office of the Communist Party also started to publish its own newspaper: *Chongno*, literally 'the Correct Way'. Initially a weekly, *Chongno* was gradually published more frequently as time passed.

While *Chongno* inevitably gave its readers a very rosy image of the country, early North Korea was not a pleasant place to be. With the colonial government gone and the new state institutions yet to be established, the economy was dysfunctional, and the man in charge—Colonel-General Chistyakov—was doing little to help alleviate the situation.

One of the most fascinating documents of the era is the report of two courageous Soviet officers, Lieutenant-Colonel Georgiy Fyodorov and Major Yuriy Livshits.[31] Written after spending about six weeks in North Korea, the report sharply and objectively described the situation in the Soviet occupation zone. The report was disturbing—economic life had come to a halt with the end of colonial rule, and the economy was crumbling: trains had stopped running, factories were shutting down and, given the lack of fertiliser, the agricultural sector could not produce enough food to meet the people's needs. Many

Soviet soldiers and even officers behaved abhorrently. They got drunk, shot wildly in the air, robbed and beat Korean men and raped Korean women. Moreover, the new authorities resettled the Japanese people in ghettos, with dozens dying in appalling conditions every day.

Chistyakov carried personal responsibility for the situation, as the Colonel-General blocked his subordinates from helping the populace. In one example, he refused the request of Major-General Andrei Romanenko and Colonel of State Security Colonel Gerasim Balasanov to allocate rice to the starving ghetto dwellers: the Colonel-General stated that the rice was a 'trophy' that 'has already been inventoried by the intendancy'.[32]

In an act of unprecedented bravery, Fyodorov and Livshits chose to defy the all-powerful general and report him to his superiors. It seems the intervention was a success and their letter reached Chistyakov's commander, Marshal Meretskov, who ordered Chistyakov to feed the starving Japanese;[33] the following month, in January 1946, Shtykov replaced Chistyakov as the senior officer in charge of North Korea.

Meanwhile, in December 1945, Moscow decided that it would be Kim Il-sung who would lead the nascent nation.[34] Previously, Kim had been 'promoted' by the generals of their own volition, but now this line was formally sanctioned by the Kremlin.

Moscow's decision, naturally, caused changes in Korea as well. The first signs of a nascent cult of Kim Il-sung started to appear. On 14 December 1945, *Chongno* published a message from an organisation called the 'Seoul Section of the all-Korea Union of Youth Organisations' in which Kim Il-sung was called 'Commander', 'True Patriot' and 'Great Chief'.[35] The situation in the Party's Branch Office leadership soon changed too. On 18 December, Kim Yong-bom resigned, and Kim Il-sung took his place as the chief secretary of the Northern Branch Bureau of the

Communist Party of Korea. This was his first position where he would be in charge of North Korea.[36]

On 21 December, the very first official biography of Kim Il-sung appeared in *Chongno*. While being closer to the real narrative than any of the subsequent ones, it already showed signs of significant falsification. Kim, the newspaper said, had been working for the revolution since he had been a student. In 1927, he had joined the youth league of the Communist Party of China. In 1929, he became the youth league's secretary in Eastern Manchuria. He joined the Party itself at the age of twenty-one and in 1931 organised and led the 'People's Anti-Japanese Guerrilla Unit in Eastern Manchuria'. In 1933, as the unit grew, he became its political officer. In 1936, he became a division commander in the Second Army of the NAJUA and later a member of the Communist Party's Special Committee for Eastern Manchuria. After becoming chief of the Second Army, he returned home when the Red Army liberated Korea. He switched his membership from the brotherly CPC to the Communist Party of Korea and now enforces the party line and 'iron discipline'. His life was a life of Bolshevist struggle, concluded the piece.[37]

This biography was already quite farfetched. Kim Il-sung had never joined the CPC youth league. He had not organised any independent partisan unit but had instead joined the existing one. His positions in the NAJUA were also inaccurate. Still, the biography at least acknowledged that Kim used to be a member of the CPC—a fact that was soon to become completely taboo in North Korean historical hagiography.[38]

The North Korean proto-government

In late December, US Secretary of State James Byrnes, UK Secretary of State for Foreign Affairs Ernest Bevin and the USSR's

People's Commissar for Foreign Affairs Vyacheslav Molotov met in Moscow. Among many other topics concerning the post-world order, they also discussed Korea. Washington, London and Moscow agreed to place the peninsula under a trusteeship of four powers—themselves and China—for five years, while the Americans and the Soviets would set up a provisional government for a united Korea.[39] The decisions of this Moscow Conference were immediately made public.

The trusteeship clause proved highly unpopular among the contemporary Korean elite, as it meant that for five more years the country would be mostly or exclusively run by foreigners. Only communists, instructed by Moscow, duly supported the conference's decisions, and even they initially expressed their opposition to the trusteeship idea before the Kremlin ordered them to relent.[40]

Meanwhile, the year 1946 dawned—the first New Year since Korea's liberation from Japan. In one of his first actions as the man in charge, Kim Il-sung made his first New Year address to the Korean people, which was published on the front page of *Chongno* on 1 January 1946.[41] Interestingly, in the speech Kim spoke positively about all of the Allied Powers: not just the USSR but also Britain, the United States and the Republic of China. The Cold War was yet to begin. Since then, every New Year Kim Il-sung would deliver a lengthy speech where he presented the nationwide audience with his vision of the country's present and tasks for the future.

It was also in early 1946 that the United States and the Soviet Union started long and ultimately unsuccessful talks about the creation of a unified government in Korea. The chief of the Soviet delegation was Colonel-General Shtykov, previously political officer of the First Far Eastern Front who had replaced Chistyakov as the de facto senior Soviet officer in North Korea.[42]

Shtykov was a very different person from Chistyakov. Whereas the commander of the Twenty-Fifth Army was a professional military man, Shtykov was a politician—and a rising star. A friend and protégé of Politburo member Andrei Zhdanov, who at the time was perceived as a potential successor to Stalin, Shtykov was one of very few political officers at the time to reach the three-star rank of Colonel-General.

Shtykov's background and personality were also quite unusual for a general. He never received any advanced education, having only graduated from a middle school. He was a rather simple person, and this simplicity could mean greater kindness as well as greater cruelty. For North Korea in the second half of the 1940s, his appointment led to a change for the better. His predecessor, Chistyakov, ruled the North as an occupier in the worst sense of the word. Shtykov, on the other hand, felt responsible for those under his rule, and he and his subordinates bombarded Moscow with requests to send aid to Korea.[43] Kim Il-sung and Shtykov liked each other and soon became close friends. They spent a lot of time together and sometimes played cards: in a revealing custom, the loser had to climb under the table.[44] For Kim, this friendship was most useful, as it greatly contributed to him staying in power.

Meanwhile, North Korea was preparing for the formation of its proto-government. Stalin's instructions were to organise all parties into one bloc with a single platform: support the decisions of the Moscow Conference.

However, the Democratic Party's chairman, Cho Man-sik, refused to perform his assigned role. As well as failing to endorse the Moscow Conference, the Party formally voted to condemn it.[45] The Soviets saw this as crossing a red line. On 5 February, under instructions from the Soviet administration, Cho Man-sik's deputy Choe Yong-gon purged the organisation of nationalists and took over the leadership of the Party, which was soon reduced to a compliant puppet of the communists.

As a union between the 'purified' Democratic Party and the communists would have looked far from convincing as a bloc supposedly representing the 'whole of Korean society', two more political parties were formed, the first of which was the Party of Young Friends of the Heavenly Way.

The Heavenly Way was a religion founded in the early twentieth century. Popular among nationalists, it had become especially prominent in the colonial era, when some had perceived it as a national alternative to both the State Shinto of Japan and the Christianity of the West. Since many of its followers were at the time quite young, the 1920s saw the formation of a number of youth organisations of Heavenly Way believers, culminating in the establishment of the Party of Young Followers of the Heavenly Way in 1923.[46] This organisation was dissolved by the militarist regime of Governor-General Minami Jiro in 1939.[47] The North Korean party was thus a recreation of this colonial-era organisation.

The other was the New People's Party (NPP), created by Kim Du-bong, a linguist and communist nationalist close to Mao Zedong, who had been one of the rejected candidates on the list of potential occupants of the North Korean throne. A leftist nationalist party such as the NPP[48] was exactly what the Soviets needed for the bloc, known as the 'United Front' in the parlance of the day, which now comprised communists, 'rightist' democrats, leftist nationalists and a group representing a local religion. Such a combination looked sellable as the legitimate representative of all 'progressive' North Koreans.

Thus, with the Democratic Party subjugated and the Heavenly Way and NPP established, the preparations for the formation of the North Korean proto-government were complete. Despite the government being marketed as 'democratic', it was not established by any election whatsoever. Instead, in February 1946 the Soviets organised an event verbosely called the 'Extended Conference of all Political Parties, Social Organisations, Various Administrative Bureaus and Province-, City- and County-Level People's Committees of North Korea'. It was this conference that endorsed the formation of the Provisional People's Committee for North Korea (PPCNK), with Kim Il-sung at its head.[49]

The Soviet Army sent formal greetings to the PPCNK. Notably, as archival documents show, mention of the Moscow Conference, present in an earlier draft, was removed from the final version of the letter.[50]

The PPCNK was under the Soviet Union's complete control. The decisions it passed were prepared by a group of Soviet officers headed by Major-General Romanenko, typed in Russian and then translated into Korean and passed on. The translation quality was often substandard, and the Korean outcome often featured distinctly Russian expressions. However, the PPCNK rubber-stamped the translated documents as is, without even a stylistic correction.[51] In May 1947, the group was eventually reformed into the Directorate of the Soviet Civil Administration (DSCA), which controlled most aspects of life in North Korea.[52]

However, to the general public, the PPCNK was presented as if it were actually in charge. It should be said that while it was not, and though some Soviet officials wanted to maintain full control, others genuinely believed that the local administration should eventually take over.[53]

Soviet policy in North Korea, which Kim Il-sung duly signed into law, was similar to the policy adopted in the many countries that had fallen under the USSR's rule by the end of the Second World War. The general line was to confiscate property from the rich and give it to the poor, ban large companies and nationalise a substantial part of the economy. However, the fact that Korea used to be a colony added some specifics. While only the property of rich Koreans was to be confiscated, each and every Japanese person was to lose their possessions and be deported to the Japanese archipelago.

Land reform was another important policy of the Soviet administration. Formulated by Romanenko's team, the reform plan prescribed that, as well as the Japanese, rich Koreans would also lose their land, which was then to be given to poor farmers, with no compensation given to the previous owners. The latter aspect was the major difference from what was going on in the South, where the local administration decided that the landlords should be compensated for the land they were losing.[54] This difference mattered a lot, since most of the landlords were Koreans, not Japanese, and these were wealthy but not obscenely rich people—for many of them, the land reform in the North was an abrupt end to their financial viability.

In the autumn of 1946, North Korea established a public distribution system of basic nutrition, initially targeted solely at government employees.[55] This was intended to be a provisional measure until the economy recovered from the crisis, but in 1947 it was expanded to include some industrial goods as well.[56] In the years to come, it would become one of the cornerstones of the economic system of Kim Il-sung's North Korea.

The Japanese had invested heavily in northern Korea's industry,[57] and soon nearly the entirety of it was given to the North Korean proto-state.[58] Thus, the Soviets created a huge state sector in the economy. However, at the time, neither private trade nor small business was considered illegal in the North.[59] The private sector was limited but by no means destroyed.

The yen was to be replaced with a new currency, first as a provisional measure, by the won of the Red Army command, and then, two years later, by the North Korean won,[60] with the banknotes being printed in the USSR. Although credited to the 'people's government' led by 'Commander Kim Il-sung', all of these decisions were made by the Soviets.

Support and opposition

In the very earliest publications, Kim Il-sung was presented as an equal to Kim Du-bong, whom the Soviets intended to put in charge of the North Korean proto-parliament (also not elected by the people).[61] Soon, however, Kim Il-sung became the only 'Leader of the Korean people'.

The leader needed a good biography, and, instructed by General Romanenko, in late 1946 a group of DSCA employees started to compile one. No references to Kim's Soviet past were to be made,[62] and his earlier years were also to be rewritten. The major twist to the emerging official version of Kim's biography was that he was no longer a member of the partisan movement led and organised by the Chinese but rather led his own force, allegedly called the 'Korean People's Revolutionary Army' (KPRA).[63] This claim, which had no relation to reality and well-documented history, was inserted to 'nationalise' his past.[64]

It is not psychologically easy to participate in manufacturing fake history, and the head of the project, a Soviet Korean Pak Il, eventually asked Romanenko to accept his resignation on ethical grounds. The general himself seemingly understood that what they were doing was morally dubious, so he told Pak Il that while they were being watched and thus could not just abort the project, he would do his best to relieve Pak Il from this unscrupulous assignment as soon as possible.[65]

Yet the myth lived on, and a significant number of North Koreans believed it and trusted Kim Il-sung. Indeed, it is very hard for any political system to survive without at least a substantial minority of the population supporting it, and early

North Korea definitely had some popular support. Who were these people?

The first were the communists, who, naturally, saw the Red Army's arrival as the realisation of their most cherished dreams and were willing to accept Kim Il-sung as the head of the nascent state. These were left-wing intellectuals who thought that the new regime would be a definite improvement over its colonial predecessor, not least as it would not treat Koreans as second-class citizens. They also thought that, compared with its counterpart in the South, it would be fairer to the common man and strive to enlighten the people. Unlike Pyongyang, Seoul compensated the landlords for the lost land. Unlike in the North, big businesses— including those that had been closely affiliated with the colonial regime—were welcome to continue operating in the South.

Naturally, quite a few farmers—Korea at the time was an agrarian country—appreciated being given their landlords' land and no longer having to pay rent for it. There were also those who bought into the Soviet rhetoric about 'democracy'. This may seem somewhat surprising given that only people approved by the Soviets were eligible to run in the elections, but it should be remembered that most Koreans had been disfranchised under the Japanese. Having little to no experience in democracy, they did not comprehend that passive suffrage (the right to stand for election) is as much a necessity for a democratic system as active suffrage (the right to vote).

But the new regime also met with opposition from some quarters. There was a significant number of farmers who, to the utter shock of the Soviet administration, opposed the land reform, saying that it made them feel like thieves and that the landlords should at least be compensated for their property.[66] Along with businessmen and most of the colonial elite, the landlords themselves did not appreciate being treated as traitors at worst and suspicious elements at best solely for being successful under the previous administration. There were also rightists: those who were ideologically opposed to the communists and wanted their country to become more like the United States than the USSR. And local Christians were, of course, not happy that half the country would now be controlled by a regime openly pursuing a policy of state atheism.

The most radical opposition mostly consisted of right-wing nationalists. Forced to go underground in September and October 1945, they believed that it was their duty to resist the new foreign power that had replaced the Japanese order with a communist one.

One of the prominent nationalists, Kim Jong-ui, founded a group called the 'White Shirts Society' that engaged in terrorist attacks with the aim of overthrowing the nascent communist regime. The group plotted to kill Kim Il-sung and, hopefully, take the lives of some Soviet generals with him as well.

A good opportunity to do so came on 1 March 1946, when Kim Il-sung was scheduled to talk on the occasion of the first post-independence celebration of the anniversary of the 1 March movement, when some Soviet generals would also be in attendance. Several armed members of the White Shirts went there too. The man who conducted the attack was called Kim Hyong-jip.

'I threw the grenade and ran for 200 metres or so'—testified Kim Hyong-jip. 'I understood from the talking I heard that there were no dead from the blast. I wanted to repeat the attack, but after I returned to the tribune, I was arrested and did not manage to throw the second grenade on the tribune.'[67] What Kim Hyong-jip did not see was that a junior Soviet lieutenant, Yakov Novichenko, caught the grenade and covered it with his body. The officer was carrying a book, which ultimately served him as a glorified flak jacket. Thus, while Novichenko was wounded, he was not killed. After capturing Kim Hyong-jip, the

Soviets soon tracked down the entire organisation. Kim Jong-ui and Kim Hyong-jip, along with other members of the White Shirts, were tried in the court of the Soviet Maritime District. Both Kims were found guilty and executed.[68]

Vision for a unified Korea

In the meantime, preparations were being made for the first talks with the United States about Korea's future. Documents show that in March 1946 Shtykov outlined his project for a hypothetical government for a unified Korea after discussing it with Kim Il-sung and Pak Hon-yong.[69] His candidate for the position of head of state—the prime minister—was not Kim Il-sung. The man whom Shtykov envisioned as the leader of the government was Yo Un-hyong, a leftist independence activist who had met Lenin but was not himself a communist. While he may have looked like a compromise candidate, there was little evidence of compromise in the composition of the cabinet.

All important positions were to be controlled by the communists. A communist was to be appointed as one of the two deputy prime ministers, as well as holding positions as ministers of internal affairs, of foreign affairs, of industry, of education and of propaganda; a communist was also appointed as chairman of the Committee for Economic Planning. Kim Il-sung was to become the minister of internal affairs and thus placed in charge of the police, and Pak Hon-yong was appointed deputy prime minister.[70]

A few amendments were made to the second edition of the proposal, the most important of which was the creation of the position of the minister of the armed forces. This position was to be taken by Kim Il-sung, with responsibility for the Ministry of Internal Affairs being given to Choe Yong-gon.[71] A former member of the CPC, Kim took to heart Mao's famous words: 'Political power grows out of the barrel of a gun.'

Indeed, if accepted, such a configuration could easily have led to a communist takeover of the entire nation. A similar scenario later unfolded in Czechoslovakia: after solidifying control over the key ministries in 1946, the communists led by Prime Minister Klement Gottwald went on to usurp power from President Edvard Beneš in 1948.[72] However, this second proposal was not even properly tabled.[73] The Joint Soviet–American Commission of Korea was consumed by mutual distrust almost from the outset. Every suggestion was debated, every sentence and phrase questioned. As time went by, hope for a compromise faded further away.

Meanwhile, a cult of personality continued to grow around Kim Il-sung in North Korea. According to the then established tradition, every top communist leader was supposed to be a master of political theory: accordingly, on 23 March 1946 Kim published his first theoretical work, *A Political Manifesto of Twenty Points*. The manifesto basically reflected the then-Soviet view of North Korea's future: a welfare state in which citizens would supposedly be equal and with a universal franchise. Naturally, it omitted the key points constituting the new order: that this would be a highly authoritarian state led by the Communist Party, which, in turn, would answer to Moscow and the Soviet Union.

The manifesto was forever enshrined in the first song to glorify Kim, the 'Song of Commander Kim Il-sung', which described him as the 'saviour of the masses' and the 'Great Sun' and called on Koreans to unite 'around the Twenty Points'. In the decades to come, this became one of the most frequently sung songs in North Korea.[74]

On 30 May 1946, Kim Jong-suk gave birth to Kim Il-sung's first daughter. The girl was also given a Russian name: Tatyana.[75]

However, she is better known under her Korean name, Kyong-hui.[76]

In July, soon after Tatyana was born, Kim Il-sung was summoned to Moscow to talk to Joseph Stalin himself. Although Stalin met a number of leading figures of the nascent socialist bloc in that month,[77] this meeting was unique in that it was not a formal one and thus not mentioned in official records. While the meeting was very briefly mentioned in a later document,[78] historians have largely been forced to rely on eyewitness testimonies to reconstruct what happened. Fortunately, one of the participants—General Lebedev—gave a detailed interview revealing how the meeting came about.[79]

According to Lebedev, as well as other sources, Kim Il-sung was summoned to Moscow together with Pak Hon-yong, the leading South Korean communist at the time.[80] They were accompanied by Generals Lebedev, Shtykov and Romanenko, Anatoliy Shabshin, the former Soviet deputy consul in Seoul, as well as Pak's and Kim's personal secretaries. Kim's secretary was Mun Il, who thus once again became privy to history-altering decisions.[81]

It was during this meeting that Stalin commanded Kim to proceed with the 'Sovietisation' of North Korea.[82] From then on, the Kremlin viewed a unified Korea merely as a plan B, one that was unlikely to be put into motion. The primary scenario for the future was the creation of a separate communist state in the North.

The Communist Party of North Korea

When Kim Il-sung returned from Moscow, his family hired a female Japanese servant, Hagio Kazuko, a former girls' high school student in Manchukuo's capital who had been forced to flee the city when the war began.[83] She was sixteen and worked for the Kims for one year before leaving Korea with the other Japanese.

As Kazuko later remembered, at the time she mostly cooked Russian food for the Kims, although Kim Il-sung also had a taste for Japanese *gyoza* dumplings. Breakfast was to be served at 10 a.m., lunch at 3 p.m. and dinner at 9 or 10 p.m. Evidently, Kim was a night owl. While he had not been able to follow such a routine in his partisan unit or in the Red Army, now, finally, he could sleep for as long as he wanted.[84] Kazuko was evidently a good cook—in 1946, Kim gained a significant amount of weight.

As for Korea, one of the signs the division was increasingly likely to persist was the gradual change in the name the North Korean party organisation used to describe itself. On 22–3 May 1946,[85] the 'Northern Branch Bureau of the Communist Party of Korea' was renamed the 'Communist Party of North Korea'. While no formal decision seems to have been made on its renaming, the party's new name showed that 'North Korea' was becoming a separate entity.[86]

The second stage took place a little later. In the mid-1940s, Stalin's policy was to conceal the strengthening Soviet control over newly acquired satellites. One of the ways in which this was done was to merge a local Communist Party with a social democratic one. On the one hand, a united left would have more legitimacy, while on the other, the unified party and thus the country would be still controlled by the communists.

The first satellite subjected to this process was the Soviet occupation zone in Germany, where, by orders from Moscow on 21 April 1946, the Communist Party was merged with the Social Democratic Party of Germany to form the Socialist Unity Party of Germany. A similar scheme was imposed on North Korea as well. By Stalin's direct order,[87] the Communist Party was merged with the NPP, forming the Workers' Party of North Korea (WPNK).

By July 1946, the decision to merge the parties had already been made.[88] The process was smoother than in Soviet-occupied Germany, as the NPP was not an independent political force to begin with, and its members were also communists in all but name. The inaugural congress of the WPNK, held in August 1946, formally approved the merger.[89] The Communist Party's *Chongno* and the NPP's *Chonjin* (lit. 'Advance') were also merged to form a new newspaper: *Rodong Shinmun* (lit. 'Labour Newspaper').

It appeared as if the Communist Party had simply swallowed the NPP, as the WPNK became the main tool of the Soviet administration in ruling the North. But it is not that simple. The chairman of the WPNK's Central Committee was not Kim Il-sung. Instead, Kim Du-bong was appointed to that position, with Kim Il-sung becoming one of two vice-chairmen (the second was Chu Nyong-ha, who later became the DPRK's first ambassador to the Soviet Union).

The congress was also the first major event to mention the name of the future North Korean state: the Democratic People's Republic of Korea, or DPRK.[90] This long and unusual name was the product of a peculiar political intrigue.[91]

At the time, communists in general were as obsessed with the minutiae of political terminology as religious fundamentalists are with their scriptures. Thus, the exact phrasing of the name of the new country was considered to be of huge significance. The word 'socialist' could not have been used, since the country was not officially a socialist republic, as acknowledging that would cause it to be regarded as a Soviet satellite. However, for many, the question of whether to call it, say, a 'People's Republic' or a 'Democratic Republic' was of paramount importance.

The moniker of a 'People's Republic' was pushed by those close to Pak Hon-yong, who advocated the name 'Korean People's Republic', which had been briefly proclaimed in South Korea in

1945. The alternative, 'Democratic Republic', was advocated by the Kim Du-bong camp. A few months before Japan's surrender, Mao Zedong created the concept of New Democracy, as opposed to the 'Old Democracy' of the West and the early Soviet Union's 'dictatorship of the proletariat'. This concept was endorsed by Kim Du-bong. After learning about the debate, Kim Il-sung proposed merging both variants into the sobriquet 'Democratic People's Republic', which appeared to be a compromise between the two while also having the benefit of putting the word promoted by the more dangerous Pak Hon-yong in second place.

It was, naturally, the Soviet Army that made the final decision, and this was also another occasion when Mun Il played a crucial role in one of Kim Il-sung's plans. In a conversation with Mun Il, General Lebedev remarked: 'It seems that you've surpassed the "people's" stage. But I'd say you are yet to reach the "democratic" one. Let us call the country a "People's-Democratic" one.'[92]

Mun Il reported the discussion to Kim Il-sung, and Kim came up with an ingenious idea: call the country 'People's Democratic Republic' in Russian as instructed but 'Democratic People's Republic' in Korean. Thus, while it appeared to the Soviets that he was being obedient, it appeared to the Koreans that his position had been endorsed.

This intrigue was one of the first manifestations of Kim Il-sung's masterful ability to slowly chart the way to his own political independence—a goal that, as readers will see, he achieved in the decade following these events.

The 38th parallel

For Kim Il-sung, the late 1940s was also a time of tragedy, as his younger son Shura drowned while playing in a swimming pool. Kim was overcome by grief: he drank so much that at one point Mun Il refused to bring him another bottle of vodka.

Kim tearfully remembered his brother Chol-ju, who had been captured by the Japanese. He said he had seen Chol-ju in a dream the previous night. His comrades spent the entire day with the inconsolable father bereft of his dear son.[93]

Meanwhile, by 1947 the members of the Joint Soviet–American Commission for Korea had come to the realisation that it would be impossible to arrive at a compromise. Both sides began to recognise that Korea's division was likely to be permanent. A prominent sign of this was the North Korean proto-government's decision to drop the word 'provisional' from its name. As of 22 February 1947, it was just 'People's Committee for North Korea'.

On 3 September 1947, General Lebedev wrote in his diary that 'one can have a funeral service of this commission'.[94] On 26 September, the Soviet side suggested that talks should be put to rest and that both US and Soviet troops should depart from Korea. On 18 October, the Joint Commission suspended itself until the Korean problem was solved by the UN. In other words, the talks had ended in failure: Korea was not to be unified.

As time went by, the 38th parallel was gradually transformed from a provisional demarcation line to a permanent one. Soon, it would become a real border and, ultimately, a part of the impenetrable Iron Curtain.[95] In a telling incident, even as early as October 1946, Pak Hon-yong could not visit the North legally and was instead carried there in a coffin, pretending to be deceased.[96]

In the late 1940s, this border saw numerous tensions and armed provocations. It seems that the South Korean side was more active in engaging in them due to Seoul's autonomy from the United States and the bellicose nature of the contemporary South Korean leadership. The Kremlin, which at the time had no plans for a military intervention in Korea, feared that Seoul's actions could escalate to a conflict—something Stalin wanted to avoid.[97]

For the Korean people, the most notable sign of the permanent division was the change of flag. Since independence, both Koreas had used the country's traditional flag, poetically called the Flag of the Great Extremes due to the yin–yang symbol in its centre. This has been South Korea's flag ever since. However, in the North, this flag was abandoned for a completely different one.

How the flag was changed reveals much about the nature of North Korea at the time. The idea to adopt a new flag for the North seemingly appeared in the mind of General Lebedev after Kim Du-bong explained the symbolism of the Flag of the Great Extremes, leading Lebedev to conclude that the old flag was medieval and superstitious. The design of the new flag was sent from Moscow, and thus North Korea became the only communist state with a flag not designed by the locals, further reflecting the level of Soviet control over the nascent state.[98]

Initially, the new flag was quite unpopular, to the point that one deputy of the North Korean proto-parliament, the People's Assembly for North Korea, breaking all unwritten rules of behaviour, gave a speech suggesting that the old flag would be retained.[99] However, this opposition did not last long, and the North Koreans quickly grew accustomed to the new national symbol.

What concerned Kim Il-sung, however, was not symbols but the country's armed forces. Ever since he had come to power, he had been bombarding the Soviets with requests to arm and train North Koreans so that the nascent state would have its own army, navy and even air force.[100] The Soviets agreed but were initially hesitant to make the process too obvious, as they were still ostensibly working to create a united Korea. Thus, the armed forces were initially presented as an assemblage of paramilitary units and formations, and only in February 1948, after one more push from Kim Il-sung,[101] did Stalin's Politburo approve the formal creation of an army.[102] The first parade of the KPA was held on 8 February.

The same month saw the demise of the last semi-independent political force in North Korea: the Party of the Young Friends of the Heavenly Way. Seeing that the permanent division of the country was imminent and that this would mean that the North would remain under communist rule, the Heavenly Way's leadership started to organise peaceful anti-communist demonstrations scheduled for the anniversary of the 1 March uprising. The parallel would have looked impressive: Koreans protesting against foreign conquerors in 1919 and again in 1948. However, the party's leader, Kim Dal-hyon, betrayed his own comrades by alerting the authorities to their plans and even letting them arrest a messenger carrying the party's instructions on how to proceed. Mass arrests followed. This was the end of the Party and, with it, all political life in North Korea outside the WPNK and the Soviet administration.[103] Even Kim Dal-hyon eventually met a grim fate—he was purged in the late 1950s.[104]

The birth of two Koreas

By the spring of 1948, there was little hope that a compromise could be reached that would allow a united Korean government to be established. Both sides blamed the other. In April 1948, the People's Assembly for North Korea adopted the constitution of the DPRK.[105] While the constitution was not yet enforced, it was inevitable that it would be at some stage in the near future. In May, South Korea held elections for the Constitutional Assembly, demonstrating that it was preparing to proclaim a separate state in the South.

The name of the leader of the nascent South Korean state may be familiar to readers. He spelt it as Syngman Rhee. One can see where this man's sympathies lay simply by looking at his name: instead of keeping the traditional Eastern name order where the family name precedes the given one and/or splitting his given name with a space or a dash, Syngman Rhee wrote his name in English in a completely Western way. Formerly an independence activist, he hoped that Korea's independence would be brought about by the United States—and for the South, his dream came true. Married to Franziska Donner, an Austrian (i.e. foreign) woman, he was one of the most pro-Washington politicians on the peninsula.

Korea's division became irreversible on 10 July 1948. After the above-mentioned South Korean elections, the Soviet Politburo instructed Shtykov to implement the constitution of North Korea,[106] which the People's Assembly for North Korea formally voted to do. Dramatically, immediately after midday, Kim Du-bong removed the old Flag of the Great Extremes from its place in the presidium of the voting hall and hoisted the new one in its place. Choe Yong-gon announced: 'Long live the constitution of the Democratic People's Republic of Korea!'[107] Thus the new state was officially born.

The constitution proclaimed that the DPRK's capital was Seoul, not Pyongyang.[108] An earlier version had stated that 'Pyongyang shall be the capital until the formation of the unified government',[109] but this clause was dropped, as Kim Il-sung's government was to claim legitimacy as the unified one. The way this decision was made is most curious. The People's Committee for North Korea was to be transformed into the Cabinet of Ministers of the DPRK on the first session of the reorganised parliament, the Supreme People's Assembly (SPA). Elections to the SPA in the North took place on 25 August, with the state reporting a 99.97 per cent participation rate. Naturally, there was only one candidate on the ballot in each district—a standard practice in communist countries.

However, Pyongyang claimed that secret, underground elections to the SPA had also taken place in South Korea. While it is not impossible that some South Korean communists secretly participated in the election, the announced participation rate left no room for doubt. Pyongyang claimed that 77.52 per cent of adults in the South—more than three-quarters—voted in these clandestine elections.[110]

While this was obviously propaganda, there are good reasons to think that the Soviet authorities were delusional enough to actually believe these reports. By 26 July, wrote Shtykov in his diary, 110,000 eligible Seoulites out of 600,000 had already voted. Similar numbers were given for another large city—Inchon. His source was Pak Hon-yong's statements, which Shtykov simply believed.[111] Thus, 77.52 per cent was also the number the Soviets reported to Moscow.[112]

South Korean records do not mention this supposedly massive underground election at all. The falsification happened further down the hierarchy—activists sent to 'collect votes from South Koreans' claimed total success, and both Pak Hon-yong and the Soviets accepted these inflated results. It should be remembered that the Soviet generals at the time viewed themselves as being definitively on the side of the righteous—people who had liberated Korea from the evil Japanese and brought them socialism, the most progressive form of governance. Nonetheless, the level of self-delusion still looks remarkable. To both the North Korean leadership and to the Soviets, this number alone also suggested that the South Korean regime was enormously unpopular and that a country-wide rebellion could be sparked with little effort. This was one of the factors that ultimately led to the Korean War. As readers will see, the North thought that with such numbers on their side, they would be victorious in no time.

The first session of the SPA opened on 2 September. The main question was the composition of the cabinet, and, like all other decisions, this was not for the SPA itself to decide. Shtykov wrote a preliminary composition of the cabinet in his diary on 27 August[113] and the final one on 30 August,[114] which was formally adopted on 8 September. Kim Il-sung became premier and Pak Hon-yong a deputy premier and simultaneously the minister of foreign affairs.

On 1 December 1948, South Korea enacted the National Security Act, which made all communist activity illegal. By that time, the Workers' Party of South Korea was already de facto an underground organisation, and its members were fleeing to North Korea. Thus, a decision was made to merge the parties of the North and the South, as the unified party would have legitimacy over the entirety of Korea. And here the Soviets were faced with a dilemma: Who would lead the Party? As Kim Il-sung's party position was that of vice-chairman of the WPNK, he was still formally subordinate to Kim Du-bong. Pak Hon-yong, the chairman of the southern Workers' Party, also had his own ambitions.

This was a decision that was not only bound to have lasting consequences but also required authorisation from the very top. An eyewitness testified how a team of Soviet officials came to the North to talk to potential candidates. After a series of interviews, Kim Il-sung's final ascension to the position of head of the Party was confirmed.[115] We do not have adequate historical records to ascertain why he was picked over the other candidates, but the deed was done. The Southern and Northern parties were merged in June 1949, and Kim became the chairman of the Central Committee of the new, unified, Workers' Party of Korea (WPK). Kim was now unquestionably the top man in North Korea, second only to the Soviet ambassador.

Kim was not just concerned with politics. In the late 1940s, he also started looking for his first wife, Han Song-hui, whom the Japanese had captured back in the 1930s. After she had been released from prison, Song-hui had married again—to a Korean farmer. The couple was probably quite shocked to learn that Song-hui's ex-husband was now in charge of the country and decided to keep a low profile.

Yet when Kim Il-sung found his old love, he acted honourably. He met with Song-hui and told her he had found and punished those who had betrayed her to the Japanese. He remembered how she had woven him socks out of her own hair and told her he would never forget her kindness. He respected her wishes to remain with her new husband, with whom she was happily married, and the two remained friends through the years to come.[116]

His relationship with his second wife was less bright—there are reports that Kim Il-sung regularly cheated on her with a number of mistresses.[117] Jong-suk could do little but complain, and Il-sung ignored her grievances.[118]

In September 1949, Kim Jong-suk died while delivering a stillborn baby.[119] Losing a wife and another child must have been heart-breaking. Yet what Kim Il-sung made the country experience very soon brought inestimably greater sorrow and pain to incalculably more families.

6

KIM IL-SUNG'S WAR

The Korean War (1950–3) is the most destructive conflict the peninsula has ever seen, with over one million victims. After the hostilities ended, and throughout the Cold War, most of the academic community assumed the war had been instigated by Moscow. Indeed, at the time, the DPRK was a puppet state of the Soviet Union, and Kim Il-sung was following Stalin's lead. It appeared a logical supposition.

Thus, one of the most shocking discoveries historians made after the opening of the Russian archives in the early 1990s was that it was the North Korean side that conceived the idea of invading the South, and that initially Stalin was actually against it.

The two officials lobbying Stalin were Kim Il-sung himself and his second-in-command Pak Hon-yong. Kim wanted to 'liberate' South Korea and rule over the unified nation, while for Pak unification would also mean the restoration of his power base—South Korean communists, who could support him as the new leader or at least strengthen his position.

Kim Il-sung had pushed for a strong military almost since he had been appointed to lead North Korea. As both Soviet and

American occupation forces were leaving Korea in 1948–9, this presented the two men with a golden opportunity to seize South Korea by force. One of the signs of the continuous militarisation was the creation of a new province, Chagang, which was to host most of the North Korean military–industrial complex.[1] Located in the North Korean north-west, it has been the most closed part of the country ever since.

In his New Year speech on 1 January 1949, Kim angrily denounced 'traitors in the South Korean separatist puppet government' who opposed the American withdrawal from South Korea. The 'traitors' were apparently claiming that this withdrawal would lead to a North Korean invasion, and, as everyone in Korea would soon learn, this was exactly what would happen.[2]

Kim was not the only one contemplating a military solution to the political impasse. Mao had considered it even before he triumphed in the Chinese Civil War. As early as 17 May 1949, Mao mentioned to the Soviets that, in the case of an inter-Korean war, China would provide food and military assistance to the North Korean Army.[3]

Appealing to the Soviets

However, a decision to invade the South had to be personally authorised by Stalin. A direct request was unlikely to be approved, and thus Kim and Pak started probing Ambassador Shtykov. Perhaps if the senior Soviet representative agreed, he would be able to present their suggestion to Stalin himself.

The first attempt was made on 12 August 1949, soon after Kim had been put in charge of the WPK. Initially, the ambassador was sceptical. He said that unless the South attacked first, an outright invasion was out of the question.[4] He was only willing to consider a limited operation, targeting the Ongjin peninsula, which had been cut off from the rest of South Korea by the 38th parallel.[5]

This was yet another time when Mun Il played a crucial role in North Korean history, as it was after his visit to Grigoriy Tunkin, the Soviet *chargé d'affaires*, on 3 September 1949 that the embassy started to waver in its opposition. Previously, the Soviet diplomats had disapproved of Kim and Pak's bellicose plans; this time, however, Tunkin's report to Moscow was more neutral.[6]

After learning about the suggestions of Kim and Pak, Stalin told Tunkin to talk to Kim Il-sung and obtain an assessment of the South Korean Army and of Kim's own forces.[7] Tunkin complied: after assessing the capabilities of both armies and the international situation, he advocated against an invasion.[8] Stalin agreed and banned the limited strike on the Ongjin peninsula as well.[9] Kim and Pak, naturally, were not exactly pleased but had no choice but to acquiesce.[10]

This was, however, a temporary retreat. At a lunch on 17 January 1950 in Pyongyang, a highly agitated Kim Il-sung addressed the Soviet diplomats, stating that South Koreans needed to be liberated and that he could not help but constantly think about their plight. He continuously requested Stalin's approval for invading the South.[11]

This time, Stalin was more open to suggestions. What had swayed him? The decisive factor may have been the communists' spectacular victory in the Chinese Civil War—the government of Chiang Kai-shek lost mainland China and in December 1949 retreated to the island of Taiwan, while the rest of the country fell to Mao. Indeed, around the time Stalin received Shtykov's request for an invasion of South Korea, the Soviet leader held several meetings with a Chinese delegation headed by Mao and Chinese Foreign Minister Zhou Enlai.[12]

On 30 January 1950, Stalin telegraphed Shtykov, saying that any such invasion 'would need extensive preparations' and that 'it should be organised without taking too big a risk'.[13] This changed everything. With Stalin's approval, preparations for the invasion were put in motion.

After learning that his plan to launch the invasion had been approved, Kim Il-sung was filled with joy and delight, as observed by Shtykov.[14] He told the ambassador that he would prepare to meet Stalin.[15] On 2 February, Stalin instructed Pyongyang to keep the plan secret—even from the Chinese, for security purposes.[16] In fact, he had talked with Mao, who at the time was in Moscow, about providing military assistance to the North without telling the Chinese leader that the ultimate purpose of this assistance was to support the invasion of South Korea.[17] Once Kim's request to divert Soviet funds to arm three more divisions was approved by Moscow,[18] Kim repeatedly asked Shtykov to relay his gratitude to Stalin.[19]

Kim spent almost a month in Moscow, from 30 March to 25 April, during which time the Korean leadership and the Soviets finalised the invasion plan.[20] Pak Hon-yong and Mun Il accompanied him.[21] After the plan had been finalised, Stalin informed Mao the invasion had been confirmed.[22] On 15 May, Kim also met the Chinese leader and was assured of Mao's full support. According to Pak, who was also present at the meeting, this time Mao promised that 'if the Americans would enter the war, China will help North Korea with troops'.[23]

Kim assembled his inner circle and informed them of the plan to invade the South. Apart from Pak Hon-yong, those entrusted with this information were party Vice-Chairman Aleksei Hegay, head of the SPA Presidium Kim Du-bong, Minister of National Defence Choe Yong-gon and Minister of Justice Lee Sung-yop. Reportedly, only Choe was sceptical, fearing American intervention.[24]

Kim Il-sung suggested the invasion would start in late June. Soviet generals thought the army needed more time to prepare, but as the rain season was due to begin in July, which would make it hard for the KPA to advance, they ultimately accepted Kim's proposal.[25] On 15 June, the invasion date—Sunday, 25 June—was set.[26] From 12 June to 23 June, the North Korean troops were repositioned along the 38th parallel. At the last minute, the invasion plan was changed from focusing on several key directions to a massive assault across the entire frontier, as Kim Il-sung feared the enemy might have suspected that an invasion was imminent.[27] On 24 June, division commanders received the invasion order.[28] The war would begin the next day. The KPA's operational plan assumed the enemy would be completely defeated in twenty-two to twenty-seven days.[29]

War begins

The attack, undertaken by the KPA at 4:40 a.m.,[30] took South Korea completely by surprise.[31] It took the South Korean Army more than four hours to even reach the president.[32] As testified by Rhee's secretary, the head of the South Korean state was enjoying his usual Sunday fishing—the president liked the solitude of one of Seoul's palace gardens, where he could reflect on state affairs troubled by no one but his fishing rod.[33]

On the night of 25 June, Kim had Hegay call members of the cabinet and several other high-ranking officials to summon them for an emergency meeting. When everyone arrived, Kim announced that South Korea had attacked the North and he, as the commander-in-chief, had instructed the military to launch a counteroffensive.[34] Technically, Kim was not yet the commander-in-chief—he would be formally appointed on 4 July, as instructed by the Soviets[35]—but this was not an issue. Upon hearing of 'the enemy attack', the elite unanimously supported Kim's line. This has been the official North Korean stance ever since. Naturally, it was false, but given that South Korea had previously engaged in several provocations—duly reported and sometimes exaggerated in the North Korean press—many in the North also believed these claims, at least initially.[36]

The war immediately led to a change in Kim Il-sung's status: the press started calling him 'Leader', a title previously reserved for Lenin and Stalin. He, the Leader of the Korean people, was leading them to victory—asserted Pyongyang.[37]

In the initial days of the Korean War, many in the North Korean leadership anticipated that the invasion would end in a swift victory. The plan was to take the enemy capital, after which they expected that a massive rebellion in South Korea would cause the Rhee regime to collapse.[38] Korea would thus be unified under the DPRK's leadership, and the capital would be moved to Seoul, which North Korea had already named as the capital in its 1948 constitution. Indeed, after a few days of fighting, it became perfectly clear that the North Korean Army, armed with Soviet weaponry, was superior to the South in every way. As it was advancing on Seoul, people started fleeing the city. The retreat became a rout. The most tragic episode was when a South Korean colonel, instructed to blow up a bridge across the Han River bisecting the capital, detonated the charges without checking for civilians present on the bridge. About 800 people were killed.

Seoul fell on 28 June, and Kim Il-sung issued a proclamation to the 'liberated capital of the DPRK'.[39] Yet the government in the North decided to stay in Pyongyang for the time being. Instead, Kim dispatched Lee Sung-yop to govern Seoul. The army in Seoul started celebrating the takeover instead of advancing further, as Choe Yong-gon had previously ordered that the army would have three days of rest after occupying the capital.[40]

Meanwhile, it increasingly appeared that things were not going as planned. There was no general uprising in South Korea, and the situation on the diplomatic front was also far from promising. The USSR had been boycotting the UN Security Council since 13 January 1950 in protest at its refusal to grant membership to the recently formed People's Republic of China (PRC). The United States used this situation to push through several resolutions condemning the North Korean invasion and creating a UN mandate for intervention, which the boycotting Soviets were unable to veto. Days after the war began, North Korea was subjected to bombing by the US Air Force. While not nearly as heavy as the later bombing campaigns, the very fact of an immediate American intervention was enough to seriously affect the North Korean elite's morale. By early July, many had already started questioning whether they would win the war. Kim Du-bong began pestering Kim Il-sung, constantly asking him what actions the Soviet Union intended to take. Pak Hon-yong said they should directly ask the USSR for air support and for China to intervene. Kim scolded them and told them not to upset him further, as he was already nervous enough.[41]

The Leader's optimism continued to hold out.[42] As of mid-July, he had high hopes for the battle for Taejon, where the KPA successfully engaged the advance forces of the United States, which had sent ground forces to Korea on 29 June, along with the South Korean Army. Growing impatient, Kim scolded front commander Kim Chaek and front chief of staff Kang Gon for their lack of progress.[43] Meanwhile, in the 'liberated territories', the DPRK enforced North Korean land reform, while soldiers taught the locals the 'Song of Commander Kim Il-sung', hoisted new flags and organised rallies hailing Kim Il-sung and Stalin.[44] Local men were conscripted into the ranks of the KPA, and many South Korean officials who had failed to flee ever southward were arrested and even executed.[45] Their sentences were passed down by 'people's courts', an expression that in South Korea remains synonymous with the English term 'kangaroo courts'. Taejon fell to the KPA on 20 July. The KPA not only managed to capture the city but also to take prisoner the American commanding officer, Major-General William Dean; however, the victory proved to be a pyrrhic one. The front was stabilised, and there was no quick victory ahead.

By mid-August, Kim understood that something had gone terribly wrong. Mun Il told the Soviets he had never seen Kim in such a state.[46] The enemy frontline refused to collapse, and the threat of a full-scale American invasion was looming. By the end of August, Kim admitted to Mun Il that he was unsure whether North Korea could win the war on its own and that he wanted to ask China for help. Mun immediately relayed this to the Soviets.[47] And then everything changed.

War comes to the North

On 15 September, the United States and its UN allies launched an amphibious operation in Inchon—the city port of Seoul. The force, consisting of more than 260 vessels and 75,000 soldiers, was far superior to anything North Korea could have defeated on its own. The KPA launched a series of counterattacks, but these resulted in the loss of nearly all the attacking troops as the UN Army advanced towards Seoul. Kim Il-sung understood that, if left on its own, North Korea was doomed. On 21 September, the WPK's Political Council officially asked China for support.[48] The situation was becoming desperate. All contact with the command in Seoul, headed by Minister of National Defence Choe Yong-gon, was lost. Kim relieved Choe of his duties and appointed himself minister.[49] Here, Kim was probably mimicking Stalin's behaviour during the war with Germany: in July 1941, the Soviet leader had replaced Semyon Timoshenko, the People's Commissar for Defence, with himself. However, in Kim's case this appears to have been an emotional and sporadic decision, as by the following month Choe had regained his position.[50]

Seoul was retaken on 28 September. The next day, President Rhee returned to the liberated capital, and General Douglas MacArthur, commander of the UN Army, proudly announced to him that Seoul once again belonged to South Korea. The UN command decided not to stop at retaking South Korea but to bring the war to the North. By 1 October, Stalin realised that, as he put it, 'the situation of the Korean comrades is getting desperate'.[51] He concluded that the PRC should immediately assist North Korea, although he left the ultimate decision with Beijing.[52] On 2 October, Mao replied. The answer was clear: there would be no assistance. It would not be easy to turn the tide by sending a few divisions, explained the Great Helmsman, and Chinese intervention could trigger a world war with the United States. All plans for the reconstruction of China would have to be aborted, and the public would be unlikely to agree with the intervention. Therefore, concluded Mao, it would be for the best if the DPRK suffered a 'temporary defeat'.[53]

The Soviets were puzzled by Mao's change of heart:[54] back in May, the head of the Chinese state had promised that China would intervene if necessary,[55] but now he was insisting that an invention could provoke a world war and that the Chinese Army was too weak to fight the Americans.[56] Kim felt this was the end. Broken, he summoned Mun Il and told him that North Korea was doomed and the war was lost, and that if the foreign allies would not help, they would lose Korea forever. This was recorded on the same day by the Soviet ambassador.[57] Indeed, the history of North Korea could have ended at this point. However, what Mao said made a lot of sense: sending China into yet another war would have been a very dangerous endeavour, and his caution looked highly reasonable.

South Korea, preparing for celebration, printed postal marks commemorating the reunification, showing a South Korean flag hoisted at the top of Mount Paektu. As for Kim Il-sung, defeat would mean that he would again have to live as a hunted partisan or leave the country to live as an exile in China or the Soviet Union. There was every prospect the DPRK would become a historical obscurity: a state that existed for about two years and was destroyed due to the failure of its leadership to assess the risks of launching a war that ultimately involved superpowers that were far stronger than he had realised.

But North Korea's fate was different. After being pushed by Stalin, Chairman Mao reconsidered his original decision.[58] At 6:00 a.m. on 8 October, Kim Il-sung received a telegram through which China informed him that help would be coming.[59] Both Kim Il-sung and Pak Hon-yong were overjoyed,[60] but, in fact, the final decision had not yet been made. Fierce debates continued in Beijing. Gao Gang, the vice-chairman of the central government, firmly supported the intervention,[61] but Mao was still not sure it was the correct course of action. On 12 October, the Chinese leader again contacted Moscow's representative, saying he would not be sending any troops.[62]

Upon learning this, Stalin ordered Kim to evacuate from North Korea.[63] It seems the decisive factor that pushed Mao to finally approve the intervention was that at the time Zhou Enlai was in the USSR, and when Stalin met him, the Soviet leader made it very clear that Moscow favoured China's entry into the war and was willing to assist.[64] On 13 October, Mao finally agreed to intervene.[65] The next day, Stalin informed North Korea of the momentous decision.[66] Thus, although the enemy was advancing on Pyongyang, Kim Il-sung knew he was safe. Yet there was not much time to prepare for the evacuation, and it was quite chaotic—some state organisations simply ordered their employees to march 100 miles north to the city of Kanggye, which became North Korea's provisional capital.[67]

One of the problems the authorities faced was what to do with the inmates held in Pyongyang's prisons. Some were shot, while some were forced to march north to Kanggye. One of the people killed in Pyongyang was Cho Man-sik, who back in 1945 was briefly considered one of the candidates to the North Korean throne and had later headed the Democratic Party.[68] One of those who perished in the death march was Lee Kwang-su, considered the founding figure of modern Korean literature.[69]

Kim stayed in the capital until mid-October and then left.[70] He went in the direction of Sinuiju; on 25 October, he sent a telegram to Stalin from nearby Taeyu district.[71] Eventually, he reached Kanggye, and given the situation on the frontline, it is highly likely that he went there through China.

Chinese intervention

The disastrous outcome of the assault on South Korea had repercussions for one of its instigators: Ambassador Terentiy Shtykov. On 22 November, Shytkov was dismissed from participating in all military affairs, which were to be conducted by the newly arrived Lieutenant-General Vladimir Razuvayev. Kim Il-sung felt that he himself might be the next to go. Perhaps feeling that this was unavoidable, Kim suggested to Shtykov and Pak Hon-yong that he should also resign from the position of supreme commander.[72] In short order, the Soviet Politburo recalled Shtykov home[73] and later demoted him from Colonel-General to Lieutenant-General.[74] He never returned to Korea. Although Shtykov later served in semi-important positions, such as ambassador to Hungary,[75] his subsequent career was forever hobbled by the Korean War.

As for Kim Il-sung, it was during this time in Kanggye that he received a new secretary, a young woman named Kim Song-ae, who was assigned to Kim Il-sung as his 'attendant secretary', akin to a housekeeper. The premier and his secretary became intimate. In 1951, Kim Song-ae informed Pak Chong-ae, chairwoman of the Democratic Women's Union of Korea, that she was pregnant. Kim Il-sung and Kim Song-ae then had something of a shotgun wedding.[76] It seems that Kim Il-sung's second daughter was born from this pregnancy, although her name and fate are unknown. While it is likely that Kim Il-sung was a loyal husband to his first wife—there is, at least, no evidence suggesting otherwise—he was faithful to neither Kim Jong-suk nor Kim Song-ae. He took a number of mistresses,[77] and in a few years after his rise to power, his harem had become semi-institutionalised. Pak Chong-ae was said to be in charge of the harem, thus making it quite reasonable for the pregnant Kim Song-ae to ask her what to do.

In the meantime, the tide of war was turning. The Chinese Army started to cross the border on 19 October. While the southern coalition expected the war to be over by the end of 1950, this was not to happen. The Chinese had been massing their troops for a month, while the advancing UN forces remained complacent. After a probing attack, the Chinese launched a full-scale counteroffensive in late November. After a few decisive actions, the UN–South Korean coalition was in full retreat. Pyongyang was abandoned without a fight—a decision for which General Walton Walker was widely criticised—and Kim Il-sung triumphantly returned to the city.

Mao had underestimated his own army. The Chinese People's Volunteers, as they were called, proved themselves a formidable force: they pushed the allies further and further southwards, and communist victory became a real possibility.

The Chinese Army was put under the command of one of the most prominent PRC military men, Peng Dehuai. Peng and Kim Il-sung did not like each other. The Chinese commander was angry that the PRC had to cover up for Kim's mistakes, at great cost to the Chinese people. Peng also made no effort to hide his opinion of Kim Il-sung's military skills.[78] Reportedly, Peng asked Kim directly: 'Tell me, who started the Korean War? Was it American imperialism or was it you?'[79] Peng's attitude towards Kim is further revealed by an episode in the archival documents: on one occasion, when Kim arrived at Peng's headquarters, he was detained and held for an extensive period despite being the head of state of an ally nation.[80]

Nevertheless, notwithstanding these squabbles at the top, the People's Volunteers fought with great efficiency. On 4 January 1951, Seoul again fell to the communists. This time, the capital had been properly evacuated, and the city was empty. At the time, the allies even thought that the DPRK would be able to take over the entire Korean Peninsula and were thinking about evacuating the South Korean government to the island of Cheju, located to the south of the Korean mainland (the plan was further complicated by the lack of drinking water on Cheju).[81]

But the fortunes of war shifted once again. Matthew Ridgway, the new commanding officer of the US Eighth Army, who replaced General Walker after the latter was killed in a traffic accident, proved himself a competent and skilful commander. He managed to boost the troops' morale and halt the Chinese advance. Seoul was retaken again—two months after it had fallen to the communists for the second time. Mao's position played a role in the victory: he thought that China's goal in the war was to restore the *status quo ante bellum* rather than the conquest of South Korea and was thus unwilling to spend excessive force to defend the conquered territory to the south of the 38th parallel.[82]

As time went on, the frontline stabilised. Understanding where his salvation ultimately lay, Kim Il-sung took good care that the DPRK would continue to supply the Soviet Union with promised mineral resources—even though the war was still raging and the North Korean economy was in ruins.[83]

Negotiations or nuclear strikes?

Although Kim wanted China to retake Seoul for the third time,[84] Beijing and Moscow thought that the time had now come for armistice talks. The communist coalition and the UN commenced talks in July 1951, a little over a year after the conflict had begun, in the city of Kaesong, just to the south of the pre-war border.[85] No ceasefire was called, and the war continued even as the negotiations went on.

By that time, both sides realised that the war would end in a compromise. Neither North nor South Korea was going to disappear. Both sides also accepted the idea of a demilitarised zone (DMZ) between the two nations.[86]

Yet some points remained to be negotiated. The first was the issue of the border. Would it be reversed to the pre-war 38th parallel? Or would it follow the current frontline? The communist side insisted on the former and the UN on the latter.

Second, what would happen with the prisoners of war? The UN suggested that both those who wanted to leave and those who would prefer to stay where they were should be given an opportunity to do so. The communist side, however, insisted that all prisoners should be exchanged. This suggestion was unacceptable to the Americans, and the talks broke down.

At the next stage, which started on 25 October 1951, the talks were moved from Kaesong to a new location further east—the village formerly called Nolmulli but renamed Panmunjom specifically for these talks, as the old name could not be properly reflected in Chinese characters. Thus, essentially, the renaming was done for China's convenience. The new name, meaning 'the Wooden Door Point', had been in unofficial use since the Imjin War of the late sixteenth century and was a fitting name for a place that eventually became the gateway between the Koreas.

While the negotiations continued, the US Air Force launched a massive bombing campaign in North Korea. The use of incendiary bombs meant that even if the targets were military, the bombings were bound to cause substantial civilian casualties—and they did. Ultimately, more than three-quarters of the buildings in North Korean cities were incinerated.[87]

Not everyone supported the idea of peace. General MacArthur, the former commander of the UN forces, suggested that the United States should use its weapon of last resort and annihilate the enemy through atomic firepower.[88] At the time, the thermonuclear bomb had yet to be invented, and atomic weapons were not subject to outright rejection as a matter of course.

Was MacArthur indeed a madman, willing to see hundreds of thousands, if not millions, burn in an atomic holocaust? Or was he Asia's Churchill, whose actions could have spared China its Great Leap Forward and the Cultural Revolution and North Korea seven decades of Kim family rule? This author does not propose an answer. However, MacArthur's urge for a massive atomic strike did have one lasting consequence in that it became known in the North and was later used for propaganda purposes. Although it is impossible to know if this was what triggered Kim Il-sung's interest in obtaining nuclear weapons for North Korea, he nevertheless began to show an interest in atomic weaponry soon afterwards. The first signs of the DPRK pursuing its own nuclear programme appeared in the late 1950s,[89] and this programme was crowned with a successful nuclear bomb test twelve years after Kim's death.

With the frontline stabilised, Kim started to dedicate more time to non-military issues. When he turned forty on 15 April 1952, an updated version of his biography appeared. In this new version, his 'KPRA' was presented as the force that participated in the 1945 campaign against Japan in Korea.[90] Only seven years had passed since the fall of the Japanese Empire, but the myth of the KPRA, which had been invented by the Soviets, was already beginning to grow. This was the same year the North Korean press started to call Kim Il-sung 'Great Leader', although this sobriquet only became his standard title in the 1960s.[91]

The question of prisoners caused the talks to drag on until 1953. It seems that Moscow and Seoul were quietly sabotaging the talks. For Stalin, war meant that the United States would remain focused on Korea rather than increasing its presence in Western Europe.[92] Stalin may have even wanted China to stay in the war as long as possible—although it is not very likely that he foresaw the possibility of a future split with Beijing. As for President Rhee, he still hoped the war could be won and unification be achieved, and the idea of formally surrendering half of Korea to the communists was repellent to him.

Armistice

In 1952, a peculiar incident occurred during a meeting of the leadership of the USSR, the PRC and the DPRK. The meeting, which was being held to discuss a unified strategy for the armistice talks, vividly highlighted Kim's stance towards Stalin at that time. On 4 September, Stalin asked Peng Dehuai if the Chinese Army had any military decorations. After receiving a negative answer, the Soviet leader gave the Chinese delegation a brief lecture, emphasising that a real army should have orders, ranks, insignia and everything else; otherwise, it would be a large partisan unit, not a proper army.[93] Kim, who was present at the meeting, felt this criticism could also be applied to the DPRK. The KPA had been formed from paramilitary forces, and as of September 1952, officers of the North Korean Army only had positions (e.g., battalion commander) rather than ranks, reminiscent of the early days of the USSR.

To forestall any potential displeasure from Stalin, Pyongyang introduced ranks for KPA officers on the last day of 1952.[94] Both the rank system and corresponding uniforms were copied from the USSR, with the only notable difference being at the very top.[95] Very soon, the beneficiaries of these alterations became obvious: on 7 February 1953, Kim Il-sung received the highest rank of Marshal of the DPRK, and Minister of National Defence Choe Yong-gon the second-highest rank of Vice-Marshal.[96] Kim's uniform closely resembled Stalin's, complete with the iconic communist marshal's star. However, there were some subtle differences: Kim's rank insignia, for example, did not precisely mirror the Soviet style. In Stalin's uniform, a coat of arms was positioned alongside a five-pointed star, while Kim's uniform featured the coat of arms superimposed on to the star. Evidently, at that time Kim was hesitant to symbolically elevate himself to the same level as Stalin.

However, in the months following Stalin's death on 5 March 1953, Kim adjusted his insignia to match Stalin's design, clearly feeling emboldened to make this change with the Kremlin's master no longer in the picture.[97]

After Stalin's death, North Korea went into mourning with the rest of the communist bloc. The government issued a proclamation on the death of 'Generalissimo Stalin—the bright and wise Leader and the Teacher of all the working people of the world, the liberator and the closest friend of the Korean people.'[98] A delegation was sent to Moscow to offer formal condolences.

With the 'Leader of the Nations' gone, the armistice talks made more progress, as the new Soviet leadership was more willing to compromise.[99] The question of prisoners was finally settled when Seoul unilaterally set free those prisoners of war who did not want to return to the communist side. Although this was, perhaps, the most humane decision of President Rhee's entire career, it should be remembered that this was also done for political reasons, as it nearly caused another breakdown of the talks, which was what Rhee had hoped for; however, the two sides finally managed to reach an armistice agreement that was acceptable to both.

The agreement prescribed a new border, which adhered to the frontline of July 1953. This has since become the border between the two Korean states and, at the time this book was being written, still is. North Korea lost more territory than it gained—including Kim's own villa near the town of Sokcho—though it did secure control over the major city of Kaesong.

Finally, it was settled. The Soviet Union instructed Kim not to go to Panmunjom to sign the armistice on his own, fearing for his safety.[100] Instead, another North Korean official, General of the Army Nam Il, was to represent the DPRK at the signing ceremony on 27 July. South Korea, adamant in its rejection of the armistice, never signed it. Seoul did, however, send a representative to observe the ceremony. This man was Lieutenant-General Choe Tok-shin, who later ended up living in North Korea (at the time of writing, it is not clear whether he was abducted or went there by his own volition).

At 10:11 a.m. on 27 July 1953, amid the gloomy atmosphere of a still ongoing war, General Nam Il, commander of the Chinese Army Peng Dehuai and UN representative William Harrison signed the armistice agreement in Panmunjom. Nam Il left the building without saying a word and departed for Pyongyang to deliver a copy for Kim Il-sung to sign. General Harrison politely declined to comment for the press. He took a helicopter to the UN base in the town of Munsan, where the agreement was signed by Mark Clark, the commander-in-chief of the UN coalition.[101] In Pyongyang, Kim, dressed in his white marshal's uniform, signed the agreement in the presence of several top officials and in front of a camera.[102]

The agreement entered into force at 10 p.m. on the same day, and the bloodiest and most destructive conflict in Korean history came to an end. The number of victims was close to one million.

The North Korea authorities quickly understood that the armistice should be portrayed not as the stalemate it was but rather as a glorious victory.[103] This is the narrative North Korea has pushed ever since. State-approved publications about the war were never about the tragedy of mass fratricide but rather about the glory found in annihilating the regime's enemies.

* * *

It is said there were no victors in the Korean War. Yet there was one man who greatly benefitted from the deadly conflict: Kim Il-sung. The war gave him much-needed political autonomy from total Soviet control, which he immediately started to use to eliminate his opponents and solidify his control over the country.

7

CLEANSING THE WAY

With the fighting over, rebuilding commenced. The American bombing campaign had left North Korea in ruins, but thanks to the massive aid provided by the Soviet Union and China, the recovery process was comparatively swift.[1] Kim Il-sung himself also got a new home—near Mansu Hill in Pyongyang. It was a pleasant location as well as being a convenient one: the Soviet embassy was nearby.[2]

Apart from its normal police functions, the North Korean Ministry of Internal Affairs was tasked with supplying Kim Il-sung with food—for free, of course. A special state farm grew vegetables and fruits for him and the rest of the leadership, and the Great Leader's house received a supply of Kangso mineral water. Wherever he went, a truck carrying whatever he might need accompanied him. A cook was always part of his entourage.[3] In all, Kim owned eight cars—five Soviet and three American.[4]

Life was good for Kim Il-sung. Now the armistice had been signed, he switched his attention to domestic policy. Here, his goal was to obtain political independence from the Soviet Union. During the Cold War, South Korean media often denounced the North as 'a puppet regime'. Before the Korean War began, this description had largely been accurate, as all important and even some not-so-important decisions in the North had been prepared by the Soviets. With the beginning of the war, however, the situation changed. Stalin wanted Kim to show some initiative and not merely wait for the Soviets to decide on every issue.[5] In war, time is of the essence, and Stalin's experience of the war with Germany showed to him that giving local commanders some freedom of decision was beneficial, as they could assess the situation better than he could from the Kremlin.

'Red tyranny, cursed be thy name'

The post-war North Korean leadership was an uneven community, consisting of four rough groups.[6] The first group was made up of Kim's own comrades from the partisan movement in Manchuria and the Eighty-Eighth Brigade. Next were Soviet Koreans. Chinese Koreans, who had been affiliated with Mao and later returned to Korea after 1945, made up the third group. Finally, there were those who had been involved in the underground communist movement in colonial Korea. This was the general scheme. Although it was quite accurate, it should be noted that there were some non-guerrillas who had pledged their total and complete allegiance to Kim from the very beginning, the most notable example being the founder of the North Korean secret police, Pang Hak-se, a Soviet Korean who had served the Soviet prosecution during Stalin's Great Purge.[7] His loyalty would later save his life.

Kim Il-sung's goal was thus to promote people loyal to him personally while getting rid of the rest. Before the war began, the DPRK's senior leadership comprised the chairman of the party's Central Committee Kim Il-sung, Vice-Chairmen Pak Hon-yong and Aleksei Hegay, chairman of the SPA Presidium

1. South Pyongan province, where Kim Il-sung was born, in the 1910s.

2. Shang Yue, Kim Il-sung's middle school teacher.

3. Major-General Nozoe Masanori, commander of the anti-partisan liquidation unit.

4. Han Song-hui, an anti-Japanese partisan and Kim Il-sung's first wife.

5. Anti-Japanese partisans in Manchuria, 1939.

6. Former partisans in the Soviet Union, early 1940s.
Kim Il-sung can be seen lying down; his second wife
Kim Jong-suk is in the front, wearing white.

7. General Iosif Apanasenko, commander of the Soviet Far Eastern Front, early 1940s.

8. Captain Kim Il-sung (front row, second from the right) in the Eighty-Eighth Brigade, 1943.

9. The *Emelian Pugachev*, the ship that brought Kim Il-sung back to Korea after World War Two.

10. Demonstration in Pyongyang in honour of the Red Army, 14 October 1945.

11. Kim Il-sung's first public appearance, 14 October 1945.

12. A 1946 North Korean stamp, featuring Kim Il-sung, the traditional Korean flag and the stamp's value written in Russian.

13. Kim Il-sung, his second wife and three children.

14. Kim Il-sung (left) with his wife Kim Jong-suk (second from the left), brother Kim Yong-ju (right) and children Kim Jong-il and Kim Kyong-hui.

15. Kim Jong-suk with her first son Yura (aka Kim Jong-il).

16. The fall of Seoul. The North Korean flag is hoisted near the government building.

17. North Korean victory stamp featuring a flag hoisted above the Central Government Office in Seoul.

18. South Korean victory stamp featuring a flag hoisted above the Heavenly Lake of Mount Paektu.

19. Pyongyang is taken. South Korean and UN flags decorate government buildings.

20. Kim Il-sung (right) and Commander of the Chinese Volunteer Army Peng Dehuai (left).

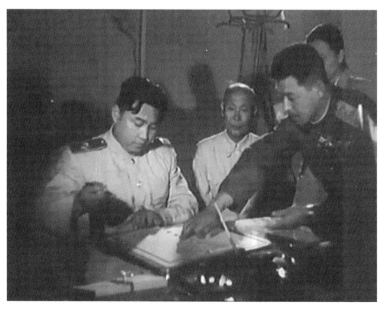

21. Kim Il-sung signs the armistice agreement. Later, this chronicle will be heavily edited in North Korea to remove the purged officials from it.

Kim Du-bong, Minister of Justice Lee Sung-yop and Minister of National Defence Choe Yong-gon. These were the only people who had been entrusted with planning the invasion. By the time Kim Il-sung was done, all except Choe Yong-gon were dead, and even he had been stripped of all power and placed in a ceremonial position.

Before Kim made any move against the other leaders or factions, there was one man who realised the situation was changing: Mun Il. A man of unparalleled intuition, he noted that Kim was beginning to display occasional displeasure with him, and he wisely chose to leave quietly for the Soviet Union in 1951.[8]

Mun was right to leave, as things began to change soon after he had left the country. The first target was Hegay. Kim did not yet dare purge him outright, as Stalin was unlikely to endorse such a decision, but in November 1951 he demoted him from deputy chairman of the Party to deputy premier.

The next targets were Pak Hon-yong and Lee Sung-yop. Both were former communist activists operating in colonial Korea and represented the only rival faction that did not have the protection of a fellow communist state and were thus an easy target. In the spring of 1953, as the armistice appeared imminent, Pak and Lee were relieved of all duties and accused of high treason.[9] Lee was formally arrested soon after the accusations were made,[10] while Pak was initially placed under house arrest.[11] Soon after Stalin's death, the USSR sent a delegation to the North, which met Kim Il-sung and hinted that 'old methods no longer work'[12]—but to no avail.

Kim then refocused his sights on Hegay. Already stressed by his demotion, Hegay was again subjected to a very heavy criticism session by Kim Il-sung and other members of the top leadership. His request for help from the Soviet embassy was met with a cold and formal response.[13] On 2 July 1953, he was found dead;

we will likely never know for sure whether he had been killed or committed suicide.[14]

August saw the overt, public condemnation of Lee Sung-yop via a newspaper campaign alleging that he, along with his co-conspirators, were American spies.[15]

In 1955, Kim Il-sung made a move against the Chinese Koreans as well. Pak Ir-u, who formerly served as the minister of internal affairs and later as minister of communications, was arrested and interrogated.[16]

The shrewder members of the other factions started to suspect that unless they resisted, they would also end up badly. The most serious attack on Kim Il-sung was launched by Deputy Premier Pak Chang-ok. In April 1955, this cynical and cold-hearted Soviet Korean, whose character was somewhat similar to that of Kim Il-sung himself, joined forces with Kim Du-bong, the formal head of the SPA, to table a motion calling for Kim Il-sung's resignation from the premiership. The motivation was simple in its sheer audacity: Kim, they said, had 'too many tasks' on his hands. While Kim was supposed to lose his position as premier, he was to remain the chairman of the party's Central Committee.[17]

Events in Bulgaria and Hungary, which unfurled roughly at the same time, suggest that Pak Chang-ok's proposal could have led to Kim Il-sung losing power. In both countries, dictators were removed in two steps. The first involved him losing his position as head of state and then, second, as head of the Party.

The power of Bulgaria's Stalinist dictator, Valko Chervenkov, was weakened in 1954 when the Bulgarian Communist Party liquidated his position of general secretary. In 1956, Chervenkov was demoted from premier to vice-premier, thus ending his rule over the country, while the much more liberal Todor Zhivkov took his place.[18] A similar scenario unfolded in Hungary: in 1953, the man in charge—Mátyás Rákosi—was removed from the premiership, and in July 1956, under Soviet pressure, Rákosi resigned from the position of first secretary of the Party as well.[19]

Thus, should Kim Il-sung have been forced out of the premiership, it is quite possible that he would have soon stopped being the Party chairman as well.

However, unlike Chervenkov and Rákosi, Kim managed to ride out the storm. First, he postponed the discussion on his potential resignation, and next, he suggested the least popular member of the Political Council[20]—Choe Yong-gon—as his replacement. The thought of having someone they regarded as a lummox as their boss was unbearable for most of the members, who instead chose to accept Kim Il-sung as the lesser evil for the time being.[21] Many of them later paid for this mistake with their lives.

Meanwhile, the purges continued. On 15 December 1955, the Special Tribunal of the Supreme Court passed triple death sentences and triple sentences of confiscation of his entire estate on Pak Hon-yong.[22] Available documents and testimonies reveal that Pak was torn between his understanding that the entire proceeding was a farce and his desire to prove his innocence to the court and his former comrades.[23]

To some of the other people put on trial, the situation was clearer. Before he was shot, Lim Hwa, a famous leftist poet in the colonial era and now Pak's co-accused, reportedly wrote his last poem: 'Red Tyranny, Cursed Be Thy Name'.[24]

The state decided to release a transcript of the proceedings against both Pak and Lee Sung-yop.[25] For later political trials, this Stalinist tradition was deemed too revealing and discontinued. Had Pak Hon-yong—or, for that matter, any of the other accused—genuinely been a spy, this would have undoubtedly provoked panic from Kim Il-sung and the Soviets. All the information Pak could potentially have had access to would need to be checked, and all the cyphers in the military would need to be changed. Such a huge and glaring hole in the country's security would have been remembered for decades. Unsurprisingly, none of this happened. Everyone understood that the trial was purely political and that the accusations were false.[26] As a Soviet diplomat sarcastically remarked in 1957: 'In the WPK, "enemy and anti-Party groups" happen to appear too frequently', revealing that Moscow understood—and tacitly endorsed—what Kim Il-sung was doing.[27]

Many other officials, including those at lower levels, were purged as well, but not every one of them was shot. The fate of the accused depended on political circumstances and on Kim's current mood. Some were permitted to leave the country, whereas others were merely demoted. Nevertheless, they were no longer a threat.

Severing Soviet ties

Purges were useful to solidify Kim's position and weaken Soviet political control over the DPRK. But it was not the only method he used. Another was an appeal to nationalism, which exerts a powerful emotional force, as people generally do not like feeling that they are controlled by an outside power. As the history of decolonisation shows, replacing a dictator appointed by a foreign power with a local tyrant can easily be sold as 'liberation', even if the lives of locals turned out to be less free and less prosperous under the native boss.

Thus, Kim Il-sung started to assert that education should be less Soviet-oriented, that the DPRK would be perfectly fine on its own and that Koreans should focus on their history and traditions first and on the Soviet experience second.[28] As the USSR's ideology allowed for greater tolerance of the nationalism of 'smaller' nations, this campaign ran unopposed by Moscow, especially since the ever-cautious Kim Il-sung refrained from attacking the USSR directly and regularly paid lip service to the Soviet Union's greatness.

Loanwords—an object of many nationalists' hatred—were purged from North Korea as well. By that time, the North Korean language had borrowed a large number of words and expressions from Russian, and the state started to replace names like *kkomissiya* (commission) with more traditional ones like *wiwonhoe*.[29] However, it should be noted that many distinctly Soviet expressions still survived in North Korea for decades. This campaign was about Kim gaining power, and nationalism was merely a tool.

The post-war years saw another, yet unseen battle between the two Koreas being waged—a battle for the hearts of Koreans in Japan. When the empire surrendered in 1945, there were more than two million Koreans living in Japan. Some went to the metropole in search of a better life, some went to study and many others were subjected to labour conscription in the last years of the Second World War.[30] When Japan signed the San Francisco Peace Treaty (1952) with the Allies and restored its independence after seven years of American occupation, it also recognised Korea's independence—and that in turn meant that these people no longer had Japanese citizenship and had to choose between Seoul and Pyongyang.

That South Korean President Rhee was fanatically anti-Japanese greatly helped Pyongyang's efforts. Under his rule, Seoul refused to maintain any relationship with Japan, even to the point of refusing Tokyo's help during the Korean War.[31] Perhaps unsurprisingly, therefore, Rhee made it very difficult for Japanese Koreans to return home.[32]

With the Japanese Koreans abandoned by the South, Pyongyang launched a repatriation campaign in Japan. To facilitate the campaign, North Korea created an Association of North Korean Citizens in Japan (ANKCJ). In the mid-

1950s, many Koreans answered the ANKCJ's call and left for the North—never to be permitted to leave North Korea again. The campaign was tacitly endorsed by Tokyo, believing it would be in Japan's best interests to have this potentially problematic population leave the country.

It was also during this time that North Korea started using a word many readers may already be familiar with: 'Juche'. More accurately pronounced as 'Chuche', the word is a translation of the German word *Subjekt*, which is often translated into English as 'subject'.[33] This translation reflects one particular meaning of this word: 'main driving force'. Saying, for example, that something is the 'subject of history' would mean that something is the main driving force of history, while something being an 'object of history' would mean that this something has no will of its own.

As of the mid-1950s, this word was simply part of the campaign against the Soviet Union: it called for the North to be the 'subject', that is, to stand on its own instead of following a foreign example. The idea of using this word was probably conceived by Kim Chang-man, one of Kim Il-sung's deputies— at least, this is what the Soviet embassy papers say.[34] It was not until much later that the DPRK started to promote 'Juche' as the state ideology.

In this campaign against Soviet control, Kim had to constantly watch for the reaction of the Soviet ambassador, as the head of the USSR's mission could have had him removed if he strayed too far. And here, fate smiled upon Kim once again. On 17 June 1955, the USSR appointed a new ambassador to the DPRK, Vasiliy Ivanov, whose appointment marked the beginning of a new Soviet policy. Before his assignment to Pyongyang, Ivanov was a deputy prime minister of the Russian Soviet Federative Socialist Republic (RSFSR), by far the largest and most important of the

Soviet Union's constituent republics. The appointment was a major demotion.

The policy of using the position of Soviet ambassador to North Korea as a dumping ground for disgraced officials, rather than appointing experienced diplomats to serve in Pyongyang, continued until the 1960s, and, as readers will see, it had catastrophic consequences for the USSR. Both of Ivanov's successors—Aleksandr Puzanov and Vasiliy Moskovskiy—had a similar background. Before their demotions, both Puzanov and Moskovskiy were also deputy premiers, just like Ivanov. While Moskovskiy, in defiance of stereotypes, proved himself more than capable of diplomatic work, by the time of his appointment in 1962, the mediocre Ivanov and the completely inept Puzanov had already ruined everything: by the mid-1960s, all of Moscow's previous control over Pyongyang had been lost (see Chapter 9).

Collective farms and Chollima

Despite the impotence of the ambassadors, North Korea continued to follow the Soviet example, even if the USSR's direct political control over the country was gradually decreasing. Kim saw Stalin's USSR as a worthy model. Thus, when he proceeded with the creation of collective farms, he did it with great vigour.[35] And just like in the USSR, the state's resources were poured into heavy industry.

Following the Soviet example was considered perfectly legitimate as far as communist ideology was concerned. At the time, North Korea was considered a 'People's Democracy': a pre-socialist nation that was to follow the USSR's example before advancing from socialism to the communist utopia as envisioned by Marxism–Leninism. Following Stalin's death, many in Moscow started to have doubts about whether Stalin's economic management had been correct, but such a policy had yet to be officially condemned.

Collectivisation had already brought gruesome results by late 1954, with North Korea failing to produce enough grain to feed itself. Attempting to fulfil the economic plans, officials tried to extort even higher taxes from farmers, leaving them unable to support themselves.[36] In some cases, the tax collected was twice as high as the one prescribed.[37] Some North Korean officials shared their concerns with the Soviet embassy.[38] Kim Il-sung's initial reaction was to organise a crackdown, and, on 5 December 1954, the government banned private rice trade in the country.[39] But this measure only intensified the crisis. Reports on death from malnourishment and starvation started to appear, with the toll eventually rising to more than 1,000.[40]

Facing a nationwide crisis and under pressure from the Soviet embassy,[41] Kim retreated. The government reduced the tax on farmers and purchased the necessary grain from abroad.[42] This was a life-saving measure. The problem was that the Great Leader saw this retreat as a purely tactical step. Neither then nor in the decades to come would he realise that a planned economy is fundamentally unable to meet consumer needs.

For those from more liberal communist nations, the situation in North Korea was horrific. A Bulgarian diplomat confessed to his Soviet colleagues that he had been shocked to see dystrophic North Koreans during his visit to a hospital in Kanggye and regretted that Pyongyang was concealing what was going on from the diplomatic corps.[43]

Another development that followed the Stalinist model was the beginning of the Chollima movement. Named after a legendary Pegasus-like animal, the Chollima movement was a typical communist campaign of economic mobilisation. The idea was to use propaganda to motivate workers to labour harder without increased pay. While such campaigns are not very efficient, the DPRK would launch them repeatedly in the years to come.[44]

Thus, after the death of Stalin, Stalinist methods of governance continued to evolve in the North. Kim Il-sung's methods of political-economic management were distinctly Stalinist. In some ways, he was even less flexible than Stalin had been in his later years.[45] While he was open to the idea of products for his family being bought in marketplaces,[46] when it came to the country in general, Kim was a firm believer in a planned economy, maximum centralisation and state distribution of goods. In the mid-1950s, he was still limited by post-Stalin-era reformists in Moscow and could not fully implement his vision. This was to change in later years.

One final Stalinist trait was a paranoid obsession with foreign spies, and North Korea of the mid-1950s very much followed in this tradition, with the state producing manuals on how to find and catch foreign agents.[47]

Kim Il-sung's family grew up during this post-war period. Kim Song-ae gave birth to two sons: Phyong-il was born in 1954 and Yong-il in 1955. However, it was also during these years that Kim Il-sung lost one of his closest and dearest friends, his ex-wife Han Song-hui. Testimonies from people who escaped the DPRK suggest that at some time around 1956, Song-hui confronted Kim Il-sung, seeing how the Great Leader enjoyed his life with Kim Song-ae. She, so goes the story, said that forming yet another family after Jong-suk had died was a sign of disrespect to her memory and to the love Il-sung and she, Song-hui, used to have. Kim Il-sung was insulted by this, and the two stopped talking. The Great Leader cut all support he had provided to Han Song-hui, and she later died as a simple worker.[48]

Before proceeding to the next chapter, a synoptic glance at the political situation of North Korea as of early 1956 is in order. Kim Il-sung had already annihilated the faction of Pak Hon-yong and his communist comrades from colonial times and weakened the position of the Soviet Koreans, who started to form an informal coalition with the Chinese faction. The final battle for power in North Korea was now to be waged between Kim and this unofficial opposition bloc.

8

THE VICTORY OVER THE OPPOSITION

On 25 February 1956, the communist world changed forever. On the last day of the Twentieth Congress of the Communist Party of the Soviet Union (CPSU), First Secretary Nikita Khrushchev delivered a speech openly denouncing Joseph Stalin, accusing him of heinous crimes against the Soviet people.[1]

Khrushchev's so-called 'Secret Speech' sent shockwaves around the world and paved the way for a dramatic liberalisation of communist countries. Political prisoners were freed, censorship was relaxed, and for the first time in decades, people felt less afraid that the state would come after them. No speech in human history has changed the lives of so many people for the better in such a short space of time.

North Korea was one of the countries directly affected. The DPRK's representative to the congress, Vice-Marshal Choe Yong-gon, together with other foreigners, was not permitted to be present at the speech, but it is unlikely he expected Khrushchev to say anything close to what he actually did. For some members of the North Korean elite, Khrushchev's speech was a signal of change. Stalin was accused of creating a cult of personality, of usurping the leadership from the Central Committee and of arrogant and inept leadership during a war—and the North Korean elite could have pointed at a certain someone guilty of similar, if not identical acts.

A conspiracy started to brew.[2] The major drivers of the conspirators were former Chinese Koreans, as Soviet Koreans had already been weakened, and the 'native' communists who operated clandestinely in colonial Korea had nearly been annihilated. The conspirators' unofficial leader was Choe Chang-ik, one of Kim Il-sung's deputies in the Cabinet of Ministers. Had the opposition been victorious, Choe would have become the country's new leader.[3] Choe hailed from the Chinese faction, spending about ten years in China cooperating closely with Mao's Communist Party.

It was an odd alliance of individuals who wanted change, did not like Kim Il-sung, wanted to remove their opponents from the Central Committee or simply wanted power. Some of them, such as Choe Chang-ik, had assisted Kim in his previous attacks, including the one on the Soviet Koreans.[4] But now they were bound together by a single goal: overthrow Kim Il-sung.

Yet the conspirators proved inept when it came to political intrigue, which ultimately proved their undoing, especially as their enemy was such a skilful and manipulative schemer.

Third Congress of the WPK

On 19 March, Kim Il-sung received a copy of Khrushchev's momentous speech.[5] He immediately realised that the speech posed a major threat to his power and that he had to do something and do it fast. His first attempt was to claim that there was indeed a problem with a cult of personality in the country, but that the cult centred on Pak Hon-yong rather than

Kim Il-sung, and now that Pak had been purged, the problem had been solved.[6]

Not satisfied with this, the oppositionists started to probe other members of the committee for their support. However, they eventually encountered loyalists, who reported what they had heard to Kim Il-sung.

The first major party event after Khrushchev's speech was the Third Congress of the WPK. The congress opened on 23 April—the day after Lenin's birthday—and lasted for six days. By that time, the opposition was yet to be shaped as a single bloc. Instead of launching a coordinated attack, one of the Leader's opponents, Lee Sang-jo, North Korea's ambassador to the Soviet Union, decided to act on his own. He twice sent notes to the congress's presidium demanding that the meeting discuss the personality cult in the WPK.[7] All speeches to be read at the congress were censored by the Central Committee's departments loyal to the Leader, and thus, naturally, this move was successfully neutralised.[8]

Lee Sang-jo continued to stand by his views even when he was later confronted by Kim's supporters after the congress. However, all this accomplished was to alert the Leader. While more hot-headed loyalists called for the ambassador's credentials to be revoked immediately, the Machiavellian Kim Il-sung did not want to alarm Moscow with such a move, and for the time being, Lee was free to return to the USSR.[9]

In any case, after the congress it looked like Kim's position had become stronger. As a representative of the British Foreign Office observed less than a month after the end of the Third Congress: 'It can be said that so far Kim Il Sung has succeeded in the attack on the cult of the individual, for which he would seem to be an obvious target. His personal position appears unimpaired and the Congress re-elected him as the Chairman of the Party's Central Committee.'[10]

Another sign that the old Stalinist order was not about to disappear was that, according to the contemporary testimony of a Bulgarian diplomat, North Korean officials still referred to Kim Il-sung as 'master'.[11]

In order to achieve its goals, the opposition had to remove Kim Il-sung from the highest position in the country: chairman of the Party's Central Committee. The organisation that was de jure empowered to do so was the Central Committee itself.[12]

To remove Kim, they needed a majority. There were seventy-one members on the committee, and thus thirty-six votes were required for a majority. The initial situation did not appear favourable for the opposition: thirty-four out of seventy-one members had been appointed to the committee at the recent Third Congress. Many of them lacked the courage to attack the chairman. Out of eleven full members of the committee's presidium, only about two or three appeared to be with the opposition.[13] Moreover, some oppositionists did not have complete confidence in their cause, feeling that their old comrade, Kim Il-sung, should be subject only to fraternal criticism rather than being removed from office.

A prudent approach would have involved appearing loyal at all party meetings while secretly asking the Soviet Union to formally recommend Kim's dismissal and supporting his removal when the time came. Yet the oppositionists did not act with due prudence. They expressed vocal disapproval of the situation in the country during official meetings of the Party leadership[14] and even during unofficial meetings with the Leader.[15] All that achieved was to alert Kim Il-sung of where their loyalties lay.

However, the battle was merely postponed. Even before the congress, Kim Il-sung seemingly suspected Choe Chang-ik of disloyalty and considered expelling him from the Central Committee's presidium, although he ultimately chose not to act.[16] Kim's official memoirs state that several officials, including

Nam Il,[17] had informed him about the conspiracy, and other documents seem to corroborate this statement.[18] One—maybe the earliest—of the reports about the plot came when the Leader was visiting the USSR, and his suddenly gloomy mood revealed to those around him that he had taken it most seriously.[19] It seems that Kim was not completely sure if Nam Il was playing both sides and subjected him to criticism in May along with Choe Chang-ik.[20] It was an uncertain, stressful time for the Leader.

Manoeuvres and counter-manoeuvres

Kim had one more reason to be stressed: he was summoned to the USSR by the presidium of the CPSU's Central Committee and scolded for his cult of personality and disregarding his people's well-being. It seemed that Kim's overseers were considering replacing him, and should that happen, there seemed to be no way for him to directly resist the Kremlin. Furthermore, the Soviet criticism of Kim was revealed to the opposition by a high-ranking diplomat, counsellor S.N. Filatov.[21]

Emboldened by the Soviet Union's actions, the more naive part of the opposition thought that the best course of action would be to take the news to Kim Il-sung and force him to make concessions. But this simply further alerted the Leader to their plans. Kim did his best to calm the opposition, promising them reforms and changes while mobilising his supporters for the coming power struggle.[22]

In the meantime, the smarter oppositionists started to do what they should have done months ago and approached the Soviet embassy. On 5 June, Choe Chang-ik scheduled a meeting with Ambassador Ivanov,[23] who met him on 8 June as planned. Choe complained of a great many issues within the senior leadership: factionalism, nepotism, attacks on the Soviet Koreans, denunciations of the late Hegay, incompetence on the part of some of Kim Il-sung's underlings, pervasive poverty, refusal to follow the spirit of the Twentieth Congress of the CPSU and the personality cult of Kim Il-sung.[24] He did not explicitly say he wanted Kim Il-sung to be removed but said that Kim should be given advice he would listen to.[25] However, by early August, the opposition was getting desperate. The Soviet embassy did not intervene explicitly, and in case of a direct attack, there was a good chance they would not get the thirty-six votes necessary to pass a resolution removing Kim from power.

Another of the conspirators' ideas was to weaken the Kim Il-sung faction by expelling some of his supporters from the Central Committee so that it could be reconfigured in a way that would be more favourable to them.[26] Kim reacted masterfully to this, suggesting that he himself was partly to blame for his supporters' alleged misdeeds—by sharing responsibility, he ensured that none of them would lose their positions.[27]

However, the opposition had another very important supporter. Lee Sang-jo, the then-ambassador to the Soviet Union, had direct access to the Kremlin and thus could have asked the Soviets to assist his comrades. On 9 August, Lee relayed the conspirators' plan to Moscow. The key idea was to remove Kim Il-sung from the position of head of the Party and to replace him with Choe Chang-ik. While Kim would remain as premier, the position of supreme commander would be given to Choe Yong-gon instead.[28] At the time, the opposition thought that Choe Yong-gon, who had been there in Moscow when Khrushchev was delivering his momentous speech, would join their cause, although he later chose not to.[29]

Yet, rather than proceeding covertly, the leaders of the opposition continued to openly criticise Kim Il-sung, even as the plenum of the Central Committee was approaching. Perfectly aware of their plans, Kim was making his final preparations for the fight, passing instructions to his supporters while placing pressure on some of the oppositionists in order to silence them.[30] Pang Hak-se, minister of internal affairs, and loyal to Kim, mobilised the police to monitor Pyongyang.[31]

Decisive battle

The final confrontation took place on Thursday, 30 August. History knows fateful days that set the course of history for decades to come. For North Korea, this was one of them.

By the time the plenum of the Central Committee convened, Kim Il-sung knew who was going to attack him and when. He had a majority on his side, and he was ready. The plenum opened with Kim making a report on his visit to the USSR and other socialist countries. The Leader mentioned the personality cult at the end of his speech. He said that the problem had existed in the WPK but that it had not been serious and was nearly completely solved.

Next was Kim Thae-gun, the Party chief for North Hamgyong province. He praised the party's policy while attacking trade unions and the Ministry of Trade, organisations led by opposition figures.[32]

The third to speak was a member of the opposition, Trade Minister Yun Kong-hum. Yun stood up and said: 'My speech will be focused on the personality cult, which exists in our party, and its serious consequences' and started delivering his speech.[33] Although he was eventually interrupted and never finished speaking, the full draft of the speech he intended to give actually survives in the Russian archives.[34] Accusing Kim of 'flagrantly trampling upon democracy inside the Party and stifling criticism', Yun declared that 'these actions completely contradict the party's charter and the Leninist norms of party life'. 'The department of agitation and propaganda of the Central Committee of the party ruthlessly suppressed all views relating to the analysis of the state of affairs existing in Korea, which do not coincide with the views given by Comrade Kim Il-sung', he continued. 'The Central Committee should make a decision on the ideology of the personality cult', Yun concluded, 'the centre of which is Comrade Kim Il-sung.'

The speech was written in an orthodox communist style and was not particularly radical. It did not call for Kim's immediate removal from power but merely for the condemnation of his cult of personality. However, everyone, including Yun Kong-hum and Kim Il-sung, knew that such a condemnation was bound to eventually produce—to borrow another communist term—'organisational conclusions'. In other words, a man condemned by the Central Committee could no longer lead it, and a subsequent meeting would have had him removed.

Kim Il-sung could not allow that to happen. Yun Kong-hum's speech was interrupted by Kim's supporters,[35] who started shouting: 'Why are you slandering?', 'Are you saying that the WPK is a fascist party or a bourgeois one?'[36] Only Choe Chang-ik spoke out in his support.[37] Yun retorted that the party bylaws had been violated and pointed to Minister of National Defence Choe Yong-gon's appointment as a vice-chairman as an example.[38] Infuriated, Choe shouted: 'You son of a bitch! What were you doing when I was fighting Japan? Shouting "hosanna" to the emperor, that's what you did!'[39]

The plenum now looked more like a bar brawl than an organised meeting of the party leadership. Screams and insults were flying around. Two members of the Central Committee, Pak Chang-ok and Pak Ui-wan, called for order.

Kim Il-sung responded to Yun's speech by saying there was no need to allow these reactionary anti-party elements to talk and suggested a vote on closure and terminating the discussion immediately. This turned out to be a vote on the future of North Korea.[40]

Only seven members of the Central Committee voted against the closure. The majority supported Kim Il-sung, making it clear to everyone in the room that the Leader was winning. Choe Chang-ik and Pak Ui-wan immediately suggested revoking the decision on closure, but this desperate proposal failed. Nam Il attempted a compromise: he condemned Yun but said he should be allowed to finish his speech. This suggestion was also voted down. The loyalists started shouting: 'Crush and destroy! Crush and destroy!', referring to the future fate of the opposition.[41] Seeing that he was receiving no support, Yun Kong-hum left the hall. Kim Il-sung announced a recess.[42]

The rest of the day was dedicated to the ardent and loud denunciation of the opposition, as Kim Il-sung's loyalists made speeches promising to eradicate those who opposed the Leader. Choe Chang-ik tried to speak but was immediately silenced by Kim's supporters.[43]

When Yun Kong-hum did not return after the break, Kim Il-sung quickly took advantage of his absence:

> Yun Kong-hum is absent here. For a party committee member to be absent at a meeting without any reason is a violation of the party bylaws. This is an act against the party. I thus propose to expel him from the party as a punishment. Those in support—raise your hands.

This time, only one man dared vote against the Leader's suggestion.[44] This man was So Hwi, the head of the DPRK's trade unions. From what we know about him, he was both the bravest and most liberal politician in all of North Korea's history.

On 31 August, with the majority on Kim Il-sung's side, the plenum adopted a resolution condemning the opposition for 'factionalist conspiracy'.[45] While the resolution still called them 'comrades' and even mentioned 'the personality cult, which existed in a slight form in the ideological sphere in our party', it was clear the oppositionists were doomed, and they knew it.

On 30 August, Yun Kong-hum and So Hwi discovered that their home phones had been cut off,[46] and they concluded that their only chance to physically survive was to immediately flee to China. They took two other officials from the Chinese Korean faction with them, boarded a car that belonged to one of the officials in order to evade detection—Yun's and So's registration plates were well known to the authorities—and rushed headlong to the Yalu River marking the border between the DPRK and the PRC.

They arrived in the morning and saw a fisherman on a boat. They summoned the man, who was shocked to see such a high-ranking group in front of him, and offered to buy his fish for a hefty price. The fisherman agreed, and they took his boat for a picnic. Sailing to the island in the middle of the river, the group stayed there for some time—probably to avoid arousing suspicion—and then waded across the river to China. They were detained by the Chinese border guard before Mao eventually granted them refuge in the PRC.[47]

Although these men were saved, the opposition to Kim Il-sung had been crushed. The four runaways were in China, never to return, while the others sat in Pyongyang awaiting their fate. However, it was not over yet. Far away in Moscow, Ambassador Lee Sang-jo received the news that his comrades had failed. It was now up to him, and him alone, to save the cause.

The USSR and China enter the fray

Lee Sang-jo decided to write directly to Khrushchev, asking the first secretary to intervene in the North Korean affair. His letter complained about people being unjustly expelled from the Central Committee for criticising Kim Il-sung and made several proposals on what could be done, the most radical of which was to send a representative of the Soviet Central Committee to Korea and have him convene a new plenum in Pyongyang and 'fix the shortcomings' of the previous meeting.[48]

What ultimately doomed the conspiracy was Lee's lack of resolve. He dared not directly suggest to Khrushchev that Kim should be removed from power. Moreover, it seems that he himself was torn over the situation: on the one hand, Lee Sang-jo understood that Kim either had to be removed or his, his comrades' and his country's fate was sealed. On the other hand, he desperately wanted to believe that the situation had simply resulted from a misunderstanding between good comrades, and if subjected to fraternal criticism, Kim Il-sung, a fellow communist and a revolutionary, would repent.

Lee Sang-jo's plan was implemented in its entirety; in fact, the Soviets did even more than he had asked for. After deliberating among themselves and consulting with the Chinese,[49] the Soviet leadership dispatched a joint delegation with China to the North. The delegation was co-headed by Khrushchev's deputy, Anastas Mikoyan, and the former commander of the Chinese forces in Korea, Peng Dehuai. Mikoyan and Peng forced Kim Il-sung to take a step back. On 23 September 1956, a new plenum, conducted under Soviet and Chinese surveillance, grudgingly admitted that the 'comrades' had been punished too harshly and partly reversed the decision. However, notably, despite Soviet and Chinese pressure,[50] Choe Chang-ik was only reinstated to the Central Committee, not the higher body, its presidium, to nullify any chance he might again challenge Kim and to show that he was still guilty.[51]

Kim used his usual strategy here. When presented with outside pressure, he yielded as much as he absolutely had to, knowing that otherwise he would run the real risk of being removed. He then waited for the outsiders to become distracted before quietly putting his plans back into full motion. Kim may well have learned this most useful skill back in his guerrilla years, having used the same tactic to save his life during the purge of the members of the GPW. And here it bore fruit once again. As readers will see in the next chapter, soon the opposition was purged again.

This was a huge success for Kim Il-sung. Initially, he felt that Mikoyan and Peng could end his reign. North Korea later made both men, to borrow George Orwell's expression, non-persons. Neither Anastas Mikoyan nor Peng Dehuai are ever mentioned in encyclopaedias published in North Korea, even though Peng was the commander of the Chinese Army during the Korean War.

Kim's triumph was complete. The events of August 1956, which initially appeared to pose a serious threat to his position, had ultimately strengthened his rule.

However, it would be too simplistic to view the August plenum and subsequent events as a struggle between Stalinists and moderates. Both Soviet and Chinese factions had advocates for moderation as well as supporters of the Stalinist orthodoxy. However, the man the opposition intended to put in power—Choe Chang-ik—had given no indication of being a moderate or a reformist. Before 1956, he was eager to participate in Kim Il-sung's purges and was also accused of corruption.[52] There is no evidence that he had shown any leniency to anyone before 1956, and, even during the time the conspiracy was being prepared, he looked to be a man interested in power, not reforms.

Moreover, Choe Chang-ik was a protégé of China, and by 1956 the Chinese Army was still stationed on North Korean soil, allowing China to influence policy in Pyongyang with relative ease. If Choe had triumphed over Kim Il-sung, North Korea could easily have become a client state of the PRC, with the regime being forced to adopt Maoism in its entirety.

That said, Choe Chang-ik was still a preferable option to Kim Il-sung. The most important reason for this is that it is unlikely he would have ever appointed his son a successor, and thus Maoist North Korea would have died with him, whereas the Kimist one outlived Kim Il-sung for nearly three decades and counting. Moreover, in the years to come, Kim's economic policy was reminiscent of the worst excesses of China's Great Leap Forward. Like Mao's China, Kim Il-sung's North Korea descended into extreme forms of war communism. The only major difference was that the DPRK was spared the Cultural Revolution. However, as readers will see, the events of the late 1960s in North Korea were, if anything, even worse.

9

HIS LAST BOW

Mikoyan and Peng's failure to remove Kim Il-sung from power was not the end of the matter. The opposition had lost, but the Soviet Union still exercised a considerable degree of control over North Korea. It took one more intrigue to shift the political balance away from the USSR.

After Stalin's death, the Soviet Union increasingly emphasised the concept of 'collective leadership', according to which power should be divided between the leading members of the political elite.

In accordance with this Soviet principle, not long after Khrushchev's historic speech, the Soviet embassy in Pyongyang started advising Kim Il-sung to divide power in North Korea. By that time, Kim occupied two positions: that of premier, thus making him the leader of the government, and that of chairman of the Central Committee of the WPK, meaning that he was also in charge of the party. The Soviet embassy directly recommended to Kim that he should yield one of these two positions to someone else.

When Kim heard the phrase 'the Soviet Union recommends', he did not know how to act. Officially, the DPRK was an independent country, and the USSR did not officially intervene in its internal affairs. However, before Stalin's death, when a Soviet ambassador gave 'advice', it was a de facto order that Kim had to follow. But now the situation appeared to have changed.

Testing Soviet control

Kim wanted to retain both positions, as this gave him nearly unlimited power inside the country. However, should the Soviets insist, he was prepared to do as he was told. In this case, Kim was planning to yield one of the two positions to one of his trusted lieutenants, likely with the aim of taking it back again in a year or so.

The first candidate Kim suggested to the Soviet embassy was Choe Yong-gon, his second-in-command, who, back in 1955, had been put forward as a potential premier when Pak Chang-ok suggested that Kim should resign from the position.

By the mid-1950s, Choe Yong-gon was probably the most influential person in North Korea after Kim Il-sung himself. He occupied the positions of deputy premier and minister of national defence and was the only person in the country holding the second-highest military rank of Vice-Marshal.

What kind of politician was Choe Yong-gon? When in mid-1956 Kim Il-sung informed the Central Committee's presidium that Pak Ir-u, the former minister of internal affairs who had been accused of counterrevolutionary activities,[1] had been found innocent by investigators, Choe reacted with a suggestion to have Pak executed.[2]

Yet Kim trusted Choe, who had been one of the most vigorous defenders of the Great Leader during the fateful August plenum, and this trust was largely not misplaced. So, it was a logical choice for Kim to choose Choe to assume one of his positions, should the USSR insist, expecting that his friend would willingly yield the position to him again when the time came.

But in 1957, something changed, and Kim ceased to view Choe as an acceptable candidate. Despite initially proposing him as a replacement, Kim began a campaign to persuade the Soviet embassy against Choe's possible appointment. What reasons could have influenced him? Since Kim never discussed his motivations with anyone, we can only speculate. First, it seems that Choe was growing overly ambitious. For example, the KPA regulations of 1955 signed by Choe Yong-gon spoke extensively about the rights of the Vice-Marshal and minister of national defence—that is, Choe Yong-gon himself—at the expense of the Marshal and Premier: Kim Il-sung.[3] Perhaps Kim feared that, trusted with one of the two highest offices in the country, Choe would start to plot his own removal.

Another likely factor was the purge of the army Kim was preparing to conduct. In the winter of 1956–7, Choe Yong-gon and his chief aide, Chief of the General Staff Kim Kwang-hyop, following Kim Il-sung's instructions, prepared an emergency mobilisation plan for the armed forces, with several other top generals participating in its creation as well. The plan's purpose was to crush any uprising in the event of the DPRK experiencing civil disorder similar to the recent Hungarian popular uprising. However, at some point the leadership began to speculate that this plan could be used as a pretext to stage a coup and overthrow Kim Il-sung. This is likely the main reason why Choe fell out of favour with Kim.[4]

Furthermore, Choe's wife, Wang Yuhuan, was Chinese. Kim well remembered that the August conspiracy against him was led by Choe Chang-ik, the leader of the pro-Chinese faction. Moreover, since this event took place soon after the visit of

Mikoyan and Peng in September 1956, Kim had every reason to believe that China was opposed to him staying in power.

The alternative candidate to Choe was Kim Il. He was also a member of the anti-Japanese partisan movement and a former serviceman of the Eighty-Eighth Brigade. In the North, Kim Il became a member of the party's highest ruling body—the presidium of the Central Committee—as early as 1946. By 1956, he held the positions of deputy premier and vice-chairman of the Central Committee. The major difference between the two is that Kim Il was never considered an independent figure. Choe was in charge of the army. Kim Il's career consisted of him occupying a position as someone's deputy or being in charge of a relatively minor government department, such as the ministry of agriculture. Thus Kim Il-sung had more reason to believe that Kim Il would not 'misuse' the position, should he be entrusted with it.

Over the next few months, Kim Il-sung and his lieutenants— former Soviet Koreans Nam Il and Pak Chong-ae—probed the Soviet embassy to assess the degree of political independence allowed to Kim. If it was mere autonomy, he would have yielded the lesser position of premier to one of his own men.[5] Here, he also tested whether the embassy would insist on Choe or agree to his own choice. If, however, it was real independence, Kim Il-sung would continue to hold both positions and thenceforward ignore his former master's instructions.

One of the main reasons for Kim's success was the personality of the then-Soviet ambassador, Aleksandr Puzanov, who like his predecessor Ivanov was a demoted Soviet official.[6] As a man with little diplomatic experience and excessively cautious due to his recent fall from grace, Kim Il-sung could not have asked for a better man than Puzanov in order to achieve his aims.

Ambassador Puzanov proved himself to be incompetent. When North Korea cautiously talked to him about 'the division of power', he did not provide any meaningful response whatsoever. Kim grew increasingly bold. Even after the regime suggested that Kim should simply retain all power,[7] there was still no response from the Soviet embassy. On 3 September, Kim decided to pay the embassy a personal visit and reiterated the proposals that had already been made by his aides: that he should remain the premier for some time ('two years or so') and that Choe Yong-gon was a poor candidate for the post. Choe was instead to be appointed chairman of the SPA presidium instead. Eventually, perhaps, Kim Il would be appointed premier, he added.

Once again, the ambassador did not respond directly, merely noting in his journal: 'I got the impression that Kim Il-sung himself also does not want to quit the premier's office.' As for the position of the premier, 'I offered no opinion on the subject', wrote Puzanov.[8] Nor did he offer an opinion on the following day, when Nam Il informed him that it was the opinion of the entire Central Committee's presidium that Kim Il-sung should stay.[9]

The ambassador's silence revealed to Kim that trying to set his plan in motion would be unlikely to result in Soviet retribution, and he started to look for a convenient moment to implement it. The opportunity very soon presented itself. From 11 to 28 September, Puzanov was in Moscow on an assignment.[10] And while Puzanov was absent, Kim made his move.

A country of Kim Il-sung's creation

On 20 September, the new cabinet was formed. Choe Yong-gon was relieved of the position of Minister of National Defence and stripped of the rank of Vice-Marshal.[11] Kim Il-sung retained the premiership[12] and remained Chairman of the Central Committee as well. As this directly contradicted the ambassador's 'advice', Kim had to wait for the ambassador to return to present him with the new arrangement as a *fait accompli*. As he hoped, the Soviet reaction never came. In fact, the following month, on 22 October 1957, the ambassador received instructions telling him not to act on the issue, apart from giving advice to the North Koreans to implement a division of power sometime in the future.[13]

It was over. If the Soviet Union did not interfere when its advice on the issue of the top leadership was not followed, then its advice and commands could be ignored from now on. Thus, from the autumn of 1957, the USSR started to lose control over North Korea. Thereafter, the DPRK was increasingly a country of Kim Il-sung's creation, a fact that everyone in the DPRK would come to appreciate. Pak Chong-ae and Nam Il, who were instrumental in this final victory, were no exception: Pak was purged, and Nam lived the rest of his life in fear, hopelessly dreaming of being allowed to return to the USSR before ultimately perishing in a suspicious car accident in 1976.[14] His son later went to the North from the Soviet Union to learn about his father's death, but Pang Hak-se, the former chief of the secret police, advised him to return as quickly as possible and not to meddle in affairs that did not concern him.[15]

The other country that concerned Kim Il-sung was China. At the time, Chinese troops were still stationed in North Korea, meaning that Beijing could still use them against Kim if necessary. Yet Kim managed to outsmart Mao as well. When Kim met Mao in November 1957, the Chinese leader said that China had been wrong to intervene in the WPK's internal affairs and that nothing like the Mikoyan–Peng delegation would ever happen again.[16] The withdrawal of Chinese troops, which was already underway, was completed on 28 October 1958.[17] With the troops gone, Chinese control over North Korea also came to an end.

North Korea was rapidly becoming a very different place. Earlier, Kim Il-sung pushed a decision that set the foundation for a social structure that would define North Korea for decades to come. It was called 'On Making the Struggle with the Counterrevolutionary Elements into the Movement of All the Party and of the All the People'. Adopted on 30 May 1957, it prescribed the division of the entire population into three strata— 'nucleus force', 'middle force' and 'people of counterrevolutionary components'.[18] While each stratum initially corresponded to exactly one-third of the population, these three groups later started to diverge in size.[19] Belonging to one of these three strata had a major impact on a North Korean's life. Those belonging to the lowest group were unlikely to be able to attend a good university or get a good job and were also subject to more severe punishments if convicted of a crime.[20] Reportedly, the person put in charge of implementing the policy was Kim Yong-ju, Kim Il-sung's brother.[21]

As for the elite, since the oppositionists were no longer protected by either the Soviets or the Chinese, Kim took the opportunity to purge them completely and utterly. Kim chose to crown this process with a spectacular event—a party conference. Conferences were considered emergency meetings of the communist parties, and the Chinese had just held one in 1955: to purge those deemed disloyal to Mao.[22] The conference convened in early March 1958. After extended criticism, the conference formally voted to remove the opposition leaders from their positions and to expel most of them from the party.[23] They were later arrested and were either shot or died in prison.

By the late 1950s, North Korea had ceased to even formally condemn the cult of personality around Kim Il-sung. While the 1957 edition of the *Dictionary of Political Terms for the General Population* stated that 'the ideas of the personality cult have no relation to Marxism–Leninism and thus cause tremendous harm to unity of the party ranks and revolutionary activities',[24] any reference to the cult of personality had been dropped in the 1959 edition.[25]

Purging the opposition, securing the state

The purges caused a massive exodus of Soviet Koreans back to the USSR. Most Soviet Koreans had come to the North with a genuine desire to help the land of their forefathers; now they were fleeing for their lives. The decision of whether to let someone go or not was arbitrary. Kang Sang-ho, former vice-minister of internal affairs, remembered how, after he had been arrested, interrogated and tortured for three months, he was finally allowed to leave:

> Honestly speaking, even after I and my wife received entry visas to the USSR in the Soviet consulate and up to the moment when we crossed the border to the Union, I still did not believe that I managed to break free of this place. Dozens, hundreds of my friends, colleagues and compatriots perished in prisons and labour camps with their wives and children. I remember, when we were crossing the border, my wife and I started softly singing the song 'Soviet land, so dear to every toiler'. It was only then that we fully understood this was not a dream. But how painful it was to think about those who would never come back, those who already drank their cup of suffering to the bottom, and those who only had to drink it in the future.[26]

Others were less lucky. Pak Il-san, son of Pak Chang-ok, one of the August conspirators, remembered his sister Galina, who did not manage to escape:

> Galina wanted to leave with assistance of one Czech man, but someone reported that their marriage was a pro forma one. She was not allowed to leave the country and about 1960 we received a letter from her—from North Hamgyong province. She could not write anything real—

just vows of loyalty to Kim Il-sung. I sent her a parcel, but it came back with a note 'the receiver no longer lives at this address'.[27]

The Chinese faction was targeted as well. One of the many people who suffered was a KPA division commissar named Kang Su-bong. He spent fifteen years in camps and escaped to China, later writing about what he had experienced in the North after he had been released.[28] Many, many more never managed to flee.

In all, the period 1958–9 saw such a massive purge of high-ranking officials that the North Korean rubber stamp parliament—the SPA—lost more than a quarter of its members, even though it had only been elected in August 1957. Pyongyang conducted a formal by-election in July 1959, although, strangely enough, the leadership chose not to announce the election in the press. Only fourteen voters out of about 1.2 million chose to vote against the suggested candidates—the last people to ever do so in Kim Il-sung's North Korea.[29] From the next elections in 1962, the official result of all North Korean elections under his rule has been the same—100 per cent in support of the only candidate on the list.

As the terror campaign intensified, the DPRK moved to create a network of concentration camps, with the Cabinet of Ministers instructing their creation in January 1959.[30] The North Korean camps are often compared to Stalin's Gulag, but this comparison is somewhat incorrect. These camps, officially called 're-education centres', resemble Soviet camps in many, even minute, details.[31] However, the darkest part of the DPRK's penitentiary system originated not in the Gulag but in a less well-known aspect of Stalin's terror policy: settlements for people sentenced to exile.[32]

North Korea's horrific analogue is called 'centres for administration of re-settlers'. Here, people were and are sentenced not by a court but by a decision of a local Security Committee.[33] These committees are normally composed of the local chairman of the police, as well as prosecution and party bureaucrats. Normally, when an individual is sentenced, the entire family shares their fate. Centres for administration of re-settlers are further divided into 'zones of revolutionisation', from which people are occasionally released, and 'zones of absolute control', where people are essentially held as slaves and forced to work in appalling conditions until they die.

As North Korea approached its tenth anniversary in 1958, Pyongyang moved to cautiously rewrite not only the pre-1945 biography of Kim Il-sung but also the history of the country itself. Three topics concerned the censors. The first was those who had been purged. Following the Stalinist example, the DPRK's official history writers simply pretended they had never existed by removing them from historical photos. The second was the traditional flag of Korea, which was replaced in the North on 10 July 1948 and was now firmly associated with the South. As well as also being excised from photos, North Korea now started to pretend that the flag had never been used.[34] The third and most important topic was the very fact of Soviet rule in the North in the 1940s. As Kim asserted his independence, he felt the time during which he had been subservient to Moscow was best forgotten. At the time, he dared not completely rewrite the history of the first years of independence, but Soviet influence nevertheless started to be downplayed in contemporary publications.

In 1961, Kim Il-sung's political manoeuvrings approached their final stage. On 6 July, the DPRK signed a Treaty of Friendship, Cooperation and Mutual Assistance with the Soviet Union, in which both countries pledged to assist each other with all necessary force should either be attacked, thus creating a formal military alliance. While Moscow thought that Pyongyang was siding with them, in just five days, on 11 July, Pyongyang signed a nearly identical treaty with China, thus firmly securing its place in the middle of the two great communist powers, whose relations were deteriorating with every month.

As for domestic policy, the major event of 1961 was the Fourth Congress of the WPK. Conducted in September of that year, the congress saw those loyal to Kim Il-sung take over all key positions. After the congress, there were no known opposition sympathisers left among the North Korean political elite. The Fourth Congress was enshrined as 'the congress of the victors' in North Korean historiography. This epithet was borrowed from the Soviet Union, where it had been used in reference to the Seventeenth Congress of the Bolshevik Party (1934)—the first congress after Stalin had solidified his rule. However, since the Korean language has a less clear distinction between singular and plural nouns than English or Russian, the Korean name of the Fourth Congress can be translated as 'the congress of the victor', which would perhaps be a more accurate definition.

Kim Il-sung was, indeed, the victor: his triumph over his foes was complete. No longer hindered by anyone inside or outside the country, he was in total control of North Korea.

PART III

UNDER THE RED SUN

10

PREPARATIONS FOR A SECOND KOREAN WAR

Moscow's political dominance and the possibility of the Central Committee voting Kim Il-sung out of office had been the only restrictions on Kim's power. With these restrictions gone, his rule became absolute, and he started to reshape the country according to his own ideas.

The Great Leader started with the economy. The North Korean public distribution system (PDS), established in 1946, distributed goods provided by the state in quotas, with the people paying only a symbolic sum for the goods they received. Although similar systems existed in various other countries, they were usually established to provide welfare to the poor or to feed the population in times of a dire emergency. This is how the PDS had been perceived by the DPRK in the 1940s and 1950s, with the state press occasionally reporting on the abolition of a socialist country's PDS as an achievement.[1] Yet instead of abolishing the PDS, Kim began transforming it into the only mechanism through which people could receive any goods in North Korea. The state again banned the private grain trade in

1957, forcing the people to rely solely on the PDS.[2] The goal of this policy was for private trade to disappear completely.[3]

Kim's other economic policies were similarly radical. When Pyongyang outlined North Korea's first five-year plan in 1957, the Soviet State Planning Committee argued that the plan was unrealistic and placed too much emphasis on heavy industry, neglecting light industry and agriculture.[4] However, now Kim could ignore such advice—and that is exactly what he did.

A gun in one hand and a hammer and sickle in the other

In 1960 and 1961, Kim enforced two doctrines that prescribed the creation of an ultra-centralised economy. These were the 'Chongsanni method' and the 'Taean work system', named after the places where Kim uttered his instructions. The 'Chongsanni method', which was adopted first, envisioned agriculture being directly controlled by local party bureaucrats; any alteration of the plan required pre-approval by a superior party organisation. The 'Taean work system' commanded that the same be done in industry.

What Kim really wanted was complete personal control of the economy rather than central planning alone. He had little real respect for economic plans. Indeed, from January 1957 to the summer of 1958, the DPRK's economy operated without a general plan, which was yet to be adopted. Kim also felt free to alter the plan whenever he wanted. After a five-year plan was finally adopted in 1958, Kim started arbitrarily changing it, demanding much higher productivity without any consideration of the original goals or economic realities.[5]

Kim's tendency to set unfulfillable economic goals created a further problem. Fearing punishment for not fulfilling the goals, North Korean officials tended to distort the statistics they reported to Pyongyang. A vivid example of this was when the number of tractors for a statistical reference were calculated not in actual machines but in imaginary 'tractor units', arrived at by adding up the engine power of all the country's tractors and dividing the figure by an arbitrarily selected coefficient. Due to these kinds of issues, even Kim Il-sung did not get a fully objective image of what was actually going on in the economy.[6] The situation was further complicated due to many cadres of the Central Statistics Bureau of the DPRK's Cabinet of Ministers having fallen victim to the purges of the 1950s.[7]

The situation was also affected by Kim's new hobby, 'on-the-spot guidance'.[8] This involved the Great Leader travelling across the country and inspecting various locations, such as farms, schools and factories, and issuing instructions. Sometimes, he arrived by car, and sometimes he used his personal train.[9] Naturally, the local officials, being warned of the coming inspection, did their very best to prepare a Potemkin-like setting, and thus Kim Il-sung usually 'saw' that everything was going well and was left with a very rosy image of the country. Kim even started to believe that these 'on-the-spot guidance' sessions were the best way to oversee the economy in general and commanded local officials to do the same on a regular basis.[10] The time wasted on these inspections did little to contribute to the country's economic performance.

Such drastic mismanagement meant that only the parts of the economy Kim considered a priority—heavy industry and particularly the military industries—would be developing properly. In the rest of the economy, it was almost as though Kim's command to workers from 1962, to 'hold a gun in one hand and a hammer and a sickle in the other one',[11] had been implemented literally.

In the meantime, South Korea was experiencing unprecedented political turmoil. In the spring of 1960, President Rhee attempted to rig vice-presidential elections in favour of the candidate he supported, triggering widespread protests across the country. Eventually, even members of his cabinet suggested that the president should resign, as did the American ambassador, Walter Patrick McConaughy. Rhee fled to the United States, never to return home.[12]

The new-born Second Republic was a short-lived one. In May 1961, the military orchestrated a coup, dissolved the government and announced the country would now be ruled by the Supreme Council for National Reconstruction, chaired by Lieutenant-General Chang Do-yong. In fact, however, General Chang ruled the nation for less than two months, as on 2 July he was deposed and arrested. Chang's former deputy, Major-General Park Chung-hee, then assumed power.[13]

Park Chung-hee ruled South Korea for eighteen years and presided over a period of spectacular economic development. However, Kim Il-sung had no way of knowing that would be the case in 1961. From his perspective, the South was in revolutionary turmoil, having experienced three successive, successful attempts to overthrow the head of state. Thus, decided Kim, perhaps this was the time for a rematch: the Second Korean War.

Readers should not be surprised, as he was not the only person dreaming about a second Korean war just two years after the first one had ended. In 1955, his South Korean counterpart, Rhee, had also expressed a desire to attack the North.[14] At the time, neither Rhee nor Kim could start such a war, as neither Washington nor Moscow would have given their approval; now, however, things were different in the North. Moreover, Kim Il-sung had already instigated a war in Korea—and it was not stopped by a change of heart but because the war could not be won. Thus, with the possibility of victory given the turmoil in the South, Kim started planning.

Many things needed to be done. First, North Korea had to be much better armed than the South, and the difference would have to be even greater than it had been in 1950. Next, the South Korean people would have to be made sympathetic towards the North so that they would welcome the KPA as liberators. The American Army would also have to be forced to leave the South. And, of course, North Korea would need to secure the international assistance of Mao's China or Khrushchev's Soviet Union.

This was an ambitious plan, and it would require several years to be fulfilled. The first task was to promote militarisation in the economy. Originally, the seven-year plan, scheduled to begin in 1961, promoted light industry, agriculture and public welfare above heavy industry and the military. These goals were now jettisoned and replaced by the primacy of the rapidly growing military–industrial complex. The militaristic doctrine culminated in December 1962, when a plenum of the Central Committee announced four new policy doctrines: arming the people, making the entire country a fortress, making the entire army a cadre one[15] and modernising all regular armed forces. The following years saw an expansion of both regular military forces and paramilitaries. Massive construction projects were launched, with the workers mobilised to build fortifications across the country.[16]

Pivot to China

As for foreign policy, the international situation once again proved beneficial for Kim Il-sung. Since Khrushchev's denunciation of Stalin, Mao had been growing increasingly distrustful of Moscow. As time went by, the two greatest communist powers steadily grew further apart. Politically, Kim was now an independent actor and could decide whom to support. Economically, however, the country was dependent on Moscow and Beijing. To lessen this dependence, Kim decided that while North Korea would not seek to alienate the Kremlin, the country would provide more vocal support for the leader with whom Kim felt more affinity: Chairman Mao.

Not only was Mao's pro-Stalin line much closer to Kim's own views—as opposed to Khrushchev's reformism and calls for coexistence with the capitalist world—but he also understood that the USSR would never give its blessing for a second Korean war. As only a few years had passed since the PRC's annexation of a group of small islands in Taiwan's Zhejiang province in 1955, Kim believed that China may well have been willing to offer such support.[17]

Perhaps the most vivid manifestation of this pro-China line was an article, 'Let Us Defend the Socialist Camp', which was published in *Rodong Shinmun* on 28 October 1963 before later being reprinted in other major newspapers and journals.[18] This lengthy editorial attacked the USSR and praised China. While Khrushchev was not named directly, the article condemned those who 'do not distinguish between their revolutionary comrades and class enemies' and their calls for amicable coexistence with the West. The USSR had previously been the only base of socialism, the article explained, but at present one country did not and could not represent the entire socialist bloc. Attempts to isolate China were merely attempts to divide the socialist camp, continued the piece.

This was an open declaration of support for Mao in the Sino-Soviet dispute. However, the DPRK also made it clear that it was going to support the PRC as an equal and had no intention of becoming a client state of Beijing. The North Koreans would obey Kim Il-sung and him alone.

Once Kim thought the preparations were complete, it was time to involve China in his plans. In the autumn of 1965, Kim met the PRC's ambassador, Hao Deqing, who was leaving Pyongyang for Beijing, and told him: 'Sooner or later, there will be a fight in Korea. This is unavoidable. This problem cannot be solved otherwise. The Korean people must experience it':

> The struggle of the South Korean people intensifies. If the contradictions are sharp, they will rise to fight. We have already thought about it. We are ready. We also wish it to happen. We are old comrades-in-arms and our meetings went very well. We ask your army to participate in the future conflict![19]

Nothing ultimately came of this endeavour, presumably because China refused to approve Kim's plans. Mao remembered how Kim had started the war in 1950, how enormously costly it had proved for China and how little had been gained. It was a mistake they would not seek to repeat. When the plan for a joint invasion of South Korea fizzled away, North Korea's friendship with China vanished along with it.

11

CHARTING OUR OWN PATH

The following year, 1966, saw a rapid decline in relations between China and North Korea.

Apart from Mao's refusal to start a second Korean war, the most important reason for the downturn in Chinese–North Korean relations came in May 1966, when Mao announced the Great Proletarian Cultural Revolution. The Cultural Revolution was very different from anything the communist world had ever seen. Mao asserted that the leadership of the party—apart from his infallible self, of course—had become corrupt and called on the revolutionary masses—particularly young men and women—to 'bombard the headquarters'. In the ensuing years, the country saw squads of Red Guards—young people fanatically devoted to Mao—beating, torturing and killing anyone they considered disloyal to the Great Helmsman.[1] This was definitely not the way Kim Il-sung envisioned running a country. His rule prioritised rigid order, not controlled chaos. Terror was to be carried out by the secret police, not an angry mob. Thus, Mao's Cultural Revolution was a further reason to distance North Korea from Beijing.

The new era was heralded by a *Rodong Shinmun* editorial published on 12 August 1966. Headlined 'Let Us Protect Independence', the article attacked both 'modern revisionists' and 'dogmatists', that is, the Soviets and the Chinese respectively. Both countries were henceforth considered equally hostile.[2]

The tensions between China and North Korea eventually resulted in a border conflict after North Korea installed posters with anti-Mao slogans along the border, which remained there until 1968.[3] Encouraged by the propaganda, North Korean children near the border city of Shinuiju would regularly go to the bank of the Yalu River and throw rocks in the direction of China.[4] Meanwhile, Beijing was pressuring North Korea to relinquish parts of Mount Paektu, which straddles the Sino–North Korean border. They even threatened North Korea with a military operation if it failed to comply.[5]

At the same time, North Korea itself experienced a student riot that was indirectly instigated by China. The students were not actually North Koreans but rather members of the country's 10,000-strong Chinese diaspora.[6] In May 1966, when Mao proclaimed the Cultural Revolution, some of them organised a patriotic hike in Pyongyang—waving the Chinese flag and shouting 'Long live Chairman Mao!' and 'Long live the Communist Party!' The school's WPK secretary attempted to stop them, arguing that 'if the American bastards saw this, they'd say the Volunteers' Army is back!' The students thought this was a direct infringement of their rights as Chinese citizens.

Similar episodes followed. Pyongyang initially tried to broker a compromise, but its approach changed after 23 August, when the students stormed the secretary's office. They were acting exactly like the Red Guards in China, whose actions they were seeking to emulate. The authorities viewed the students' behaviour as crossing a red line and closed the school. Similar incidents with students from the Chinese diaspora also took place in rural areas.[7] The situation culminated in the state threatening to cut the country's Chinese citizens off from the North Korean PDS unless they either naturalised or left. It was the Chinese diaspora's darkest hour, and soon they were nearly completely destroyed as a social group.[8]

Remoulding the country: national isolation and Juche Thought

Given the sorry state of relations with China, Kim started to probe the Soviet Union with the aim of rekindling the friendship between the two states. In 1966, he even met the new Soviet leader, Leonid Brezhnev, who had replaced Khrushchev in 1964. At a summit held aboard a Soviet missile cruiser near Vladivostok, Brezhnev and Kim decided to set the past aside and work towards a better relationship.[9]

However, Kim's demands went far beyond what Moscow was willing to consider. As later talks showed, he was ready to criticise Mao and vocally support Moscow's policy, such as the Soviet invasion of Czechoslovakia in 1968, but in return he demanded not only economic assistance but also that the USSR supply him with secret intelligence about other countries and comply with his requests regarding Soviet domestic policy: specifically, Kim wanted Khrushchev, whom he blamed for the attempts to oust him in 1956, to be publicly condemned in the Soviet press.[10] Thus, the 'great friendship' was not reborn, even though the official media of the two countries continued to project an image of the DPRK and the USSR as close allies.

One of the few foreign heads of state who visited the DPRK during this period was Norodom Sihanouk. An eccentric Cambodian king, he had actively collaborated with both Vichy France and imperial Japan during the Second World War before abdicating in 1955 to lead the nation as the head of an organisation called the Community of the Common People. One could hardly expect such a person to bond with Kim Il-sung, but the two in fact became close friends, and Kim even allowed Sihanouk to be published in *Rodong Shinmun*.[11]

However, Kim's main priority was North Korea's domestic policy. In October 1966, he convened the Second Party Conference. At the time of writing, very little is known about this event. What we do know is that Kim's position at the top of the party was renamed to 'general secretary'. This, of course, was a gesture towards the Soviet Union: 'chairman of the Central Committee' was the name of the top position in the CPC, whereas, in 1966, Brezhnev had changed the name of his own position from first secretary to general secretary. It appears that Kim also used the conference to blame a number of officials for the failure of his increasingly combative policy towards South Korea.

However, the conference was chiefly significant for ushering in a new policy on North Korean ideology. From this point on, the country would be remoulded in Kim's image, making him not merely the supreme ruler but the man whose ideas would be the sole and mandatory form of guidance for every person in the country.[12]

Since North Korea now wanted to present itself as an alternative to both Moscow and Beijing, the country needed an ideology that could be marketed as superior to Marxism–Leninism and Mao Zedong Thought. With this came perhaps the most comical episode in North Korean history.

Among those purged around the time of the Second Conference was Kim Chang-man, who had coined the term 'Juche' in the 1950s, a concept that had been used to convey the idea of being the 'main driving force' in history and to justify the DPRK's growing independence from the USSR. In the following years, and though it was periodically mentioned in party publications, North Korea did little to actively promote the concept of 'Juche'.

With Kim Chang-man removed, Kim Il-sung decided to appropriate this concept for his own ideology. The Leader commands, and the party obeys. Beginning in 1966, North Korea's internal and external propaganda started to promote the word with extreme vigour. The problem was that Kim Il-sung never received a higher education and was not particularly well versed in any branch of philosophy, including Marxism. For him, Juche was little more than a means to assert North Korea's independence from Moscow. And the system of total obedience to the Leader he was creating prevented his underlings in the ideological departments from reformulating it into a more intelligible form. Thus, when it came to explaining what 'Juche' thought actually is, North Korean ideologues limited themselves to just one sentence: 'Man is the master of all things', repeated and rephrased over and over. They had to wrap this single sobriquet as the apex of all philosophy, leading to extremely repetitive texts like the following, taken from the *Grand Encyclopaedia of Korea*:[13]

> The Juche Thought is formed from philosophical principles and socio-historical fundamentals, from guiding doctrines of revolution and construction. The philosophical principle is an important component of the Juche Thought. Among the philosophical principles of the Juche Thought, the most important ones are the one which sets man into a place in the world and the one which shows man's fundamental qualities. Among the philosophical principles of the Juche Thought, the most important one is the one which shows the role which man plays in the world, that principle that man is the master of all things and decides everything.[14]

Readers should be applauded for wading through the above paragraph. For the encyclopaedia's authors, it must have been even more excruciating to write, but given that Kim Il-sung himself had a very limited understanding of what 'Juche Thought' was actually about, they had no other choice. 'Man is the master of all things' is not exactly a meaningful sentence. Generations of foreign observers spent much time and effort trying to understand 'Juche Thought', attempting to find some philosophical substance akin to that of Soviet or Chinese ideology.

It is an open secret that many academics outside the Korean Peninsula who brand themselves as researchers of North Korea have little, if any, actual command of the Korean language. Thus, many of them had no idea how to correctly translate the word 'Juche'. This has often led to a perception of Juche as an Oriental enigma that a Western mind is unable to fully comprehend.[15] In fact, however, there is nothing 'Oriental' or enigmatic about this word. As mentioned earlier, it was initially created to translate a purely Western concept—the German word *Subjekt*. It is no more or less comprehensible than other Korean words for philosophical concepts—*muljil* (matter), *kwannyomnon* (idealism) or, for what it matters, *juche*'s antonym, *kaekche* (object)—all of which were created in the nineteenth century to convey Western terms and concepts in a Korean context.

Juche Thought did not sell abroad at all. Apart from tiny 'Juche Thought study groups' sponsored by DPRK embassies all over the world, virtually no one was willing to become a follower of one nebulous sentence—and even those study groups were simply offering their vocal support to the North rather than actually studying anything. The only time anyone inspired by North Korea has sought to take power was in Bulgaria in 1965, before Juche Thought started to be promoted.[16]

Raids on the South: the Vietnamese model

As for South Korea, Kim Il-sung did not give up completely. Although an invasion would have been doomed without Chinese help, Kim thought he might have some success by applying the Vietnamese model. Like Korea, Vietnam was divided into a communist North and a capitalist South. During the civil war of the late 1950s, the South was constantly being harassed by communist guerrillas and underground activists. By the late 1960s, it was increasingly likely that North Vietnam would win the war, and hence its example was attractive to North Korea. Thus, the late 1960s saw a series of provocations, incidents and attacks aimed at destabilising South Korea that were fashioned after those launched by North Vietnam. In the West, these provocations are sometimes called 'the Second Korean War', although this name is both misleading and disrespectful to the victims of the actual war. In fact, these limited skirmishes happened precisely because there was no second Korean war.

The first, and perhaps most important of these incidents was the attempted assassination of South Korean President Park Chung-hee. The DPRK trained an elite group of commandos for this operation. The group, dressed in South Korean military uniforms, covertly crossed the inter-Korean DMZ and on 21 January 1968 approached the vicinity of the presidential residence. They were intercepted, and a police officer—Chief Superintendent Choe Gyu-shik—began to question the group. Choe grew more and more suspicious and eventually pulled out his pistol. As soon as he did, shooting began. Officer Choe gave his life in the ensuing battle, and almost all of the North Korean commandos were also killed, with one managing to escape back and another captured. The escapee, Pak Che-gyong, later became a four-star general in the KPA,[17] while the prisoner, Kim Shin-jo, lived the life of an ordinary South Korean citizen.[18]

Another major event took place just two days later—and this time the target was the United States. On 23 January, the North Korean Navy seized an American signals intelligence ship, the USS *Pueblo*. As Kim Il-sung himself later testified, the capture of the ship took him by surprise: he was called by his chief of staff, General O Jin-u, who reported that 'we just captured an

American ship'. Kim's first reaction was 'Now, why did you have to do it?', but after receiving a more detailed report, he agreed that the navy had acted correctly. The vessel was taken to Wonsan, where the crew was detained[19] and subject to brutal treatment while in captivity. A report based on an eyewitness's testimony—Tatyana Lee, a Soviet Korean woman who lived in Wonsan—describes the prisoners being beaten and robbed by North Korean soldiers amid the cheering of young North Korean civilians and the silent protest of others.[20]

Pueblo's crew was held in the North as prisoners of war until December, when they were returned to South Korea.[21] Meanwhile, the North Korean operations continued.

On 9 December 1968, a squad of North Korean commandos murdered a South Korean boy, Lee Sung-bok, after being sent to the South to establish a network of sympathisers. The child was killed on his birthday; he was only nine.[22] The tragedy shocked the South Korean public. The senseless killing led many to question whether this incident had been invented or at least exaggerated by South Korean conservatives. However, a later investigation, carried out long after the triumph of democracy in the South and under a left-wing administration, confirmed that Sung-bok had indeed been murdered by North Koreans.[23]

Another incident took place on 15 April 1969, Kim Il-sung's fifty-seventh birthday, when KPA fighters shot down a US Navy Lockheed EC-121 Warning Star reconnaissance aircraft flying over the Sea of Japan near Chongjin. All thirty-one of its crew died. The North Korean government's position was that the imperialists had been warned not to infringe on their sovereignty and had been taught a lesson.[24]

One of the final episodes in this series of confrontations was the hijacking of an entire South Korean plane, complete with its passengers. On 11 December 1969, a Korean Air Lines plane flying from the city of Kangnung on the shore of the Sea of Japan to Seoul was hijacked by North Koreans who forced the pilots to take it to the North. Thirty-nine out of fifty-one passengers were later returned; the other passengers—and the crew—never came back.[25]

This was a time of uncertainty. The Great Leader was under a lot of stress and suffering from a sleep disorder.[26] By that time, North Korea had developed an extensive infrastructure to attend to Kim's personal needs, from dozens of luxurious villas[27] to a personal clinic with ultra-modern equipment.[28] But even the best North Korean medics had failed to cure Kim's insomnia, and, as archival documents show, Pyongyang had to ask Moscow to send a Soviet neuropathologist to Pyongyang to treat Kim Il-sung.[29] Within the space of a year, another request was sent—not only was Kim still struggling to sleep; he was also suffering from severe pain due to inflammation in his right shoulder.[30]

Kim had good reasons to be stressed, since Pyongyang had failed where Hanoi had succeeded. South Korea proved to be much more stable than South Vietnam, and Kim failed to create any meaningful partisan movement there. By the early 1970s, Kim also recognised that his tactics had failed, and the attacks on the South finally stopped, at least for the time being.

Kim appears to have envied the Vietnamese. When Saigon fell on 30 April 1975, for example, the announcement of the Vietnamese communists' victory[31] was dwarfed in North Korea's *Rodong Shinmun* by a huge editorial: 'The Revolutionary Great Deed of Our Working-Class and Our People, Who Receive the Wise Leadership of the Great Leader, Is Ever Victorious and Never Failing'.[32] The Vietnamese created a communist regime in Saigon, and the formal unification of Vietnam was proclaimed the following year. The ambassador of the communist Republic of South Vietnam later complained to the Soviets that during his tenure in 1975–6 neither Kim Il-sung nor even his deputy had ever granted him an audience.[33]

12

THE LONG NIGHT BEGINS

To outside observers, the introduction of 'Juche Thought' and the attacks on South Korea appeared to be of major significance. Yet, however important these developments may have been, the consequences of what was happening inside the DPRK were wider and far more enduring, as the new order being set would affect the lives of every single man, woman and child in North Korea for decades to come.

In 1967, Kim Il-sung moved to create a truly totalitarian regime. The new order has a name: Singular Thought System. This system prescribed that Kim's ideas would guide every aspect of life in the country and that no discussion or even independent thought apart from his ideas would be allowed. It was an open declaration of a totalitarian state. Kim first mentioned the Singular Thought System in March, saying that everything that had unfolded since 1956 had led to its creation.[1]

Like many key decisions, the Singular Thought System was formally introduced at a meeting of the party's leadership—the fifteenth plenum of the Fourth Central Committee. The meeting lasted from 4 to 8 May 1967 and proceeded in the deepest secrecy:[2] for a few years, North Korean encyclopaedias omitted any reference to the fifteenth plenum altogether, skipping from the fourteenth to the sixteenth.[3]

The fifteenth plenum's proceedings were recorded on tape, which was distributed to local party committees and later played to ordinary party members,[4] who would thus have been able to hear the Leader accusing other functionaries of 'injecting feudal, Confucian ideas' into the party, failing to fulfil the production plans and not having enough faith in the slogans of Kim Il-sung. Kim Il-sung's son, Kim Jong-il—formerly known as Yura—also made a speech at the plenum, as he was already a high-ranking official. He said that some of the party members had rejected the sole guiding role of the Leader in an attempt to turn the party into an undisciplined mob. Thus, the party must be strengthened with the Singular Thought System. Henceforth, there would be one will, one thought. With this, the party would succeed in building socialism and, eventually, communism.[5]

Later that month, on 25 May, Kim Il-sung gave a secret speech to a group of WPK propagandists called 'On the Immediate Tasks in the Directions of the Party's Propaganda Work'. Often referred to as simply the '25 May Instructions', this speech was a watershed that marked the transformation of the country into a truly totalitarian state.[6] This new order was based on six pillars: the cult of personality, control, secrecy, hierarchy, exploitation and terror. Based on the '25 May Instructions', these six pillars have shaped North Korea for more than half a century—and at the time this book was being written, no one can convincingly predict how many more it will last.

The cult of Kim Il-sung

The first pillar—the cult of Kim Il-sung—anchors the new order. In less than a year since the '25 May Instructions', Kim's cult of personality surpassed that of Stalin, and after a few years it had surpassed anything the communist bloc had ever seen. The new cult of personality was pioneered in the ANKCJ, the publications of which started to hail Kim Il-sung with unprecedented vigour as early as 1965.[7] In 1967, the cult was introduced into the DPRK itself.

The first step in this process involved the name 'Kim Il-sung' becoming sacred in North Korea, to the extent that in 1974 all North Koreans named Kim Il-sung were ordered to change their names.[8] Every time the name 'Kim Il-sung' appeared in writing, it had to be accentuated with different typography, such as bold or a bigger font. For example, it was always '**Kim Il-sung** University' and never 'Kim Il-sung University'. When crossing out a sentence containing one of the names, the Leader's name was not to be crossed out. Instead, it had to be placed in a frame with a squiggle showing that the name had been written by mistake.

Even Korean grammar was altered to accommodate the cult of personality, with sentences being routinely butchered to place Kim's name in a dominant position, leading to phrases like 'The Great Leader Comrade **Kim Il-sung**'s immortal classical works newspapers, journals and media of several countries have published.'[9]

Finally, the Kim name even affected the way Chinese characters were taught in the DPRK's schools. While in South Korea students usually started learning with the simplest characters like 'one', 'two' and 'three' (一, 二, 三), in the North they began with 'gold', 'sun' and 'become' (金, 日, 成), pronounced as, respectively, 'kim', 'il' and 'sung'.

Next were the titles. North Korea developed several titles that were mandatory when referring to Kim Il-sung. The most popular of these was 'Great Leader', and in the 1970s, they customarily added 'of the Revolution'. The second was 'Respected and Beloved Leader'. There were myriad others such as 'Great Marshal', 'Unsurpassed Genius' and 'Sun of the Nation'. The loftiest of these titles was:

> The great thinker, theoretician and philosopher, whom our nation came to deeply venerate for the first time in its half-10,000 years of history, peerless patriot, legendary hero, excellent military strategist, ever-victorious iron-willed brilliant commander, the one who is deeply adorated by each and every person in the world, the great man among the great ones, Respected and Beloved Leader Comrade **Kim Il-sung**.[10]

In many cases, the Leader's name was nearly fused with his standard title. Even the country's encyclopaedias and reference books reflected this. While Kim Il-sung's biography preceded any other entries, articles dedicated to other things related to Kim were placed not under the letter K but under the letter 'wi'—the first letters in the word *widaehan*, 'great'—meaning that all the articles about Kim had to contain the title 'Great Leader'.

Kim Il-sung's birthday, 15 April, became the central day in the DPRK's calendar.[11] On this day, people were given special gifts from the state, ranging from simple candies to substantial items such as refrigerators and TV sets. In the army, promotions to the top ranks were normally made just before 15 April, so that the promoted generals would celebrate with exceptional vigour.

Moreover, the fact that Kim was born in 1912 meant that the traditional Chinese zodiac was banished from the DPRK—the year 1912 was the year of the rat, unbefitting the Great Leader.

Kim Il-sung's portraits were also mass produced and elevated to the status of sacred objects. Only specially qualified people—called 'painters of the First One'—were authorised to produce them.[12] Each household was and is required to have a standard set of portraits on a wall where nothing else is allowed to hang. Portraits were hung in offices, factories, Pyongyang metro cars, on the streets, virtually everywhere. When children received their breakfast in school, when a patient was healed in hospital, when voting and on many other occasions, everyone was supposed to bow to a portrait and thank the Fatherly Marshal for his grace. Stories began to appear in North Korean publications applauding people who died saving the portrait from some natural disaster or even those who preferred saving the portraits over saving their own children.[13]

Stealing a portrait of Kim Il-sung was made punishable by death,[14] while recycling or throwing away a paper portrait is forbidden—the only appropriate way to dispose of an image of Kim Il-sung is to burn it.

Even thieves do not dare steal these portraits—they know they will be punished by death if they are caught.

All photos of the Great Leader are also supposed to be taken from the left in order to obscure an unsightly but benign tumour on the right side of his head.[15] Statues of Kim also proliferated during the 'Singular Thought System' era, with locals expected to bring flowers and bow to them regularly, and from 1979, Kim Il-sung also featured on 100 won banknotes (the highest denomination available).

Kim Il-sung's 'on-the-spot guidance' visits were now treated as life-defining events for those graced with his presence. During the visit, all of Kim's remarks, even the smallest ones, were recorded, processed into a detailed plan to be implemented and then hung on walls and duly observed by the workers. A plaque with the dates of the Great Leader's visit would be placed on the door and updated in case of future visits. Anniversaries of Kim's visit are also celebrated, and the state press was instructed never to cover any visit by any other official, no matter how important it was. Only Kim Il-sung had that right.

All things and objects honoured with the Leader's presence were immediately sanctified. Chairs and benches on which the

Leader sat were preserved, with no one allowed to sit on them again. The same fate usually awaited the pens he used to sign documents. There are even a number of special shelters, called Veneration Rooms, designed specifically for the preservation of statues, plaques, portraits and other objects of the cult in case of an emergency. In later years, the party's Central Military Commission ordered that, in case of war, all revered objects should be moved immediately to the Veneration Rooms, an act seen as an even greater priority than evacuating civilians.[16]

The cult of Kim Il-sung manifested itself in every sphere of life. Journal articles included quotes by Kim even if the subject was unrelated, and sportspeople dedicated their victories to the leader when they won their medals. Actors who played Kim— who would never be credited for doing so[17]—were subsequently banned from playing any other role.[18]

Regular and ideological meetings at workplaces, dedicated above all else to extolling the Leader's greatness, were conducted several times a week, and participation was mandatory. Only children, the very elderly and those incarcerated in prisons and camps were exempted. A multitude of songs, poems and books lauding Kim Il-sung were produced. On 20 March 1972, the DPRK introduced the Kim Il-sung Order, ranking it above all other military decorations.[19] The supreme award thus joined the nation's top university and Pyongyang's central square, built after the war, on the list of things named after Kim Il-sung.

The cult was expensive to maintain, especially for a nation as poor as North Korea. Statues, portraits and other holy objects, as well as their maintenance, cost money. Time wasted on ideological meetings could have been used for real work to improve the economy. Ultimately, this became much more than just a means to accommodate the ego of Kim Il-sung. In the ensuing decades, the cult has remoulded North Korean culture, literature, education, economy, patterns of life, historical studies and even aspects of military service.

The cult obviously required justification, which the North Korean authorities sought to find by rewriting history to glorify Kim Il-sung. In the new version of North Korea's history, Kim Il-sung's family were not middle-class rural intellectuals but legendary heroes who had been fighting for the nation for decades. Kim Il-sung's paternal great-grandfather Kim Ung-u was claimed to have led the fight against the *General Sherman*, a US merchant ship that entered Korean territorial waters in 1866. His father Kim Hyong-jik did not just join the 1 March movement but was its most prominent leader.[20] His mother Kang Ban-sok organised women for anti-Japanese resistance in Manchuria.[21]

Kim Il-sung himself was described as having been a natural leader since a very early age. He founded his first anti-Japanese organisation—the 'Down-with-Imperialism Union'—when he was only fourteen. North Korean propaganda now claimed he had led the entire anti-Japanese movement in Manchuria and had only cooperated with the Chinese communists; his CPC membership was never to be mentioned. Chinese comrades respected his wisdom and guidance and asked for his advice.[22]

Finally, the myth of the KPRA was taken to a completely new level. As readers may recall, the idea that Kim Il-sung created and led this 'army' in Manchuria was coined by the Soviet administration in the 1940s, and in the 1950s the KPRA was shown as an auxiliary force to the Red Army during the war with Japan. Now it was presented as the main fighting force: it was the KPRA that had defeated Japan in 1945, with the Allies, including the USSR, playing a secondary role in the war.

The entire period of Soviet administration was removed from North Korean history books, while Stalin was relegated to the status of leader of a junior nation who bowed before the Leader of the World—Kim Il-sung.[23]

Official versions of this history of Korea were taught in North Korea at all stages of education, from kindergarten to university. Kim Il-sung's biography became a separate subject in 1968.[24] Needless to say, both the Soviets and Chinese perceived this as a bitter betrayal by a former comrade-in-arms. Yet in both China and the Soviet Union, critics were silenced by the state. Both countries were trying to sway North Korea, and Pyongyang cleverly played both sides. It was not until the late 1980s that truthful publications on the subject could finally emerge—first in the Soviet Union, and then, from the early 1990s, in China.[25]

The cult made Kim believe in his own greatness, and he did not like being reminded of his past. A revealing incident occurred in 1979, when Kim Il-sung met his old associate, General Lebedev, who came to visit Kim in Pyongyang.[26]

The two were standing in front of a plaque hailing Kim Il-sung when Lebedev started to recall their common past. 'Kim!', said the general: 'Think of it, we were laying just here, you do remember, don't you? We were so young, so stupid then ...' And then Lebedev saw how Kim Il-sung's bodyguards flinched, how all of them at once put their hands on their weapons. The Leader himself blanched. 'Yes', he said, after recovering: 'You were indeed so young. And very stupid.' After this incident, Lebedev was never again invited back to the North.[27]

State control over the individual

Control was the second pillar of Kim's new order. North Koreans could not travel freely. The year 1967 saw the introduction of local government-issued travel certificates that were normally required before leaving one's county of residence.[28] Special types of permits existed for those wishing to travel to the capital or an area near the border. International travel was severely restricted, almost to the point of being banned, even before 1967.[29]

Under the new system, people could not stay at their friends' or relatives' house without first informing the state. The person in charge was a chairwoman of the local 'people's group'— an otherwise unemployed woman charged with monitoring newcomers to the local community. The chairwoman's responsibilities also include surprise night checks: accompanied by a police team, she knocks at random flats and checks whether anyone is staying illegally.

Every North Korean who is not a child or in prison must be a member of a political organisation. These include the party, for the society's elite; the Children's Union and the Youth League[30] for young people; and labour unions, the Women's League and Union of Agrarian Labourers for the rest.

The primary duty of these organisations was to arrange daily ideological meetings.[31] During these mandatory meetings, North Koreans studied Kim Il-sung's works, his official biography, listened to recent news as presented and interpreted by the state and took part in criticism and self-criticism sessions. Participants would stand up in turn to accuse their 'comrades' of petty offences, which could be anything from being late for work or not washing their hands often enough. Accusations would be followed by correctional quotes from the Great Leader's writings. The accused would then admit their wrongdoing and pledge to try being a true 'Kimilsungist' in future. A similar model was used for self-criticism. A particularly heated session, especially in the early 1970s, could result in a criticised person being physically beaten. Needless to say, this system was highly effective at making individuals doubt themselves and their friends, as well as ensuring obedience to the state.

Another aspect of life that is ubiquitous in North Korea is the KPA and its associated paramilitaries. Created between the late 1950s and the early 1970s, these paramilitary organisations' structure, purposes and goals were strongly influenced by Mao's China, in contrast to the regular armed forces, which were modelled after the USSR.

As a teenager, North Koreans spend around two weeks receiving basic military training in the Young Red Guard Corps. After graduating from school, a typical North Korean normally joins the army or one of the paramilitary organisations. One of these is the University Military Training Corps, where students are trained to become officers; the alternative is the Corps of Speed Battle Young Stormtroopers: militarised labour brigades, whose members participate in various construction projects. Next, an adult becomes a member of the Workplace Military Training Corps and then Corps of Workers or the Farmers' Red Guards, which keep people in shape in case they are mobilised. Naturally, life in the military and in the paramilitaries is an ideal way to keep the people compliant and indoctrinate them in the state's ideology. This is probably one of the reasons why the length of service in the KPA has gradually been expanded, from three and a half years in the 1950s to a record high of ten by the end of the Kim Il-sung era in 1994.[32]

Secrecy and censorship

The third pillar of the system is secrecy and the censorship implemented to facilitate it. Kim Il-sung banned all foreign radio and media in North Korea, and 'foreign' did not just mean 'capitalist': the Soviet Union's *Pravda* and China's *Renmin Ribao* became as illegal as *The New York Times* or Japan's *Asahi Shimbun*. Only radios that could be set solely to state-prescribed channels were allowed.

So extreme was this isolation that Kim Il-sung's North Korea even refused to acknowledge that man had landed on the moon.[33] At the time this book was being written, the only people who had ever walked on the surface of Earth's satellite were US citizens, and for decades the DPRK did not acknowledge this symbolic victory of North Korea's greatest enemy. When Neil Armstrong made his iconic 'small step' in 1969, Pyongyang did not report on it; the moon landing was only mentioned for the first time in the *Grand Encyclopaedia of Korea* around a decade after Kim Il-sung's death.[34]

The state press was prohibited from publishing anything negative about life inside the country, including such trivialities as a minor official being rude to some random person or supplies for some small event not being delivered on time. State media were instructed to project an image of a flawless nation of perfect and happy people led by the great Kim Il-sung, the supreme incarnation of love and morality (which was also one of his many official monikers).

The new order meant banning foreign literature as well, including that from the communist countries. In the late 1960s, works of Marx, Engels, Lenin, Stalin and Mao were removed from libraries to restricted access rooms as part of a campaign called 'arrangement of books'. These books were inconvenient to the regime for many reasons, including Marxism's claim that history is driven by economic factors rather than great individuals, given that the DPRK asserts the opposite: great people, and especially Kim Il-sung, are those who ultimately change history.

Soviet and Chinese culture was considered suspicious and duly banned. The ban even extended to the small diaspora of foreign nationals living in the country. In 1972, when the son of a Soviet mother and a Korean father was caught reading Maxim Gorky by his teacher, the teacher hit the child with a book and told him that what the boy was doing was revisionist.[35] A Korean child would probably have received a much harsher punishment.

Eventually, the ban was partly reversed, but until the early 1970s, for example, no Soviet songs could be heard in North Korea.[36]

From the late 1960s to the late 1980s, North Korea almost completely stopped publishing any laws. Everything—including, for example, the Criminal Code of 1974—was classified. This meant that people without proper clearance did not even know what activities were prohibited. Even such an innocent object as a list of deputies to the SPA—the country's rubber-stamp parliament—went unpublished. North Korea duly held the elections, announced, as usual, that 100 per cent of the voters had participated and that 100 per cent of the voters had endorsed the only candidate, but the list of the elected deputies was never released.[37]

No economic statistics were published.[38] Fiction books published in the country were not supposed to mention the names of their Korean authors. And state institutions did not have plaques with their names on the front door, as strangers were not allowed to know what government buildings were being used for.

Stratifying citizens

The fourth pillar of the Kim Il-sung system is hierarchy. North Korea has perfected a system of social stratification. First created in the late 1950s, the system has been through several revisions. At some point in the 1970s, for example, all DPRK citizens were reportedly divided into one of twenty-three categories[39] and at another point into fifty-one.[40]

By the end of the Kim Il-sung era, the situation had become even more complex. According to secret regulations composed in 1993 that were subsequently leaked from the country,[41] each North Korean citizen had three statuses assigned at the age of seventeen. The first two were 'origins' and 'social status'. Social status is an individual's occupation and origins—the occupation of their closest relative, normally the father. The third one—'layer'—is calculated from an individual's origins and social status as well as other factors. There were dozens of categories in each of the three designations, and 'layers' were further divided into three groups: 'basic', 'complex' and 'hostile'. The names for the strata differed from time to time—'nucleus' was sometimes used instead of 'basic' and 'wavering' instead of 'complex'—but the general outline has remained the same.

'Demobilised soldiers' were explicitly assigned to the basic group,[42] 'religious people' to the complex[43] and 'businessmen' to the hostile group.[44] There were also more exotic categories: individuals who had been granted an audience with Kim Il-sung or Kim Jong-il, who had risen to the position of the second man in the country by the early 1990s, were upgraded to the basic strata, for example,[45] while both 'former inmates of concentration camps for political criminals' and 'heroes, who came to the North from the South' were assigned to the complex group, and 'wealthy farmers' and 'pro-American elements' to the hostile one.[46]

While the North Korean system somewhat resembles the Indian caste system, it should be noted that it is more flexible than in India and thus somewhat less unfair. The division was organised so that an individual could, in some cases, cleanse their original status—by becoming a worker or serving in the KPA, for example—or at least influence the status of their children. Thus, according to North Korean internal statistics obtained by South Korean intelligence, in 1971 the proportion of 'nucleus', 'wavering' and 'hostile' classes, as they were called at the time, was 27–22–51, while five years later, in 1976, this had changed to 25–35–40.[47] A majority were still assigned to the least-trusted strata, but this figure was rapidly shrinking, to the point that the secret regulations of 1993 noted that the hostile class had become very small.[48]

This was of course small consolation to those whose lives had already been ruined. Only individuals with a very high status could enter the elite. Those below a certain threshold could not attend university. As of the mid-1970s, an individual of a lower status was only permitted to do farm work. Next were those forced into hard labour, and, finally, those kept under guard solely for belonging to the lowest stratum.[49]

Inter-strata marriages were discouraged and could result in a 'nobler' spouse being downgraded or even expelled from the party.[50] A brave few still married people of different strata, proving that love can sometimes prevail against all odds.[51]

Another aspect of the hierarchy was the special status of the capital city and its residents. While the system of stratification in the capital was later perfected by Kim Jong-il, who ordered that Pyongyang dwellers be issued special IDs, Pyongyang residents were first given a special status under Kim Il-sung. People of tainted origins were evicted from the city as part of a campaign to make it 'the capital of the revolution'.[52] Although the inhabitants of other cities could also be relocated, such relocations were mostly done to ensure the regime's stability, such as preventing people in Wonsan from fleeing to South Korea.[53]

People with disabilities were also evicted from the capital. Under Kim Il-sung, people with disabilities were divided into two groups with very different rights. The first were 'honoured soldiers'—as the name suggests, the state actively sought to provide them with assistance. The second were what the regime calls 'invalids' (*pulguja*), who were treated as useless and thus evicted from the 'capital of the revolution'.[54] Kim Dok-hong, a former employee of the Party History Institute who fled from North Korea in 1997, remembered that a person with disabilities needed the Leader's personal authorisation to be admitted to a college. He could recall only one case where this permission was granted—to the son of one of Kim Il-sung's old comrades.[55]

Kim Il-sung personally commanded that the capital's provisioning be a priority, arguing that Pyongyang was the face of the country.[56] Only Pyongyang schoolchildren were granted free milk from the state,[57] and no other North Korean city has an underground transportation system, even though the Pyongyang metro system opened as long ago as 1973.

The DPRK has also perfected a system where party members have a privileged status. Party members were of course privileged under all communist regimes, but most countries still allowed for exceptions to exist. North Korea eliminated those exceptions. Rising above a certain level requires membership in the WPK.

One of the paradoxical consequences of this policy is that the party stopped being perceived as a political party in the conventional sense. In Hitler's Germany, Nazi Party membership was voluntary, and those who joined were later perceived as 'Nazis'—real believers in Hitlerism. In the USSR, joining the Communist Party could serve as a means of career advancement, but since it was not strictly mandatory, it was also perceived as a gesture of loyalty towards the state. In North Korea, membership of the party is seen as a way to gain extended rights and nothing else.[58]

But what about the other two parties? What became of the Democratic Party and the Young Friends of the Heavenly Way? Even before the Korean War, these two were completely stripped of any autonomy, and in the late 1950s their organisations below the central committees were dissolved. All that remained were central organisations, maintained solely for interaction with foreign leftists, and especially South Koreans. In 1981, the Democratic Party was renamed the Social Democratic Party at a ceremony featuring a huge portrait of Kim Il-sung.[59] All members of these small parties are also members of the WPK, and hence all members of the DPRK's elite must ultimately belong to the WPK.

This social hierarchy was somewhat paradoxical. Demotion to worker status was considered punishment, and those with tainted origins were forced to become manual workers. However, this clashed with the communist dogma about workers being the most progressive class: thus, the children of these workers were considered to have noble origins. This did at least allow for some social mobility within this otherwise rigid and inflexible system.

Exploiting the population

Another paradox was the fifth pillar of Kimilsungism: the DPRK's exploitation of working people and thus North Korea's treatment of welfare. Welfare was a major object of pride for post-Stalinist communist nations, and the DPRK's publications extolled the virtues of free medicine and education.

Yet in the 1970s the state also organised a propaganda campaign hailing extended workdays. 'Extended' is an understatement, as in the 1970s it was normal for a North Korean to work twelve to fourteen hours each day without weekend holidays.[60] This was actually presented as an achievement,[61] and the fact that some nations, like the Soviet Union, had a shorter workday and workers had the freedom to choose where they would work was seen as a sign of laziness and a factor in economic destabilisation.[62]

Far-left rhetoric was of course employed as well. For example, the regime distrusted the idea that people should be paid more if they worked harder, with the very concept itself sometimes being publicly rejected as bourgeois.[63] Naturally, this meant that people would be much less motivated; the state compensated for this lack of motivation with propaganda and punishment for those who did not work with sufficient enthusiasm.

This was not about being right or left: it was about forcing the masses to work as hard as possible for as little pay as possible.

Terrorising the people

The system's sixth and final pillar was terror. Little is known about the true extent of the state's repression under Kim Il-sung, as is often the case with especially repressive regimes: when the state is exceptionally good at subjugating society, little information leaks outside, as very few victims can escape. However, the available testimonies about life in the DPRK from the early 1970s unanimously depict a country in which terror ran amok.

There was no need for a judicial or even Security Committee decision for people to be punished. The secret police were authorised to execute people without trial for acts as trivial as accidentally spoiling Kim Il-sung's portrait or uttering a single statement that might be interpreted as a sign of disrespect towards the Great Leader. One of the first to reveal how someone could expect to be punished for damaging an image of Kim Il-sung was Kong Thak-ho, a captain of the DPRK secret police from the city of Kaesong who accidentally dropped ink on a portrait of Kim Il-sung during a lecture. Someone later reported this unforgivable crime, and being a member of the secret police, he knew the accusation would mean death. He only survived by sheer luck: his superiors did not arrest him on the spot, Kaesong was close to the South Korean border and he had a standing permit to visit the DMZ that enabled him to escape to the South.[64]

Another witness was Venezuelan poet Ali Lameda. A leftist sympathetic to North Korea, he went to Pyongyang in 1966. Unlike many of the DPRK's supporters, Lameda spoke Korean and used his language skills to assist Pyongyang in translating propaganda material. As such, he was in the DPRK when the Singular Thought System was first introduced. After cautiously voicing his disapproval of the new policy, he was arrested within a few days and spent seven years in prison camps before being

183

released due to the efforts of organisations such as Amnesty International and political leaders such as Romania's Nicolae Ceaușescu.[65]

Lameda was subjected to a show trial: 'The tribunal did not make any specific accusations—there were no formal charges— but the accused has to accuse himself before the tribunal. Thus, there was no necessity for the tribunal to produce any evidence. I had no right to defend myself, I could only admit guilt.'[66] Many others did not even get that luxury, as the state was condemning denizens to imprisonment and death with little concern over judicial protocol.

In 1974, the earlier-mentioned secret Criminal Code was promulgated, seemingly to place this terror campaign on a formal legal basis, as well as establishing at least some limitations. The code's purpose, outlined in Article 4, was to

> protect the President of the DPRK,[67] accomplish protection of the Republic government's line and policies, preserve the revolutionary accomplishment of the authority of workers and farmers, protect constitutional rights and life of the people and the property and to accomplish the great deed of establishing the revolutionary order in all spheres of life and making the entire society monochromatically coloured with Juche Thought.[68]

Composed of 215 articles, the code prescribed capital punishment with confiscation of an individual's entire estate for 'counterrevolutionary crimes'. Among other things, the latter included 'reactionary propaganda' and 'opposition to the socialist state and the revolutionary people'. The death penalty itself was described as 'the merciless iron hammer of the revolution which brings the ultimate stop to the dirty fate of class enemies, the legal means to preserve the ensured triumph of the class struggle in the most forceful way'.[69]

Much of what is known about North Korea's concentration camps comes from the testimonies of people like Kang Chol-hwan, who was sent to Yodok camp in 1977 when he was still a child.[70] An Myong-chol, a junior sergeant who served as a guard in several concentration camps between 1987 and 1994, also wrote a book about his experience after fleeing the country.[71] Conditions in the camps ranged from prison settlements where people were kept under constant guard to places where people toiled in mines like the slaves of ancient Rome—until they died. Hundreds of thousands of unfortunates went through these camps.

* * *

That was the system Kim Il-sung established. But it did have a weak point: he was mortal, and his death would run the risk of destabilising the machine the state had built around him. He was fully aware this flaw existed and did his best to preserve the system through a truly ingenious stratagem.

13

HEIR TO THE GENERAL SECRETARY

On 14 April 1969, just a day before Kim Il-sung's birthday, the CPC adopted a new constitution. While the constitution, as usual, extolled the virtues of Marxism–Leninism and Mao Zedong Thought, one paragraph was particularly significant: 'Comrade Lin Biao has consistently held high the great red flag of Mao Zedong Thought and most loyally and firmly defended and carried out the proletarian revolutionary line of Comrade Mao Zedong. Comrade Lin Biao is a close comrade and the successor of Comrade Mao Zedong.'[1]

This was a major innovation: no communist nation had ever appointed a successor to a living leader. Officially, they still pretended to be democracies, and the leader was to be elected at a plenum or a congress, not appointed beforehand. This was a major change to the unwritten rules. Vice-Chairman of the Central Committee of the CPC Lin Biao was now the designated successor to Mao while the Great Helmsman was still alive.

This seems to have given Kim Il-sung an idea of how he and his regime could avoid the fate that Stalinism suffered after Stalin's death in 1953. Kim saw how, just a month after Stalin's death, the Soviet press had stopped hailing the Father of the Nations and how Stalin had been openly denounced in 1956, and then again in 1961 at the Twenty-Second Congress of the CPSU. If a successor could be handpicked, Kim could choose someone who would not betray his memory.

A reactionary system

The normalisation of Sino-North Korean relations meant the Chinese example was now acceptable. In April 1970, when Premier Zhou Enlai, China's third in line after Mao and Lin, visited North Korea, the two sides agreed to end the Sino-North Korean split.[2] Befriending China was a necessity, since the North Korean economy was in a very sorry state. The seven-year plan, adopted in 1961, had not been fulfilled, and the North needed more economic aid. The regime tried to obtain loans from socialist countries; however, the 'brotherly nations' soon tired of subsidising the DPRK's economy and did not fulfil North Korea's requests in their entirety. Pyongyang then approached capitalist nations—Japan, West Germany and France, among others—and borrowed extensively from them. The DPRK ultimately defaulted on the loans, though the regime never planned to repay them in any case.[3]

The alternative to closer relations with China would have been to befriend the Soviet Union, and Kim did in fact meet Brezhnev in 1966.[4] However, since the meeting and subsequent diplomacy with Moscow had not yielded the expected results, Pyongyang sought to mend Sino-DPRK relations, and Beijing reciprocated. 'Dogmatist Mao' and 'revisionist Kim' were no more: both Mao and Kim started to call each other 'Great Leader' of the Chinese and Korean people respectively. An important sign of the new era was the publication of an article, 'Let Us Adhere to Proletarian Dictatorship and Proletarian Democracy',[5] in the

North Korean press. Appearing on 4 February 1971, the article mirrored the piece that had been published in 1963, 'Let Us Defend the Socialist Camp' (see Chapter 10), including in the way it suddenly quoted Lenin, whose works North Koreans were banned from reading. The article was a message to China: the DPRK is again at your side; the past has been forgotten.

There was one social group in North Korea that immediately benefitted from the warming of relations between Beijing and Pyongyang. Former North Korean Chinese were allowed to restore their citizenship. Regaining their citizenship involved a monumental amount of bureaucracy, but those willing to complete the process (the vast majority) ultimately succeeded.[6]

In 1970, a major party event took place: the WPK's Fifth Congress.[7] The congress was supposed to be dedicated largely to economic affairs.[8] However, Kim Il-sung's son, Kim Jong-il, used the event as an opportunity to strengthen his position by pandering to his father's ego. By that time a high-ranking party official, he reportedly suggested that everyone in the DPRK be mandated to wear badges with Kim Il-sung's portrait.[9] This suggestion was put in motion, with a multitude of badges subsequently being produced. Reportedly, at one point, different versions even reflected the social status of the wearer.[10]

In 1971, however, the possibility of emulating China and appointing a successor was complicated by Lin Biao's fall from grace. Just a year after anointing Lin his heir, Mao started to undermine his position, and in September 1971 the 'close comrade and the successor of Comrade Mao Zedong' died in a plane crash in Mongolia.[11] Posthumously, Lin Biao was accused of plotting a coup against Chairman Mao, and it is likely these accusations were correct. Kim Il-sung therefore concluded that it was vital to exercise great care when designating a successor. The designated successor could not just be some high-level party cadre: even those most loyal to Kim could follow Lin's example and stab the Leader in the back. It would have to be someone whose very legitimacy was bound to him, someone who would have a vested interest in being loyal to Kim Il-sung even after he died, someone who would be in danger of being overthrown should he choose to oppose Kim Il-sung's legacy. Someone like his son, Kim Jong-il.

A son as the successor to the supreme leader—for a communist country, this was an extremely counterintuitive idea. It can partly be explained by North Korean nepotism: by the late 1960s, quite a few of Kim Il-sung's relatives occupied important positions in the country. According to a Soviet intelligence report from 1969, Kim Yong-ju—Kim Il-sung's brother—was at that time the head of the Organisation and Guidance Department of the Central Committee.[12] Kim Il-sung's wife Kim Song-ae was first deputy chairwoman of the Union of Democratic Women of Korea[13] and was soon to rise to the position of chairwoman.[14] The chairwoman she replaced was Kim Ok-sun, another relative of Kim Il-sung, and Kim Ok-sun's husband Choe Gwang was a general in the KPA.[15]

Both Kim Song-ae's brothers—Song-yun and Song-gap— were also not forgotten. Kim Song-yun occupied a position in the Cabinet of Ministers and was responsible for delivering 'Kim Il-sung's gifts'[16] to the masses; Kim Song-gap was employed in the Ministry of Social Security, under the command of Minister Kim Byong-ha, the husband of yet another relative of Kim Il-sung.[17]

Kim Il-sung's cousin, Kim Jong-suk,[18] was deputy chair of the Youth League, and her husband, Ho Dam, became the first deputy foreign minister. Another cousin of the Great Leader, Kim Shin-suk, headed Kim Il-sung University's history department. Her husband Yang Hyong-sop was the minister of higher education.[19]

Thus Kim Jong-il's career was not exactly unusual. A graduate of Kim Il-sung University,[20] he started in the Central Committee

Department for Agitation and Propaganda and the Department of Organisation and Guidance.[21] By 1969, he had been appointed head of Kim Il-sung's personal guard, showing himself to be a loyal son above all else and giving him additional access to his father.[22]

But the very notion of hereditary succession was contradictory to communist ideology. The 1970 edition of North Korea's *Dictionary of Political Terms* defines a 'system of hereditary succession' as a 'reactionary system set in law in exploitative societies in which the class that has a status granting special privileges passes down its position or property to the next generation'.[23] Yet this 'reactionary system' was about to be implemented in communist North Korea.

The Adored Leader versus the Respected Chairwoman

The earliest available document lauding Kim Jong-il is a vow to be loyal to him, signed by members of one of the country's musical ensembles on 2 November 1971, exactly one year after the Fifth Congress.[24] The date was likely intentional: North Korea treats the anniversaries of all ideological events as a very big deal. The document states: 'In front of the party we, the Great Leader's personal guard, a suicide unit, all as one, upholding his noble will, being the followers of the eternally living and never dying Kimilsungism, solemnly pledge to become the loyal stormtrooper unit to the Adored Leader.'

This was the rhetoric of the 1970s. Everyone was supposed to be a loyal stormtrooper, a member of a personal guard and of a suicide squad. The state called for the highest degree of mobilisation and readiness at any second, despite the reduction in inter-Korean tensions during this period; indeed, in July 1972 both Koreas signed a de facto non-aggression pact.[25] Reflecting the improved relationship, in December 1972 North Korea adopted a new constitution that finally recognised that the capital of the DPRK is Pyongyang, not Seoul, in contrast to what had been claimed since 1948.[26]

The unusual part of the document, however, was the mention of the Adored Leader. Much later, after both Kim Il-sung and Kim Jong-il died, North Korean publications revealed that this had been one of the earliest monikers for Kim Jong-il.[27] The Adored Leader was not described as the successor, at least not yet. More importantly, he also had a competitor, the Respected Chairwoman, the title given to Kim Il-sung's wife, Kim Song-ae, who had become chairwoman of the Union of Democratic Women of Korea in 1971. Importantly, while the title Adored Leader was only used in a document relating to a small session of art workers, the title Respected Chairwoman was used in a wide range of publications.[28] It goes without saying that all this was authorised by Kim Il-sung, who wanted to promote his family members to special positions. However, Kim Jong-il had every reason to be worried. His mother, Kim Jong-suk, had died in 1949, and Kim Song-ae had two sons of her own—Kim Phyong-il and Kim Yong-il—both of whom were also potential successors.

One of the first signs that Kim Il-sung favoured Kim Jong-il came in 1972. In that year, another 'election' to the SPA took place. The newspapers reported that 'Respected and Beloved Leader Comrade Kim Il-sung' had run from district 216.[29] Though seemingly of little significance, the true meaning of the choice of district number later became clear: the number 216 symbolised the sixteenth day of the second month of the year, February, when Kim Jong-il was born; in the years to come, number 216 became his semi-official symbol.[30]

Kim Song-ae resisted and continued to promote herself as Kim Il-sung's successor. In 1973, for example, the army launched a campaign calling on soldiers to venerate the Respected Chairwoman as their 'representative'.[31]

Kim Jong-il appears to have retaliated by using his position as de facto head of North Korea's film industry. In 1973, a film named *Our Family's Problem* was shown in North Korean cinemas. Uncharacteristically for the DPRK, the movie presented a negative North Korean character: the evil wife of a good official who was the chief of a post office. The film shows the woman manipulating the man, ruining his life. Even more uncharacteristically, the film has an unhappy ending: it concludes with the chief, his career completely ruined by the malevolent woman, simply walking near a river bank. Han Gil-myong, the actress who played the villainess, bore a striking resemblance to Kim Song-ae.

The most important person in the film's target audience appears to have been Kim Il-sung, with the film acting as a warning from Kim Jong-il. The son slowly began to usurp the stepmother, as the 1973 edition of the *Political Dictionary*, in a telling move, dropped negative references to 'hereditary succession'.[32] At the same time, Kim Jong-il was appointed a secretary of the Central Committee and put in charge of the Propaganda and Agitation Department.[33] The process of appointing the successor was progressing.

The Dear Leader

In February 1974, the struggle ended in victory for Kim Jong-il. He was turning thirty-three, which may have been one of the reasons his father decided to proceed with the final promotion: Kim Il-sung himself was exactly thirty-three when he was chosen to lead North Korea in 1945. The eighth plenum of the Fifth Central Committee formally proclaimed Kim Jong-il successor and bestowed upon him membership of the Political Council—second only to the position of the general secretary himself.

In private, Kim Song-ae still tried to present herself as a superior figure, stressing that Kim Jong-il was her son as well as Il-sung's,[34] but it was too late. After the February plenum, Kim Song-ae appeared less frequently in North Korean media, and all references to her were eventually removed from North Korea's history books. The last time she was mentioned by name in the state media was on a published list of members of Marshal O Jin-u's funeral committee. In the long list of officials, she was number 101.[35]

Another potential successor was Kim Jong-il's uncle, Kim Yong-ju. By the early 1970s, he had risen to the helm of the prestigious Organisation and Guidance Department of the Central Committee. It was he who signed the Joint Declaration with the South during the brief inter-Korean détente. With Kim Jong-il's ascension, he was demoted to the role of deputy chairman of the Administrative Council and eventually vanished from public view.[36]

Informally designating Kim Jong-il as the successor created certain difficulties for North Korea's propaganda department. Kim Il-sung did not want Kim Jong-il's promotion to become known outside the country. The most likely reason for this is that he still did not want to finalise a decision that would be costly to reverse. Inside the country, he could have made Kim Jong-il disappear from the state narrative as easily as Kim Song-ae. However, appointing and then dismissing a successor would make him look weak to the outside world. Thus, it was safer to avoid releasing any information about the arrangement until Kim Il-sung was sure he had made the right decision.

Hence the 'outer-track'[37] press—the one that was sent abroad as well as being read by ordinary North Koreans—was forbidden from mentioning Kim Jong-il by name. Instead, they had to use a strange moniker: the 'Party Central'.[38] An outsider would have assumed they were talking about the Party Central Committee, the name of which was often shortened to 'Party Central'. Reportedly, Kim Jong-il himself told his subordinates to address him in writing as 'Party Central Committee, Kim Jong-il' instead of, say, 'Adored Leader'.[39] The 'Party Central' may have originated as a shorter form of this.[40]

There were no such restrictions for 'inner-track' publications intended solely for a domestic audience, which frequently emphasised that the people deeply venerated Kim Jong-il, or the Dear Leader as he started to be called.[41] Much later, North Korea claimed that the 'Dear Leader' moniker had been formally prescribed by the Central Committee.[42]

Initially, the cult of personality around Kim Jong-il was more intense in organisations responsible for the arts, which was Kim Jong-il's personal domain. For example, in September 1974, a Soviet diplomat noticed Kim Jong-il's portrait hanging in Pyongyang cinema studio '8 February'.[43] Later, the cult of personality was disseminated to every corner of North Korean society.

The Dear Leader needed a fitting biography, and Pyongyang started to write one. As always, historical facts were sacrificed to political necessity. According to the official version, taught at least from 1976, Kim Jong-il was not born in the Soviet Union but in a 'secret camp' on Mount Paektu.[44] The question of why Kim Il-sung made his wife climb hundreds of yards up a mountain to give birth to a child behind enemy lines was naturally omitted.

Kim Il-sung himself instructed his subordinates to 'find' this camp, and they did.[45] Unsurprisingly, the camp was located on the Korean side of the mountain, not the one that was part of China. Moreover, it was located exactly 216 metres from the mountain's Commander Peak.[46] In August 1988, Kim Il-sung ordered that Commander Peak be renamed 'Jong-il Peak'.[47]

Détente and diplomacy

The period 1973–4 seemed like a suitable point to start promoting a successor, as the North Korean economy was growing,[48] likely because the inter-Korean détente of 1972 had pushed the DPRK into spending less on the military. Built with China's assistance,[49] the Pyongyang metro opened in 1973.[50] In 1974, North Korea abolished the formal taxation of private individuals,[51] albeit without acknowledging that such taxation had contributed only a small amount to the state budget.[52] Nevertheless, many North Koreans interpreted this as a positive sign.

However, on 18 August 1976, the DPRK faced an unexpected crisis at the inter-Korean border in Panmunjom. Known under the clumsily translated name of 'axe murder incident', the crisis began when a team of American and South Korean military personnel started cutting down a poplar tree in Panmunjom that was blocking their view from the South. The North Koreans suddenly intervened, with a KPA lieutenant demanding that the Southerners stand down—he claimed the tree had been planted by Kim Il-sung and was not to be touched. When they were ignored, they attacked the US–South Korean team, leaving two US military officers dead and many wounded. UN troops, still stationed in the country after the end of the Korean War, responded with a show of force, sending a detachment of soldiers to cut the tree down, while aircraft patrolled the sky near Panmunjom. Interestingly, one of the soldiers serving in Panmunjom was Moon Jae-in, president of South Korea in 2017–22.[53] The crisis resulted in North Korea being put on high alert[54] while US and South Korean military personnel cut the tree down in Operation Paul Bunyan. Fortunately, the crisis was defused, with Kim Il-sung sending a letter of regret to the UN side.[55]

During this period, one of the aims of North Korean diplomacy was to gain admission to the United Nations, a goal shared by Seoul. This resulted in both Koreas having their own version of the scramble for Africa, with Seoul and Pyongyang courting various African leaders and dictators to garner support for their admission to the UN among members of the General Assembly. Seoul, for example, managed to sway Gabon,[56] while Pyongyang established very close relations with Zimbabwe, even training soldiers for the country's dictator Robert Mugabe.[57]

This diplomatic offensive was accompanied by an ideological one: the DPRK launched a campaign to promote 'Juche Thought' in the Third World.[58] However, this campaign proved an utter failure—an ideology without content simply does not sell.

Around 1977, Pyongyang seemingly commanded the ANKCJ to start cautiously mentioning Kim Jong-il, as his photos and brief mentions of his name began appearing in their publications about Kim Il-sung's greatness, albeit without any explanation of who this young man was.[59] Here is a typical quote, coming from 'Merciful Sun', an official biography of Kim Il-sung: 'After receiving this request, Dear Comrade Kim Jong-il wrote to the construction workers: "Do it the way the Leader ratified it."'[60] Kim Jong-il was yet to become an independent actor in his own right, but his special status within the system was becoming increasingly clear.

The regime seemed to be coming close to officially revealing Kim Jong-il to the outside world, but in 1978 Kim Il-sung appears to have had doubts about his decision. An Chan-il, a former North Korean non-commissioned officer who had served in the DMZ before fleeing to South Korea, told this author that around 1978 all portraits of the Dear Leader were removed from his unit's barracks and that his unit was no longer obliged to praise Kim Jong-il. The directive from the Central Committee commanding these changes explained that Kim Jong-il had ordered them himself, since he was a very modest man.[61] Adrian Buzo, an Australian diplomat who served in Pyongyang at the time, also noticed that references to the 'Party Central' had suddenly stopped.[62] That this was linked to Kim Jong-il falling out of favour seems to be confirmed by a report from the Hungarian embassy to Budapest, which claimed that Kim Jong-il was no longer being promoted as the heir apparent.[63] However, sometime in late July 1979, Kim Il-sung appears to have changed his mind once again.[64] On 29 July, Kim Jong-il was again lauded by the military newspaper *Choson Inmingun*;[65] the campaign was back on track.[66]

At the same time, momentous events were unfurling in South Korea. It had been seven years since 1972, when President Park Chung-hee transformed the country from a semi-democracy to a dictatorship by forcing upon it a new, highly authoritarian constitution. He was no longer elected directly; instead, every seven years the country voted for candidates to an electoral college, the name of which literally translated as 'Citizens' Congress for Unification and Juche'.

The North Korean connotations were remarkably appropriate, given that only loyalists were allowed to take part in the elections. Following the elections, the Citizens' Congress for Unification and Juche overwhelmingly re-elected the president, adhering to article 39 of the newly adopted constitution, which mandated this process to be conducted 'without any discussions'. There was no sign suggesting that this established order would falter, until a fateful event on 26 October 1979, when President Park was assassinated by the chief of South Korean civil intelligence.[67]

This abrupt end to the eighteen years of the Park era ushered in a new age of instability. His successor, Choi Kyu-ha, was a weak leader, and in a few months, a new coup took place. Major-General Chun Doo-hwan seized power, formally deposed Choi and made himself president. This happened a few months before Kim Jong-il finally appeared in public as Kim Il-sung's successor.

Terror and transparency

Kim Jong-il's final ascension was to be completed at a party congress, and, on 13 December 1979, the decision to convene the congress appeared in open publications.[68] However, though Kim Jong-il's birthday in February 1980 was celebrated with exceptional vigour, there was still no mention of him in the outer-track press—this only happened after the congress.

This grand party meeting took place in October 1980. Exactly one day before it began, Shin Hyong-nim, the DPRK's ambassador to Switzerland, publicly announced *urbi et orbi* that the rumours were true: Kim Jong-il was indeed the anointed successor to Kim Il-sung.[69]

At the congress, Kim Jong-il was duly elected to all senior positions in the party leadership—secretary, member of the Central Military Commission and of the Politburo Standing Committee[70]—and his name finally appeared in the outer-track press.[71] In the following year, the Dear Leader was hailed in outer-track publications with the same vigour as had previously been the case in the inner-track ones. And a further twist was added to his official biography—from 1982, North Korea started to claim he had been born in 1942, not 1941.[72] There was no particular need for this, apart from creating an aesthetically pleasing thirty-year gap with Kim Il-sung.

The appointment of a successor meant that Kim Il-sung no longer held an absolute monopoly on power. However, the final ascension of Kim Jong-il did not immediately have a major effect on North Korea's policy towards South Korea. For Kim Il-sung, the situation in the South looked much like the situation in the early 1960s, and the North's policy towards the South was for him to administer and guide.

Once again, the Great Leader returned to his cherished dream: that perhaps by some miracle he would be able to destabilise the South and unify the peninsula. There are records of him fantasising about the rival government collapsing after taking too many loans or about Pyongyang implementing the Hong Kong-style 'one country, two systems' in South Korea.[73] Ultimately, Kim Il-sung used a new method to weaken the South, a method that was becoming increasingly prevalent across the world: terrorism.

In the 1980s, the DPRK conducted at least three terrorist attacks on South Korea. The first was aimed at Chun Doo-hwan. During a trip to Burma in October 1983, Chun was scheduled to pay a visit to the mausoleum of the country's founder Aung San. North Korea dispatched explosives to the DPRK's embassy in Burma, which North Korean agents planted in the mausoleum roof. The explosion killed twelve high-ranking and four lesser members of the South Korean government as well as a journalist, but President Chun was not present at the time and survived. The Burmese government was furious: not only did it sever diplomatic relations with Pyongyang; it even stopped recognising the DPRK as a state.[74]

Next was a terrorist attack on Seoul's Kimpo Airport. As Japanese researcher Murata Nobuhiko later discovered from East German documents, North Korea had contracted a Palestinian terrorist leader named Abu Nidal to do their work. His agents planted a bomb there, killing five people and wounding thirty-eight.[75]

Finally, on 29 November 1987, North Korea engaged in another terrorist attack when two North Korean agents planted a bomb on a Korean Air flight from Baghdad to Seoul, killing 115 people. The perpetrators tried to escape, but upon being detained in Bahrain on their way back to North Korea, they tried to commit suicide. One succeeded, but another, Kim Hyon-hui, was brought to trial in South Korea and sentenced to death—she was ultimately saved by a presidential pardon. Eventually renouncing Kim Il-sung and the North Korean regime, Kim Hyon-hui wrote two memoirs recalling her painful past.[76]

Even if Kim Jong-il had disagreed with the attacks, he could not openly object at the time. Inside the country, however, the atmosphere was beginning to feel different as the influence of the somewhat more moderate Kim Jong-il started to be felt. The first signs of a slight liberalisation started to appear in the 1980s, corresponding to the rise of Kim Jong-il.

One of the first signs of change was that in 1982 North Korea decided to publish the list of deputies elected to the SPA. This was, of course, a purely symbolic gesture given that the SPA held no real power, but it was the first time such a list had been made public since 1977. This suggested the country was now beginning to relax its control over information, even if only slightly. The difference may have been tiny, but for the first time in decades, it was a move in the direction of more transparency, not less. Ideological campaigns in the country also started to be conducted with slightly less vigour. People were no longer physically beaten during the mandatory criticism and self-criticism sessions, and the sessions themselves became less intense and less frequent.

Even state propaganda began to cautiously suggest that times were changing. The 1986 film *The Problems of Our Family Began Again*, for example, which was released while Kim Jong-il was still in charge of North Korea's film industry, suggested that the main character was wrong for criticising people over minor transgressions.

Kim Jong-il did his best to improve North Korea's film industry. The man Kim Jong-il tasked with making high-quality films was Shin Sang-ok, a South Korean director abducted from British Hong Kong by North Korean agents in January 1978. His studio started to produce films that were ideologically correct but where characters could talk about their daily lives, hopes and dreams rather than robotically venerating Kim Il-sung, the

Eternal Sun of the Nation.[77] The change was more than welcome, and Shin Sang-ok's films were enormously popular among North Koreans.[78]

Another sign of this quasi-thaw was that North Korean legislation began to be published again in the DPRK. Since the mid-1980s, more and more laws have been published, including the Criminal Code of 1987, which replaced the more repressive and classified Criminal Code of 1974.[79]

North Korean authors, too, were allowed to put their names on the books they wrote rather than having to publish them anonymously, as had usually been the case previously. It seemed that cracks were starting to appear in the Singular Thought System and that the madness of the 1970s was easing. However, there were still obvious limits to the extent of Kim Jong-il's reformism.

Token reforms

By the early 1980s, North Korea was still leaning towards China in the wake of Zhou Enlai's visit of 1970. After Mao died in 1976, Chinese reformists, led by Deng Xiaoping and supported by the military, seized control of the party from conservatives and radical Maoists. Greenlighted by the Central Committee in December 1977, Deng launched a policy of reforms and openness from 1978, resulting in dramatic liberalisation and economic growth in the world's most populous nation.[80] For North Korea, this proved to be a challenge. Some officials saw the benefits of the new policy and started cautiously lobbying the North Korean leadership to adopt the Chinese approach, as the country desperately needed reforms.[81]

One of the main areas in which reforms were badly needed was the North Korean agricultural sector, which was woefully inefficient due to the farming methods used in the country. As well as the inefficiency of collective farms, North Korea's food security was threatened by a lack of mechanisation and the underdevelopment of infrastructure, in addition to Pyongyang's failed experiments with terrace farming, which had denuded the hillsides.[82]

However, even though Kim Il-sung privately admitted to Deng Xiaoping that the South Korean economy was superior to that of the North,[83] he felt that Chinese-style reforms could potentially undermine his system. Ultimately, the changes in North Korean economic policy in the 1980s amounted to a tiny package of minor reforms that paled in comparison to anything done by the great Chinese reformer.

The first economic reform implemented in the North was the 3rd of August movement, named after a speech by Kim Jong-il on 3 August 1984, 'On Some Issues of Improving the Supply of Goods to the People', which was a campaign to recycle waste materials.[84] Following the adoption of subsequent measures officially called '3rd of August Movement to Create Consumer Goods for the People', the movement eventually expanded to the hand-manufacturing of essential goods that were in short supply. Importantly, the movement gave people the opportunity to work outside the state sector: after registering as a participant, she or, less often, he, no longer had to work at a factory or another state enterprise. These handmade goods were substandard to the degree that '3rd of August' generally became a euphemism for low quality in general. For example, '3rd of August couple' in the North meant a couple that cohabitated but were not married.[85]

On 8 September 1984, around a month after the beginning of the 3rd of August movement, the DPRK passed a Joint Enterprise Law.[86] The law was likely adopted partly due to the failure of the DPRK's second seven-year plan (1978–84), as the regime began to consider alternative sources of income. It allowed for the creation of joint DPRK–foreign enterprises, with both foreign companies and individuals being able to participate.

This was the first in a long list of unsuccessful attempts by Pyongyang to attract foreign investment. Ultimately, only fifty-three joint enterprises were created, twenty-seven of which—more than a half—were established by members of the ANKCJ.[87] Thus, while attracting much attention from foreign observers, the law had very little effect on the North Korean economy.

Rejection of Chinese reformism meant that the DPRK had to start courting Moscow, and around 1982, for the first time in two decades, relations between the two nations started to improve. At the time, the USSR was still ruled by Brezhnev, and this aging, narcissistic man appeared much less threatening than the energetic and Machiavellian Deng. This warming in Soviet–DPRK relations continued under Brezhnev's two successors: Yuri Andropov and Konstantin Chernenko, with Kim Il-sung even travelling to Moscow to meet with Chernenko in 1984. While meeting Chernenko, Kim received gifts from the Soviet leader[88] and said he would like both countries to produce a film about the past, specifically about the attempted assassination of Kim Il-sung in 1946, from which Kim was saved by a Soviet officer, Yakov Novichenko (see Chapter 5). The USSR greenlighted the project and negotiations began. However, the problem was that by that time the two countries had very different understandings of what had happened in Korea in the 1940s, and a compromise was not easy to broker. In a telling example, the film referenced the Soviets fighting side by side with the 'KPA' instead of the mythical 'KPRA'. Naturally, the KPA did not even exist in 1945, but at least it was a real organisation. The Korean dub, however, duly replaced the KPA with the KPRA. Titled *One Second for a Feat* in Russian and *Comrades-in-Arms Forever* in Korean, the film ultimately ended up being something of a compromise between Soviet and North Korean filmmakers. No wonder that it was popular in North Korea and a complete flop in the Soviet Union.[89]

While the Brezhnev era has deservedly been nicknamed the 'age of stagnation', the USSR at the time was quite popular in North Korea. While visiting the West was out of the question even for most of the country's elite, the Soviet Union became sort of a substitute West for North Korea: a land of (relative) prosperity and freedom. Kim Il-sung's daughter, Kim Kyong-hui, went to study at Moscow State University,[90] and other members of the 'royal' family—especially women—often visited the Soviet capital city.[91]

Securing the dynasty

By this time, the Kim family had become a unique legal entity that was no longer subject to the country's normal legal system. From what is now known, its members are excluded from all official state records and are not subject to the system used to categorise ordinary North Koreans, so when Kim Jong-il married someone, this was de jure a different act from a marriage among those outside the Kim dynasty.

The heir to the throne had many wives. The first was reportedly Hong Il-chon. They married in 1966 and divorced in 1969. She gave birth to Kim Jong-il's first child: Kim Hye-gyong. The divorce appears to have been amicable—the Dear Leader later had his ex-wife employed as the president of Kim Hyong-jik University.

Kim Jong-il's second wife was Song Hye-rim, the mother of his eldest son, Kim Jong-nam. Kim Il-sung did not approve of the marriage, and thus Kim Jong-nam was raised in isolation from both the common people and the elite.[92]

Kim Jong-il was not Song Hye-rim's first husband. She had previously been married to Lee Phyong, son of Lee Gi-yong, arguably the most prominent writer in the DPRK. Song Hye-rim died in Moscow in 2002, and Kim Jong-nam attended to her grave until his assassination in Kuala Lumpur in 2017, most likely on the orders of his half-brother Kim Jong-un.[93]

Kim Jong-il's third wife was Kim Yong-suk. Unlike Song Hye-rim, this marriage was approved by Kim Il-sung. They had two daughters with Jong-il: Kim Sol-song and Kim Chun-song; it is said that Kim Il-sung personally chose the name for Sol-song.[94]

The fourth wife of Kim Jong-il was Ko Yong-hui: on 8 January 1984, she gave birth to Kim Jong-un, the sixth of Jong-il's seven known children, who succeeded his father, against all expectations, in 2011.[95] There were two other children from this marriage: son Kim Jong-chol and daughter Kim Yo-jong.

Ko Yong-hui was born in Osaka in 1952, and her family moved to the North when she was ten. She became a dancer in the most prestigious North Korean music band, Mansudae, and it was through her performances with the band that she first came to Kim Jong-il's attention. On the last day of 1972, *Rodong Shinmun* published one of Kim Il-sung's first orders as president of the DPRK in which he gave twenty-year-old Yong-hui the title of Merited Actress.[96]

After his father's death, Kim Jong-il married for the fifth and final time, to Kim Ok. Much younger than Kim Jong-il, Kim Ok was a very ambitious woman: after Kim Jong-un came to power, he reportedly dispatched his stepmother to a concentration camp.[97]

Things start to change

To contemporary observers, it looked as if North Korea could continue in its current state almost indefinitely, but this was to change when momentous events started to unfurl in the Soviet Union. In March 1985, General Secretary Chernenko died after just thirteen months in office. The Politburo convened to elect his successor, and Foreign Minister Andrei Gromyko suggested the Politburo's youngest member—Mikhail Gorbachev. Gorbachev launched a policy of radical reforms that ultimately brought an end to the Warsaw Pact, the CPSU and ultimately the Soviet Union itself.

Not long before Gorbachev was elected general secretary, South Korea's capital region was struck by a flood after the heaviest recorded rainfall in South Korean history. Pyongyang responded to the flood by offering its assistance. It is possible that North Korea expected the South to reject North Korean aid, thus making it appear as though the South was callously refusing Pyongyang's help for ideological reasons. Unexpectedly, however, and after considerable deliberation, Seoul chose to accept the proffered aid.[98]

This new and somewhat odd atmosphere of cooperation paved the way for an agreement that led to what is perhaps the most touching event to have happened on the peninsula during the Cold War: the first meeting of divided Korean families. Hundreds of thousands of people had relatives on the other side of the DMZ, which was far less permeable than the Iron Curtain had ever been in Europe.

Due to the efforts of diplomats on both sides, two reunions took place in September 1985. Northerners met in Seoul and Southerners in Pyongyang. Cultural performances also took place in both capitals.

The South Korean press reported how, for the first time in decades, South Koreans had been able to cross the military demarcation line to their homeland. They were taken to Pyongyang, where, on the second floor of the Koryo Hotel, they finally saw their loved ones after decades of separation. For three days, people were able to talk to their relatives until they had to return home, likely never to see them again.[99]

Let's play 'Sudden Death'

The following summer, in 1986, Kim Il-sung suffered a heart attack and went into a coma, which came close to bringing his rule to an abrupt end. Kim Jong-il did his utmost to keep his father alive. He approached the Soviet ambassador and pleaded with him to immediately call the Kremlin and ask for Soviet doctors to be dispatched to Kim Il-sung's villa in the Myohyang Mountains. The request was approved, and Kim Il-sung was saved.[100] This event reminded Kim Il-sung of his own mortality. A few months later, in November 1986, the world witnessed one of the most bizarre, if largely forgotten, events in all of North Korea's history.

Kim Il-sung seemingly wanted to test the world's reaction to his future death. For almost three days, 16–18 November, North Korean loudspeakers across the entire DMZ broadcast the shocking message that Kim Il-sung had died. The messages sparked a great deal of confusion in the South, but Seoul ultimately decided to wait for official confirmation from Pyongyang, which, naturally, never came.[101] The very fact that such an unprecedented operation took place—and no leaks of it have appeared since—shows how tightly the country was controlled at the time.

In 1987, nearly fifteen years of military dictatorship effectively came to an end in South Korea. General Chun Doo-hwan, who had seized power in 1979–80, refused to change the constitution to allow for direct presidential elections. This decision sparked massive demonstrations in Seoul and other cities, leading the government to consider using the army to supress the protestors. Eventually, prudence prevailed. On 29 June, General Chun's second-in-command—acting chairman of the ruling Democratic Justice Party Roh Tae-woo—appeared in front of the cameras and announced that the government would yield. The demonstrators' demands would be met in full. Political prisoners would be released, and there would be direct, free and fair elections for the presidency.[102]

A new constitution was adopted, and its system of political checks and balances—including a one-term limit for the presidency—has allowed South Korean democracy to flourish ever since. This also meant that the upcoming 1988 Summer Olympic Games in Seoul would become a celebration of the new age of democracy and openness. Previous games in Moscow and Los Angeles were boycotted by most of the capitalist and communist world respectively. This time, after debates in the Politburo, Moscow decided to participate. Deng's China also took part in the Games.

Pyongyang was furious. The DPRK's press issued a barrage of editorials demanding that it be allowed to co-host the Games and condemning the South Korean government as traitors.[103] No one paid any attention. South Korea answered to these hateful headlines with a message of peace: the official song of the 1988 Olympics was 'Hand in Hand', which is still quite popular in the South. The DPRK attempted to counteract the Olympics by hosting the Thirteenth World Festival of Youth and Students, an international leftist sporting event.

The Thirteenth Festival of 1989 was mostly notable for the sudden visit of a South Korean student, Lim Su-kyung. The twenty-year-old received assistance to go to the North through Tokyo and East Berlin, and her appearance caused a sensation in the North. Lim was met by Kim Il-sung in person, and she called the Great Leader 'father'. However, the biggest surprise for North Koreans came when they later learned that her family was neither killed nor imprisoned after she returned to the South.[104]

Preparing for the festival, North Korea started the construction of the grandest hotel in the country. Called Ryugyong after the old name of Pyongyang, this pyramid-style building was intended to tower over the capital, with its majestic design being the manifestation of the multitudinous successes of socialist Korea. Instead, it turned out to be an utter and highly visible failure. The North Korean economy's continuous decline ensured that the project would be aborted mid-way. The grey pyramid with empty windows, crowned by a towering crane, was left standing in the centre of the capital as an iconic symbol of Kim Il-sung's unfulfilled ambitions.

The festival was the last major international event to be held in North Korea under Kim Il-sung. Gorbachev's reforms led to a tectonic shift in geopolitics. One by one, communist regimes in Eastern Europe started to implode. In the USSR itself, the CPSU yielded its monopoly on power in March 1990. All of which inevitably meant that North Korea could no longer maintain good relations with Moscow. North Korea recalled its students first from Eastern Europe and then from the Soviet Union in 1989–90, and once again retreated into isolation.

The march of history seemed unstoppable. The rapid democratisation of Eastern Europe meant these countries no longer had restrictions on establishing relations with Seoul. On 30 September 1990, South Korea established formal diplomatic relations with the Soviet Union as well. On 17 September 1991, both Koreas entered the United Nations. China opened an embassy in Seoul in 1992. South Korea's isolation from the moribund Eastern bloc was over, and the DPRK's decades-long diplomatic efforts to sequester the South had proved to be utterly and permanently in vain. Even more importantly, the Soviet Union informed North Korea that the generous economic assistance it had provided would now be severely curtailed.[105] Worse, China would not fill the unfathomable void, given that their relationship with the North greatly suffered when Beijing decided to open an embassy in Seoul. These changes were bound to create an economic catastrophe, but it seems that Kim Il-sung was neither aware of this nor even particularly concerned.

Looking backwards

As the Great Leader aged, he played less of a direct role in governing the nation, with Kim Jong-il effectively becoming his regent. On 24 December 1991, Kim Jong-il was proclaimed the supreme commander of the KPA; in April 1993, he became the supreme commander of all armed forces of the DPRK. In April 1992, just before his eightieth birthday, Kim Il-sung was promoted to the newly created rank of Generalissimo of the DPRK. In the entire communist bloc, such a rank previously existed only in the USSR and in the PRC, respectively, for Stalin and Mao. Both men had second thoughts about the position: Stalin continued to wear a marshal's uniform instead of a generalissimo's uniform, while Mao simply refused the rank after it had been established. Kim Il-sung, however, accepted the promotion, and portraits of him wearing the generalissimo's uniform soon started to appear.[106]

As he aged, Kim Il-sung increasingly focused on his past. In May 1991, for example, Kim Il-sung met a South Korean student, Kim Yong-hwan, who was at the time a member of the pro-North Korean underground in South Korea (he later changed his views and became a prominent human rights activist). Most of the meeting was dominated not by a discussion of the prospects of a South Korean revolution but rather by Kim Il-sung monologuing about his life in the 1930s and the early 1940s. The old man's body was still in very good shape, but he found the daily routine of ruling to be tiresome and tedious.[107]

What concerned Kim Il-sung was not the prospect of North Korea's rapid economic decline nor the sorry fate of the communist camp or indeed even his past as leader of the DPRK. His mind

211

instead returned to his childhood in colonial Korea, to Yuwen Middle School and his long and arduous partisan career in the Manchurian forests and hills.[108] During his tenure there, he had mostly spoken Chinese and, in 1992, highly uncharacteristically, he wrote a poem in the classical form of this language.[109] The poem, in the spirit of reverse Confucianism, was dedicated to the greatness of Kim Jong-il, and this expression of paternal piety has been studied in North Korean schools ever since.

Kim Il-sung's focus on the past did have one positive effect: as all opposition to him was long gone, the Great Leader decided to show mercy to some of those who had previously been purged. Kim Il-sung's brother, Yong-ju, exiled from politics since the 1970s, was given a ceremonial position as one of the DPRK's vice-presidents in 1993. Some of the purged were quietly pardoned, while some of those who had already died were given a proper burial in prestigious cemeteries.[110] Tellingly, however, the official biographies of those who were rehabilitated at this time fail to mention that they had once been purged. Some of the diplomats who were in North Korea and observed the rehabilitations believed that Kim may have been paving the way for his son, as some of those who had been pardoned, feeling less enmity towards the regime, would be less likely to oppose him.[111]

During a short visit to the USSR in July 1988, the Great Leader even considered visiting Vyatskoye village, although he ultimately cancelled this sentimental trip.[112] Pyongyang instead dispatched some officials to erect gravestones to the partisans who had died during their service there.[113] By that time, Kim's life in the Soviet Union had been fully erased from North Korean history, but, as the Great Leader was constantly talking about his past to his subordinates, it was now reincorporated again, albeit in a completely perverted form that rendered the story politically harmless.

In the early 1990s, the DPRK started to publish Kim Il-sung's official memoirs, titled *With the Century*.[114] The final two volumes of this eight-volume work were published after Kim Il-sung's death, but their general narrative had definitely been approved by Kim Il-sung as they first featured in a party textbook that was published while the Great Leader was still alive.[115] *With the Century* speaks about Kim's life before 1945, with its narrative being very loosely based on actual events.

Although *With the Century* mentions places like Yuwen Middle School, where he had studied, the county of Fusong, where he had lived, and the people with whom he had been close, the information it presents is twisted beyond recognition. According to his memoirs, Kim was a natural leader whose wisdom had been revered ever since his childhood. Naturally, he was not a member of the Chinese resistance but rather a commander of his own KPRA—these falsifications remained unchanged.

What was new was the claim that Kim Il-sung was in Manchuria in the 1940s but visited Khabarovsk 'from time to time' before the attack on Japan had begun. According to the book, in the USSR he met some of the top Soviet military commanders—including Marshals Vasilevskiy, Meretskov and Malinovskiy.[116] Meretskov, the book claims, told Kim: 'In a war against Japanese imperialism, Korean comrades are our seniors. The role of Korean comrades in military operations against the Japanese is very important; we have high hopes for you.'[117]

According to *With the Century*, Kim Il-sung also visited Moscow before the war with Japan and met Politburo member Andrei Zhdanov, who told Kim that he had 'heard many things about a Korean partisan Kim Il-sung from Stalin and Shtykov'.[118] Apparently, Zhdanov was delighted to hear from Kim that Koreans did not really need any aid in national construction and intended to build the new state on their own.[119] According to his memoirs, Kim later instructed the command of the Soviet

First Far Eastern Front on the tactics of war, and his KPRA not only liberated Korea but also participated in the war against the Kwantung Army in Manchuria, liberating several major cities.[120] Soviet soldiers apparently told Kim that 'Korean guerrillas are the greatest.'[121] This self-flattery was the final version of Kim Il-sung's biography. It was and remains the official narrative propagated in the DPRK.

14

THE DEAD HAND OF THE GREAT LEADER

The final years of Kim Il-sung's rule over North Korea were marked by the beginning of a nuclear crisis—the first of many.

When the DPRK gravitated away from Deng's China to Brezhnev's Soviet Union in the early 1980s, Moscow proposed building a nuclear power plant in the DPRK. Very well aware and distrustful of North Korea's nuclear ambitions, Moscow's precondition for its involvement was that North Korea had to join and abide by the Treaty on the Non-Proliferation of Nuclear Weapons (NPT).[1] The DPRK agreed and acceded to the treaty on 12 December 1985.[2] This later proved to be a miscalculation, as the prospects of a Soviet power plant being built in the North fizzled out along with the very existence of the Soviet Union itself.

As of 1991, foreign observers could still have been forgiven for believing in a nuclear-free future for Korea. In September 1991, President George H.W. Bush announced that the United States would withdraw all nuclear weapons stationed on foreign soil. In one of his last decisions as president of the Soviet Union, Gorbachev reciprocated.

In 1992, North and South Korea signed the comprehensive Joint Declaration on the Denuclearisation of the Korean Peninsula. Both sides pledged not to 'test, manufacture, produce, receive, possess, store, deploy or use nuclear weapons' and to 'use nuclear energy exclusively for peaceful means'. They also pledged not to 'possess nuclear reprocessing and uranium enrichment facilities'.

If North Korea had adhered to this agreement, the peninsula would now almost certainly be free of nuclear weapons. However, that was not to be. NPT-prescribed inspections by the International Atomic Energy Agency (IAEA), which started in 1992, resulted in the conclusion that North Korea was in violation. The IAEA inspectors identified two sites where they believed Pyongyang was storing used fuel rods that could be reprocessed to extract weapons-grade plutonium. In February 1993, the North formally refused to allow the IAEA access to its nuclear facilities. The crisis escalated to the point where, on 8 March, the DPRK announced a state of pre-war readiness[3] and, on 12 March 1993, that it intended to withdraw from the NPT, a decision that would come into effect in three months' time, as mandated by the treaty.[4]

While the regime's propaganda, including the official KPA newspaper *Choson Inmingun*, asserted that the mobilisation was primarily aimed at resisting the 'aggressive' US–South Korean joint military exercise 'Team Spirit-93',[5] the real reason was the North Korean withdrawal from the NPT and the subsequent escalation of tensions on the peninsula. There was speculation about an upcoming war, but, ultimately, after a series of talks with the United States, the DPRK agreed to retract its declared intention to withdraw from the NPT on 12 June 1993, literally on the final day before it would have entered into force. In exchange, North Korea was to receive significant economic assistance; the United States and the international community also pledged to build two light-water nuclear reactors in the DPRK.

Lightning and darkness

The late 1980s and early 1990s witnessed a worldwide political shift in the direction of liberation. The fall of communism in the USSR, Eastern Europe and Mongolia, the collapse of right-wing dictatorships in South Korea, Paraguay and Chile, the democratisation of Taiwan and the end of apartheid in South Africa—spectacular events followed one after another, leading American scholar Francis Fukuyama to make his famous prediction of the 'end of history': the complete and irreversible triumph of liberal democracy everywhere on Earth.[6]

Such an atmosphere inevitably led to suspicions that the Kimist regime in North Korea would be the next to fall. Kim Jong-il felt it, too. In 1992, in a speech to North Korean intelligence officers, he said: 'The Soviet Union and the Eastern European countries are no more. If we are lax now, there will be no tomorrow for us. When socialism falls, party and security personnel are the first ones to be purged.'[7]

Kim Jong-il's fears were by no means unfounded. A number of people who escaped North Korea testified that in the year Kim gave his speech, a group of officers had been planning a coup with the aim of murdering Kim Jong-il, his father and most of the political elite. According to these accounts, the conspirators were officers who had studied in Gorbachev's Soviet Union. Caught up in the spirit of liberalisation, these military men wanted their own country to change, but they knew there would be no change while the Kims remained in power.

Reportedly, the plan was to conduct the attack during a military parade on 25 April 1992. They planned to load one of the tanks in the parade with a real shell and fire on the tribune where the Kims were standing, obliterating the Great Leader, the supreme commander and the entire leadership in a single shot. Yet a twist of fate led them to abort the plan. An unsuspecting official changed the roster of tanks participating in the parade, and the conspirators never got an opportunity to proceed. The plot was later discovered, and a massive purge of officers and their relatives ensued.[8] The Kims' rule was saved.

Even as Kim Il-sung turned eighty-two, he felt he still had long to live. When in May 1994 he met his childhood acquaintance Son Won-thae, the Great Leader told him: 'Don't worry about me; I plan to live a long life.' Fate, however, had a different plan.[9]

In the summer of the same year, Kim Il-sung started preparing for a spectacular event: the first ever inter-Korean summit meeting. He invited South Korean President Kim Young-sam to visit Pyongyang. On 28 June 1994, it was announced the summit would take place in Pyongyang between 25 and 27 July.[10]

Ten days after the announcement, on the night of 7–8 July, a storm swept through Pyongyang. It did not rain; it poured. Residents said they had never seen such a tempest. One observer recalled hearing North Koreans saying that 'the heavens have gone crazy'.[11] It is said that on this night, Kim Il-sung felt seriously unwell. He was at his villa in Myohyang Mountains, which had been built ten years earlier, in 1984.[12] No qualified medics were available, and they had to be summoned from Pyongyang. It was not flying weather, but a team of doctors took a helicopter and rushed into the storm to assist Kim Il-sung. However, the helicopter plunged into a neighbouring reservoir, taking the lives of everyone on board.[13] Kim Il-sung could not receive the help he needed, and in the midst of the raging storm, lightning and darkness, he died. It was 2:00 a.m. on 8 July 1994.

Reportedly, Kim Jong-il had wanted to rush to his father, but his wife and guards had stopped him. If he had done so, his life would have ended the same day as that of his father near his Myohyang villa, terminating the line of succession and, undoubtedly, signalling the beginning of unprecedented turmoil in North Korea.[14]

By the morning of 8 July, the storm had abated. People went to work and school, unaware that the life of the man who was watching over them from their portraits at home, at work and in the streets, the man quoted in every book and whom the entire country worshipped had ended while they were sleeping.

On Saturday, 9 July, Korean Central Television alerted its viewers that there would be a special announcement at noon.

Then noon came. The country's most famous television anchor, Chon Hyong-gyu, appeared on TV screens across the nation. The presenter was sitting in front of a light blue wall; he was wearing a dark grey suit with one of the earliest versions of the Kim Il-sung badge pinned on it. Chon Hyong-gyu started reading the message:

> A proclamation to all the party members and all the people
>
> All of our working class and collective farm farmers, commanders and soldiers of the People's Army, intellectuals, youth and students!
>
> The Central Committee of the Workers' Party of Korea and the Central Military Commission of the Workers' Party of Korea, the National Defence Commission of the Democratic People's Republic of Korea and the Central People's Committee, the Administrative Council, announce with a heart most grieving that the General Secretary of the Central Committee of the Workers' Party of Korea, the President of the Democratic People's Republic of Korea, the Great Leader Comrade **Kim Il-sung** at two hours of the eighth of July of the year one thousand nine hundred ninety four passed away from a sudden attack of illness.[15]

The format of the proclamation was not original—its wording and structure followed the prototype of the Chinese announcement of Mao's death in 1976,[16] which, in turn, had been inspired by the Soviet announcement of Stalin's death in 1953.[17] And, as had been the case in 1953 and 1976, the news came as a shock to virtually everyone who listened.

Most North Koreans who heard the news simply could not believe it.[18]

Chon Hyong-gyu continued:

> Today Comrade **Kim Jong-il**, the great successor of the great deed of the Juche revolution and the outstanding leader of our party and the people and the supreme commander of our revolutionary armed forces, stands at the head of our revolution. The refined guidance of our party thus secures that the great deed of the Juche revolution, which was founded and led by the Great Leader Comrade **Kim Il-sung** will be brilliantly upheld and fulfilled through generations.[19]

This was a remarkably accurate statement. In the years to come, the world would witness the dark brilliance of Kim Il-sung's decision to appoint his son as his successor.

Eternal President of the Republic

When Stalin died, everyone around and closest to him, from the more liberal Deputy Premier Malenkov to the notorious former chief of secret police Beria, understood that the country desperately needed reforms. When Mao died, there were those who had supported his policies, but they were soon removed by reformists supported by the military. In Albania—the most repressive country in Eastern Europe—Enver Hoxha, who ruled the nation from 1944 to his death in 1985, handpicked a successor, Ramiz Alia. Alia's reforms were very moderate but were enough to signal to the people that times were changing. After massive demonstrations in Tirana, Alia's regime fell.

Not so in North Korea. Kim Jong-il's legitimacy was based on him being Kim Il-sung's son and on his loyalty to his father and his policies. Any meaningful reforms would have disrupted the continuity of the regime. Moreover, he knew very well that liberalisation usually makes a country less stable, and he was not a man who liked risk. His first speeches stated that Kim Il-sung's line would be continued without deviation. This was the safest way to go.

Thus, the dead hand of Kim Il-sung has continued to hold North Korea in its grip ever since his death, steering it towards the edge of economic catastrophe. Decades of mismanagement plagued the agricultural sector, with state-sanctioned farming methods leading to soil erosion and the silting of water reservoirs. During the Cold War, the nation had relied heavily on generous economic aid from the USSR and China to sustain its populace. However, with the collapse of the Eastern bloc and the cessation of aid from Moscow and Beijing, North Koreans bore the brunt of Kim Il-sung's disastrous policies. Without aid, North Korea could not produce enough chemical fertiliser or electricity for agricultural pumps, resulting in diminished harvests. Silted reservoirs exacerbated the problem, leading to floods that decimated what little harvest remained. Rather than implementing reforms, the state urged its citizens to eat less. Famine ensued, claiming lives on a scale comparable to the casualties of the Korean War. This famine marked the most devastating crisis in East Asia since Mao's Great Leap Forward.[20]

Yet, Kim Jong-il, who had just witnessed the collapse of most of the communist bloc, decided not to risk major reforms. Instead, he sought to amplify his father's cult of personality even further. Kim Il-sung's presidential palace was reconstructed into a colossal mausoleum to preserve Kim Il-sung's corpse for the whole world to see, with the state press proudly presenting this luxurious building to the starving multitude.[21] The body was embalmed and put in the central room—and Kim Il-sung's head was cosmetically altered to have his disfiguring tumour removed.[22]

On 8 July 1997, the third anniversary of Kim Il-sung's death, the DPRK introduced the new Juche calendar that commences with the year 1912, when Kim Il-sung was born. His birthday was proclaimed the 'Day of the Sun'.[23] After two months, the decision went into force, and 1997 became Juche 86.[24]

The Gregorian calendar, the dating system used by most countries, is based on the birth year of Jesus Christ, albeit as miscalculated by a monk called Dionysius Exiguus. North Korea thus put Kim Il-sung on the same level as Jesus. Both calendars are normally used together (e.g., '13 September Juche 85 (1996)'), although there are instances when only the Juche calendar is used.

Even after his death, Kim Il-sung remains the formal president of the country. Although the North Korean leadership initially considered appointing Kim Jong-il to his late father's position,[25] the new Great Leader insisted that no such change be made:[26] henceforth, Kim Il-sung would be the Eternal President of the Republic.[27]

'The Great Leader Comrade **Kim Il-sung** is always with us'— proclaimed the Stelas of Eternal Life, pillars Kim Jong-il ordered to be installed across the nation. And, indeed, he, the Eternal President of the Republic, still is.

15

KIM IL-SUNG'S LEGACY

Few rulers have had such a drastic impact on the history of their country as Kim Il-sung. He has had a greater lasting influence on North Korea than, say, Franklin Roosevelt or Lyndon Johnson on the United States, or Clement Attlee or Margaret Thatcher on the United Kingdom.

A dictator's legacy rarely survives their death, even when they go to some length to ensure the survival of their system. Oliver Cromwell, Joseph Stalin, Mao Zedong and Francisco Franco all have one thing in common: a few years after their deaths, their country started to move in a very different direction. Either their regimes collapsed, or their successors did their best to undo most of their gruesome legacy. This was not the case in North Korea.

In the first years after Kim Il-sung's death, North Korea went through an enormous crisis. Abandoned by its former allies, the country experienced an economic collapse and a massive famine. Many expected that the regime would soon meet its end. That this failed to happen is at least partly due to Kim Jong-il having learned from the best, as his father truly was a genius when it came to the preservation of power through tyrannical rule.

Now, decades after Kim Il-sung's death, the DPRK still looks very much like the country he envisioned and shaped during his rule.

First, the rule of the Kim family has been preserved. Just as Kim Il-sung planned, Kim Jong-il succeeded him in 1994. Not only that, eventually, the second Kim, though somewhat reluctantly,[1] chose to follow his father's example as well. In early 2009, Kim Jong-il appointed his son, Kim Jong-un, to succeed him.[2] The third Kim ascended to power in 2011. Thus, North Korea has been ruled by Kim Il-sung's descendants for at least quarter of a century since his death.

Second, Kim Il-sung managed to avoid the posthumous fate of Stalin. Both of his successors have had a vested interest in glorifying him—the infallible founder of the state—and have even been willing to present themselves as figures somewhat lesser than the colossus of the Great Leader. Not a single aspect of his cult of personality has been abolished under Kim Jong-il, and, at the time of writing, it seems very unlikely that Kim Jong-un would ever choose to do so either.

As I type these words in 2024, almost three decades after his death, it is mandatory for each and every book or article published in North Korea to include a quote from Kim Il-sung or one of his successors. Kim's portraits still hang in every North Korean household; songs glorifying him are played on every TV and radio channel every single day. Needless to say, talking about the Great Leader—his life, character and/or achievements—in any way other than that prescribed by the state still results in forced labour or, for those who are particularly unlucky, capital punishment.

Third, in the DPRK's state ideology, Kim Il-sung's policies remain the only acceptable policies. Of course, it would be wrong to say Kim Jong-il did not alter any aspect of the regime his father had built: he made it so that people were punished for their relatives' political crimes only as an exception rather than a rule, as had been the case previously, for example.[3] After the country had experienced famine for several years, Kim Jong-il led the regime through an uneven, weak and indecisive reform process that oscillated between his father's ideology and the people's objective needs.[4] Yet, ultimately, Kim Jong-il still moved the country in the direction of economic reform, with the state eventually tacitly recognising the right of citizens to engage in private business. This development was continued by Kim Jong-un in his first few years in power.[5] Kim Jong-il liberalised the arts, allowing authentic paintings and innovative music to reappear in the North following decades in which the country had known nothing but crude propaganda.

Yet, these changes were miniscule compared to the reforms implemented in the other surviving communist nations. Additionally, though the changes were realised, they were not announced publicly at all, including the pro-market reform package of 2002 and the currency reform of 2009,[6] or they were simply downplayed as something completely in line with Kim Il-sung's teachings.

At its core, the country's education system has largely remained the same: every single stage, from kindergarten to postgraduate education, is completely infused with the cult of the Kim family, with Kim Il-sung tacitly shown as the greatest of them all.

Decades after the Great Leader's demise, the official historical narrative in the DPRK remains the one present under Kim Il-sung: a crude mix of Marxist–Leninist dogma, some Korean nationalism and an enormous dose of glorification of Kim Il-sung and his successors. Yet it is the part of the narrative about Kim Il-sung that remains the most detached from reality. Just as had been the case in the early 1990s, North Koreans are still taught that it was he who had crushed imperial Japan, had defeated the

'American imperialists' in the Korean War and led Korea on the road to glory from the very beginning.[7]

Censorship in the country has continued to be as omnipresent as it was under Kim Il-sung. All information continues to be monitored, and access to all foreign media is restricted. North Korea chose not to connect the country to the global Internet. An exception is only made for a tiny number of people, each of whom needs to be personally approved by the Supreme Leader. Even heavily restricted Internet access would have made the regime too vulnerable, as people might have started to question its legitimacy.

Even suggesting that the present system might benefit from 'reform' became anathema in North Korea. How could one even think about making alterations to the great Kimilsungism, the pinnacle of human thought? Thus, in 1999, after the country had experienced a catastrophic famine in which hundreds of thousands died, Kim Jong-il publicly announced that 'under no circumstances can we be involved in these "reforms" and "openness" the imperialists babble about. "Reforms" and "openness" are the way to the destruction of the state. We cannot allow "reforms" and "openness" even in the slightest.'[8]

The quasi-monarchy established by Kim Il-sung has arguably enforced the continuity of his policies better than an actual monarchy. A new king is usually expected to differ from his predecessor. But this is not the case in North Korea. The ingenious system invented by Kim Il-sung made the entire legitimacy of Kim Jong-il's rule flow from his adherence to the ideas of his father. The very justification of Kim Jong-il's ascension was that he was the most ardent and pious Kimilsungist in the world. The same applied to Kim Jong-un.

Yet, even an autocracy built on the foundation of a single family does not necessarily behave in this way. For example, in Taiwan, Chiang Kai-shek's son, Chiang Ching-kuo, chose not to keep his country as the Chiang's family domain but to actively dismantle the system. The reforms launched by Chiang Ching-kuo eventually resulted in a bloodless transition to democracy. In Cuba, Fidel Castro died after forty-nine years in power, the same amount of time as Kim Il-sung ruled over North Korea. After Castro's death, power passed to his brother Raúl, who launched sweeping economic reforms, legalised private property and later initiated a transition of power to Miguel Díaz-Canel, thus voluntarily ending Castro family rule over the country.

In short, the future is never set in stone, and there is always a choice involved. And perhaps this was why Kim Il-sung chose Jong-il, as opposed to one of his other sons, to succeed him. Perhaps Kim Il-sung knew that it would not be in Kim Jong-il's character to reform the system, and, perhaps, Kim Jong-il thought the same thing about his third son and successor, Kim Jong-un.

Another aspect of the Great Leader's legacy is that North Korea remains an extremely militarised state—just the way Kim Il-sung built it. The focus has somewhat shifted from an offensive war to 'liberate the South' to a defensive war 'against the imperialists', but the nature of the country has not changed. By the early 2020s, the nearly decade-long period of military conscription[9] had still not been abolished, even though the country has developed nuclear weaponry and ballistic missile technology. Military service is not simply about the regime's survival. The Kim Il-sung model allowed for the immediate mobilisation of soldiers to work on any project, whether military or otherwise—be it gathering the harvest or the construction of a dam. The model also allowed for the youth to be kept in the armed forces, where they can constantly be monitored by the state and indoctrinated in its ideology. All this was too convenient for Kim Il-sung's successors to abolish.

North Korea's foreign policy continues to follow the doctrine the country unofficially adopted after Kim Il-sung broke free from Soviet control. North Korea has neither any real friends nor any trustworthy allies. All rhetoric of friendship is merely a bargaining tool to score an economic or political advantage. Earth is a dog-eat-dog world where all relationships are of convenience and all diplomacy is about cheating your partner to maximise your profits. There are no long-term profits to be made nor any strategic goals to be set. Any tactical advantage gained should be immediately exploited; long-term consequences be damned.

Kim Il-sung bequeathed his heirs not only a regime but also a loyal political elite. Although purges played a significant role in securing their allegiance, the elite's loyalty also stems from the potential consequences of the Kim family's rule coming to an end, as this would likely lead North Korea to lose its status as an independent state. In a unified Korea, Seoul would govern the whole country, and the new regime would face political and moral pressure to hold the old elite accountable for the atrocities committed during the Kim era. Consequently, many within the elite concluded that it was in their best interests to prevent such a scenario from ever materialising.

Kim Il-sung thus proved to be an extraordinarily talented dictator. He showed that it is possible to stay in power for decades while presiding over an exceptionally repressive and cruel system, and that this system, if crafted well, can even survive the physical death of the tyrant with almost no concessions made to the people.

The enormous cost of his rule can never be wholly assessed, as, when it comes to the suffering of so many of his victims, there has been no written or even oral evidence left to tell the world of their stories. The heart-breaking fate of tens of millions of innocents whose lives were twisted and brutalised by the will of this man remains the most important and lasting legacy of Kim Il-sung.

Could North Korea's fate have been different? If the South had not existed, most would have answered 'no' to this question. Most historians would probably conclude that Korea, a country that has never known anything even resembling democracy in all its long history and has only extremely limited experience of self-governance, was bound to become one of the most closed, poorest and least free societies on the planet. It is easy to imagine books talking about the legacy of 'traditional Confucian culture' and its rejection of progress, the 'reactionary and cruel mentality of an agricultural society', the culture of the absolute monarchy and the influence of the fanatic militarism of the Japanese Empire of the 1940s.

But the real Korea is a unique place, and the South's experience shows that history can be very flexible indeed. The South's example proves that the North's fate was in no way set in stone. On the contrary: if the cards had been played only slightly differently, the lives of tens of millions could have been completely different.

A mere twist of fate—say, the United States dropping the atomic bomb on Japan two weeks earlier in 1945—could have ended up in the empire surrendering to the Allies before the Soviet entry into the war, thus preventing North Korea from ever coming into existence. It could have spared millions from the tragedy of the Korean War and the subsequent decades of terror, poverty and suffering.

Moreover, it was by no means preordained that Kim Il-sung would lead the North in 1945. If Zhou Baozhong had not sent his letter, Kim Il-sung could have stayed in the USSR for longer, missing the critical period during which a leader was chosen. Or Beria might not have approached Stalin to talk about Kim's candidacy. Or Stalin could simply have picked someone else. Yet, out of all possible candidacies to the role of 'little Stalin', North Korea got this ruthless man, the one as skilled in scheming and preserving his power as he was inept in economic management and deaf to the plight of the common people.

Events could still have turned out differently. The Soviets could have reached an agreement with the Americans, and Korea could have been unified under Yo Un-hyong or someone else. Kim Il-sung could have been killed in a terrorist attack in 1946. If Mao had stuck to his initial idea of not interfering in the Korean War, Kim Il-sung's rule would have been over by the autumn of 1950. If in the mid-1950s the opposition had been better prepared, they could have done what Hungary and Bulgaria did and replace Kim Il-sung with another leader. If Lee Sang-jo had been more insistent, Anastas Mikoyan could have demanded Kim's dismissal in 1956. And even after all this, in 1957 Ambassador Puzanov still had a chance to strip Kim of his unlimited power.

Only by the late 1950s was the fate of North Korea sealed. A master of political manipulation, Kim Il-sung managed to free his country from complete Soviet control while the Cold War was still going on.

The country was immediately subjected to Kim's ideas of how a country should be run. The economy was to be as centralised as possible, though Kim expected the nation to jettison previously adopted plans and adapt itself to new goals as soon as he felt like announcing them. Factories and collective farms were to be run by party bureaucrats, completely abandoning the stated communist goal of workers' and farmers' self-governance.

The country's entire culture was nearly completely separated from the rest of the world and remoulded to serve one overriding goal: worshipping Kim Il-sung. His portraits were to hang in every home, his name mentioned and glorified in virtually every text. Not a day was to pass without every man and woman in

North Korea praising him. The state ideology was eventually subsumed and supplemented by the cult of Kim, which did not need any additional justification.

It would be wrong to say that Kim Il-sung was a man of pure evil. He was a brave and cunning man, but he was not completely incapable of kindness, forgiveness and mercy. Yet there can be little doubt that Kim Il-sung is the darkest figure in all of Korea's history. He was the man who instigated the most destructive war Korea has ever seen, the man who created one of the most repressive states in human history, the man whose economic policy ended in mass famine and the man who did his utmost to ensure this order would be preserved after his death.

He was, to a certain extent, both a communist and a nationalist. Ultimately, however, his loyalty was not to an ideology or a specific group but rather to himself. His ego and his cult had a mutually amplifying effect that eventually led the Great Leader to completely cease believing that he might be wrong on any issue. He made himself believe that any problems the country faced came from the stupidity, laziness or ineptitude of his subordinates, not from the way he ran the country.

Yet, the legacy he cared about most—the social and political system he had built—has outlived him. As I pen these closing words, the regime, now led by Kim Il-sung's grandson, remains unyielding in the face of all challenges, dominating the lives of over 20 million North Koreans, with no apparent end in sight.

TIMELINE OF THE LIFE OF KIM IL-SUNG

15 April 1912	The future Great Leader is born in Chilgol village in colonial Korea. The eldest son of Kim Hyong-jik and Kang Ban-sok, he is given the name Kim Song-ju.
October 1917 (O.S.)	Communist revolution in Russia.
17 May 1918	Revolt of the Czechoslovak Legion begins in Russia, signalling the start of the Russian Civil War.
March 1919	Massive rebellion against the colonial authorities in Korea. Kim's father Kim Hyong-jik is an active participant.
2 March 1919	Communist International is established.
May 1919	The Kim family moves to Manchuria.
23 July 1921	CPC is formed.
30 December 1922	The Soviet Union is formed.
17 June 1923	Surrender of the last anti-Bolshevik unit in Russia. End of the Civil War.
1927	Kim Song-ju enrols in Yuwen Middle School.

December 1928	Most of China is unified under the leadership of Chiang Kai-shek.
Circa 1929	Joseph Stalin solidifies his power in the Soviet Union.
May 1929	Kim Song-ju joins the Communist Society of the Korean Youth. It is disbanded after less than a week, and Kim Song-ju is arrested.
October 1929	Kim Song-ju is released from prison after several people vouch for him.
Circa 1930	Kim Song-ju joins the KRA of the National Chamber.
1930	Kim Song-ju is appointed a member of the Organisation Committee for Fusong and Antu of the Korean Farmers' General Union in Eastern Provinces.
Circa 1930	Lee Jong-nak, one of the National Chamber's cadres, sends Kim Song-ju to study at the lyceum of South Manchuria.
Circa 1930	Lee Jong-nak and leftist members of the National Chamber quit the National Chamber and create the Army of the World Fire. Kim Song-ju becomes a member of its Military Political Council.
18 September 1931	Following a false flag attack, the Kwantung Army invades Manchuria, conquering the region in about five months.
Circa 1931	Kim Song-ju changes his name to Kim Il-sung.
Circa 1931–2	Kim joins the CPC, with Lee Chong-san as his guarantor.

February 1932	Wang Delin organises the Chinese People's National Salvation Army.
March 1932	The state of Manchukuo is proclaimed. Puyi (of the clan Aisin-Gioro), the last Qing emperor, is made its chief executive.
Spring 1932	Kim Il-sung joins the Chinese People's National Salvation Army as a propagandist.
Mid-1932	Following pressure from Nanjing, Wang Delin starts expelling communists from the Chinese People's National Salvation Army, and Kim Il-sung has to leave the organisation.
Circa 1932	Kim Il-sung joins the Antu partisan unit.
Circa November 1932	Kim Il-sung is appointed political commissar of the Wangqing Anti-Japanese Partisan Unit.
30 January 1933	Adolf Hitler becomes the chancellor of Germany.
Circa 1935	Kim Il-sung is appointed chief of staff and political commissar of the Third Regiment of the Independent Division of the Second Army of the North East People's Revolutionary Army.
20 February 1936	The North East Anti-Japanese United Army is formed by the CPC.
Circa 1936	Kim is appointed commander of the Sixth Division of the Second Army of the North East Anti-Japanese United Army.
4–5 June 1937	Kim Il-sung's unit conducts a surprise attack on the police station in Pochonbo.
8 July 1937	The Second Sino-Japanese War begins.

Circa 1938	Kim Il-sung is appointed commander of the Second Area Army of the First Route Army of the North East Anti-Japanese United Army.
Late 1930s	Kim Il-sung marries his first wife Han Song-hui.
October 1939	Major-General Nozoe Masanori is appointed the commander of the anti-partisan liquidation unit. He starts a campaign to eradicate the partisan movement in Manchukuo.
Summer 1940	Kim Il-sung's first wife, Han Song-hui, is arrested by the Japanese.
Second half of 1940	Kim Il-sung marries his second wife, Kim Jong-suk.
Autumn 1940	Kim Il-sung flees to the USSR.
January 1941	Along with other partisans, Kim Il-sung is evaluated by a team of four Comintern officials. He is considered trustworthy.
16 February 1941	Kim Il-sung's eldest son Yura is born. He will later be known as Kim Jong-il.
9 April 1941	Kim Il-sung is appointed commander of one of the two units tasked with looking for Wei Zhengming, the commander of the First Route Army of the North East Anti-Japanese United Army, and is sent back to Manchukuo.
13 April 1941	The Soviet Union and the Japanese Empire sign the Neutrality Pact.
22 June 1941	Nazi Germany launches a surprise attack on the Soviet Union, plunging the country into a cataclysmic war.

28 August 1941	Kim returns with a part of his team empty-handed, reporting that Wei Zhengming is already dead.
14 September 1941	Kim Il-sung goes back to Manchuria for the second time to meet the rest of his unit.
12 November 1941	Kim Il-sung and his unit return to the USSR. Kim Il-sung is settled in partisan camp V by the Far Eastern Front.
31 March 1942	After many guerrillas depart to camp A near Vyatskoye, Kim Il-sung is appointed chief in military and political affairs among the partisans who remain in camp V.
July 1942	As more troops are recalled to fight at Stalingrad, General Iosif Apanasenko, the commander of the Far Eastern Front, decides to create the Eighty-Eighth Separate Infantry Brigade.
16 July 1942	Kim Il-sung comes to Khabarovsk from camp V (Okeanskaya) to meet with General Apanasenko.
17 July 1942	Kim Il-sung is admitted to the Red Army, commissioned as captain and appointed commander of the First Battalion of the Eighty-Eighth Separate Infantry Brigade.
22 July 1942	General Apanasenko briefs Zhou Baozhong, Li Zhaolin and Kim Il-sung on the purposes on the newly created brigade.
23 July 1942	Kim Il-sung arrives at camp A (Vyatskoye) to serve in the Red Army.
15 May 1943	Communist International is dissolved.

1 December 1943	In the Cairo Declaration, agreed at a conference in the previous month, the Allies promise to restore Korea's independence after Japan is defeated.
1944	Kim Il-sung's second son, Shura, is born.
July 1944	At a conference involving the Eighty-Eighth Brigade, some servicemen accuse Kim Il-sung of having committed crimes before becoming a partisan. They claim he was a marauder and was slaughtering communists in the early 1930s. Kim counteracts by claiming he murdered Trotskyists. No political consequences follow.
February 1945	During the Yalta Conference, Churchill and Roosevelt push Stalin to attack Japan. Stalin agrees to do so after Germany capitulates.
Spring 1945	The Soviets start to look for a possible candidate to rule post-war Korea. Mun Il, a Soviet Korean, mentions Kim Il-sung to the authorities.
5 April 1945	The USSR nullifies the Neutrality Pact with Japan.
May 1945	Nazi Germany surrenders unconditionally to the Allies.
6 August 1945	Atomic bombing of Hiroshima marks the first time an atomic weapon is used in wartime.
8 August 1945	The Soviet Union declares war against Japan, effective the next day.
9 August 1945	The Soviet-Japanese war begins, as the Red Army attacks Japan through Manchukuo.

22. Kim Il-sung in his marshal's uniform. This portrait was widely used in the mid-1950s.

23. Kim Il-sung, Kim Jong-suk, Kim Du-bong, Aleksei Hegay and other North Korean politicians of the 1940s.

24. From left to right: Kim Chaek, Aleksei Hegay and Kim Il-sung.

25. Vice-premier Choe Chang-ik, who conspired against Kim Il-sung in an attempt to replace him as the North Korean leader.

26. From left to right: Soviet ambassador Vasiliy Ivanov, Kim Du-bong, unknown Soviet official, Kim Il-sung and the future Soviet leader Leonid Brezhnev, 1956.

27. Kim Il-sung's second cabinet, September 1957. The day it was formed marked the success of his long game to become politically independent from Moscow.

28. Kim Il-sung and Chinese premier Zhou Enlai after the signing of the 1961 Treaty.

29. A North Korean poster from the 1960s commemorating the fifteenth anniversary of the founding of the North Korean army.

30. Hao Deqing, People's Republic of China ambassador to North Korea from 1961 to 1965.

31. Chinese schoolchildren in Pyongyang, 1966, possibly participants in or witnesses to a student riot that occurred in the North Korean capital that year.

32. Kim Il-sung's main statue in Pyongyang. Erected in 1972, it became a major place of worship and pilgrimage in North Korea.

33. The Kim Il-sung Order. This variant was used in the 1970s–80s.

34. 100 won banknote from 1978, the first one to feature
Kim Il-sung's portrait.

35. From left to right: Kim Jong-il, Kim Il-sung and
Kim Kyong-hui.

36. The Sixth Congress of the WPK in 1980, where Kim Jong-il was revealed to the world.

37. Kim Il-sung, accompanied by Kim Jong-il and several officials, conducts 'on-the-spot guidance' at the construction site of the Nampho Dam, one of North Korea's most expensive and least useful construction projects, 1985.

38. North Korean painting of Kim Il-sung and Kim Jong-il, 1990s.

39. Kim Il-sung in his generalissimo uniform. He was the second generalissimo, after Stalin, in any Communist country.

40. Kim Il-sung and Mao Zedong. This snapshot of a video chronicle allows one to see Kim's tumour.

41. Kim Il-sung in his coffin. The flowers by his body are 'kimilsungias'.

42. Kim Il-sung's statue inside his mausoleum, flanked by a guard of honour.

10 August 1945	Colonels Bonesteel and Rusk outline a plan to divide Korea at the 38th parallel. The plan is approved by both Washington and Moscow.
15 August 1945	Emperor Hirohito addresses the nation to announce Japan's surrender on the Allies' terms.
Mid-August 1945	On behalf of Marshal Meretskov, Lieutenant-Colonel Grigoriy Mekler visits the Eighty-Eighth Brigade. He writes a highly positive assessment of Captain Kim Il-sung.
August 1945	The Communist Party of Korea is reborn.
24 August 1945	Zhou Baozhong, commanding officer of the Eighty-Eighth Separate Infantry Brigade, writes a letter to Marshal Aleksandr Vasilevskiy asking him to use the brigade to assist Soviet authorities in the newly occupied territories.
25 August 1945	Being presented with a choice by Marshal Meretskov, Colonel-General Ivan Chistyakov chooses Pyongyang over Hamhung as the administrative centre of North Korea.
25 August 1945	The Soviet Army creates a plan to dispatch the Koreans of the Eighty-Eighth Brigade to North Korea. Kim Il-sung is to become a deputy to the commandant of Pyongyang.
26 August 1945	Chistyakov accepts the surrender of the Japanese Army in northern Korea.
30 August 1945	Captain Kim Il-sung receives the Order of the Red Banner.
2 September 1945	The Empire of Japan formally surrenders. The Second World War ends.

19 September 1945	Kim Il-sung returns to Wonsan on the Soviet ship Emelian Pugachev with other partisans. Colonel Vladimir Kuchumov, commandant of Kangwon province, welcomes them.
Late September 1945	Mun Il introduces Kim Il-sung to Major-General Lebedev.
Late September 1945	The Soviets compile a list of candidates to lead the North Korean proto-state.
13 October 1945	The Northern Branch Office of the Communist Party of Korea is set up. Kim Yong-bom is appointed first secretary; Kim Il-sung becomes a member of the Organisational Bureau.
14 October 1945	Kim Il-sung speaks at the mass demonstration hailing the Soviet Army.
Late October 1945	In a letter to the Soviet leadership, Kim Il-sung is recommended as the leader of the North Korean proto-government.
18 December 1945	Kim is appointed chief secretary of the Northern Branch Bureau of the Communist Party of Korea, becoming the top party official in the North.
27 December 1945	At the Moscow Conference, heads of the foreign policy departments of Britain, the United States and USSR agree on the establishment of a five-year trusteeship over Korea. This plan proves to be widely unpopular among Korean elites.
1 January 1946	Kim addresses the North Koreans with his first New Year speech.

8 February 1946	Kim Il-sung becomes chairman of the PPCNK, putting him at the head of the North Korean proto-government.
21 April 1946	By orders from Moscow, the Communist Party and the Social Democratic Party of Germany are merged into the Socialist Unity Party. This is the first merger of its kind in the communist bloc.
22–3 May 1946	Northern Branch Bureau of the Communist Party of Korea becomes the Communist Party of North Korea. The party is thus officially split in two.
30 May 1946	Kim Il-sung's eldest daughter Kim Kyong-hui is born.
August 1946	With the merger of the Communist Party and the NPP, the WPNK is formed. Kim Il-sung becomes vice-chairman of the Central Committee.
1 October 1946	Kim Il-sung University is established.
February 1947	Kim Il-sung becomes chairman of the People's Committee for North Korea.
1947	Kim Il-sung's second son, Shura, drowns.
21 October 1947	The USSR withdraws from the Joint US–USSR Commission on Korea, formally ending the talks on the creation of a unified government.
10 May 1948	South Korea holds elections for its Constituent Assembly, marking the first step in creating a separate state in the South.

10 July 1948	The DPRK's constitution is enforced in northern Korea, solidifying the division of the peninsula. The new flag is hoisted for the first time in Pyongyang.
15 August 1948	The Republic of Korea is proclaimed in Seoul.
8 September 1948	Kim Il-sung becomes premier of the Cabinet of Ministers.
June 1949	Following another evaluation from Moscow, Kim is appointed chairman of the Central Committee of the WPK, finally putting him in charge of both the government and the party.
12 August 1949	Kim Il-sung and Pak Hon-yong start probing the Soviet ambassador, Shtykov, for an invasion of South Korea.
22 September 1949	Kim Il-sung's second wife, Kim Jong-suk, dies.
1 October 1949	Mao Zedong proclaims the PRC.
30 January 1950	Stalin agrees to attack South Korea. The plans are formulated and finalised.
25 June 1950	North Korea launches a surprise attack against the Republic of Korea. The Korean War begins.
27 June 1950	With the Soviet delegate absent, the UN Security Council adopts Resolution 83, authorising its members to help South Korea by all means necessary.
28 June 1950	Seoul falls, and Kim Il-sung issues a proclamation to the city's residents.
4 July 1950	Kim Il-sung is appointed supreme commander of the KPA.

15 September 1950	The United States launches the Inchon landing operation, turning the tide in the Korean War.
28 September 1950	Seoul is retaken by the US and its allies.
7 October 1950	Chinese intervention in the Korean War is confirmed.
Middle October 1950	Kim Il-sung retreats from Pyongyang for Kanggye pending the capital's immediate occupation by the allied forces.
25 October 1950	The Chinese Army enters the Korean War, turning the tide once again.
Autumn 1950	Kim Il-sung marries his third wife, Kim Song-ae.
6 December 1950	Pyongyang is retaken by the Chinese Army.
4 January 1951	Seoul falls to the Chinese advance.
15 March 1951	Seoul is retaken by the UN Army.
July 1951	Armistice talks begin in Korea.
7 February 1953	Kim Il-sung receives the newly established rank of marshal of the DPRK.
5 March 1953	Joseph Stalin dies.
Spring 1953	Kim Il-sung purges his major rivals Pak Hon-yong and Lee Sung-yop together with a number of other communists.
2 July 1953	Aleksei Hegay, one of the top-ranking Soviet Koreans in the North, dies. While he likely committed suicide, his family is doubtful and suspects he was killed on Kim Il-sung's orders.
27 July 1953	The armistice effectively ending the Korean War is signed in Panmunjom.

August 1953	Kim Il-sung launches collectivisation in North Korea.
1 October 1953	Mutual Defence Treaty between the Republic of Korea and the United States of America is signed.
1954	Thousands of people die in North Korea as a result of the collectivisation policy.
10 August 1954	Kim Il-sung's third son, Kim Phyong-il, is born.
19 January 1955	China starts its invasion of Taiwan's Dachen archipelago, culminating in the islands being annexed by the PRC.
14 May 1955	The Warsaw Pact is established.
1955	Kim Il-sung's fourth son, Kim Yong-il, is born.
Circa 1955	Kim Il-sung starts a campaign against Soviet influence in the country.
April 1955	Deputy Premier Pak Chang-ok suggests removing Kim Il-sung from premiership. Kim manages to outmanoeuvre Pak and keep the position.
25 February 1956	Nikita Khrushchev formally denounces Stalin and the concept of the personality cult.
30 August 1956	A group of conspirators unsuccessfully tries to attack Kim Il-sung at a plenum of the Central Committee.
September 1956	Lee Sang-jo, DPRK ambassador to the Soviet Union, orchestrates Soviet–Chinese joint intervention, forcing Kim to temporarily suspend the purges against his opponents.

October–November 1956	The Soviet Union invades Hungary in order to suppress an anti-communist uprising.
September 1957	Kim Il-sung strips of rank and removes from power Vice-Marshal Choe Yong-gon, his second-in command.
20 September 1957	Despite pressure from the Soviet embassy, Kim Il-sung de facto refuses to share power, reappointing himself as premier.
22 October 1957	The Soviet embassy is instructed not to take any action on Kim's reappointment. The USSR begins to lose control over North Korea.
March 1958	Kim Il-sung purges the opposition at the First Party Conference.
August 1958	The Beidaihe Conference of the Chinese Politburo signals the beginning of the Great Leap Forward.
28 October 1958	Chinese troops are withdrawn from the DPRK.
22 January 1959	Order 7 of the DPRK's Cabinet of Ministers prescribes the establishment of a network of labour camps across the nation.
February 1960	Kim Il-sung enforces the 'Chongsanni method', putting party officials in direct control of agriculture.
April 1960	An attempt to rig elections leads to a popular uprising in South Korea. President Rhee is overthrown.
16 May 1961	The military seizes control in South Korea. Eventually, Major-General Park Chung-hee emerges as the incoming military junta's leader.

6 July 1961	North Korea signs a Treaty of Friendship, Cooperation and Mutual Assistance with the Soviet Union.
11 July 1961	North Korea signs a Treaty of Friendship, Cooperation and Mutual Assistance with the PRC.
September 1961	The Fourth Congress of the WPK sees Kim's supporters appointed to the senior positions in the party, completely solidifying his control over the nation.
December 1961	Kim Il-sung enforces the 'Taean work system', putting party officials in direct control of industry.
18 October 1963	With the pro-Chinese article 'Let Us Defend the Socialist Camp' appearing in major newspapers, the DPRK officially and openly sides with China against the USSR in the Sino-Soviet conflict.
14 October 1964	Leonid Brezhnev takes power in the USSR following the dismissal of Nikita Khrushchev.
22 June 1965	Treaty on Basic Relations between Japan and the Republic of Korea is signed.
Autumn 1965	Kim Il-sung asks the PRC to assist him in a new invasion of South Korea. The request is denied.
12 August 1966	Rodong Shinmun publishes article 'Let Us Protect Independence', signalling the end of the pro-Beijing line in North Korea.
12 October 1966	At the Second Party Conference, Kim's position in the party is renamed 'General Secretary'.

4–8 May 1967	The fifteenth plenum of the Fourth Central Committee is convened, passing instructions on the Singular Thought System, signalling the transformation of the DPRK into a truly totalitarian state.
25 May 1967	Kim Il-sung gives a classified speech, 'On the Necessary Directions of the Party Propaganda Work', giving instructions for the implementation of the Singular Thought System.
21 January 1968	Kim Il-sung unsuccessfully tries to assassinate South Korean President Park Chung-hee.
23 January 1968	The American signals intelligence ship USS Pueblo is detained by North Korea, triggering tension with the North unprecedented since 1953.
20–21 August 1968	The Warsaw Pact invades Czechoslovakia to depose its reformist government.
14 April 1969	Lin Biao is endorsed as Mao Zedong's successor in China, marking the first case of an anointed successor in the communist bloc.
15 April 1969	On Kim Il-sung's birthday, the North Korean Air Force shoots down an American EC-121 reconnaissance plane.
December 1969	North Korean agents infiltrate north-east South Korea and brutally murder a nine-year-old child, Lee Sung-bok. The murder causes a public uproar against the North in South Korea.

April 1970	Zhou Enlai visits North Korea, marking the beginning of a thaw in relations between Beijing and Pyongyang.
4 February 1971	An article, 'Let Us Adhere to Proletarian Dictatorship and Proletarian Democracy', signals Pyongyang's return to the pro-Chinese line. This time, however, North Korea's support for China is more cautious.
13 September 1971	Lin Biao dies in a plane crash, probably following an abortive coup against Mao in China.
15 April 1972	Kim Il-sung's sixtieth birthday marks the peak of the personality cult. His statue in Pyongyang is unveiled.
4 July 1972	In a joint declaration, Pyongyang and Seoul pledge mutual non-aggression.
17 October 1972	President Park Chung-hee announces a state of emergency in South Korea that eventually leads to the adoption of an authoritarian constitution that transforms him into its dictator.
28 December 1972	Following the adoption of the new constitution, Kim Il-sung becomes the president of the DPRK.
February 1974	Kim Jong-il is formally appointed Kim Il-sung's successor.
April 1974	North Korea publishes 'Ten Principles on the Party's Singular Thought System', calling for complete and unconditional loyalty to Kim Il-sung.
15 August 1974	A North Korean sympathiser attempts to assassinate South Korean President Park Chung-hee and kills his wife in the process.

30 April 1975	The fall of Saigon. The Vietnam War ends.
2 July 1976	The unification of Vietnam.
18 August 1976	A small skirmish in Panmunjom, known as the 'axe murder incident', creates tension in Korea, prompting the DPRK to announce a state of pre-war readiness.
9 September 1976	Mao Zedong dies in China.
December 1978	The third plenum of the Eleventh Central Committee of the CPC marks the beginning of the policy of reforms and openness.
26 October 1979	President Park Chung-hee is killed by the chief of the South Korean civil intelligence, ending his eighteen-year rule in South Korea.
May 1980	A crackdown on pro-democracy demonstrations in Kwangju, South Korea, results in thousands of victims.
1 September 1980	General Chun Doo-hwan is inaugurated as president of South Korea after his successful coup.
October 1980	As the Sixth Party Congress convenes, the DPRK officially announces to the outside world Kim Jong-il as Kim Il-sung's successor.
15 April 1982	On Kim Il-sung's seventieth birthday, Juche Tower and Arch of Triumph are unveiled in Pyongyang. The latter commemorates his alleged victory over imperial Japan in 1945 and thus becomes the world's largest monument commemorating an imaginary 'event'.
9 October 1983	Kim Il-sung's operatives unsuccessfully try to assassinate South Korean President Chun Doo-hwan in Rangoon (Burma).

8 January 1984	Kim Jong-il's son, Kim Jong-un, is born.
March 1985	Mikhail Gorbachev becomes the general secretary in the USSR. Eventually he launches a radical reform policy, known as perestroika.
27–30 May 1985	The first meetings of the families divided by the Korean War take place in Seoul and Pyongyang.
Summer 1986	Kim Il-sung suffers a stroke. For some days, he lies in a coma. Eventually, he is saved by Soviet doctors.
14 September 1986	Agents of Palestinian terrorist leader Abu Nidal are contracted by Pyongyang to plant a bomb in Kimpo Airport in Seoul. Five people are killed, thirty-eight are wounded.
November 1986	For several days, broadcasts along the DMZ announce Kim Il-sung's death, sparking concern in South Korea.
29 June 1987	The democratic movement triumphs in South Korea, marking the end of the military dictatorship.
29 November 1987	North Korean agents detonate a bomb on board a Korean Air Lines flight from Baghdad to Seoul, killing 115 people.
17 September 1988	Despite Pyongyang's best efforts, the XXIV Olympics open in Seoul. Both China and the Soviet Union participate, ending South Korea's diplomatic isolation from the communist bloc.
July 1989	Pyongyang hosts the Thirteenth World Festival of Youth and Students. A visit by a South Korean student Lim Su-kyung to the festival becomes its central event.

1 December 1989	The People's Chamber of East Germany votes to end the Socialist Unity Party's rule over the country.
14 March 1990	The CPSU relinquishes its monopoly on power over the country.
30 September 1990	South Korea establishes diplomatic relations with the Soviet Union.
3 October 1990	The reunification of Germany.
1 July 1991	The Warsaw Pact is formally dissolved.
17 September 1991	Both South Korea and the DPRK join the United Nations.
6 November 1991	The CPSU is outlawed.
13 December 1991	In the Basic Agreement between the two Koreas, Pyongyang and Seoul pledge to recognise and respect each other's political systems.
24 December 1991	Kim Il-sung appoints Kim Jong-il as supreme commander of the KPA.
26 December 1991	The Soviet Union is formally dissolved.
13 April 1992	Kim Il-sung receives the rank of generalissimo of the DPRK, making him the second generalissimo in the communist bloc after Stalin.
25 April 1992	Reportedly, a group of rebellious officers plans to kill Kim Il-sung and Kim Jong-il during a parade by firing on a tribune from a tank. The tanks are changed at the last moment, and the plan fails.

24 August 1992	South Korea establishes diplomatic relations with the PRC.
12 March 1993	North Korea announces its withdrawal from the NPT, signalling the beginning of the first of many nuclear crises and negotiations surrounding the country's nuclear weapons programme.
9 April 1993	Kim Il-sung appoints Kim Jong-il chairman of the National Defence Commission.
28 June 1994	Both Koreas agree to hold a summit in Pyongyang in late July 1994.
8 July 1994	Kim Il-sung dies from a heart attack at the age of eighty-two.

NOTES

1.   FROM KOREA TO MANCHURIA

1. Chilgol is the Korean name of the village. It should be noted that at that time in English (and other European languages), Korean names were written according to the Japanese pronunciation of the characters, and the full address of Kim Il-sung's homeland at the time would have been 'Nanatani, Shitasato, Ryōzan district, Heijō, South Heian province, Korea, Empire of Japan.' However, these Japanese names mostly fell into obscurity after 1945, and thus in the main text of the book I employ Korean names for the period of Japanese colonisation as well.

2. *Man'gyŏngdae*, Pyongyang: Kungnip Misul Ch'ulp'ansa [Fine Art State Publishing House], 1960, p. 19; 'Ch'ilgol saramdŭl' [The Chilgolians], *Rodong Shinmun*, 4 June 1960, p. 3; Ŏm Ju-yŏp, '21seginŭn nuga tŏ yŏllin sahoe ro kanŭnyaesŏ sŭngbu' [In the twenty-first century, those who establish a more open society will win, and those who do not will lose], *Munhwa Ilbo*, 1 Jan. 2016, http://www.munhwa.com/news/view.html?no=2016010101032939173001 (accessed 22 Sept. 2023).

3. The information about Ryong-ho comes from a North Korean book about Kim Il-sung's childhood published in 1964. Kang Hyo-sun, *Noŭl pikkin Man'gyŏngbong* [Sunset's light over the Mangyong peak], Pyongyang: Chosŏn Sahoejuŭi Rodong Ch'ŏngnyŏn Tongmaeng ch'ulp'ansa, 1964, p. 1. All mention of him was erased from the subsequent official discourse.

4. Chōsen sōtokufu seimukyoku [Department of Government Affairs of the Government-General of Korea], 'Futei-dan kankei zakken: Chōsenjin-no bu; Zai naichi; Ni' [Various incidents related to disloyal organisations: Section of the Koreans; On the mainland, volume 2], n.p.: n.p., 1918, http://db.history.go.kr/item/level.do?setId=3&itemId=haf&synonym=off&chinessChar=on&page=1&pre_page=1&brokerPagingInfo=&position=0&levelId=haf_108_0610 (accessed 22 Sept. 2023).

5. 'Kolmok taejang Kim Il-sŏng-ŭl kiŏk'anŭn 102se kohyang hubae' [102-year-old fellow villager remembers the 'cocky boy' Kim Il-sung], BBC K'oria [BBC Korea], 3 Sept. 2021, https://www.bbc.com/korean/media-58430776 (accessed 22 Sept. 2023).

6. Ŏm Ju-yŏp, '21seginŭn nuga tŏ yŏllin sahoe ro kanŭnyaesŏ sŭngbu' (2016); Anatoliy Zhurin, 'Sdelan v SSSR' [Made in the USSR], *Sovershenno sekretno*, 9, no. 268 (2011), https://web.archive.org/web/20150628072203/http://www.sovsekretno.ru/articles/id/2889 (accessed 22 Sept. 2023). Zhurin's article is based on the interview his friend Boris Krishtul conducted with General Nikolay Lebedev in 1984.

7. Hilary Conroy, *The Japanese Seizure of Korea, 1868–1910: A Study of Realism and Idealism in International Relations*, Pennsylvania: University of Pennsylvania Press, 1960, p. 367.

8. Chŏng Il-sŏng, 'Hasegawa Yoshimich'i', in *Inmullo pon ilche Chosŏn chibae 40nyŏn* [Forty years of Japanese rule in Korea: Personal portraits], P'aju: Chishik saŏp sa, 2010, pp. 155–84.

9. 'Stories of Cruelty (March 20)', in *The Korean 'Independence' Agitation: Articles Reprinted from the Seoul Press*, Keijo: Seoul Press, 1919, p. 4.

10. 'Rikugun gawa chōsa ni kakaru Ōryoku-kō engan chihō Shina chi ni okeru zaijū Chōsenjin no toguchi sono ta ni kansuru ken' [Cases related to Korean households residing on the Chinese side of the Yalu River and others, in relationship with the investigation of the army], 1925, p. 24, http://db.history.go.kr/id/haf_095_0230 (accessed 22 Sept. 2023).

11. Ibid.

12. On Zhang Zuolin, see Chi Man Kwong, *War and Geopolitics in Interwar Manchuria: Zhang Zuolin and the Fengtian Clique during the Northern Expedition*, Leiden: Brill, 2017.

13. 'Rikugun ...' (1925), p. 24.

14. The average income in Manchuria at the time was about 16 silver US dollars per month, and the exchange rate was about 2.44 yen per

dollar. See Robert C. Allen et al., 'Wages, Prices, and Living Standards in China, 1738–1925: In Comparison with Europe, Japan and India', London School of Economics, Working Papers no. 123/09, July 2009, http://eprints.lse.ac.uk/27871/1/WP123.pdf (accessed 22 Sept. 2023), and 'Exchange Rates between the United States Dollar and Forty-One Currencies', MeasuringWorth, https://www.measuringworth.com/datasets/ exchangeglobal (accessed 22 Sept. 2023).

15. Traditionally, the navy was more liberal than the army, and appointing a retired naval officer seemed like a good compromise between the armed forces and civilian officials. The background to Saito's appointment is discussed in an excellent study by Chon Sang-suk: *Chŏn Sang-suk, Chosŏn ch'ongdok chŏngch'i yŏn'gu* [Study of the policy of the governor-generals of Korea], P'aju: Chisik sanŏpsa, 2012, pp. 127–31.

16. See the chronological table in Suh's classic biography of *Kim Il-sung: Dae-Sook Suh, Kim Il Sung: The North Korean Leader*, New York: Columbia University Press, 1988, p. 333.

17. Chen Zhiyan, Liao Weiyu and Jia Chengsen, *Jin Richeng zai Jilin Yuwen Zhongxue* [Kim Il-sung's tenure in the Yuwen Middle School of the Jilin province], Jilin: Jilin yuwen zhongxue, 1997, p. 2.

2.   FROM MANCHURIA TO THE SOVIET UNION

1. Guo Fuchang and Wu Degang, *Jiaoyu gaige fazhanlun* [Reform and development of education], Shijiazhuang: Hebei jiaoyu chubanshe, 1996, p. 214.

2. Shang Yue, *Shang Yue shixue lunwen xuanji* [Selected works of Shang Yue on historiography], Beijing: Renmin chubanshe, 1984, p. 590.

3. Chen Zhiyan, Liao Weiyu and Jia Chengsen, *Jin Richeng zai Jilin Yuwen Zhongxue* (1997), p. 2.

4. Ibid.

5. Vladimir Lenin, *Imperializm kak vysshaya stadiya kapitalizma* [Imperialism, the highest stage of capitalism], in *Polnoye sobraniye sochineniy* [Complete collection of works], 5th edn, vol. 27, Moscow: Gosudarstvennoye izdatel'stvo politicheskoy literatury, 1969, pp. 299–426.

6. Zhurin, 'Sdelan v SSSR' (2011).

7. Lee Yong-sang, *Samsaek-ŭi kunbok* [Three colours of the uniform], Seoul:

Hanjulgi, 1994, p. 5. Lee Yong-sang, the author of these memoirs, knew Kim Yong-ju personally. He only learned his real name—and that he was Kim Il-sung's brother—in 1945. In the years to come, this accidental acquaintance proved useful, as the South Korean government, including President Park Chung-hee, took an interest in him. Fully understanding his duty to history, Lee Yong-sang wrote these memoirs cautiously, recalling every meeting with Yong-ju in the most detailed and neutral way possible.

8. Kobayashi Kazuko, 'Atakushi-wa Kin Nissei shushō-no komazukai datta' [I was a maid of Premier Kim Il-sung], in *Zaigai hōjin hikiage-no kiroku: Kono sokoku-e-no setsu naru bojō* [Records of the evacuation of the overseas compatriots: Desperate love for the motherland], Tokyo: Mainichi Shimbunsha, 1970, pp. 119–22. Kazuko, who served in Kim Il-sung's house in 1946, recalled that Yong-ju's Japanese had been indistinguishable from that of a native speaker.

9. Lee Yong-sang, *Samsaek-ŭi kunbok* (1994), p. 259.

10. Zai Kitsurin sōryōkikan [Consulate-General in Jilin], 'Chōsen Kyōsan seinenkai soshiki no ken' [The case of the formation of the Korean Youth Communist Society], in *Gaimushō keisatsushi* [History of the police of the Foreign Ministry], vol. 13.3, *Manshū no bu* [Manchurian Bureau], Tokyo: Fuji Shuppan, 1997, pp. 172–3, lists 9640–3.

11. Leonid Vasin, 'Tovarisch kapitan' [Comrade Captain], *Sovershenno sekretno*, no. 7 (1991), p. 25.

12. 'Lichnoye delo Tszin Zhi-chena' [Jin Richeng's personal file], Russian State Archive of Socio-Political History, collection 495, inventory 238, file 60.

13. Zai Kitsurin sōryōkikan, 'Chōsen Kyōsan seinenkai soshiki no ken' (1997), pp. 172–3, lists 9640–3.

14. In other words, both his original and new names were 'Kim Song-ju', but the first one was spelt as 金聖柱 and the second one as 金成柱. The second character was different. For the second variant of the name, see *Gaiji keisatsu-hō dai hyakunijuyon gō* [Bulletin of foreign and police affairs, issue 124], 1932, p. 83, https://www.digital.archives.go.jp/das/image/F0000000000000093102 (accessed 22 Sept. 2023).

15. Chang Se-yun, 'Chosŏn Hyŏngmyŏnggun yŏn'gu' [Study of the Korean Revolutionary Army], in *Han'guk tongnip undongsa yŏn'gu* [Studies of the

Korean independence movement], vol. 4, Chonan: Tongnip Kinyŏmgwan Han'guk Tongnip Undongsa Yŏn'guso, 1990, pp. 315–43.

16. 'Chōsen kyōsan-tō kankei' [Things related to the Communist Party of Korea], in *Nippon Kyōsan-tō kankei zakken* [Various matters related to the Communist Party of Japan], vol. 5, n.p.: n.p., 1930, section 5, p. 485, https://www.jacar.archives.go.jp/aj/meta/image_B04013181300 (accessed 22 Sept. 2023).

17. Lee Myŏng-yŏng, *Pukkoe koesu Kim Il-sŏng chŏngch'e: 4inŭi 'Kim Il-sŏng'e kwanhan yŏn'gu* [The true nature of Kim Il-sung, head of the North Korean puppet regime: A study of four Kim Il-sungs], Seoul: Minjok munhwasa, 1975, pp. 108–9. While the quality of Lee Myŏng-yŏng's research is questionable—he credits most of Kim Il-sung's career in the 1930s and the early 1940s to other people—this information seems to be trustworthy. Lee directly quotes Kim's education in the lyceum of South Manchuria from an interview with an eyewitness, and Kim Song-ju's affiliation with Lee Jong-nak is further corroborated by contemporary Japanese documents.

18. *Gaiji keisatsu-hō* ... (1932), p. 83.

19. Chō Kōhō [Zhang Hongpeng], 'Endō Saburō to Manshū-koku' [Endo Saburo and Manchukuo], *Journal of Modern Chinese Studies*, 5, no. 2 (2013), pp. 35–55, https://aichiu.repo.nii.ac.jp/record/8630/files/04%20 %E5%BC%B5%E9%B4%BB%E9%B5%AC.pdf (accessed 22 Sept. 2023).

20. Chōsen sōtokufu keimukyoku [Police Department of the Government-General of Korea], *Kokugai-ni okeru yogi Chōsenjin meibo* [List of suspicious Koreans living abroad], Keijo: Gyōsei gakkai, 1934.

21. 'Lichnoye delo ...', p. 12.

22. 'Zhongguo Gongchandang Dangzhang' [Constitution of the Communist Party of China], in 'Zhonggong Zhongyang Wenjian Xuanji Si' [Document collection IV of the Central Committee of the Communist Party of China], http://cpc.people.com.cn/GB/64162/64168/64558/4428362. html (accessed 22 Sept. 2023).

23. Gao Qianyi, 'Wang Delin', Zhongguo Junwang [Chinese Military Network], http://www.81.cn/yljnt/2018–02/14/content_7945180.htm (accessed 22 Sept. 2023).

24. 'Lichnoye delo ...', p. 12.

25. Li Yanlu (1895–1985), a native of Jilin province, was a soldier from

1919 and then an officer of the military; he later worked in the police troops in Jilin. In 1931, he joined the CPC and was sent to Wang Delin's army. After the defeat of Wang Delin's troops, Li Yanlu was one of the organisers of the partisan movement in Manchukuo. In 1936, he left for Moscow, then stayed in an unoccupied part of China, the USSR and Europe, before settling in Yan'an after 1938. After the war, Li held leading administrative positions in North East China.

26. Zhou Baozhong (1902–64), a Chinese politician of Bai ethnic origin, born in Yunnan, joined the Communist Party in 1927 and studied in the USSR in 1928–31. He was later one of the leaders of the partisan movement in Manchuria and a member of the local Communist Party organisation. In 1937–41, he was the chief commander of the Second Route Army of the North East Anti-Japanese United Army and the secretary of the Communist Party's Committee for East Manchuria. In 1940, Zhou Baozhong moved to the territory of the USSR; in 1942, he was appointed the commander of the Red Army's Eighty-Eighth Separate Infantry Brigade, where Kim Il-sung served under his command.

27. Xiao Xue and Liu Jianxin, *Ranshaode heitude: Dongbei kangzhan jishi* [Burning black land: A documentary on the North East War of Resistance], Beijing: Tuanjie chubanshe, 1995, p. 131; 'Stenogramma zasedaniya politsekretariata IKKI' [Stenographic record of meeting of the political secretariat of the Executive Committee of the Communist International], in *VKP (b), Komintern i Kitay: Dokumenty*; 1931–1937 [All-Union Communist Party (Bolsheviks), Communist International and China: Documents, 1931–7], Moscow: ROSSPEN, 2006, pp. 230–41.

28. Ryŏ Jŏng, *Pulgke muldŭn Taedonggang* [The Taedong River runs red], Seoul: Tonga Ilbosa, 1991, p. 112.

29. 'Yugongja chŏngbo: Kim Il-sŏng' [Information about a meritorious person: Kim Il-sung], Ministry of Patriots & Veterans Affairs, http://e-gonghun.mpva.go.kr/user/ContribuReportDetail.do?goTocode=20001&mngNo=7201 (accessed 22 Sept. 2023).

30. 'Kohŏn shilgi' [Kohŏn's true records], *Tongnip kinyŏmgwan*, p. 3, https://search.i815.or.kr/sojang/read.do?isTotalSearch=Y&book=&adminId=1-000919-002#infomation (accessed 22 Sept. 2023).

31. Kim Chŏng-u, National Institute of Korean History, http://db.history.go.kr/id/im_101_03235 (accessed 22 Sept. 2023).

32. *Kanpō* [Official gazette], 31 May 1911, Colonial government of Korea, http://dl.ndl.go.jp/info:ndljp/pid/2951737/6 (accessed 22 Sept. 2023).

33. *Chosŏn-ŭi Nap'olleong Kim Kyŏng-ch'ŏn Changgun* [Commander Kim Kyong-chon, Korea's Napoleon], YTN, 27 Jan. 2019, https://www.youtube.com/watch?v=Q0HBuRVjCVA (accessed 22 Sept. 2023).

34. The last years of Kim Hyon-chung's life can be reconstructed through this memorial database of victims of Stalin's terror: Kim Ken Chen [Kim Kyŏng-ch'ŏn], 'Otkrutyy spisok' [Open list], https://ru.openlist.wiki/%D0%9A%D0%B8%D0%BC_%D0%9A%D0%B5%D0%BD_%D0%A7%D0%B5%D0%BD_(1885) (accessed 22 Sept. 2023). Kim Kyŏng-ch'ŏn is another alias of Kim Hyon-chung.

35. *Chosŏn-ŭi ...* (27 Jan. 2019).

36. Lee Yong-sang, 'Che85hwa: Naŭi ch'in'gu Kim Yŏng-ju; 'Kim Il-sŏng' ŭro tun'gap' [Episode 85: My friend Kim Yong-ju; Becoming 'Kim Il-sung'], *Chungang Ilbo*, 27 May 1991, p. 9, https://news.joins.com/article/2567178 (accessed 1 Oct. 2020).

37. Wangqing fanri youjidui [Wangqing Anti-Japanese Partisan Unit], Jilin Sheng difangzhi bianzuan weiyuanhui [Jilin Provincial Local Chronicles Compilation Committee], http://dfz.jl.gov.cn/jldywh/dbkl/201806/t20180606_5217625.html (accessed 1 Oct. 2020).

38. 'Zhonggong Dongman tewei shuji Feng Kang de baogao (zhi yi): Guanyu Dongman Tewei shudangtuan ganbu he Renmin Gemingjung anbu jianli (yijiusanwu nian shier yue ershi ri)' [Report of Feng Kang, secretary of the Special Committee for Eastern Manchuria of the Communist Party of China (Part 1); Resume on the party committee and the People's Revolutionary Army cadres of the Special Committee for Eastern Manchuria (20 Dec. 1935)], in *Dongbei diqu Geming Lishi Wenjian Huiji* [Documents of the revolutionary history of the north-east], vol. 67, Harbin: Heilongjiangsheng chubanzongshe, 1989, p. 180.

39. *Ch'angssi kaemyŏng* [Policy of adopting Japanese-style names], ed. Chŏng Un-hyŏn, Seoul: Hanminsa, 1994. This book, written in a clear and engaging style, is an exemplary study of the colonial era.

40. One of the better studies on this subject is C. Sarah Soh, *The Comfort Women: Sexual Violence and Postcolonial Memory in Korea and Japan*, Chicago: University of Chicago Press, 2008.

41. For an excellent study of the subject, see Chong-Sik Lee, 'Witch Hunt

among the Guerrillas: The Min-Sheng-T'uan Incident', *The China Quarterly*, 26 (Apr.–June 1966), pp. 107–17.

42. 'Zhonggong Dongman tewei shuji Feng Kang de baogao (zhi yi) ...', vol. 67 (1989), p. 180.

43. Lee, 'Witch Hunt among the Guerrillas', pp. 107–17.

44. 'Shōwa jūni nen go gatsu chū Kantō (Konshun ken wo fukumu) oyobi setsujō chihō chian jōkyō hōkoku no ken' [May 1937: Reports on security situation in Jiandao (including Hunchun) and near Heijō], p. 8, https://library.korea.ac.kr/kyungsung/index.php?id=46010268#dflip-ebook/31/ (accessed 22 Sept. 2023).

45. There is a conspiracy theory claiming that Kim Il-sung, the commander of the Sixth Division who organised the Pochonbo raid, was not the same person as the future ruler of North Korea. The following Japanese document provides definitive and final counterproof to this theory, as it states the birthplace of the Kim Il-sung who organised the raid, which is the same as that of Kim Il-sung of North Korea. See 'Kankyō-nandō kokkyō chitai sisō jōka kōsaku gaikyō' [An outlook on the work on ideological purification in the near border area of South Kankyō province], in 'Shisō ihō' [Ideological reports], vol. 20, 31 Aug. 1939, pp. 7–41, http://e-gonghun.mpva.go.kr/portal/url.jsp?ID=PV_SS_0020_00000005 (accessed 22 Sept. 2023).

46. 'Ponsa t'ŭkp'awŏn Pak Kŭm sugi o. Suji-e kŏlli-n p'okp'o ullim-e iljosŏkkyŏng' [Diary of our correspondent Pak Kum: Part 5; A stone trail through the forest of sorrow; Waterfalls among the trees and their branches], *Tonga Ilbo*, 7 Aug. 1929, p. 5.

47. 'Poch'ŏnbo p'isŭp sagŏn sokpo' [Breaking news about the attack on Pochonbo], *Tonga Ilbo*, 6 June 1937, p. 1.

48. Kankō chihō hōin [Kankō regional court], 'Keizan jiken hanketsu shosha' [Written sentence on the Keizan incident], 1941, pp. 70, 101.

49. Chōsen sōtoku fu Kankyō-nandō keisatsu bu [Police department of the South Kankyō province of the colonial government of Korea], 'Chūgoku kyōsan-tō no Chōsen nai jinmin sentō kessei oyobi nichishi jihen kōhō kakuran jiken' [Communist Party of China's organisation of anti-Japanese people's struggle in Manchuria and disturbances after the start of the Sino-Japanese War], Keijo: Chōsen sōtoku fu Kankyō-nandō keisatsu bu, 1940; 'Kankyō-nandō ...' (1939), pp. 7–41.

50. 'Poch'ŏnbo sŭpkyŏk sokpo' [Breaking: There has been an attack on

Pochonbo], *Tonga Ilbo*, 5 June 1937, p. 1; 'Kyōsan hi nihyaku mei ekkyō shi yūbinsho, gakkō nado-o osōfu: Zakkashō-o yuzuru-no hōka Keizansan jōryū Futenhō-o zenmetsu' [200 communist bandits cross the border and strike at post office, school: All inventory in a general store is burnt; Pochonbo fort, up the river from Hyesanjin, is annihilated], Keijō Nippō, 6 June 1937, p. 2; 'Poch'ŏnbo sagŏn sokpo' [Breaking: A report on the Pochonbo incident], Maeil Shinbo, 6 June 1937, p. 3.

51. 'Hamnam Poch'ŏnbo-rŭl sŭpkyŏk up'yŏnso, myŏnso-e ch'unghwa' [There has been an attack on Pochonbo (South Hamgyong): Post office and township office were burnt], *Tonga Ilbo*, 5 June 1937, p. 1.

52. 'Kim Il-sŏng p'isal?' [Was Kim Il-sung killed?], *Tonga Ilbo*, 18 Nov. 1937, p. 2.

53. 'Kankyō-nandō ...' (1939), pp. 7–41.

54. In some existing works, including Dae-sook Suh's biography of Kim Il-sung, General Nozoe's personal name is incorrectly given as 'Shotoku'.

55. Some information on Nozoe Masanori's biography can be obtained through an account written by his descendant Kanamori Ko: Kanamori Ko, 'Sofu-no mochimono-to sore-ni matsuwaru hanashi' [My grandfather's belongings and stories about them], http://alpha.bccks.jp/viewer/21896/ (accessed 22 Sept. 2023).

56. For some reason, in Suh Dae-sook's biography of Kim Il-sung this man's name is spelt as 'Fukube'.

57. Dae-Sook Suh, *Kim Il Sung* (1988), p. 24.

58. Keijō kōtō hōin kyoku shisō bu [Ideological section of the prosecution department of the Keijo High Court], 'Chūkyō-tō Nanman shō iinkai shoki ken Tōhoku kōnichi dai ichi rogun fuku shirei Gi Jōmin yori Kokujo kyōsan-tō Chūgoku daihyō iin-tō ni zutsu taru jōkyō tsuge (ichi kyū yon rei nen shi gatsu)' [Report on the current situation by Wei Zhengming, deputy commander of the First Route Army of the North East Anti-Japanese United Army and the secretary of the South Manchurian Committee of the Communist Party of China to the representative member of China in the Communist International (Apr. 1940)], in 'Shisō ihō' [Ideological reports], vol. 25, Dec. 1940, pp. 62–75.

59. Zhonggong Liaoning sheng weixuan chuanbu, Gongqingtuan Liaoning sheng weiyuanhui, Dongbei xinwen wang [Propaganda Department of the CPC Liaoning Provincial Committee, Communist Youth League Liaoning Provincial Committee, North East News Network], *Liaoning*

kangzhan wangshi [Memories of the anti-Japanese war in the Liaoning province], Shenyang: Liaoning Renmin chubanshe, 2015, p. 80

60. Keijō kōtō hōin kyoku shisō bu, 'Chūkyō-tō Nanman shō iinkai shoki ken Tōhoku ...' (Dec. 1940), pp. 62–75.

61. *Dongbei diqu Geming Lishi Wenjian Huiji* [Documents of the revolutionary history of the north-east], vol. 42, Harbin: Heilongjiangsheng chubanzongshe, 1991, p. 284. Volumes 40 to 43 of this collection contain the diaries of Zhou Baozhong, one of the commanders of the guerrilla resistance in Manchuria. They were also published in the PRC as a single volume; however, that edition (Zhou Baozhong, *Dongbei kangri youji riji* [Diary of the north-east Anti-Japanese guerrilla struggle], Beijing: Renmin chubanshe, 1991) was evidently censored, as some information present in the document collection was removed from it. Hence, I have instead used the more complete version found in this collection co-signed by the Central Archives of China and Archives of Heilongjiang, Jilin and Liaoning provinces: Zhou Baozhong, *Dongbei kangri youji riji* [Diary of the north-east anti-Japanese guerrilla struggle], Beijing: Renmin chubanshe, 1991, pp. 544–55.

62. Rin In [Lim Ŭn], *Kita Chōsen ōchō seiritsu hishi: Kin Nissei seiden* [The secret story of the creation of the North Korea dynasty: Kim Il-sung's true nature], Tokyo: Jiyusha, 1982, p. 56; *Chŭngŏn Kim Il-sŏng ŭl marhanda: Yu Sŏng-ch'ŏl I Sang-jo ga palk'in Pukhan chŏnggwŏn ŭi shilch'e* [Testimonies on Kim Il-sung: Yu Song-chol and Lee Sang-jo shed light on the North Korean regime], Seoul: Hanguk Ilbosa, 1991, pp. 69–70.

63. 'Kim Il-sŏng ŭi aech'ŏ ga kwisun' [Kim Il-sung's wife submits to the legal authorities], Chosŏn Ilbo, 5 July 1940, p. 2.

64. Rin In, *Kita Chōsen ōchō seiritsu hishi* ... (1982), p. 55.

65. Although North Korea later altered her birth year to 1917, her 1949 obituary gives the correct date of 1919. See 'Aedomun' [Obituary], *Rodong Shinmun*, 23 Sept. 1949, p. 2.

66. 'Lichnoye delo ...'

67. Ryŏ Jŏng, *Pulgke muldŭn Taedonggang* (1991), pp. 113–14; Georgiy Tumanov, 'Kak izgotovlyali velikogo vozhdya' [How the Great Leader was manufactured], *Novoye vremya*, no. 16, 1993, pp. 32–4. 'Georgiy Tumanov' was a pseudonym that was likely assumed by Soviet journalist Ivan Loboda, who was also known to be linked to Soviet intelligence.

68. 'Dongbei kang lian diyi lujun yuejing renyuan tongjibiao' [Statistical

table on the personnel of the First Route Army of the North East Anti-Japanese United Army crossing the border], in *Dongman diqu geming lishi wenxian huibian* [Compilation of documents on the revolutionary history of the area of Eastern Manchuria], vol. 1, Yanji: Zhonggong Yanbian zhouwei dang shi yanjiushi, 1988, p. 862.

69. 'Lichnoye delo ...'

70. 'Jin Richeng, An Ji, Xu Zhe gei Wang Xinlin de baogao' [A report from Kim Il-sung, An Gil and So Chol to Wang Xinlin], in *Dongbei diqu Geming Lishi Wenjian Huiji* [Documents of the revolutionary history of the north-east], vol. 60, Harbin: Heilongjiangsheng chubanzongshe, 1991, pp. 95–105; 'Perevod doklada predstaviteley Nan'man'skogo partiynogo komiteta (1-y ONRA)' [Translation of the report of the representatives of the South Manchuria party committee (First Anti-Japanese Route Army)], 1 Jan. 1941, Russian State Archive of Socio-Political History, collection 514, folder 1, item 1041, pp. 2–8.

71. 'Spravka K.F. Vilkova, I.P. Plyshevskogo, A.G. Zyuzina i A.I. Kogana "Sostoyaniye partiynyh organizatsiy i partizanskogo dvizheniya v Man'chzhurii"' [Reference letter of K.F. Vilkov, I.P. Plyshevskiy, A.G. Zyuzin and A.I. Kogan 'On the situation with the party organisations and the partisan movement in Manchuria'], 23 May 1941, Russian State Archive of Socio-Political History, collection 514, folder 1, item 944, pp. 14–104.

72. Georgi Dimitrov, *Dnevnik: 9 mart 1933–6 fevruari 1949* [The diary: 9 Mar. 1933–6 Feb. 1949], Sofia: Saint Clement of Ohrid, 1997, p. 220.

73. It is unknown whether either of these full names were actually used in daily life, as all available contemporary documents exclusively use 'Yura' to refer to him. See, for example, Kobayashi, 'Atakushi-wa Kin Nissei shushō-no komazukai datta' (1970), pp. 119–22.

74. Kim Ch'an-jŏng, 'Ppalch'isan man'ga: Kim Il-sŏng-gwa 88tongnip yŏdan' [Partisans' dirge: Kim Il-sung and the Eighty-Eighth Separate Brigade], *Shindonga*, no. 7, 1992, pp. 360–87.

75. Igor Morozov, 'Koreyskiy poluostrov: Shvatka vnich'yu' [The Korean Peninsula: A draw fight], in *NKVD*, no. 22 (1995), pp. 42–9.

76. Nikitenko's order certificate confirms that he was a medic (platoon commander in a medical company), held the rank of major and served in the same unit as Kim Il-sung. 'Frontovoy prikaz 10/n' [Front order 10/n], 29 Aug. 1945, Central Archive of the Ministry of Defence of Russia, collection 33, inventory 687572, item 2317.

77. Kim Ch'an-jŏng, 'Ppalch'isan ...' (1992), pp. 360–87.

78. Li Zaide was a Chinese Korean woman; her Korean name was Lee Chae-dŏk. She later worked in a government office under the PRC's parliament.

79. Kim Ch'an-jŏng, *Pigŭg-ŭi hangil ppalch'isan* [Tragic anti-Japanese partisans], Seoul: Tonga Ilbosa, 1992, p. 13.

80. Okeanskaya camp, evidently much smaller than the one at Vyatskoye, is referenced in Andrei Lankov's interview with Yu Sŏng-ch'ŏl, 18 Jan. 1991, Tashkent, and in 'Kin Nissei no katsudō jōkyō' [Current status of Kim Il-sung's activities], *Tokkō Geppō* [Monthly bulletin of the Special Higher Police], Nov. 1944, pp. 76–8.

81. *Kunan yu douzheng shisi nian* [Fourteen years of suffering and struggle], Beijing: Zhongguo dabaikequanshu chubanshe, 1995, p. 350.

82. Ibid., p. 351.

83. Dimitrov, *Dnevnik: 9 mart 1933* (1997), p. 244.

84. 'Jin Richeng gei Zhou Baozhong, Jin Ce de xin' [Kim Il-sung's report to Zhou Baozhong and Kim Chaek], in *Dongbei diqu Geming Lishi Wenjian Huiji* [Documents of the revolutionary history of the north-east], vol. 61, Harbin: Heilongjiangsheng chubanzongshe, 1990, pp. 371–81.

85. 'Zhou Baozhong-zhi Wang Xinlin-de xin' [Letter of Zhou Baozhong to Wang Xinlin], in *Dongbei diqu Geming Lishi Wenjian Huiji* [Documents of the revolutionary history of the north-east], vol. 65, Harbin: Heilongjiangsheng chubanzongshe, 1990, p. 338; 'Zhou Baozhong-gei Jin Ce, Zhang Shoufa-de xin' [Letter of Zhou Baozhong to Kim Chaek and Zhang Shoufa], in *Dongbei diqu Geming Lishi Wenjian Huiji* [Documents of the revolutionary history of the north-east], vol. 65, Harbin: Heilongjiangsheng chubanzongshe, 1990, p. 347.

86. *Dongbei diqu Geming Lishi Wenjian Huiji* [Documents of the revolutionary history of the north-east], vol. 42, Harbin: Heilongjiangsheng chubanzongshe, 1990, pp. 393–4.

87. Xu Wanmin, *Zhong-Han guanxishi* [History of Sino-Korean relations], Beijing: Shehui kexue wenxian chubanshe, 1996, p. 261.

88. *Dongbei diqu* ..., vol. 43 (1991), p. 7.

3.   IN THE USSR

1. Pyotr Grigorenko, 'Dal'nevostochnyy front 1941–43 gg.' [Far Eastern Front, 1941–3], in *V podpol'ye mozhno vstretit' tol'ko krys* [There are

nothing but rats in the underground], n.p.: n.p., 1981, http://militera. lib.ru/memo/russian/grigorenko/20.html (accessed 22 Sept. 2023). Pyotr Grigorenko was a Soviet officer who served on the Far Eastern Front. In 1959, he was promoted to the rank of Major-General (one star). General Grigorenko became one of the most famous critics of the CPSU regime and an active participant in the dissident movement. In 1977, when Grigorenko was in the United States, he was stripped of his Soviet citizenship and forced to remain in America. His memoirs are a unique source on the situation in the Soviet Far East during the war with Germany.

2. One of many works on the subject is Nikolay Cherushev, *1937 god: Elita Krasnoy Armii na Golgofe* [1937: The Red Army's elite faces its Golgotha], Moscow: Veche, 2003.

3. On Shtern's fate, see Ilya Kuksin, 'General-polkovnik Grigoriy Mihaylovych Shtern' [Colonel-General Grigoriy Shtern], *Zhurnal-gazeta 'Masterskaya'*, http://club.berkovich-zametki.com/?p=34230 (accessed 22 Sept. 2023); Pyotr Grigorenko, 'Dal'niy Vostok' [The Far East], in *V podpol'ye mozhno vstretit' tol'ko krys* [There is nothing but rats in the underground], http://militera.lib.ru/memo/russian/grigorenko/16.html (accessed 22 Sept. 2023).

4. Grigorenko, 'Dal'nevostochnyy front 1941–43 gg.' (1981).

5. Ibid.

6. 'Dnevnikovyye zapisi generala armii I.R. Apanasenko' [Diary entries of I.R. Apanasenko, General of the Army], in *Arheograficheskiy Yezhegodnik za 1995 god* [Yearbook on archeography, 1995], n.p.: n.p., 1997, pp. 210–12.

7. As of 1942, the Soviet regulations stated that an infantry division was to have 11,641 men and a separate infantry brigade of 5,000 men. See 'Postanovleniye GKO SSSR № 1229ss "O formirovanii novyh 50 strelkovyh diviziy i 100 kursantskih brigad"' [Decision of the State Committee for Defence of the USSR no. 1229 (top secret) 'On the formation of fifty new infantry divisions and 100 cadet brigades'], 1 Feb. 1942, Russian State Archive of Socio-Political History, collection 644, folder 1, item 20, pp. 153–9, and 'Postanovleniye GKO ot 14 aprelya 1942 goda №GKO-1603ss "Ob organizatsii, shtatnom sostave i vooruzhenii otdel'noy strelkovoy brigady"' [Decision of the State Committee for Defence no. SCF-1603 (top secret) 'On the organisation, staffing and

armament of a separate infantry brigade'], Russian State Archive of Socio-Political History, collection 644, folder 1, item 30, p. 127.

8. In an interview with Andrei Lankov (1 Feb. 1990, Moscow), Russian military historian Georgiy Plotnikov stated that Kim Il-sung had studied at Khabarovsk Military Infantry Academy in 1942. However, I have conducted an extensive search in the Russian archives and have found no evidence to corroborate this statement. The academy's records make no mention of Kim or any other partisan; moreover, they explicitly state there had been no Chinese or Korean students in the academy in either the spring or summer of 1942. See 'Doneseniye o spisochnoy chislennosti Habarovskogo pehotnogo uchilishcha po sostoyaniyu na 1 iyulya 1942 g.' [Report on the registered number of personnel attached to the Khabarovsk Military Infantry Academy as of 1 July 1942], Central Archive of the Ministry of Defence of Russia, collection 60096, inventory 35188, file 7, p. 113. The records do not appear to have been tampered with in any way. Given this, and also the fact that the academy's graduates were given, at most, the rank of lieutenant, while Kim Il-sung was commissioned as captain and his superior Zhou Baozhong as lieutenant-colonel, it would appear that Plotnikov was mistaken.

9. Bai people are one of the ethnic minorities of China. Most Bai people live in South West China; thus Zhou Baozhong's ethnicity was even more unusual for Manchuria.

10. On Chai's biography, see 'Chai Shilong', *Lishi shang di jintian* [Today's history], 2016, http://www.todayonhistory.com/people/201708/27890.html (accessed 22 Sept. 2023).

11. After 1945, Kang became the first chief of staff of the North Korean Army. He died during the first months of the Korean War.

12. Andrei Lankov's interview with Kang Sang-ho, 7 Mar. 1990, Leningrad; Grigorenko, 'Dal'nevostochnyy front 1941–43 gg.' (1981).

13. Lankov's interview with Georgiy Plotnikov, 1 Feb. 1990, Moscow.

14. 'Kim Pong-nyul tongji ŭi sŏgŏ e taehan pugo' [Obituary on the passing of Comrade Kim Pong-nyul], *Chosŏn Inmin'gun*, 20 July 1995, p. 4.

15. Lankov's interview with Plotnikov, 1 Feb. 1990, Moscow.

16. *Dongbei diqu* ..., vol. 43 (1991), p. 57.

17. 'Zhou Baozhong-gei Ji Qing, Chai Shirong, Jin Richeng, An Ji, Cui Xian, Piao Deshan, Guo Chishan-de xin (1942nian 3yue 31ri)' [Letters from Ji Qing, Chai Shirong, Kim Il-sung, An Gil, Ch'oe Hyŏn, Pak

Tŏk-san and Kwak Chi-san to Zhou Baozhong]. Quoted from *Zhongguo-Chaoxian·Hanguo guanxishi* [History of China's relations with North and South Korea], vol. 2, Tianjin: Tianjin Renmin chubanshe, 2001, p. 882.

18. *Dongbei diqu …*, vol. 43 (1991), pp. 69–71.

19. Ibid., p. 71.

20. Kim Ch'an-jŏng, *Pigŭg-ŭi hangil ppalch'isan* (1992), p. 82.

21. 'Kanglian Diyilujun Lüeshi' [Short history of the First Route Army], in *Dongbei Kangri Lianjun shiliao* [Historical documents on the North-East Anti-Japanese United Army], Beijing: Zhonggong dangshi ziliao chubanshe, 1987, pp. 665–79.

22. Jin Yuzhong was a Chinese Korean with the Korean name of Kim U-jong.

23. Kim Ch'an-jŏng, *Pigŭg-ŭi …* (1992), p. 81.

24. 'Kanglian Diyilujun Lüeshi' (1987), pp. 665–79.

25. Wang Minggui, *Tapo xingan wanzhongshan* [Advancing through mountains of Xing'an], Harbin: Heilongjiang Renmin chubanshe, 1988, pp. 221–3.

26. 'Vypiska iz plana ispol'zovaniya 88-y otdel'noy strelkovoy brigady Dal'nevostochnogo fronta s nachalom boyevyh deystviy' [Excerpts from the plan to use the Eighty-Eighth Separate Infantry Brigade of the Far Eastern Front in case of military action], Central Archive of the Ministry of Defence of Russia, collection 2, inventory 17582, folder 1, pp. 8–12. I obtained this document as a blurred photocopy, and thus the inventory and folder number might be incorrect.

27. Wang Minggui, *Tapo xingan wanzhongshan* (1988), p. 219.

28. '6·25ttae Pukhan'gun chakchŏn kukchang Yu Sŏng-ch'ŏl / "Na ŭi chŭngŏn": 1' [Yu Song-chol, chief of department of operations of the KPA during the Korean War: 'My testimony', part 1], *Han'guk Ilbo*, 1 Nov. 1990, https://www.hankookilbo.com/News/Read/199011010041424744 (accessed 22 Sept. 2023).

29. Kim Ch'an-jŏng, 'Ppalch'isan …' (1992), pp. 360–87.

30. E. Katyshevtseva and K.-H. Min, 'Partiyno-politicheskaya rabota v 88-y strelkovoy brigade i Kim Ir Sen (1942–1945 gg.)' [Political training of the party members in the Eighty-Eighth Brigade and Kim Il-sung (1942–5)], *Voprosy istorii*, 9, 2018, pp. 101–22.

31. Kim Ch'an-jŏng, 'Ppalch'isan …' (1992), pp. 360–87.

32. Ibid.

33. 'Kin Nissei no katsudō jōkyō' [Current status of Kim Il-sung's activities],

Tokkō Geppō [Monthly bulletin of the Special Higher Police], Nov. 1944, pp. 76–8.

34. Andrei Lankov's interview with Yu Sŏng-ch'ŏl, 18 Jan. 1991, Tashkent.

35. After the fall of the communist regime in the USSR, Vyatskoye attracted considerable attention from scholars and journalists looking for information about Kim Il-sung's past. Such demand attracted a fraudster, a woman called Avgustina Segeeyevna Varduchina, who started telling journalists that she used to be a close friend of the Kims. In fact, she moved to Vyatskoye after 1945 and had never met any of them; thus her stories often contradicted the established narrative, puzzling many researchers. Sadly, the materials exposing her true nature were printed in a book published in a mere 200 copies in Kyrgyzstan and thus remained unknown for years, while Varduchina's fake stories lived on. See Geron Li, *Velikoye pokayaniye* [The great confession], Bishkek: ID Salam, 2005, p. 372.

36. Georgiy Tumanov, 'Kak izgotovlyali velikogo vozhdya' [How the Great Leader was manufactured], *Novoye vremya*, no. 16, 1993, pp. 32–4.

37. Sofiya Ivanova-Shershneva, *Davno minuvscheye* [Things long gone], Uglich: Lulu.com, 2013, p. 63.

38. 'Dokumenty o rasformirovanii 88 otdel'noy strelkovoy brigady' [Documents on the dissolution of the Eighty-Eighth Separate Infantry Brigade], Central Archive of the Ministry of Defence of Russia, collection 1896, folder 1, item 2, p. 97.

39. 'O veteranah 88-oy otdel'noy strelkovoy brigady' [On veterans of the Eighty-Eighth Separate Infantry Brigade], Association of Indigenous People of the North of Khabarovsk Region, https://shorturl.at/4xopz (accessed 22 Sept. 2023).

40. One wonders if, back in the 1940s, the Eighty-Eighth Brigade had been properly supplied or if Kim Il-sung himself had experienced first-hand the hardship of looking after the animals, perhaps future North Korean soldiers would have been spared all the time spent on farming. See Konstantin Tertitski and Fyodor Tertitskiy, 'Kim Il-sung in the Soviet Army: His Experience and Its Impact on His Future Policy in the KPA and North Korea', *Journal of Cold War Studies*, 26, no. 2 (2024), pp. 4–25.

41. Tumanov, 'Kak izgotovlyali velikogo vozhdya' (1993), pp. 32–4.

42. '88 otdel'naya strelkovaya brigada (vtorogo formirovaniya)' [Eighty-

Eighth Separate Infantry Brigade (second iteration)], Central Archive of the Ministry of Defence of Russia, collection 1896, folder 1, item 1, p. 2.

43. 'Rasporyazheniye nachal'nika shtaba Glavnogo komandovaniya sovetskimi voyskami na Dal'nem Vostoke Voyennomu Sovetu Zabaykal'skogo fronta s informatsiyey ob ispol'zovanii na razvedrabote kitaytsev i koreytsev 88-y brigady' [Ordinance of the chief of staff of the high command of the Soviet troops in the Far East to the Military Council of the Transbaikal Front with information on the use of Chinese and Korean personnel of the Eighty-Eighth Brigade in the intelligence], Central Archive of the Ministry of Defence of Russia, collection 66, folder 178499, item 11, p. 322. Quoted from V.N. Vartanov and A.N. Pochtaryov, '"Stalinskiy spetznaz": 88-ya otdel'naya strelkovaya brigada' ['Stalin's Special Forces': Eighty-Eighth Separate Infantry Brigade], in *Novyy chasovoy*, no. 5, 1997, pp. 178–9; 'Arhivnoye sledstvennoye delo v otnoshenii Tsai-Shi-Yuna' [An archived investigation case against Chai Shirong], Central Archive of the Russian Federal Security Service, item N-17437. Although access to this archive is restricted, I received the outline of the contents of the case after filing a formal request with the archive.

44. This Japanese report mentions the Okeanskaya base but has no mention of either Vyatskoye or the brigade. 'Kin Nissei ...' (1944), pp. 76–8.

45. Kim Ch'an-jŏng, 'Ppalch'isan ...' (1992), pp. 360–87.

46. Ryŏ Jŏng, *Pulgke muldŭn Taedonggang* (1991), p. 118; Kim Ch'an-jŏng, 'Ppalch'isan ...' (1992), pp. 360–87.

47. Mark Barry, 'The U.S. and the 1945 Division of Korea', NK News, 12 Feb. 2012, https://www.nknews.org/2012/02/the-u-s-and-the-1945-division-of-korea/ (accessed 22 Sept. 2023).

48. Ibid.

49. Ibid.; Lee Wan-bŏm, *Samp'al sŏn hoekchŏngŭi chinshil*, 1944–1945 [The demarcation though the 38th parallel: The true story, 1944–5], Seoul: Chishik sanŏpsa, 2001.

50. Barry, 'U.S. and the 1945 Division of Korea' (12 Feb. 2012).

51. 'Pis'mo komandira 88-y otdel'noy brigady glavnokomanduyuschemu Sovetskimi voyskami na Dal'nem Vostoke s predlozheniyami po ispol'zovaniyu brigady' [A letter of the commanding officer of the Eighty-Eighth Separate Infantry Brigade to the commander-in-chief of the Soviet forces in the Far East with suggestions on using the brigade], Central Archive of the Ministry of Defence of Russia, collection

66, inventory 3191, folder 2, pp. 14–15. Quoted from Vartanov and Pochtaryov, '"Stalinskiy spetznaz" ...' (1997).

52. Rodion Malinovskiy and Aleksandr Tevchenko, 'Doneseniye komanduyuschego voyskami Zabaikal'skogo fronta glavnokomanduyuschemu Sovetskimi voyskami na Dal'nem Vostoke o priyome komandira 88-y brigady' [A report of the commander of the Transbaikal Front to the commander-in-chief of the Soviet forces in the Far East on the audience granted to the commander of the Eighty-Eighth Brigade], 3 Oct. 1945, Central Archive of the Ministry of Defence of Russia, collection 66, inventory 178499, folder 11, p. 384.

53. One of the victims was Peng Shilu, former company commander in the Eighty-Eighth Brigade who later became a Major-General in the Chinese Army. Zhongguo lishiwang [History Network of China], 'Peng Shilu: Henan ji jiangling renwu chuanji jianjie' [Peng Shilu: An introduction to the biography of the general from Henan], 22 Oct. 2017, http://lishi. zhuixue.net/2017/1022/72253.html (accessed 22 Sept. 2023).

54. 'Sovetskiye koreytsy, nahodivschiyesya v sostave 88-y osbr (s. Vyatskoye), prednaznachennye dlya raboty v Koreye' [Soviet Koreans, who used to serve in the Eighty-Eighth Separate Infantry Brigade (Vyatskoye village) and are to work in Korea], 31 Aug. 1945, Central Archive of the Ministry of Defence of Russia, collection 2, inventory 19121, folder 2, p. 15.

55. 'Spisok lichnogo sostava 1-go batal'ona 88-y otd. str. Brigady 2-go Dal'nevostochnogo fronta, prednaznachennogo dlya raboty v Koreye' [A list of personnel of the Eighty-Eighth Separate Infantry Brigade which is to be dispatched to work in Korea], Central Archive of the Ministry of Defence of Russia, collection 3, inventory 19121, folder 2, pp. 14–15; Serafim Chuvyrin and Mikhail Ankudinov, 'Iz doklada nachal'nika RO Stavki Glavnokomandovaniya Sovetskimi voyskami na Dal'nem Vostoke Marshalu Sovetskogo Soyuza A.M. Vasilevskomu' [From the report of the chief of the Reconnaissance Department of the staff of the high command of the Soviet forces in the Far East to A.M. Vasilevskiy, marshal of the Soviet Union], Central Archive of the Ministry of Defence of Russia, collection 3, inventory 19121, folder 2, pp. 3–4.

56. 'Frontovoy prikaz 10/n' [Front Order 10/n], 29 Aug. 1945, Central Archive of the Ministry of Defence of Russia, collection 33, inventory 687572, item 2317.

57. Built on 13 Apr. 1943 by the Oregon Shipbuilding Corporation, the ship

was christened *Louis Agassiz* after a famous Swiss geologist. After being given to the USSR on 21 Apr. in the same year, it was renamed after the leader of the late eighteenth-century peasant uprising in the Russian Empire, 'Yemel'yan Pugachyov (do 21.04.1943 g. "Louis Agassiz")' [Emelian Pugachev (Louis Agassiz before 21 Apr. 1943)], https://web. archive.org/web/20210621154310/http://www.sovnavy-ww2.ho.ua/ transports/typ_liberty.htm#pugachev (accessed 22 Sept. 2023).

58. *Yemel'yan Pugachyov* [Emelian Pugachev], 'PAO "Dal'nevostochnoye morskoye parohodstvo"' [Open joint-stock company 'Far Eastern Sea Shipping'], https://www.fesco.ru/about/history/fleet-roll/12043/ (accessed 22 Sept. 2023).

59. Vasiliy Ivanov, *V tylah Kvatunskoy armii* [In the rear of the Kwantung Army], Moscow: IDV RAN, 2009, p. 215.

60. Kim Ch'an-jŏng, *Ppalch'isan ...* (1992), pp. 360–87.

61. Ibid.

62. Ibid.

63. Vasin, 'Tovarisch kapitan' (1991), p. 25.

64. Ivanov, *V tylah Kvatunskoy armii* (2009), p. 215.

4. THE ASCENSION

1. 'Doneseniye komanduyuschego voyskami 1-go Dal'nevostochnogo fronta glavnokomanduyuschemu Sovetskimi voyskami na Dal'nem Vostoke s soobrazheniyami o poslevoennoy dislokatsii voysk na Dal'nem Vostoke' [A report from the commander of the First Far Eastern Front to the commander-in-chief of the Soviet armed forces in the Far East with some thoughts about the disposition of the armed forces for the post-war Far East], 24 Aug. 1945, Central Archive of the Ministry of Defence of Russia, collection 66, inventory 117499, folder 1, pp. 376–8.

2. Colonel-General was the Soviet equivalent rank of a three-star general.

3. Given that Chistyakov had visited Hamhung on the previous day to instruct the local Japanese garrison on the provisions and procedure of its surrender, it appears the general did not like the city—at least to the extent that he did not want his headquarters based there. Ivan Chistyakov, 'Neobychnoye zadaniye' [An unusual task], in *Sluzhim Otchizne* [Serving the fatherland], http://militera.lib.ru/memo/russian/chistyakov_im/19. html (accessed 22 Sept. 2023).

4. 'Zhurnal boyevyh deystviy 25 armii s 9 po 19 avgusta 1945 g. Prilozheniye k zhurnalu boyevyh deystviy' [War journal of the Twenty-Fifth Army, 9–19 Aug. (including attachment)], Central Archive of the Ministry of Defence of Russia, collection 379, folder 11019, item 9, pp. 35–7.

5. Georgiy Fyodorov and Yuriy Livshits, 'Dokladnaya zapiska' [Memorandum], in 'Raznyye materialy, postupivshiye iz Grazhdanskoy administratsii Severnoy Korei' [Various materials received from the civil administration for North Korea], 1945, Central Archive of the Ministry of Defence of Russia, collection 172, folder 614631, item 37, pp. 14–32.

6. Born in 1883, Cho Man-sik converted to Presbyterianism when he was twenty-two. He was studying in Tokyo when Korea was annexed by Japan. After graduating from Meiji University, Cho returned to Korea to become a teacher. He participated in the 1 Mar. 1919 uprising and spent a year in prison as a result. In later years, Cho Man-sik continued his political and educational activities, and his opposition to the conscription of Koreans into the imperial army briefly brought him back to prison in 1943. By 1945, he had become a well-known and influential independence activist.

7. 'Spravka o vrazhdebnyh partiyah, suschestvuyuschih v nastoyascheye vremya v Koree' [A reference on hostile parties existing in Korea at this time], in 'Dokumenty, harakterizuyuschiye politicheskiye partii i obschestvennyye organizatsii Severnoy Korei za 1945 g.' [Documents on political parties and public organisations of North Korea of 1945], Central Archive of the Ministry of Defence of Russia collection 172, folder 614630, item 5, pp. 17–18; Morita Yoshio, 'Chōsen sōtoku Abe Nobuyuki: Minami Chōsen no seijō to chian mondai' [Abe Nobuyuki, governor-general of Korea, on the political and security situation in the southern part of Korea], in Chōsen shūsen no kiroku [Chronicles of the end of war in Korea], Tokyo: Gannandō shoten, 1964, pp. 301–12.

8. 'Spravka o vrazhdebnyh ...', pp. 17–18.

9. 'Sotsial-demokraticheskaya partiya' [Social Democratic Party], in 'Dokumenty, harakterizuyuschiye politicheskiye partii i obschestvennyye organizatsii Severnoy Korei za 1945 g.' [Documents on political parties and public organisations of North Korea of 1945], Central Archive of the Ministry of Defence of Russia collection 172, folder 614630, item 5. pp. 74–6.

10. For research on East Austria, see Barbara Stelzl-Marx, Stalins Soldaten in Österreich [Stalin's soldiers in Austria], Vienna: Böhlau Verlag, 2012.

11. 'Pechat' i radio' [Media and radio], Central Archive of the Ministry of Defence of Russia, collection of the Directorate of the Soviet Civil Administration, folder 433847, item 1, pp. 64–70.

12. 'Marshalu Vasilevskomu, Voyennomu Sovetu Primorskogo voyennogo okruga, Voyennomu sovetu 25 armii' [To Marshal Vasilevskiy, Military Council of the Maritime District and the Military Council of the Twenty-Fifth Army], Central Archive of the Ministry of Defence of Russia, collection 148, folder 3763, item 111, pp. 92–3.

13. Andrei Smirnov, 'Kim Ir Sen—podkidysh: Kak Sovetskaya Armiya vnedrila v Severnuyu Koreyu prezidenta Kim Ir Sena i yego pravitel'stvo' [Kim Il-sung the foundling: How the Soviet Army implanted President Kim Il-sung and his government in North Korea], Sovershenno sekretno, 1992, pp. 10–11.

14. Zhurin, 'Sdelan v SSSR' (2011).

15. Andrei Lankov's interview with Kang Sang-ho, 31 Oct. 1989, Leningrad.

16. Gavriil Korotkov, 'Stalin i Koreyskaya voyna' [Stalin and the Korean War], in Voyna v Koreye 1950–1953 gg.: Vzlyad cherez 50 let [War in Korea of 1950–3: Looking back after fifty years], Tula: Grif i Ko, 2001, pp. 67–89. Korotkov mentions a number of Soviet documents in this conference report; however, he often fails to provide proper references to them, possibly because they were still classified when the volume was published. One of these documents was the list of candidates to the position of the supreme leader of North Korea. Judging by Korotkov's other works, it is probably kept in the Central Archive of the Ministry of Defence of Russia; however, at the time the current book was being written, it was impossible to locate the original document, and I have thus been forced to use Korotkov's work as a reference instead.

17. Andrei Lankov's interview with Ivan Loboda, Nov. 1990, Moscow.

18. Kim Yong-bom died in 1947. Pak Chong-ae, Chang Shi-u, Kim Du-bong and probably Yang Yong-sun were purged. Aleksei Hegay died either by suicide or assassination in 1953. Yu Song-chol, Pak Pyong-yul and Kim Chan returned to the USSR to avoid sharing the grim fate of the others. Pak Chong-ho stayed in South Korea during and after the Korean War and worked there as an illegal agent—again—before he was executed in 1959. See 'Pak Chŏng-ho', in Chosŏn Tae Paekkwa Sajŏn [Grand encyclopaedia of Korea], vol. 10, Pyongyang: Paekkwa sajŏn ch'ulp'ansa, 1999, p. 340. 'Pak Chŏng-ho kanch'ŏp sagŏn' [A case of

Pak Chong-ho, the spy], in *Han'guk minjok munhwa Tae Paekkwa Sajŏn* [Grand encyclopaedia of Korean national culture], http://encykorea.aks. ac.kr/Contents/Item/E0021133 (accessed 22 Sept. 2023). Kim Gwang-jin was the only one who actually enjoyed a long life in North Korea. He died as an academician of the Academy for Social Studies—one of the highest positions a North Korean academic could have aspired to. See 'Kim Gwang-jin', in *Chosŏn Tae Paekkwa Sajŏn*, vol. 4 (1996), pp. 148–9. Mikhail Kan quietly retuned to the USSR in 1947. See Andrei Lankov's interview with Mikhail Kan's son, Vitaliy Kan, 2 Feb. 2001, Moscow.

19. 'Puk Chosŏn Rodongdang chungang ponbu kyŏlchŏngsŏ sang ilguho' [Decision no. 19 of the central headquarters of the Workers' Party of North Korea], in *Pukhan kwan'gye saryojip* [Collection of North Korea-related historical documents], vol. 1, Seoul: Kuksa P'yŏnch'an Wiwŏnhoe, 1982, p. 477.

20. Andrei Lankov's interview with Yu Sŏng-ch'ŏl, 18 Jan. 1991, Tashkent; Chang Hak-pong, 'Yu Sŏng-ch'ŏl (chŏn Inmin'gun Ch'ongch'ammobu Chakchŏnkukchang kyŏm Puch'ongch'ammojang)' [Yu Song-chol (former chief of the operations department of the general staff of the KPA and deputy chief of staff)], in *Puk Chosŏn-ŭl mand-ŭn Koryŏin iyagi* [A story of Soviet Koreans who built North Korea], Seoul: Kyŏngin munhwasa, 2006, pp. 503–45. Chang Hak-pong was a high-ranking officer in the North Korean Army. This book is a collection of memoirs written by his former comrades. Compiled by a South Korea researcher Lee Shin-chol, it is a priceless source on the early history of North Korea.

21. Andrei Lankov's interview with Pak Pyŏng-yul, 25 Jan. 1990, Moscow; Chang Hak-pong, 'Pak Pyŏng-yul (chŏn Kangdong Chŏngch'i Hagwŏn wŏnjang)' [Pak Pyong-yul (former chief of Kangdong Political Academy)] in *Puk Chosŏn-ŭl mand-ŭn Koryŏin iyagi* (2006), pp. 367–75.

22. 'Chŏngnyŏng: Yang Yŏng-sun tongji-rŭl Ch'ek'osŭllobak'iya konghwaguk chujae Chosŏn Minjujuŭi Inmin Konghwagung t'ŭngmyŏng chŏn'gwŏn taesa-ro immyŏngha-me kwanha-yŏ' [Executive order: On appointing Comrade Yang Yong-sun to the position of ambassador extraordinary and plenipotentiary of the DPRK to the Republic of Czechoslovakia], *Rodong Shinmun*, 11 Mar. 1954, p. 1; 'Praha uvítala korejskou vládní delegaci' [Prague welcomed the Korean government delegation], *Rudé právo*, 22 June 1956, p. 1.

23. Andrei Lankov's interview with Kim Ch'an, 15 Jan. 1991, Tashkent;

Chang Hak-pong, 'Kim Ch'an (chŏn Chosŏn Chungang Ŭnhaeng ch'ongjae)' [Kim Chan (former head of Korean Central Bank)], in *Puk Chosŏn-ŭl mand-ŭn Koryŏin iyagi* (2006), pp. 114–18.

24.   Zhurin, 'Sdelan v SSSR' (2011).

25.   Svetlana Vasilyeva, 'Osobyy teatr boyevyh deystviy' [Special theatre of war], *Russkiy bazar*, no. 4 (875), http://russian-bazaar.com/ru/content/111461.htm (accessed 22 Sept. 2023).

26.   Andrei Pochtaryov, 'Taynyy sovetnik "solntsa natsii"' [A secret counsellor of the 'Sun of the Nation'], in *Nezavisimoye voyennoye obozreniye*, 14 Jan. 2005, https://www.ng.ru/history/2005-01-14/5_kim_ir_sen.html (accessed 22 Sept. 2023).

27.   Kabŭril K'orot'ŭk'op'ŭ [Gavriil Korotkov], *Sŭt'allin-gwa Kim Il-sŏng* [Stalin and Kim Il-sung], vol. 1, trans. Ŏ Kŏn-ju, Seoul: Tonga Ilbosa, 1992, p. 180. This book has only been published in Korean translation, with the Russian draft possibly having been written specifically to be translated. While the translation is poor, the book contains some unique testimonies about Kim Il-sung's ascension.

28.   'Spisok lichnogo ...', pp. 14–15.

29.   Andrei Lankov's interview with Nikolay Lebedev, 19 Jan. 1990, Moscow.

30.   'Myŏngsa ŭi p'yŏnyŏng, Kim Il-sŏng ssi' [A sign of the famous warrior, Kim Il-sung], *Minjung Ilbo*, 14 Oct. 1945, p. 1.

31.   'Sekretaryu TsK VKP/b/ tov. Malenkovu, zamestitelyu narodnogo komissara oborony—general-armii—tov. Bulganinu, nachal'niku Glavnogo politicheskogo upravleniya Krasnoy Armii general-polkovniku tov. Shikinu' [To Comrade Malenkov, Secretary of the Central Committee of the All-Union Communist Party (Bolsheviks), Comrade Bulganin, Deputy People's Commissar of Defence, General of the Army, comrade Shikin—head of the Main Political Department of the Red Army, Colonel-General], Central Archive of the Ministry of Defence of Russia, collection 172, inventory 614631, folder 23, pp. 21–6.

32.   Zhurin, 'Sdelan v SSSR' (2011).

33.   Andrei Lankov's interview with Nikolay Lebedev, 19 Jan. 1990, Moscow.

5.   THE NEW BEGINNING

1.   'Prikaz komanduyuschego Sovetskoy 25 armiyey v Severnoy Koreye' [Order of the commander of the Soviet Twenty-Fifth Army in North

Korea], Central Archive of the Ministry of Defence of Russia, collection of the Directorate of the Soviet Civil Administration, folder 433847, item 1, pp. 26–7.

2. 'Direktiva stavki Verhovnogo glavnokomanduyuschego Krasnoy Armiyey Glavnokomanduyushemu sovetskimi voyskami na Dal'nem Vostoke, voyennym sovetam Primorskogo voyennogo okruga i 25-y armii o vzaimootnosheniyah voysk s mestnymi organami vlasti i naseleniyem Severnoy Korei' [A directive of the supreme commander of the Red Army to the commander-in-chief of the Soviet troops in the Far East, military councils of the Maritime Military District and of the Twenty-Fifth Army on the relations between the military and the local organs of governance, as well as with the people of North Korea]. A copy of the document is available at Central Archive of the Ministry of Defence of Russia, collection 148, inventory 3763, folder 111, pp. 92–3.

3. Yuriy Livshits, 'Informatsionnaya svodka o sostoyanii kompartii v severnyh provintsiyah Korei' [Assessment reference on the current status of the Communist Party in the northern provinces of Korea], in 'Dokumenty, harakterizuyuschiye politicheskiye partii i obschestvennyye organizatsii Severnoy Korei za 1945 g.' [Documents on political parties and public organisations of North Korea of 1945], 20 Oct. 1945, Central Archive of the Ministry of Defence of Russia, collection 172, inventory 614630, folder 5, pp. 45–51.

4. Ibid.

5. Vasin, 'Tovarisch kapitan' (1991), p. 25.

6. Valeriy Yankovskiy, *Ot Groba Gospodnya do groba Gulaga: Byl'* [From the Lord's tomb to a tomb in the Gulag: True story], Kovrov: Mashteks, 2000, pp. 89–91.

7. Vladimir Ivanov-Ardashev, 'V teni vozhdey' [In the Leaders' shadow], *Literaturnaya gazeta*, no. 33, 2012, 23 Feb. 2015.

8. Vasin, 'Tovarisch kapitan', p. 25.

9. Zhurin, 'Sdelan v SSSR' (2011).

10. 'Paek Sŏn-yŏp-kwa Kim Hyŏng-sŏk, munmu 100nyŏn-ŭi taehwa' [Paek Sŏn-yŏp and Kim Hyŏng-sŏk: Centennial solider and scholar speak], *Chosŏn Ilbo*, 2 Jan. 2020, https://www.chosun.com/site/data/html_dir/2020/01/02/2020010200287.html (accessed 22 Sept. 2023).

11. While the text of this speech was later heavily distorted in the DPRK to accommodate the state's ideological goals, the following publication

appears to be an unedited version: 'Kim Il-sŏng changgun-ŭi yŏnsŏl yoji' [Memo of the speech of Commander Kim Il-sung], in *Chosŏn Chungang Nyŏn'gam 1949* [Korean central yearbook, 1949], Pyongyang: Chosŏn Chungang T'ongshinsa, 1949, p. 63.

12. Smirnov, 'Kim Ir Sen—podkidysh' (1992), pp. 10–11.

13. O Yŏng-jin, *So kunjŏng ha ŭi Pukhan: Hana ŭi chŭngŏn* [North Korea under the Soviet military administration: A testimony], Seoul: Kukt'o t'ongirwŏn, 1983, reprinted edn, pp. 90–3.

14. That this largely ceased being a popular belief was due to the South Korean government's more permissive policy towards the study of North Korea in the 1960s, thus enabling South Korean scholars to disprove the idea that Kim Il-sung was an imposter. See Fyodor Tertitskiy, 'The "Theory of Kim Il-sŏng the Impostor": A Historiographical Study', *Archiv orientální*, 90, no. 1 (2022), pp. 183–207.

15. Video of an interview with Grigoriy Mekler (Moscow, 2004), kindly provided to this author by Nick Holt.

16. Zhurin, 'Sdelan v SSSR' (2011).

17. Ibid.

18. Hong Sun-gwan, 'Chŏn Kim Il-sŏng pisŏ shiljang ch'unggyŏk kobaek' [Shocking revelation of the former executive secretary of Kim Il-sung], *Shindonga*, Oct. 1994, pp. 188–207. Despite the provocative headline, this is actually one of the most interesting and detailed testimonies on the politics of early North Korea.

19. Pak Pyŏng-yŏp, *Chosŏn Minjujuŭi Inmin Konghwaguk-ŭi t'ansaeng* [Birth of the Democratic People's Republic of Korea], Seoul: Sŏnin: 2010, p. 47.

20. Valentin Petuhov, *U istokov bor'by za yedinstvo i nezavisimost' Korei* [At the starting point of the struggle for unity and independence of Korea], Moscow: Nauka, 1987, p. 153.

21. Ibid.

22. Author's interview with Yuriy Kang, 25 Apr. 2021, online (Seoul–Chicago).

23. Andrei Lankov's interview with Kang Sang-ho, 13 Jan. 1990, Leningrad.

24. Author's interview with Yuriy Kang, 25 Apr. 2021, online (Seoul–Chicago).

25. Valentina Berezutskaya, 'Moy udel—tyotki iz naroda' [My fate is that of an average woman], *Karavan istoriy*, 5 Feb. 2018, https://7days.ru/caravan-collection/2018/2/valentina-berezutskaya-moy-udel-tetki-iz-naroda/7.htm (accessed 22 Sept. 2023).

26. Lee Yong-sang, *Samsaek-ŭi kunbok* [Three colours of the uniform], Seoul: Hanjulgi, 1994, pp. 248–50.

27. Ibid., p. 16.

28. *Kodang Cho Man-shik* [Cho 'Ancient Temple' Man-sik], Seoul: Kodang chŏn P'yŏngyang chigan haenghoe, 1966, p. 222.

29. Leonid Vasin, 'O sozyve organizatsionnogo sobraniya Demokraticheskoy partii Korei' [On the convocation of the foundational meeting of the Democratic Party of Korea], Central Archive of the Ministry of Defence of Russia, collection of the Directorate of the Soviet Civil Administration, inventory 433847, item 1, pp. 126–8.

30. Ham Sŏk-hŏn, 'Naega kyŏkkŭn Shinŭiju haksaeng sagŏn' [The student uprising in Shinuiju: My experience], *Ssiar-ŭi sori* [Voice of a seed], no. 6 (1971), pp. 33–48; Cho Tong-yŏng, 'Naega kyŏkkŭn Shinŭiju haksaeng pan'gong ŭigŏ' [The student righteous struggle against communism in Shinuiju: My experience], *Wŏlgan Pukhan* [North Korea monthly], no. 164, August 1985, pp. 50–5.

31. Fyodorov, Livshits, 'Dokladnaya zapiska', pp. 14–32.

32. Ibid.

33. 'Postanovleniye Voyennogo Soveta 25 armii Primorskogo voyennogo okruga' [A decision of the Military Council of the Twenty-Fifth Army of the Maritime Military District], 15 Jan. 1946, in 'Postanovleniya Voyennogo Soveta 25 armii za 1946 god' [Decisions of the Twenty-Fifth Army adopted in 1946], Central Archive of the Ministry of Defence of Russia, collection 25A, folder 532092, item 1, pp. 3–5.

34. That it did not happen earlier is evident, among other things, by the fact that in Dec. 1945 Kim Il-sung was still described by the Soviets as a 'notable party member, personally widely popular among the people', not as the inbound leader of the country. See 'Spravka-doklad o politicheskom polozhenii v Severnoy Koreye' [A reference report on the political situation in North Korea]. Document from the author's collection.

35. 'Kim Il-sŏng changgun ege ponaenun messeiji' [A message for Commander Kim Il-sung], *Chŏngno*, 14 Dec. 1945, p. 2.

36. 'Pun'guk ch'aegim pisŏ-e Kim Il-sŏng tongji ch'wiim' [Comrade Kim Il-sung appointed the chief secretary of the Branch Office], *Chŏngno*, 21 Dec. 1945, p. 1.

37. 'Kim Il-sŏng tongjiŭi pinnanŭn t'ujaengsa' [Bright history of struggle of Comrade Kim Il-sung], *Chŏngno*, 21 Dec. 1945, p. 1.

38. For example, a 1946 article claimed that Kim Il-sung had joined the Communist Party of Korea, not of China, in 1931, even though the Communist Party of Korea did not even exist at the time. N. Ignatova, 'V Severnoy Koreye' [In North Korea], in *Stalinskiy sokol*, 23 Oct. 1945, p. 4.

39. 'Report of the Meeting of the Ministers of Foreign Affairs of the Union of Soviet Socialist Republics, the United States of America, the United Kingdom', Lillian Goldman Law Library, http://avalon.law.yale.edu/20th_century/decade19.asp (accessed 22 Sept. 2023).

40. 'Kak Chŏngdang Haengdong T'ongil Wiwŏnhoe, shint'ak shilshi pandae kyŏrŭihago sŏngmyŏngsŏ palp'yo' [Committee of the multiple political parties to act towards unification adopts, signs and proclaims a resolution against the trusteeship policy], *Maeil Shinbo*, 29 Oct. 1945, http://db.history.go.kr/id/dh_001_1945_10_26_0010 (accessed 22 Sept. 2023).

41. 'Sinnyŏn ul majihamyŏnsŏ uri inmin ege turim' [A message for our people on the occasion of the New Year], *Chŏngno*, 1 Jan 1946, p. 1.

42. Further evidence that Shtykov was in charge is that both Chistyakov's successors at the position of commander of the occupation force in North Korea—Lieutenant-General Gennadiy Korotkov and Major-General Serafim Merkulov—did not influence policy in North Korea.

43. See, for example, 'Doneseniya o polozhenii v Severnoy Korei za 1947 god' [Reports on the situation in North Korea in 1947], Russian State Archive of Socio-Political History, collection 17, folder 128, item 392, p. 120.

44. Andrei Lankov's interview with Vadim Tkachenko, 23 Jan. 1990, Moscow.

45. Andrei Lankov, 'Razgrom nekommunisticheskih partiy v KNDR (1945–1959)' [The destruction of non-communist parties in the DPRK: 1945–59], in *KNDR vchera i segodnya* [North Korea, yesterday and today], Moscow: Vostok-Zapad, 2004, pp. 148–73.

46. 'Ch'ŏndogyo Ch'ŏngnyŏn Dang' [Party of Young Followers of the Heavenly Way], in *Han'guk minjok munhwa Tae Paekkwa Sajŏn* [Grand encyclopaedia of Korean national culture], http://encykorea.aks.ac.kr/Contents/Item/E0078227 (accessed 22 Sept. 2023).

47. Ibid.

48. Shim Chi-yŏn, *Chosŏn Shinmindang yŏn'gu* [Study of the New People's Party], Seoul: Tongnyŏk, 1988, p. 83.

49. 'Shikin—Bulganinu' [From Shikin to Bulganin], 11 Feb. 1946, Central

Archive of the Ministry of Defence of Russia, collection 32, folder 473, item 45, pp. 104–5.

50. 'Postanovleniya narodnogo komiteta Severnoy Korei o demokraticheskom preobrazovanii za 1946 g.' [Ordinance of the People's Committee for North Korea on democratic transformation, 1946], Central Archive of the Ministry of Defence of Russia, collection 172, folder 614631, item 29, p. 5.

51. Ibid., pp. 9–12.

52. 'Doklad ob itogah raboty Sovetskoy Grazhdanskoy Administratsii za tri goda: Tom I; Politicheskaya chast' [Report on the results of work of the Soviet civil administration for three years: Volume 1; Political affairs], 1948, Archive of the Foreign Policy of the Russian Federation, collection 0480, folder 4, item 46, p. 9.

53. Nikolay Lebedev's diary, entry for 8 Sept. 1947.

54. For the South Korean reform, see Chang Shi-wŏn, 'Nongji kaehyŏk' [Land reform], in Haebang chŏnhusa-ŭi chaeinshik [Reassessment of the history before and after the liberation], vol. 2, Seoul: Ch'aek Sesang, 2006, pp. 345–89.

55. Haebang 10-nyŏn ilji 1945–1955 [Daily record of the ten years after the liberation], Pyongyang: Chosŏn Chungang T'ongshinsa, 1955, p. 62.

56. Chosŏn Minjujuŭi Inmin Konghwaguk kwahagwŏn kyŏngje pŏphak yŏn'guso [Institute for Economic and Legal Studies of the DPRK Academy of Sciences], Haebang hu uri nara-ŭi inmin kyŏngje paljŏn [Development of the people's economy in our country after the liberation], Pyongyang: Kwahagwŏn ch'ulp'ansa, 1960, p. 77.

57. The best book on the subject is Kimura Mitsuhiko and Abe Keiji, Kita Chōsen-no gunji kōgyō-ka: Teikoku-no sensō-kara Kin Nissei-no sensō-e [Military industrialisation of North Korea: From the empire's war to Kim Il-sung's war], Tokyo: Chisen shokan, 2003.

58. For Soviet economic policy in North Korea in 1945–8, see 'Doklad ob itogah raboty Sovetskoy Grazhdanskoy Administratsii za tri goda: Tom II; Ekonomicheskaya chast' [Report on the results of work of the Soviet civil administration for three years: Volume 2; Economic affairs], 1948, Archive of the Foreign Policy of the Russian Federation, collection 0480, folder 4, item 47.

59. 'Chastnaya torgovlya' [Private trade], in 'Doklad ob itogah ...', vol. 2 (1948), pp. 162–74.

60. Chŏn Hyŏn-su, '1947nyŏn 12wŏl Pukhanŭi hwap'ye kaehyŏk' [Monetary reform in North Korea, Dec. 1947], *Yŏksa-wa hyŏnshil*, Mar. 1996, pp. 175–218.

61. Smirnov, 'Kim Ir Sen—podkidysh' (1992), pp. 10–11.

62. For example, a book published in a CPC-controlled part of China in 1946 already claimed that in 1943–4 Kim Il-sung had been stationed at the border of Jilin and Liaoning provinces, yet in reality he had been in Vyatskoye at the time. See Ji Yunlong, *Yang Jingyu he Kanglian Diyilujun* [Yang Jingyu and the First Anti-Japanese Route Army of the NAJUA], n.p.: n.p., 1946, p. 119.

63. 'Kim Il-sŏng changgun-ŭi ...' (1949), p. 63.

64. We do not know who coined the name for the 'KPRA'. If Kim Il-sung himself was entrusted with inventing it, he may have taken it from the North East People's Revolutionary Army, as he had previously served in one of its battalions. Founded by the CPC in 1933, it was one of the many predecessors to the NAJUA. If, however, the name was coined by a Soviet person, then it was almost certainly taken from the armies of pre-Second World War Soviet satellite states in Asia, as Mongolia, Tuva and the Far Eastern Republic's militaries were all called 'People's Revolutionary Armies'.

65. Smirnov, 'Kim Ir Sen—podkidysh' (1992), pp. 10–11.

66. Fyodorov and Livshits, 'Dokladnaya zapiska' (1945), pp. 14–32.

67. Valeriy Usoltsev, 'Pokusheniye na vozhdya' [Assassination attempt on the Leader], *Dal'niy Vostok*, Nov. 1990, pp. 203–11.

68. Ibid.

69. 'Predlozheniye Shtykova ot 7.3.46 g. № 2776' [Shtykov's proposal, 7 Mar. 1946, no. 2776], Russian State Archive of Socio-Political History, collection 17, inventory 128, folder 998, pp. 3–4.

70. Ibid.

71. 'Harakteristika na kandidatov vo Vremennoye demokraticheskoye pravitel'stvo Koreii' [Assessment of candidates to the provisional democratic government of Korea], Russian State Archive of Socio-Political History, collection 17, inventory 128, folder 61, pp. 1–14.

72. On these events, see Václav Veber, *Osudové únorové dny* [Fateful February days], Prague: NLN, 2008.

73. Teretniy Shtykov, 'Doneseniye' [Report], 20 Mar. 1946, Central Archive

of the Ministry of Defence of Russia, collection 172, folder 614631, item 14, pp. 3–5.

74. Interestingly, another song of the era hailing the young leader mentioned 'Siberian winds and snow', implying that its author probably knew that Kim had spent several years in the Soviet Union. However, the most widely played songs of the era contained no references to the Soviet period of Kim Il-sung's life. 'Kim Il-sŏng changgun' [Commander Kim Il-sung], in *Uri-ŭi t'aeyang (Kim Il-sŏng changgun ch'anyang t'ŭkchip)* [Our Sun (special collection of texts glorifying Commander Kim Il-sung)], Pyongyang: Pukchosŏn Yesul Ch'ongryŏnmaeng, 1946, 11–7 item no. 1–100 (RG 242; National Archives Collection of Foreign Records Seized), p. 18.

75. Yuriy Kogai, 'Strana moyego detstva' [The country of my youth], 17 Feb. 2009, http://world.lib.ru/k/kogaj_j_p/infaneco.shtml (accessed 22 Sept. 2023).

76. There are also claims that Kyong-hui's Russian name was actually Era; however, these claims do not come from someone who knew her personally. See *Chŭngŏn Kim Il-sŏng ŭl marhanda ...* (1991), p. 68. It is also possible, although not very likely, that at one point she was called Era but later changed her Russian name to Tatyana.

77. *Na priyome u Stalina* [Receptions by Stalin], Moscow: Novyy Hronograpf, 2008, pp. 476–7.

78. 'Telegramma Shtykova v Moskvu' [Shtykov's telegram to Moscow], 21 Mar. 1950, Archive of the President of the Russian Federation, collection 45, folder 1, item 346, pp. 90–1.

79. 'Sŭt'allin/Kim Il-sŏng orŭn tchok anch'yŏ nakchŏm amshi/45 nyŏn-man-e palk'yŏji-n Pukhan pisa' [Kim Il-sung was sitting at the right hand of Stalin as a sign of being the chosen one: Secret history of North Korea, unveiled after forty-five years], *Chungang Ilbo*, 30 Nov. 1991, p. 3, https://news.joins.com/article/2664096 (accessed 1 Oct. 2020).

80. Ibid.; Andrei Lankov's interview with Fanya Shabshina, 23 Jan. 1992, Moscow; Andrei Lankov's interview with Viviana Pak, daughter of Pak Hŏn-yŏng, 28 Jan. 1990, Moscow.

81. 'Sŭt'allin ...' (1991), p. 3.

82. Ibid.

83. Kobayashi Kazuko (née Hagio), 'Atakushi-wa Kin Nissei shushō-no komazukai datta' [I was a maid of Premier Kim Il-sung], in *Zaigai*

hōjin hikiage-no kiroku: kono sokoku-e-no setsu naru bojō [Records of the evacuation of the overseas compatriots: Desperate love for the motherland], Tokyo: Mainichi Shimbunsha, 1970, pp. 119–22.

84. Ibid.

85. I successfully obtained *Chŏngno*'s issues for late May 1946, which have not been accessible to the academic community for a long time. On 22 May, the newspaper still called itself 'the organ of the Northern Branch Bureau of the Communist Party of Korea'. On 23 May, it became 'the organ of the Communist Party of North Korea'.

86. On this change, see Kim Ch'ang-sun, 'Chosŏn Nodongdang'-ŭi ch'angdang' [Foundation of the 'Workers' Party of Korea'], *Wŏlgan Pukhan* [North Korea monthly], Nov. 1989, pp. 38–48. 'Spravka o politicheskih partiyah i obschestvennyh organizatsiyah v sovetskoy zone okkupatsii Korei' [A reference letter on political parties and public organisations in the Soviet occupation zone in Korea], Russian State Archive of Socio-Political History, collection 17, folder 128, item 205, pp. 13–25; Andrei Lankov, *KNDR vchera i segodnya* [North Korea, yesterday and today], Moscow: Vostok-Zapad, 2004, pp. 36–7.

87. Terentiy Shtykov, 'Tovarischu Stalinu' [To Comrade Stalin], 9 Jan. 1947, Central Archive of the Ministry of Defence of Russia, collection 172, folder 614633, item 3, pp. 9–10.

88. 'Ignat'yev: Voyennomu sovetu 25 armii' [Ignatyev: To the Military Council of the Twenty-Fifth Army], 23 July 1946, Central Archive of the Ministry of Defence of Russia, collection of the Directorate of the Soviet Civil Administration, folder 102038, item 2, pp. 256–8; 'Ignat'yev: Voyennomu sovetu 25 armii' [Ignat'yev: To the Military Council of the Twenty-Fifth Army], 27 July 1946, Central Archive of the Ministry of Defence of Russia, collection of the Directorate of the Soviet Civil Administration, folder 102038, item 2, pp. 263–4.

89. The congress's minutes were later reprinted in South Korea and can be accessed here: 'Puk Chosŏn Rodongdang Ch'angnip Taehoe' [Inaugural Congress of the Workers' Party of North Korea], in *Chosŏn Rodongdang Taehoe charyojip* [Collection of documents on the WPK's congresses], vol. 1, Seoul: Kukt'o t'ongirwŏn, 1980, pp. 11–106.

90. *Chosŏn Rodongdang Taehoe charyojip*, vol. 1 (1980), p. 13.

91. Kang Ŭng-ch'ŏn, 'Chosŏn Minjujuŭi Inmin Konghwaguk kukho-ŭi kiwŏn-gwa chejŏng kwajŏng yŏn'gu' [Origins and process of adoption

of the name 'Democratic People's Republic of Korea'], MA thesis, University of North Korean Studies, 2018.

92. Andrei Lankov's interview with Nikolay Lebedev, 13 Nov. 1989, Moscow.

93. Andrei Lankov's interview with Kang Sang-ho, 13 Jan. 1990, Leningrad. See also 'Sonyŏn Kim Jŏng-il-ŭl tullŏssan 7kaji misŭt'ŏri' [Seven mysteries surrounding the youth of Kim Jong-il], *Shindonga*, 22 Sept. 2006, http://shindonga.donga.com/Library/3/01/13/100670/1 (accessed 22 Sept. 2023).

94. Nikolay Lebedev's diary, entry for 3 Sept. 1947.

95. A good article on this topic is Kim Jae-ung, 'Pukhan-ŭi 38sŏn wŏlgyŏng t'ongje-wa wŏllam wŏlbug-ŭi yangsang' [North Korea's control over the crossing of the 38th parallel and the appearances of crossing over to the North and to the South], in *Han'guk minjok undongsa yŏn'gu* [Historical studies of Korea's national movements], no. 87, 2016, pp. 189–232.

96. 'Dnevnik T.F. Shtykova' [Terentiy Shtykov's diary], entry for 7 July 1946, National Institute of Korean History, http://db.history.go.kr/item/level. do?itemId=fs&levelId=fs_010_0010_0010_0260&types=o (accessed 22 Sept. 2023).

97. Anatoliy Torkunov, *Zagadochnaya voyna: Koreyskiy konflikt 1950–1953 godov* [A mysterious war: The conflict in Korea of 1950–3], Moscow: ROSSPEN, 2000, pp. 6–28.

98. 'Pukhan in'gonggi ku-Soryŏn-sŏ mandŭrŏtta' [The North Korean flag was made in the former Soviet Union], *Tonga Ilbo*, 26 Sept. 1993, p. 14.

99. 'Puk Chosŏn Inmin Hoeŭi t'ŭkpyŏl hoeŭi hoeŭirok (1948.4.28)' [Records of the special session of the People's Committee for North Korea, 28 Apr. 1948], in *Pukhan kwan'gye saryojip* [Collection of North Korea-related historical documents], vol. 8, Seoul: Kuksa P'yŏnch'an Wiwŏnhoe, 1989, pp. 219–340.

100. The best source on the creation of the KPA is Chang Chun-ik, *Pukhan Inmin Kundaesa* [History of the People's Army of North Korea], Seoul: Sŏmundang, 1991.

101. Andrei Lankov's interview with Nikolay Lebedev, 13 Nov. 1989, Moscow.

102. 'Protokol n. 62' [Protocol no. 62], in 'Resheniya Politbyuro TsK VKP(b) za 27 yanvarya–17 marta 1948 g.' [Decisions of the Politburo of the Central Committee of the All-Union Communist Party of Bolsheviks, 27 Jan.–17 Mar. 1948], 3 Feb. 1948, Russian State Archive of Socio-Political History, collection 17, folder 162, item 39, p. 24.

103. *Pukhan minju t'ongil undongsa, P'yŏngannamdo p'yŏn* [History of the democratic and unification movements in North Korea, South Pyongan province], Seoul: Pukhan yŏn'guso, 1990, pp. 448–57; Lankov, *KNDR vchera i segodnya* (2004), pp. 148–73.

104. V. Bakulin, 'Itogi dovyborov v Verhovnoye Narodnoye Sobraniye KNDR' [Results of the by-elections to the Supreme People's Assembly of the DPRK], 11 Aug. 1959. Document from the author's collection.

105. 'Puk Chosŏn inmin hoeŭi t'ŭkpyŏl hoeŭi hoeŭirok (1948.4.28)' [Records of the special session of the People's Assembly for North Korea, 28 Apr. 1948], in *Pukhan kwan'gye saryojip*, vol. 8 (1989), pp. 219–340.

106. 'Protokol № 63' [Protocol no. 63], in 'Resheniya Politbyuro TsK VKP(b) za 26 marta–26 maya 1948 g.' [Decisions of the Politburo of the All-Union Communist Party of Bolsheviks, 26 Mar.–26 May 1948], 24 Apr. 1948. Document from the author's collection.

107. 'Puk Chosŏn inmin hoeŭi che o ch'a hoeŭi hoeŭirok (1948.7.9)' [Records of the fifth session of the People's Assembly for North Korea, 9 July 1948], in *Pukhan kwan'gye saryojip*, vol. 8 (1989), pp. 341–408.

108. 'Chosŏn Minjujuŭi Inmin Konghwaguk hŏnbŏp ch'oan' [Draft of the constitution of the DPRK], in *Puk Chosŏn T'ongshin* [North Korea's news agency], vol. 1, Pyongyang: Puk Chosŏn t'ongshinsa, 1948, pp. 1–11.

109. 'Chosŏn Minjujuŭi Inmin Konghwaguk rimshi hŏnbŏp ch'oan' [Draft of the provisional constitution of the DPRK], in *Miguk kongmunsŏ pogwanso sojang Pukhan kwallyŏn charyo mongnok* [List of documents related to North Korea kept in American archives], Seoul: Han'guk maik'ŭrop'illŭm, 1972, pp. 29–35.

110. *Pungnam ch'ongsŏn'gŏ-rŭl sŭngnijŏkŭro ikkŭshiyŏ* [He victoriously led the general elections in the North and in the South], *Uri Minjok kkiri* [Our nation and no one else], https://web.archive.org/web/20180429195205/http://www.uriminzokkiri.com/m/download.php?categ2=100&no=2952&page=20 (accessed 22 Sept. 2023). This publication even gave the number of alleged voters—6,732,407 people.

111. 'Dnevnik T.F. Shtykova', 26 July 1948, http://db.history.go.kr/item/compareViewer.do?levelId=fs_010r_0010_0040_0050 (accessed 22 Sept. 2023).

112. 'Doklad ob itogah ...', vol. 1 (1948), p. 47.

113. 'Dnevnik T.F. Shtykova', 27 Aug. 1948, http://db.history.go.kr/item/

compareViewer.do?levelId=fs_010r_0010_0040_0150 (accessed 22 Sept. 2023).

114. Ibid., 30 Aug. 1948, http://db.history.go.kr/item/compareViewer. do?levelId=fs_010r_0010_0040_0170 (accessed 22 Sept. 2023).

115. Georgiy Tumanov, 'Kak izgotovlyali velikogo vozhdya' [How the Great Leader was manufactured], *Novoye vremya*, no. 16, 1993, pp. 32–4.

116. Rin In, *Kita Chōsen ōchō seiritsu hishi* ... (1982), p. 55

117. Hong Sun-gwan, 'Chŏn Kim Il-sŏng ...' (1994), pp. 188–207; '6·25ttae Pukhan'gun chakchŏn kukchang Yu Sŏng-ch'ŏl / "Na ŭi chŭngŏn": 7' [Yu Song-chol, chief of department of operations of the KPA during the Korean War: 'My testimony', part 7], *Han'guk Ilbo*, 8 Nov. 1990, https:// www.hankookilbo.com/News/Read/199011080057393135 (accessed 22 Sept. 2023).

118. Much later, North Korean historiography started hailing Kim Jong-suk as the leader's only wife, as the 'heroine of the anti-Japanese struggle'. Yet North Korean historians do not seem to have known the name of Kim Jong-suk's mother. It would thus appear that, during all the years of the couple living together, Kim Il-sung never learned his mother-in-law's actual name.

119. '6·25ttae Pukhan'gun ...' (1990).

6.   KIM IL-SUNG'S WAR

1. 'Chosŏn Minjujuŭi Inmin Konghwaguk Ch'oego inmin hoeŭi pŏmnyŏng' [Legislative order of the Supreme People's Assembly of the DPRK] and 'Chagangdo mit Hamgyŏng-pukto Rajin-gun shinsŏr-e kwanhayŏ' [On the establishment of the Chagang province and Rajin county of the North Hamgyong province], 31 Jan. 1949, in *Chosŏn Minjujuŭi Inmin Konghwaguk pŏpkyujip* [Collection of laws of the DPRK], vol. 1, Pyongyang: Kungnip ch'ulp'ansa, 1961, pp. 93–4.

2. Kim Il-sŏng [Kim Il-sung], 'Ilgusagunyŏn-ŭl majihamyŏnsŏ chŏn'guk inmin-ege ponaenŭn shinnyŏnsa' [New Year address to the entire nation on the occasion of the new year: Year 1949], *Chosŏn Inmin'gun*, 1 Jan. 1949, pp. 1–2. Reprinted in *Pukhan kwan'gye saryojip* [Collection of North Korea-related historical documents], vol. 37, Kwach'ŏn: Kuksa P'yŏnch'an Wiwŏnhoe, 2002, pp. 435–44.

3. 'Telegramma rukovoditelya gruppy sovetskih spetsialistov v Severo-

Vostochnom Kitaye Predsedatelyu Soveta Ministrov SSSR ob itogah kitaysko-koreyskih peregovorov o sotrudnichestve v voyennoy oblasti № 54611' [A telegram from the head of the group of Soviet specialists in North East China to the chairman of the Council of Ministers of the USSR on the results of the Sino-North Korean talks on the military cooperation, no. 54611], 18 May 1949, Archive of the President of the Russian Federation, collection 4, folder 1, item 331, pp. 59–61.

Most of the Soviet documents used in this chapter are quoted from two document collections. The first was compiled by a team of Russian researchers headed by Dr Valeriy Vartanov in 1997. For some reason, it was seemingly never published as a book, but the author possesses a scanned copy of it. See Valeriy Vartanov, 'Itogovyy otchyot po voyenno-istoricheskomu trudu "Voyna v Koreye 1950–1953 gg.: Dokumenty i materialy"' [Final report on the monograph in military history 'War in Korea, 1950–3: Documents and materials'], Moscow, 1997. The second one appeared in an annotated form as a book signed by Anatoliy Torkunov, president of the Moscow State Institute of International Relations. Torkunov, *Zagadochnaya voyna* (2000). Nearly the exact same book was published in Korean by the head of the Russian Diplomatic Academy, Evgeniy Bazhanov, and his wife Nataliya Bazhanova. Despite its questionable authorship, the book itself is an excellent collection of valuable Soviet documents on the Korean War. Documents in both books include reports by Soviet diplomatic and military officials stationed in North Korea. As such, they arguably offer the most detailed and objective image of the Korean War through the eyes of the communist side.

4.   'Telegramma Shtykova v Moskvu' [Shtykov's telegram to Moscow], 12 Aug. 1949, Archive of the President of the Russian Federation, collection 3, folder 65, item 775, pp. 102–6.

5.   Ibid., 27 Aug. 1949, Archive of the President of the Russian Federation, collection 3, folder 65, item 775, pp. 112–14.

6.   'Telegramma Tunkina v Moskvu' [Tunkin's telegram to Moscow], 3 Sept. 1949, Archive of the President of the Russian Federation, collection 3, folder 65, item 775, pp. 116–19.

7.   'Telegramma Stalina Tunkinu' [Stalin's telegram to Tunkin], 11 Sept. 1949, Archive of the President of the Russian Federation, collection 3, folder 65, item 775, p. 122.

8.   'Telegramma Tunkina v Moskvu' [Tunkin's telegram to Moscow], 14

Sept. 1949, Archive of the President of the Russian Federation, collection 3, folder 65, item 837, pp. 94–9.

9. 'Postanovleniye Politbyuro TsK VKP(b) ot 24 sentyabrya 1949g. Vypiska iz protokola № 71 zasedaniya Politbyuro TsK VKP(b) № P 71/191 i prilozheniye k p. 191(OP) pr. PB № 71' [Decisions of the Politburo of the All-Union Communist Party of Bolsheviks from 24 Sept. 1949: Excerpts from protocol no. 71 of the meeting of the Politburo of the All-Union Communist Party of Bolsheviks no. P 71/191 and addendum to the protocol 191 (special folder), protocol of the Politburo no. 71], Archive of the President of the Russian Federation, collection 3, folder 65, item 776, pp. 30–2.

10. 'Telegramma Shtykova v Moskvu' [Shtykov's telegram to Moscow], 4 Oct. 1949, Archive of the President of the Russian Federation, collection 43, folder 1, item 346, p. 59.

11. Ibid., 19 Jan. 1950, Archive of the President of the Russian Federation, collection 45, folder 1, item 346, pp. 62–5.

12. 'Zapis' besedy Predsedatelya Soveta Ministrov SSSR s predsedatelem Tsentral'nogo narodnogo pravitel'stva Kitayskoy Narodnoy Respubliki po voprosam sovetsko-kitayskih mezhgosugarstvennyh otnosheniy i voyenno-politicheskoy obstanovki v Yugo-Vostochnoy Azii' [Record of the conversation between the chairman of the Council of Ministers of the USSR and the chairman of the central people's government of the People's Republic of China on the issues in Sino-Soviet relations, military and political situation in South East Asia], Archive of the President of the Russian Federation, collection 45, folder 1, item 329, pp. 9–17; *Na priyome u Stalina* (2008), p. 530.

13. 'Telegramma Stalina Shtykovu' [Stalin's telegram to Shtykov], 30 Jan. 1950, Archive of the President of the Russian Federation, collection 45, folder 1, item 346, p. 70.

14. 'Telegramma Shtykova Stalinu' [Shtykov's telegram to Stalin], 31 Jan. 1950, Archive of the President of the Russian Federation, collection 45, folder 1, item 346, pp. 71–2.

15. Ibid.

16. 'Telegramma Stalina Shtykovu' [Stalin's telegram to Shtykov], 2 Feb. 1950, Archive of the President of the Russian Federation, collection 45, folder 1, item 347, p. 12.

17. Ibid.

18. 'Telegramma Shtykova v Moskvu' [Shtykov's telegram to Moscow], 4 Feb. 1950, Archive of the President of the Russian Federation, collection 45, folder 1, item 346, p. 71.

19. 'Telegramma Tsentra Shtykovu' [Telegram from the centre to Shtykov], 9 Feb. 1950; 'Shifrtelegramma № 2429 MID SSSR' [Encrypted telegram no, 2429, Soviet Ministry of Foreign Affairs], Archive of the President of the Russian Federation, collection 45, folder 1, item 346, p. 76.

20. Torkunov, *Zagadochnaya voyna* (2000), pp. 58–9.

21. *Na priyome u Stalina* (2008), p. 533.

22. 'Telegramma Ministra inostrannyh del SSSR poslu SSSR v KNR s soobscheniyem kitayskomy pravitel'stvu ob odobrenii resheniya pravitel'stva KNDR pristupit' k ob'yedineniyu Severa i Yuga Korei № 8600' [Telegram no. 8600 of the minister of foreign affairs of the USSR to the ambassador of the USSR in the PRC informing him that the government of the DPRK's decision to unify the North and the South of Korea has been approved], 14 May 1950, Archive of the President of the Russian Federation, collection 45, folder 1, item 334, p. 55.

23. 'Telegramma Roschina Stalinu' [Telegram of Roschin to Stalin], 2 July 1950, Archive of the President of the Russian Federation, collection 45, folder 1, item 331, pp. 76–7.

24. Hong Sun-gwan, 'Chŏn Kim Il-sŏng pisŏ shiljang ch'unggyŏk kobaek' [Shocking revelation of the former executive secretary of Kim Il-sung], *Shindonga*, Oct. 1994, pp. 188–207.

25. 'Telegramma Shtykova v Moskvu' [Shtykov's telegram to Moscow], 29 May 1950, Archive of the President of the Russian Federation, collection 3, folder 65, item 829, pp. 43–4.

26. 'Telegramma Shtykova v Moskvu' [Shtykov's telegram to Moscow], 16 June 1950, Archive of the President of the Russian Federation, collection 3, folder 65, item 830, pp. 9–11.

27. 'Telegramma Shtykova Stalinu' [Shtykov's Telegram to Stalin], 21 June 1950, Archive of the President of the Russian Federation, collection 45, folder 1, item 348, pp. 14–15.

28. 'Doklad posla SSSR v KNDR zamestitelyu nachal'nika General'nogo shtaba Sovetskoy armii o podgotovke i hode voyennyh deystviy koreiskoy Narodnoy armii' [Report of the ambassador of the USSR to the DPRK to the deputy chief of general staff of the Soviet Army on the preparation and the unfurling of military actions by the Korean People's Army],

26 June 1950, Central Archive of the Ministry of Defence of Russia, collection 5, folder 918795, item 122, pp. 9–14.

29. 'O Koreyskoy voyne 1950–53 gg. i peregovorah o peremirii' [On the Korean War of 1950–3 and the peace talks], 9 Aug. 1966, Russian State Archive for Contemporary History, collection 5, folder 58, item 266, pp. 122–31.

30. This was the time in South Korea. As of 1950, South Korea, unlike the North, was using daylight saving time, and hence there was a time difference between South Korea and the DPRK at the time.

31. On the initial hours after the attack, see, for example, the following collection of interviews with John Joseph Muccio, who at the time served as the American ambassador to South Korea: Jerry N. Hess and Richard D. McKinzie, 'Oral History Interviews with John J. Muccio', Harry S. Truman Library Museum, 1971, 1973, https://www.trumanlibrary.gov/library/oral-histories/muccio (accessed 22 Sept. 2023).

32. 'Chŭngŏnnok: Myŏndam pŏnho 271 (Hwang Gyu-myŏn, 1977yŏn 7wŏl 30il)' [Testimony record 271, Hwang Gyu-myŏn, 30 July 1977], Taehan Min'guk Chŏnsa P'yŏnch'an Wiwŏnhoe [Committee for Compilation of the War History of the Republic of Korea], quoted from Pak Myŏngnim, Han'guk 1950: Chŏnjaeng-gwa p'yŏnghwa [Korea, 1950: War and peace], Seoul: Nanam, 2002, p. 144.

33. Ibid.

34. 'Ivan Afanasyeich menyaet professiyu' [Ivan Afanasyevich gets a new job], Ogonyok, Jan. 1991, pp. 25–7.

35. 'Telegramma posla SSSR v KNDR Predsedatelyu Soveta Ministrov SSSR o besede s rukovodstvom Severnoy Korei ob obstanovke na fronte' [Telegram from the ambassador of the USSR to the DPRK to the chairman of the Council of Ministers reporting on the discussion of the situation on the front with the North Korean leadership], 4 July 1950, Archive of the President of the Russian Federation, collection 45, folder 1, item 346, pp. 136–9.

36. 'Ivan Afanasyeich ...' (1991), pp. 25–7.

37. Kim Ko-mang, 'Chosŏn Inminŭi Suryŏng Kim Il-sŏng Changgun-ŭi ryŏngdo hae sŭngni-rŭl chaengch'wiha-ja!' [Let us achieve victory under the leadership of Commander Kim Il-sung—the leader of the Korean people!], T'usa shinmun, 27 June 1950, p. 2.

38. Andrei Lankov's interview with Yu Sŏng-ch'ŏl, 18 Jan. 1991, Tashkent; *Chŭngŏn Kim Il-sŏng ŭl marhanda* ... (1991), p. 77.

39. 'Uri choguk sudo Sŏul haebang-e chehayŏ' [On the liberation of Seoul—the capital of our motherland], in *Chosŏn Chungang Nyŏn'gam 1951–1952* [Korean central yearbook, 1951–2], Pyongyang: Chosŏn Chungang T'ongshinsa, 1953, p. 63.

40. Andrei Lankov's interview with Yu Sŏng-gŏl (Nikolay Yugai), 22 Jan. 1991, Tashkent.

41. 'Telegramma Predsedatelyu Soveta Ministrov SSSR o perestoyke organov urpavleniya koreyskoy Narodnoy armii i pervom otchyote yeyo boyevyh deystviy' [Telegram to the chairman of the Council of Ministers of the USSR on the restructuring of the governing bodies of the Korean People's Army and the first report on its military activities], 7 July 1950, Central Archive of the Ministry of Defence of Russia collection 5, folder 918795, item 122, pp. 168–71.

42. Ibid.

43. 'Telegramma posla SSSR Predsedatelyu Soveta Ministrov SSSR s informatsiyev severokoeyskogo pravitel'stva ob obstanovke na fronte i sostoyavshihsya kitaysko-koreiskih peregovorah o vozmozhnom vstuplenii s voynu Kitaya № 649' [Telegram from the ambassador of the USSR to the chairman of the Council of Ministers of the USSR with information from the North Korean government on the situation on the frontline and on Sino-Korean talks about possible Chinese intervention in the war, no. 649], 20 July 1950, Central Archive of the Ministry of Defence of Russia, collection 5, folder 918795, item 122, pp. 352–5.

44. One of the most fascinating testimonies on life in conquered South Korea is the diary by Kim Sŏng-ch'il, a South Korean intellectual, compiled and published by South Korean historian Chŏng Byŏng-jun. Kim Sŏng-ch'il, *Yŏksa ap'esŏ* [Facing history], P'aju: Ch'angbi, 2009.

45. For North Korea's policy in the South, see Pak Myŏng-nim, 'Hyŏngmyŏng-gwa t'ongil' [Revolution and the unification], in *Han'guk 1950* ... (2002), pp. 197–296.

46. 'Telegramma posla SSSR Ministru inostrannyh del SSSR s informatsiyey severokoeyskogo pravitel'stva ob obstanovke na fronte i pros'boy prislat' dlya prikrytiya voysk internatsional'nye aviatsionnye chasti, № 932' [Telegram from the minister of foreign affairs of the USSR with information of the North Korean government on the situation on the

frontline and request to send international air force units to cover the troops, no. 932], 19 Aug. 1950, Central Archive of the Ministry of Defence of Russia, collection 5, folder 918795, item 122, pp. 621–3.

47. 'Telegramma posla SSSR v KNDR Ministru inostrannyh del SSSR s zaprosom sovetskogo pravitel'stva po povodu vozmozhnogo vstuplenya v voynu kitayskih voysk, 981' [Telegram from the USSR ambassador to the DPRK to the USSR foreign minister requesting the assessment of the North Korean government about the position of the Soviet leadership regarding the possible entry of Chinese troops into the war, no. 981], 29 Aug. 1950, Central Archive of the Ministry of Defence of Russia, collection 5, folder 918795, item 1227, pp. 666–9.

48. 'Telegramma posla SSSR v KNDR Pervomu zamestitelyu ministra inostrannyh del SSSR s informatsiyey o zasedanii TsK Trudovoy partii Severnoy Korei. № 1258' [Telegram from the USSR ambassador to the DPRK to the first deputy minister of foreign affairs of the USSR with information about the meeting of the Central Committee of the Workers' Party of North Korea, no. 1258], 22 Sept. 1950, Central Archive of the Ministry of Defence of Russia, collection 5, folder 918795, item 125, pp. 89–91.

49. 'Telegramma predstavitelya General'nogo shtaba Sovetskoy Armii v Severnoy Koree Predsedatelyu Soveta Ministrov SSSR ob obstanovke na koreyskom fronte iz Phen'yana № 1298' [Telegram from the representative of the general staff of the Soviet Army in North Korea to the chairman of the Council of Ministers of the USSR on the situation on the Korean front from Pyongyang, no. 1298], 27 Sept. 1950, Archive of the President of the Russian Federation, collection 3, folder 65, item 827, pp. 103–6.

50. 'Telegramma posla SSSR v KNDR zamestitelyu nachal'nika General'nogo shtaba Sovetskoy armii o vypolnenii ukazaniy po otzyvu sovetskih voennyh sovetnikov iz voysk koreyskoy Narodnoy armii i napravlenii ih v Kitay dlya obucheniya vyvodimyh iz KNDR soyedineniy i chastey' [Telegram from the USSR ambassador to the DPRK to the deputy chief of the general staff of the Soviet Army on the implementation of instructions to recall Soviet military advisors from the troops of the Korean People's Army and send them to China to train formations and units withdrawn from the DPRK], no. 1566, 31 Oct. 1950, Archive of the President of the Russian Federation, collection 45, folder 1, item 347, pp. 81–3.

51. 'Telegramma Predsedatelya Soveta Ministrov SSSR poslu SSSR v KNR s rekomendatsiyami kitayskomu pravitel'stvu okazat' pomosch' KNDR voyskami' [Telegram from the chairman of the Council of Ministers of the USSR to the Soviet ambassador to the PRC with the recommendations to the PRC government to assist the DPRK by dispatching troops], 1 Oct. 1950, Archive of the President of the Russian Federation, collection 45, folder 1, item 334, pp. 97–8.

52. Ibid.

53. 'Telegramma posla SSSR v KNDR Predsedatelyu Soveta Ministrov SSSR s tekstom pis'ma Predsedatelya Tsentral'nogo Narodnogo pravitel'stva KNR o pozitsii TsK KPK po voprosu vvoda kitayskih voysk na territoriyu Korei, № 2270' [Telegram from the USSR ambassador to the DPRK to the chairman of the Council of Ministers of the USSR with the text of a letter from the chairman of the central people's government of the People's Republic of China on the position of the CPC Central Committee on the dispatch of Chinese troops to Korea, no. 2270], 3 Oct. 1950, Archive of the President of the Russian Federation, collection 45, folder 1, item 334, pp. 105–6.

54. Ibid.

55. 'Telegramma Roschina Stalinu', 2 July 1950, pp. 76–7.

56. 'Telegramma predstavitelya General'nogo shtaba Sovetskoy Armii v Severnoy Koree Predsedatelyu Soveta Ministrov SSSR s informatsiyey o koreysko–kitayskih peregovorah po povody vvoda voysk KNR na territoriyu KNDR' [A telegram from the representative of the general staff of the Soviet Army in North Korea to the chairman of the Council of Ministers of the USSR with information about the Korean–Chinese talks on the introduction of Chinese forces into the territory of the DPRK], 7 Oct. 1950, Central Archive of the Ministry of Defence of Russia, collection 5, folder 918795, item 121, pp. 705–6.

57. 'Telegramma posla SSSR v KNDR pervomu zamestitelyu ministra inostrannyh del SSR o namereniyah pravitel'stva KNDR prosit' previtel'stvo Sovetskogo Soyuza podgotovit' lyotnyye kadry i ofitserov drugih spetsial'nostey is chisla sovetskih koreytsev i koreiskih studentov, obuchayuschihsya v SSSR, № 1426' [Telegram from the USSR ambassador to the DPRK to the first deputy minister of foreign affairs of the USSR about the intentions of the DPRK government to ask the government of the Soviet Union to prepare flight personnel and officers

of other specialties from among Soviet Koreans and Korean students studying in the USSR, no. 1426], 6 Oct. 1950, Central Archive of the Ministry of Defence of Russia, collection 5, folder 918795, item 124, pp. 89–90.

58. 'Telegramma Stalina Shtykovu' [Stalin's telegram to Shtykov], 8 Oct. 1950, Archive of the President of the Russian Federation, collection 45, folder 1, item 334, pp. 112–15.

59. 'Telegramma predstavitelya General'nogo shtaba Sovetskoy Armii v Severnoy Koree Predsedatelyu Soveta Ministrov SSSR s informatsiyey ot severokoeyskogo pravitel'stva o poryadke sosredotocheniya i vvoda soyedineniy kitayskih narodnyh dobrovol'tsev na territoriyu KNDR, № 1437' [Telegram from the representative of the general staff of the Soviet Army in North Korea to the chairman of the Council of Ministers of the USSR with information from the North Korean government on concentrating and dispatching formations of Chinese people's volunteers into the territory of the DPRK 1437], 8 Oct. 1950, Central Archive of the Ministry of Defence of Russia, collection 5, folder 918795, item 121, pp. 712–13; Shen Zhihua, *Mao Zedong, Sidalin yu Chaoxian zhanzheng* [Mao Zedong, Stalin and the Korean War], Guangzhou: Guangdong Renmin chubanshe, 2004, p. 236.

60. 'Telegramma posla SSSR v KNDR Predsedatelyu Soveta Ministrov SSSR o reaktsii severokoreyskih rukovoditeley na yego pis'mo s soobscheniyem o podderzhke voyny koreyskogo naroda KNR i Sovetskim Soyuzom' [Telegram from the USSR ambassador to the DPRK to the chairman of the Council of Ministers of the USSR on the reaction of North Korean leaders to his letter informing them about the support for war of the Korean people by the PRC and by the Soviet Union], 8 Oct. 1950, Central Archive of the Ministry of Defence of Russia, collection 5, folder 918795, item 121, p. 720.

61. 'Telegramma Roschina v Moskvu' [Telegram of Roschin to Moscow], 25 Oct. 1950, Archive of the President of the Russian Federation, collection 45, folder 1, item 335, pp. 80–1; Andrei Lankov's interview with Yu Sŏng-ch'ŏl, 18 Jan. 1991, Tashkent.

62. 'Telegramma Stalina Kim Ir Senu' [Stalin's telegram to Kim Il-sung], 12 Oct. 1950, Archive of the President of the Russian Federation, collection 45, folder 1, item 334, p. 109.

63. Ibid.

64. Shen Zhihua, *Mao Zedong* ... (2004), p. 240; Andrei Lankov's interview with Yu Sŏng-ch'ŏl, 18 Jan. 1991, Tashkent.

65. 'Shifrtelegramma № 25629' [Encrypted telegram no. 25629], 13 Oct. 1950, 2 GU GSh VS SSSR [Second Main Department of the General Staff of the Armed Forces of the USSR], Archive of the President of the Russian Federation, collection 45, folder 1, item 334, pp. 111–12. See also Shen Zhihua, *Mao Zedong* ... (2004), pp. 245–6.

66. 'Shifrtelegramma № 4829' [Encrypted telegram no. 25629], 14 Oct. 1950, 2 GU GSh VS SSSR, Archive of the President of the Russian Federation, collection 45, folder 1, item 347, p. 77.

67. 'Telegramma posla SSSR v KNDR pervomu zamestitelyu ministra inostrannyh del SSSR o polozhenii v Koreye № 1468' [Telegram 1468 from the ambassador of the USSR to the DPRK to the first deputy minister of foreign affairs of the USSR on the situation in Korea], 13 Oct. 1950, Central Archive of the Ministry of Defence of Russia, collection 5, folder 918795, item 124, pp. 136–40.

68. Kim Kuk-hu, 'Hanbam P'yŏngyang hyŏngmuso-sŏ ch'ŏhyŏng / kŭkchŏk-ŭro palk'yŏji-n Cho Man-shik sŏnsaeng ch'oehu' [Shot in the Pyongyang prison in the middle of the night: Dramatic revelations of Mr Cho Man-sik's last moments], *Chungang Ilbo*, 19 July 1991, p. 3, https://news.joins.com/article/2615466 (accessed 1 Oct. 2020).

69. 'Puk, nappuk-wŏlbuk 62in P'yŏngyang myoyŏk konggae' [North Korea reveals the mass graves of sixty-two people abducted by the North], *Tonga Ilbo*, 7 July 2005, http://www.donga.com/news/article/all/20050727/8213658/1 (accessed 22 Sept. 2023).

70. Ibid.

71. Taeyu is a district in Tongchang township of Changsong county of the North Pyongan province. See 'Pis'mo Predsedatelya Kabineta ministrov KNDR poslu SSSR v KNDR s pros'boy k sovetskomu pravitel'stvu razreshit' sozdat' na territorii Sovetskogo Soyuza voyenno-morskoye uchilische i shkolu dlya podgotovki lichnogo sostava dlya VMS KNDR' [A letter from the chairman of the Cabinet of Ministers of the DPRK to the ambassador of the USSR to the DPRK with a request to the Soviet government to permit the establishment of a military academy and school on Soviet soil to train the personnel of the DPRK Navy], Archive of the President of the Russian Federation, collection 3, folder 55, item 828, p. 93.

72. 'Telegramma posla SSSR v KNDR nachal'niku General'nogo shtaba Sovetskoy Armii o besede s Glavnokomanduyuschim koreyskoy Narodnoy armii po voprosy smeny Glavnyh sovetskih voyennyh sovetnikov i o rezul'tatah soveschaniya s komanduyuschimi soyedineniyami KNA № 37' [Telegram from the ambassador of the USSR to the DPRK to the chief of staff of the Soviet Army on the talks with the commander-in-chief of the KPA on the issue of the new Soviet chief military advisor and on the results of a meeting with commanders of the KPA formations, no. 37], 22 Nov. 1950, Central Archive of the Ministry of Defence of Russia, collection 5, folder 918795, item 124, pp. 308–10.

73. 'Protokol № 79: Resheniye Politbyuro TsK; 126; O tov. Shtykove T.F.' [Protocol no 79: Decision of the Politburo of the Central Committee; Item no. 126; On Comrade T.F. Shtykov], Russian State Archive of Socio-Political History, collection 17, folder 3, item 1086, p. 24.

74. 'Protokol № 80: Ot 3.II.51 g. 175; O tov. Shtykove' [Protocol no 80: 3 Feb. 1951; Item no. 175; On Comrade Shtykov], Russian State Archive of Socio-Political History, collection 17, folder 3, item 1087, p. 34.

75. Reportedly, Shtykov did not get along with Hungary's reformist leader János Kádár; his tenure in Budapest ended abruptly when he told Kádár: 'It is a pity they did not execute you.' Shtykov died in Moscow in 1964. See Georgiy Tumanov, 'Kak izgotovlyali velikogo vozhdya' [How the Great Leader was manufactured], *Novoye vremya*, no. 16, 1993, pp. 32–4.

76. Ryŏ Jŏng, *Pulgke muldŭn Taedonggang* (1991), p. 112.

77. Hong Sun-gwan, 'Chŏn Kim Il-sŏng ...' (1994), pp. 188–207. My own interviews with North Koreans also confirm that similar rumours persisted in the North.

78. 'O Koreyskoy voyne ...' (1966), pp. 122–31.

79. Shen Zhihua, 'Peng Dehuai zhiyi Jin Richeng: Chaoxian zhanzheng jiujing shi shui fadong de?' [Peng Dehuai asked Kim Il-sung: 'Tell me, who started the Korean War?'], *Fenghuang zhoukan*, 24 Dec. 2011, http://news.ifeng.com/history/zhuanjialunshi/shenzhihua/detail_2011_12/24/11543343_0.shtml (accessed 22 Sept. 2023).

80. 'O Koreyskoy voyne ...' (1966), pp. 122–31.

81. Joint Strategic Plans Committee, 'Directive: A Preliminary Study on the Evacuation of ROK Personnel from Korea', 16 June 1951. A copy of the document is preserved in the South Korean War Memorial.

82. 'O Koreyskoy voyne ...' (1966), pp. 122–31.

83. 'Telegramma Predsedatelya Kabineta Ministrov KNDR Predsedatelyu Soveta Ministrov SSSR o hode vypolneniya postavok svintsovosoderzhschih materialov iz Korei v Sovetskiy Soyuz' [Telegram from the chairman of the Cabinet of Ministers of the DPRK to the chairman of the Council of Ministers of the USSR on the progress of shipments of lead-containing materials from Korea to the Soviet Union], 26 June 1951, Archive of the President of the Russian Federation, collection 45, folder 1, item 348, p. 35.

84. Andrei Lankov's interview with Yu Sŏng-ch'ŏl, 29 Jan. 1991, Tashkent; 'O Koreyskoy voyne ...' (1966), pp. 122–31.

85. 'Telegramma predsedatelya tsentral'nogo narodnogo pravitel'stva KNR Predsedatelyu Soveta Ministrov SSSR s informatsiyey ob itogah pervyh pyati zasedaniy peregovorov o prekraschnii boyevyh deystviy v Koreye' [Telegram from the chairman of the central people's government of the People's Republic of China to the chairman of the Council of Ministers of the USSR with information on the results of the first five meetings of the talks on the cessation of hostilities in Korea], 20 July 1951, Archive of the President of the Russian Federation, collection 45, folder 1, item 340, pp. 88–91.

86. 'Shifrtelegramma № 501869/sh' [Encrypted telegram no. 501869/sh], 1 July 1951, 8 Upr. GSh SA [Eighth Department of the General Staff of the Soviet Army], Archive of the President of the Russian Federation, collection 45, folder 1, item 340, pp. 3–4; 'Shifrtelegramma № 21726' [Encrypted telegram no. 21726], 13 July 1951, 2 GU GSh SA [Second Main Department of the General Staff of the Soviet Army], Archive of the President of the Russian Federation, collection 45, folder 1, item 339, pp. 35–42.

87. See Kim Taewoo, 'Limited War, Unlimited Targets: U.S. Air Force Bombing of North Korea during the Korean War, 1950–1953', *Critical Asian Studies*, 44, no. 3, 2012, pp. 467–92 and Kim T'ae-u [Kim Taewoo], *P'okkyŏk Mi konggun-ŭi Kongjung p'okkyŏk kirog-ŭro ing-nŭn Han'guk Chŏnjaeng* [Bombings. The Korean War read through air bombardment records of the US Air Force], Seoul: Ch'angbi, 2013.

88. Sheila Miyoshi Jager, *Brothers at War: The Unending Conflict in Korea*, London: Profile Books, 2013, p. 271.

89. 'Dnevnik posla SSSR v KNDR Ivanova V.I.' [Journal of ambassador of

the USSR to the DPRK V.I. Ivanov], 20 Jan. 1956, Russian State Archive for the Contemporary History, collection 5, folder 58, item 412, p. 120.

90. *Kim Il-sŏng Changgun-ŭi ryakchŏn* [A concise biography of Commander Kim Il-sung], Pyongyang: Chosŏn Rodongdang Chungang Wiwŏnhoe Sŏnjŏn Sŏndongbu, 1952, p. 32.

91. 'Widaehan Suryŏng-dŭrŭi ryakchŏn yŏn'gu' [Study of the concise biographies of the Great Leaders], *Rodong Shinmun*, 19 Sept. 1953, p. 3.

92. At least two documents point to such a conclusion. The first is Stalin's letter to the Soviet ambassador to Czechoslovakia Mikhail Silin outlining his thoughts on the Korean War, which was relayed to Czechoslovakian President Klement Gottwald. I am thankful to Mr Cho Gap-che for bringing this document to my attention. Filippov, 'Sovposlu' [To the Soviet ambassador], 27 Aug. 1950, Russian State Archive of Socio-Political History, collection 558, folder 11, item 62, pp. 71–2. 'Filippov' was a pseudonym used by Stalin during the war for security reasons. The second document is the record of Stalin's talks with PRC Foreign Minister Zhou Enlai, where Stalin states that the war 'is getting on the nerves of the Americans', and thus, despite all the casualties the North Korean side had suffered, it would not be in the United States' interests for it to continue. 'Zapis' besedy I. Stalina s Chzhou Enlayem' [Record of conversation of J. Stalin with Zhou Enlai], 20 Aug. 1952, Archive of the President of the Russian Federation, collection 45, folder 1, item 329, pp. 64–72.

93. 'Zapis' besedy I.V. Stalina s Kim Il Senom i Pyn De-huai' [Record of conversation of Joseph Stalin with Kim Il-sung and Peng Dehuai], 4 Sept. 1952. Document from the author's collection.

94. 'Chosŏn Inmin'gun Sanggŭp Chihwi Sŏngwŏn mit Kungwan-dŭrege Kunsa Ch'ingho-rŭl Chejŏngham-e taehayŏ' [On the introduction of military ranks to the high-ranking commanders and officers of the Korean People's Army], in *Chosŏn Minjujuŭi Inmin Konghwaguk pŏpkyujip* (1961), pp. 365–9.

95. 'Chosŏn Inmin'gun pyŏngjong changnyŏng min kun'gwan sŏngwŏndŭrŭi kyŏnjang hyŏngt'ae min tohae' [Shape and appearance of shoulder rank insignia of generals and officers of various military branches of the KPA], *Chosŏn Inmin'gun*, 3 Jan. 1953, p. 2.

96. 'Chosŏn Inmin'gun ch'oegosaryŏnggwan Kim Il-sŏng tongji-ege Chosŏn Minjujuŭi Inmin Konghwaguk wŏnsu ch'ingho-rŭl suyŏhame

kwanhayŏ' [On the bestowing of the rank of marshal of the DPRK to Comrade Kim Il-sung, the supreme commander of the Korean People's Army], *Chosŏn Inmin'gun*, 7 Feb. 1953, p. 1; 'Chosŏn Minjujuŭi Inmin Konghwaguk minjok powisang Ch'oe Yong-gŏn tongji-ege Chosŏn Minjujuŭi Inmin Konghwaguk ch'asu ch'ingho-rŭl suyŏhame kwanhayŏ' [On the bestowing of the rank of Vice-Marshal of the DPRK to comrade Choe Yong-gon, the Minister of National Defence of the DPRK], *Chosŏn Inmin'gun*, 7 Feb. 1953, p. 1.

97. '1952 nyŏn 12 wŏl 31 il chŏngnyŏng 'Chosŏn Inmin'gun Sanggŭp Chihwi Sŏngwŏn mit Kungwan-dŭrege Kunsa Ch'ingho-rŭl chejŏngham-e taehayŏ'ŭi ilbu-rŭl pyŏn'gyŏnghame kwanhayŏ' [On a partial amendment to the executive order 'On the Introduction of Military Ranks to the High-Ranking Commanders and Officers of the Korean People's Army' from 31 Dec. 1952], in *Chosŏn Minjujuŭi Inmin Konghwaguk pŏmnyŏng mit Ch'oego Inmin Hoeŭi Sangim Wiwŏnhoe chŏngnyŏngjip* [Collections of laws of the DPRK and executive orders of the SPA's Presidium], vol. 3, Tokyo: Hagu sŏbang, 1954, pp. 138–41.

98. 'Chosŏn Rodongdang Chungang Wiwŏnhoe-wa Chosŏn Minjujuŭi Inmin Konghwaguk Naegag-esŏ. Chŏnch'e Chosŏn Rodongdang tangwŏn-gwa chŏnch'e Chosŏn inmin-ege koham' [For the Central Committee of the WPK and the Cabinet of Ministers of the DPRK: A proclamation to the entire Workers' Party of Korea and to all Korean people], *Rodong Shinmun*, 7 Mar. 1953, p. 1.

99. G. Malenkov and M. Pomaznev, 'Postanovleniye Soveta Ministrov SSSR s prilozheniyem pis'ma pravitel'stva SSSR Predsedatelyu Tsentral'nogo Narodnogo pravitel'stva KNR i Predsedatelyu Kabineta Ministrov KNDR ob izmeneniyah v politike po mirnym peregovoram v Koreye i direktivy sovetskoy delegatsii na General'noy Assambleye OON po koreyskomu voprosu' [Resolution of the Council of Ministers of the USSR with the attachment of a letter from the USSR government to the chairman of the central people's government of the PRC and the chairman of the Cabinet of Ministers of the DPRK on changes in policy on peace negotiations in Korea and directives of the Soviet delegation to the UN General Assembly on the Korean issue], no. 858-372, 19 Mar. 1953, Archive of the President of the Russian Federation, collection 3, folder 65, item 830, pp. 60–71.

100. 'Telegramma ministra inostrannyh del SSSR poslu SSSR v KNDR s

rekomendatsiyami TsK KPSS Predsedatelyu Kabineta Ministrov KNDR ne uchastvovat' v podpisanii Soglasheniya o peremirii v Koreye' [Telegram from the USSR minister of foreign affairs to the USSR ambassador to the DPRK with recommendations of the CPSU Central Committee to the chairman of the DPRK Cabinet of Ministers not to participate in the signing of the Armistice Agreement in Korea], 24 July 1953, Archive of the President of the Russian Federation, collection 3, folder 65, item 830, pp. 170–1.

101. 'Truce Is Signed, Ending the Fighting in Korea: P.O.W. Exchange Near; Rhee Gets U.S. Pledge; Eisenhower Bids Free World Stay Vigilant', *The New York Times*, 27 July 1953, p. 1.

102. Later, two of them were purged and subsequently removed from all photos published by the DPRK.

103. 'Choguk-ŭl suhoha-nŭn sŏngjŏn-ŭi sŭngni-rŭl kyŏngch'ukha-yŏ P'yŏngyang-shi kunjonghoe sŏnghwangni-e chinhaeng' [Mass demonstrations in the city of Pyongyang in celebration of the victory in the holy war to protect the fatherland proceed with success], *Chosŏn Inmin'gun*, 29 July 1953, p. 4.

7. CLEANSING THE WAY

1. On the USSR and the PRC's post-war economic assistance to North Korea, see Shen Zhihua, *Zuihou-de 'Tianchao': Mao Zedong, Jin Richeng yu Zhong-Chao guanxi* [The last 'heavenly dynasty': Mao Zedong, Kim Il-sung and Sino-North Korean relations], revised edn, Hong Kong: Xianggang Zhongwen Daxue chubanshe, 2017–18, pp. 283–90.

2. Andrei Lankov's interview with Kang Sang-ho, 13 Jan. 1990, Leningrad.

3. Ibid.

4. Lee Sang-jo, 'Tovarischu Kim Ir Senu' [To Comrade Kim Il-sung], State Archive of the Russian Federation, collection R-5446, folder 98s, item 721, pp. 3–13.

5. 'Telegramma Predsedatelya Soveta Ministrov SSSR Glavnomy voyannomy sovetniku Koreyskoy Narodnoy armii s ukazaniyem razobrat'sya v suti poslannyh yemu raneye predlozheniy o povyshenii boyesposobnosti KNA' [Telegram from the chairman of the Council of Ministers of the USSR to the chief military advisor to the Korean People's Army with instructions to sort out the essence of the proposals sent earlier to him

to increase the combat effectiveness of the KPA], 3 Feb. 1951, Archive of the President of the Russian Federation, collection 45, folder 1, item 348, p. 20.

6. Probably the earliest document suggesting such a classification is a letter from Vasiliy Kovyzhenko, an officer in the Main Political Department of the Soviet Army, to Leonid Baranov, deputy chairman of the Foreign Policy Department of the CPSU. This is a remarkably detailed and honest document that reveals a great deal about the inner workings of North Korean politics. For example, Kovyzhenko noted a schism between Pak Hon-yong and Kim Il-sung as early as late 1946, and he thought that Mun Il carried a lot of the blame for their spoiled relations. See V. Kovyzhenko, 'Tov. Baranovu L.S.' [To Comrade L.S. Baranov], 20 Apr. 1948, Russian State Archive of Socio-Political History, collection 5, folder 10, item 618, pp. 30–6.

7. See my book chapter on Pang Hak-se: P'yodorŭ Tchaerŭch'ijŭsŭk'i [Fyodor Tertitskiy], 'Pukhan Powisŏng-ŭi abŏji, Pang Hak-se' [Pang Hak-se, the father of North Korea's Ministry for Protection of the State], in *Pukhan-gwa Soryŏn: It'yŏjin inmul-gwa ep'isodŭ* [North Korea and the Soviet Union: Forgotten people, neglected episodes], P'aju: Hanul ak'ademi, 2023, pp. 292–309.

8. Kim Kuk-hu, *P'yŏngyang-ŭi k'areisŭk'i ellit'ŭ-dŭl* [Soviet Koreans in the Pyongyang elite], P'aju: Hanul, 2013, pp. 192–4.

9. 'Zapis' besedy 1-go sekretarya Posol'stva SSSR v KNDR t. Vasyukevicha V.A. s sekretaryom TsK TPK Pak Chan Okom' [Record of conversation of the first secretary of the embassy of the USSR to the DPRK Comrade V. A. Vasyukevich with Pak Chang-ok, secretary of the WPK Central Committee], 4 Apr. 1953. Document from the author's collection.

10. 'Dnevnik poverennogo v delah SSSR v KNDR Suzadaleva S.P.' [Journal of the *chargé d'affaires* of the USSR to the DPRK S.P. Suzadalev], 9 May 1953. Document from the author's collection.

11. 'Dnevnik ... Suzadaleva S.P.', 27 July 1956.

12. Andrei Lankov's interview with Innokentiy Kim, 14 Sept. 2001, Moscow; *Kim Kuk-hu, P'yŏngyang-ŭi k'areisŭk'i ellit'ŭ-dŭl* (2013), pp. 274–7.

13. 'Dnevnik ... Suzadaleva S.P.', 30 June 1953.

14. There have been two attempts to systematise the information about his death. The first was done by Andrei Lankov, based, among other things, on the unique testimonies of eyewitnesses. See Andrei Lankov, *Ho Ga*

I (A. I. Hegay): Ocherk zhizni i deyatel'nosti [Hŏ Ga-I (A.I. Hegay): A sketch of his life and actions], in *KNDR vchera i segodnya* (2004), pp. 201–21. I have also written about this mysterious death: P'yodorŭ Tchaerŭch'ijŭsŭk'i [Fyodor Tertitskiy], 'Tang puwiwŏnjang Hŏ Ga-i-wa 6.25 chŏnjaeng chongnyo chikchŏn ŭimunŭi samang' [Party Vice-Chairman Aleksei Hegay and his suspicious death immediately before the end of the Korean War], in *Pukhan-gwa Soryŏn* ... (2023), pp. 310–27.

15. 'Ri Sŭng-yŏp todang sagŏn-e taehan kongp'anjŏng-esŏ p'isoja-dŭl chagi pŏmjoe haengdong-ŭl chinsul' [The accused testify about their crimes in the open proceedings against the clique of Lee Sung-yop], *Rodong Shinmun*, 7 Aug. 1953, pp. 3–4.

16. 'Dnevnik Posla SSSR v KNDR Ivanova V.I.' [Journal of Ambassador of the USSR to the DPRK V.I. Ivanov], 25 Nov. 1955. Document from the author's collection.

17. 'Iz dnevnika sovetnika posol'stva SSSR v KNDR tov. Filatova S.N. Zapis' besedy s Pak Yen Binom' [From the diary of the counsellor of the embassy of the USSR to the DPRK S.N. Filatov: Record of conversation with Pak Yŏng-bin], 25 Feb. 1956, Archive of the Foreign Policy of the Russian Federation, collection 102, folder 12, item 6, folder 68.

18. 'Za smyanata na karaula v darzhavata, za prilikite i razlikite ...' [Changing the guard in the country, the similarities and differences ...], 2 Apr. 2016, RNews.bg, https://rnews.bg/60-%D0%B3-%D0%BE%D1%82-%D0%B0%D0%BF%D1%80%D0%B8%D0%BB%D1%81%D0%BA%D0%B8%D1%8F-%D0%BF%D0%BB%D0%B5%D0%BD%D1%83%D0%BC-%D0%B2%D1%8A%D0%BB%D0%BA%D0%BE-%D1%87%D0%B5%D1%80%D0%B2%D0%B5%D0%BD%D0%BA%D0%BE/ (accessed 22 Sept. 2023).

19. Text of Rákosi's resignation letter can be found in Vladimir Popin, *1956*, n.p.: n.p., 2006, p. 45, http://mek.oszk.hu/05500/05525/05525.pdf (accessed 22 Sept. 2023).

20. The former name of the North Korean Politburo.

21. 'Iz dnevnika ... Filatova S.N.', 25 Feb. 1955.

22. Kim Nam-shik and Shim Chi-yŏn, 'Pak Hŏn-yŏng-e taehan Pukhan-ŭi chaep'an kirok' [North Korean records of trial of Pak Hon-yong], in *Pak Hŏn-yŏng nosŏn pip'an* [Criticism of the Pan Hon-yong's line], Seoul: Segye, 1986, pp. 459–535.

23. Ibid.; 'Naega ch'irŭn Pukhan sukch'ŏng (32)' [The North Korean purges I paid for, part 32], Chungang Ilbo, 16 Aug. 1993, p. 11, https://www.joongang.co.kr/article/2830546 (accessed 1 Oct. 2020); 'Naega ch'irŭn Pukhan sukch'ŏng (33)' [The North Korean purges I paid for, part 33], *Chungang Ilbo*, 14 Sept. 1993, p. 31, https://www.joongang.co.kr/article/2834135 (accessed 1 Oct. 2020); 'Naega ch'irŭn Pukhan sukch'ŏng (34)' [The North Korean purges I paid for, part 34], *Chungang Ilbo*, 28 Sept. 1993, p. 31, https://www.joongang.co.kr/article/2835979 (accessed 1 Oct. 2020).

24. Hong Sun-gwan, 'Chŏn Kim Il-sŏng ...' (1994), pp. 188–207.

25. Chosŏn Minjujuŭi Inmin Konghwaguk Ch'oego Chaep'anso [Supreme Court of the DPRK], 'Mi chegukchuŭi koyong kanch'ŏp Pak Hŏn-yŏng Ri Sŭng-yŏp todangŭi Chosŏn Minjujuŭi Inmin Konghwaguk chŏnggwŏn chŏnbok ŭmmo-wa kanch'ŏp sagŏn kongp'an munhŏn' [Materials of the open trial of Pak Hon-yong and Lee Sung-yop—spies hired by the American imperialists, who were doing espionage and conspired to overthrow the DPRK government], Pyongyang: Kungnip ch'ulp'ansa, 1955.

26. The Soviets even tried—unsuccessfully—to save Pak's life as early as April 1956. See 'Dnevnik ... Ivanova V.I.', 19 Apr. 1956.

27. 'K besede s partiyno-pravitel'stvennoy delegatsiyey KNDR' [Notes for talks with the party and government delegation of the DPRK], Archive of the Foreign Policy of the Russian Federation, collection 0102, folder 13, file 72, item 11.

28. Kim Il-sŏng [Kim Il-sung], 'Sasang saŏbesŏ kyojojuŭiwa hyŏngshikchuŭirŭl t'oech'ihago chuch'erŭl hwangnip'al te taehayŏ' [On the liquidation of formalism and dogmatism in the ideological activities and on the establishment of the subject], in *Kim Il-sŏng sŏnjip* [Selected works of Kim Il-sung], vol. 4, Pyongyang: Chosŏn Rodongdang ch'ulp'ansa, 1960, pp. 325–54. A translation of the speech can be found in Brian Myers, *North Korea's Juche Myth*, Pusan: Shtele Press, 2015, pp. 227–53. Myers has done an excellent job in tracing all the alterations made to the speech by the North Korean state in subsequent publications.

29. 'To (P'yŏngyang-shi) Tang Wiwŏnhoe nae Kŏmyŏl Kkomissiya-rŭl Kŏmyŏl Wiwŏnhoe-ro kaech'inghago kŭ yŏk'ar-ŭl chegohalte taehayŏ' [On renaming Pyongyang and provincial party inspection *kkomissiya*s to

inspection *wiwŏnhoes* and on the improvement of their roles], in *Pukhan kwan'gye saryojip*, vol. 30 (1998), pp. 845–6.

30. See, e.g., Kimura Kan, 'Sōryoku-sen taisei ki no Chōsen hantō ni kansuru ichi kōsatsu - jinteki dōin o chūshin ni shite' [Korean Peninsula during the age of total war mobilisation: Focusing on conscription of human resources], in 'Nikkan rekishi kyōdō kenkyū hōkoku-sho' [Joint research report for the history of Japan and Korea], section 3, vol. 2, 2005, pp. 321–44.

31. Nam G. Kim, *From Enemies to Allies: The Impact of the Korean War on U.S.–Japan Relations*, New York: International Scholars Publications, 1997, p. 66.

32. On the Rhee administration's policy towards Japanese Koreans, see Ogat'a Yoshihiro [Ogata Yoshihiro], 'I Sŭng-man chŏngbu-ŭi "Chaeil Tongp'o" chŏngch'aek yŏn'gu' [Study of Syngman Rhee's government policy towards the Japanese Koreans], PhD thesis, Yonsei University, 2018.

33. Myers, a fluent speaker of German and Korean, traces the origins and evolution of this word in *North Korea's Juche Myth* (2015), pp. 10–15. That the word 'Subjekt' was translated to Korean as 'Juche' can also be confirmed through the translated works of Karl Marx, which had been published in the DPRK before the proclamation of the Singular Thought System (see Chapter 12). *Maksŭ Enggelsŭ chŏnjip* [Complete collection of works of Marx and Engels], vol. 1, Pyongyang: Chosŏn Rodongdang ch'ulp'ansa, 1964, p. 186.

34. N.E. Torbenkov, 'Zapis' besedy s sovetnikom MID MNDR Pak Dok Hvanom' [Record of conversation with Pak Dok-hwan, counsellor of the DPRK's Ministry of Foreign Affairs], 1 June 1960, Archive of the Foreign Policy of the Russian Federation, collection 0102, folder 16, item 6.

35. Chosŏn Rodongdang Chungang Wiwŏnhoe [Central Committee of the Workers' Party of Korea], 'Kak to shi (kuyŏk), kun Tang wiwŏnhoe wiwŏnjang tongji-dŭr-ege: Nongŏp hyŏptong kyŏngni chojik munje-e taehayŏ' [To comrade chairs of provincial, city (district) and county party committees: On the issue of accountancy of the agricultural collectivisation]. A copy of the document is preserved in Russian State Archive of Contemporary History, collection 5, inventory 28, item 190, pp. 87–90 (reverse).

36. 'Iz dnevnika Suzdaleva S.P. Zapis' besedy s zam: Predsedatelya kabineta

ministrov i predsedatelyem Gosplana KNDR Pak Chan Okom' [From the diary of S.P. Suzdalev: Record of conversation with Pak Ch'ang-ok, deputy premier and chairman of the State Planning Committee of the DPRK], 1 Feb. 1955. Document from the author's collection.

37. 'Iz dnevnika sovetnika posol'stva A. M. Petrova i pervogo sekretarya I.S. Byakova: Zapis' besedy s predsedatelem narodnogo komiteta provintsii Chagan Pak Illarionom Dmitriyevichem' [From the diaries of A.M. Petrov, the embassy's counsellor, and I.S. Byakov, the embassy's first secretary: Record of conversation with Illarion Pak, the chairman of the People's Committee for Chagang province], 31 Mar. 1955. Document from the author's collection.

38. 'Iz dnevnika sekretarya Posol'stva SSSR v KNDR I.S. Byakova: Zapis' besedy s redaktorom zhurnala 'Novaya Koreya' t. Son Din Fa' [From the diary of I.S. Byakov, secretary of the embassy of the USSR to the DPRK: Record of conversation with Comrade Song Jin-pha], 29 Mar. 1955, Archive of the Foreign Policy of the Russian Federation, collection 11, folder 60, item 8, pp. 157–60.

39. 'Iz dnevnika sekretarya Posol'stva SSSR v KNDR I.S. Byakova: Zapis' besedy s predsedatelem provintsial'nogo komiteta provintsii Sev. Hvanhe tov. He Binom' [From the diary of I.S. Byakov, secretary of the embassy of the USSR to the DPRK: Record of conversation with Comrade Hye Bin, chairman of the Party Committee of North Hwanghae province], 18 Mar. 1955, Archive of the Foreign Policy of the Russian Federation, collection 11, folder 60, item 8, pp. 135–9; 'Zapis' besedy 1-go sekretarya Dal'nevostochnogo otdela Vasyukevicha V.A. s sovetnikom Grishayevym A.K. 8. II. 1955 goda' [Record of conversation of First Secretary of the Far Eastern Department V.A. Vasyukevich with counsellor A.K. Grishayev, 8 Feb. 1955]. Document from the author's collection.

40. 'Iz dnevnika I.F. Kurdyukova. Priyom posla KNDR v SSSR Li San Cho' [From the diary of I.F. Kurdyukov: A reception of the ambassador of the USSR to the DPRK Lee Sang-jo], 11 Aug. 1956. Document from the author's collection.

41. Natalia Matveeva, 'Why the USSR Tried—and Failed—to Slow North Korean Collectivization', NK News, 22 Apr. 2019, https://www.nknews. org/2019/04/why-the-ussr-tried-and-failed-to-slow-north-korean-collectivization/ (accessed 22 Sept. 2023).

42. 'Dnevnik ... Ivanova V.I.', 25 July 1955.

43. Ibid., 23 May 1956.
44. Balázs Szalontai, *Kim Il Sung in the Khrushchev Era*, Stanford: Stanford University Press, 2005, pp. 121–2. This book later became involved in an academic scandal when a professor named Charles Armstrong was caught plagiarising from it and using bogus sources to cover his tracks.
45. In a revealing incident, when Kim Il-sung met Stalin in 1949 it was Stalin who argued that the North Korean state should allow a 'national bourgeoisie' to exist. See 'Zapis' besedy Predsedatelya Soveta Ministrov SSSR s Predsedatelem Kabineta Ministrov Koreyskoy Narodno-Demokraticheskoy Respubliki o perspektivah sovetsko-koreyskih mezhgosudarstvennyh otnosheniy' [Record of the conversation between the chairman of the Council of Ministers of the USSR and the chairman of the Cabinet of Ministers of the DPRK on the prospects for Soviet–Korean relations], 5 Mar. 1949, Archive of the President of the Russian Federation, collection 45, folder 1, item 346, pp. 13–23, 46.
46. Kim Il-sŏng [Kim Il-sung], 'Kyŏnggongŏb-ŭl palchŏnshik'yŏ inmin saenghwar-ŭl tŏuk nop'ija' [Let us develop light industry and make the people's life even more prosperous], in *Kim Il-sŏng chŏnjip* [Complete works of Kim Il-sung], vol. 84, Pyongyang: Chosŏn Rodongdang ch'ulp'ansa, 2009, pp. 198–213. The author is thankful to Peter Ward for pointing him to the quote where Kim Il-sung states that his family was supplied from a marketplace. The quote can be found on page 203 of the book.
47. Fyodor Tertitskiy, 'The "Anti-espionage Struggle": Catching a Spy, North Korean-Style', NK News, 13 Apr. 2018, https://www.nknews.org/2018/04/the-anti-espionage-struggle-catching-a-spy-north-korean-style/ (accessed 22 Sept. 2023); *Ch'oe Sŏn-gyŏng, Pan'ganch'ŏp t'ujaeng-ŭl chŏninminjŏk undong-ŭro chŏn'gaehaja* [Let us involve all the people in the fight against spies], Pyongyang: Kungnip ch'ulp'ansa, 1955.
48. Rin In, *Kita Chōsen ōchō seiritsu hishi* ... (1982), p. 56.

8. THE VICTORY OVER THE OPPOSITION

1. Nikita Hruschyov [Nikita Khrushchev], 'Doklad na zakrytom zasedanii XX s'yezda KPSS "O kul'te lichnosti i yego posledstviyah"' [Report on the closed session of the Twentieth Congress of the CPSU 'On the cult of the individual and its consequences'], Moscow: Gospolitizdat, 1959.

2. Andrei Lankov provides extensive information on the events preceding the final confrontation between Kim and the opposition in *Crisis in North Korea: The Failure of De-Stalinization, 1956*, Honolulu: University of Hawai'i Press, 2004.

3. 'Iz dnevnika I.F. Kurdyukova: Priyom posla KNDR v SSSR Li San Cho' [From the diary of I.F. Kurdyukov: A reception of the ambassador of the USSR to the DPRK Lee Sang-jo], 11 Aug. 1956. Document from the author's collection.

4. 'Iz dnevnika sovetnika posol'stva SSSR v KNDR Filatova S.N. Zapis' besedy s chlenom Politsoveta TsK Pak Yen Binom' [From the diary of the counsellor of the embassy of the USSR to the DPRK S.N. Filatov: Record of conversation with Pak Yŏng-bin, a member of the Political Council of the Central Committee], 4 Feb. 1955. Document from the author's collection.

5. 'Dnevnik Posla SSSR v KNDR tov. Ivanova V.I.' [Journal of ambassador of the USSR to the DPRK Comrade V.I. Ivanov], 19 Mar. 1956, Russian State Archive of Contemporary History, collection 5, inventory 28, item 411, p. 164.

6. Ibid., 21 Mar. 1956. Document from the author's collection.

7. 'Iz dnevnika Samsonova G.E. Zapis' besedy s referentom ministerstva Goskontrolya KNDR Ki Sek Pokom' [From the diary of G.E. Samsonov: Record of conversation with Ki Sŏk-pŏk, analyst of the Ministry for State Inspections of the DPRK], 31 May 1956, Archive of the Foreign Policy of the Russian Federation, collection 102, inventory 12, folder 6, item 68.

8. 'Pis'mo chlena Trudovoy partii Korei So Hueya i tryoh drugih tovarischey v TsK KPK' [A letter of Sŏ Hwi, a member of the Central Committee of the Workers' Party of Korea and three other comrades, to the Central Committee of the Communist Party of China], 1956, State Archive of Russian Federation, collection R-5546, inventory 98, folder 721, pp. 170–90.

9. 'Iz dnevnika Samsonova G.E. ...', 31 May 1956.

10. 'Kim Il Sung and His Personality Cult', May 1956, National Archives of the United Kingdom, FO 1100/2287/2 (B342), pp. 1–2.

11. 'Dnevnik Posla SSSR v KNDR tov. Ivanova V.I.' [Journal of ambassador of the USSR to the DPRK Comrade V.I. Ivanov], 10 May 1956, Archive of the Foreign Policy of the Russian Federation, collection 0102, inventory 12, folder 69, item 5.

12. 'Chosŏn Rodongdang kyuyak' [Constitution of the Workers' Party of Korea], *Rodong Shinmun*, 29 Apr. 1956, p. 2. Article 35 states that 'the chairman and vice-chairmen of the Central Committee are elected by the Central Committee's plenum'.

13. Vasiliy Ivanov, 'Itogi III s'yezda Trudovoy Partii Korei' [Results of the WPK's Third Congress], Russian State Archive of Contemporary History, collection 5, inventory 28, item 411, pp. 143–5.

14. Ibid.

15. 'Pis'mo chlena ...' (1956), pp. 170–90.

16. 'Dnevnik ... Ivanova V.I.', 18 Apr. 1956.

17. *Kim Il-sŏng tongji hoegorok Segiwa tŏburŏ (kyesŭngbon)* [Comrade Kim Il-sung's memoirs 'With the Century' (post-mortem publication)], vol. 8, Pyongyang: Chosŏn Rodongdang Ch'ulp'ansa, 1998, p. 315.

18. 'Dnevnik ... Ivanova V.I.', 6 and 7 Aug. 1956.

19. Danil Svechkov, 'Pochemu Kim Ir Sen v Sverdlovske otkazalsya ot bani s Yel'tsinym?' [Why did Kim Il-sung refuse to go in a bathhouse with Yeltsin in Sverdlovsk?], *Komsomolskaya Pravda Yekaterinburg*, 6 Feb. 2015, https://www.ural.kp.ru/daily/26339.7/3221562/ (accessed 22 Sept. 2023).

20. 'Dnevnik ... Ivanova V.I.', 18 May 1956.

21. 'Pis'mo chlena ...' (1956), pp. 170–90.

22. Ibid.

23. 'Dnevnik ... Ivanova V.I.', 5 June 1956.

24. Ibid., 8 June 1956.

25. Ibid.

26. Ibid., 6 Aug. 1956.

27. Ibid.

28. 'Iz dnevnika I. F. Kurdyukova ...', 11 Aug. 1956.

29. Hong Sun-gwan, 'Chŏn Kim Il-sŏng ...' (1994), pp. 188–207.

30. 'Dnevnik Posla SSSR v KNDR V. I. Ivanova' [Journal of Ambassador of the USSR to the DPRK V.I. Ivanov], 29 Aug. 1956, Russian State Archive of Contemporary History, collection 5, inventory 28, folder 410, pp. 317–19.

31. 'Pis'mo chlena ...' (1956), pp. 170–90.

32. Ibid.

33. Hong Sun-gwan, 'Chŏn Kim Il-sŏng ...' (1994), pp. 188–207.

34. 'Proyekt vystupleniya Yun Kon Hyma na plenume TsK Trudovoy Partii

Korei v avguste 1956 goda' [A draft of the report to be read by Yun Kong-hŭm on the plenum of the Central Committee of the Workers' Party of Korea in August 1956], in 'Materialy k vizitu tov. Mikoyana v Severnuyu Koreyu' [Material prepared for the visit of Comrade Mikoyan to North Korea]. Document from the author's collection.

35. 'Pis'mo chlena ...' (1956), pp. 170–90.

36. 'Dnevnik ... V.I. Ivanova', 6 Sept. 1956, p. 328.

37. Ibid., 1 Sept. 1956, p. 320.

38. In early 1946, when the communists took over the Democratic Party of North Korea, Choe Yong-gon became the party's chairman. His role was to bring the Democratic Party into submission. At that time, he was still technically a member of the Democratic Party, not the communist one. Thus, when he was later appointed to the top position in the WPK, opposition figures tried to use his previous affiliation with a 'bourgeois' party against both him and Kim Il-sung, arguing that Choe was unfit for the role.

39. Hong Sun-gwan, 'Chŏn Kim Il-sŏng ...' (1994), pp. 188–207; 'Dnevnik ... V.I. Ivanova', 6 Sept. 1956, p. 328.

40. 'Pis'mo chlena ...' (1956), pp. 170–90.

41. Ibid.

42. Hong Sun-gwan, 'Chŏn Kim Il-sŏng ...' (1994), pp. 188–207.

43. Ibid.

44. Ibid.

45. 'Ch'oe Ch'ang-ik, Yun Kong-hŭm, Sŏ Hwi, Ri P'il-gyu, Pak Ch'ang-ok tŭng tongmu-dŭr-ŭi chongp'ajŏk ŭmmo haengwi-e taehayŏ' [On the factionalist conspiracy activities of Comrades Choe Chang-ik, Yun Kong-hum, So Hwi, Lee Phil-gyu and Pak Chang-ok], in *Pukhan kwan'gye saryojip*, vol. 30 (1998), pp. 784–879.

46. 'Pis'mo chlena ...' (1956), pp. 170–90.

47. Andrei Lankov's interview with Kang Sang-ho, 31 Oct. 1989, Leningrad.

48. Lee Sang-jo, 'Uvazhayemomu tovarischu Hruschyovu N.S.' [To esteemed Comrade N.S. Khrushchev], 3 Sept. 1956, State Archive of Russian Federation, collection R-5446, inventory 98s, folder 721, pp. 168–9.

49. 'Iz telegrammy A.I. Mikoyana v TsK KPSS o priyome Mao Tszedunom' [Excerpt of the telegram from A.I. Mikoyan to the Central Committee of the CPSU on the reception granted by Mao Zedong], 16 Sept. 1956, State Archive of the Russian Federation, collection R-5446, folder 98s,

item 717, pp. 2–3; 'Telegramma A.I. Mikoyana v Moskvu iz Pekina o vstreche s delegatsiyey WPK' [Telegram from A.I. Mikoyan describing the meeting with a delegation of the WPK, sent to Moscow from Beijing], 17 Sept. 1956, State Archive of the Russian Federation, collection R-5446, folder 98s, item 718, p. 47; 'Telegramma A.I. Mikoyana v Moskvu iz Pekina o vstreche s rukovodstvom TPK' [Telegram from A.I. Mikoyan describing the meeting with the WPK's leadership, sent to Moscow from Beijing], 19 Sept. 1956, State Archive of the Russian Federation, collection R-5446, folder 98s, item 718, pp. 35–8. These documents are reprinted in Igor Selivanov, *Sovetskiy Soyuz i sentyabr'skiye sobytiya 1956 goda v Severnoy Koreye* [Soviet Union and the events of September 1956 in North Korea], Kursk: Kurskiy Gosudarstvennyy universitet, 2015.

50. 'Zapiska A.I. Mikoyana v TsK KPSS' [Note from A.I. Mikoyan to the Central Committee of the CPSU], 21 Sept. 1956, State Archive of the Russian Federation, collection R-5446, folder 98s, item 718, pp. 12–16.

51. 'Doklad tovarischa Kim Ir Sena' [A report on Comrade Kim Il-sung], Russian State Archive for Contemporary History, collection 5, inventory 28, folder 411, p. 303–7; 'Ch'oe Ch'ang-ik, Yun Kong-hŭm, Sŏ Hwi, Ri P'il-gyu, Pak Ch'ang-ok tongmu-dŭr-e taehan kyuryul munjerŭl kaejŏng-hal-te kwanhayŏ' [On the alteration of disciplinary action against Comrades Choe Chang-ik, Yun Kong-hum, So Hwi, Lee Philgyu and Pak Chang-ok], in *Pukhan kwan'gye saryojip*, vol. 30 (1998), p. 796.

52. 'Spravka o polozhenii v Koreye' [A reference letter on the situation in Korea]. Document from the author's collection.

9. HIS LAST BOW

1. 'Pak Ir-u-ŭi pandangjŏk chongp'a haengwie taehayŏ' [On the anti-party factionalist activities of Pak Ir-u], in *Pukhan kwan'gye saryojip*, vol. 30 (1998), pp. 662–6.

2. 'Dnevnik Posla SSSR v KNDR tov. Ivanova V.I.' [Journal of ambassador of the USSR to the DPRK Comrade V.I. Ivanov], 18 May 1956. Document from the author's collection.

3. 'Chosŏn Minjujuŭi Inmin Konghwaguk inmin'gun naemu kyujŏng' [Internal service regulations of the People's Army of the Democratic

People's Republic of Korea], Pyongyang: Minjok Powisŏng Kunsa ch'ulp'anbu, 1955.

4. Ryŏ Jŏng, *Pulgke muldŭn Taedonggang* (1991), pp. 92–4.

5. 'Dnevnik Posla SSSR v KNDR A.M. Puzanova' [Journal of Ambassador of the USSR to the DPRK A.M. Puzanov], 4 June 1957, Archive of the Foreign Policy of the Russian Federation, collection 0102, inventory 13, folder 72, item 5, pp. 114–30.

6. In Puzanov's case, the demotion was even more spectacular than that of Ivanov. Just a few years before being sent to Pyongyang, Puzanov was one of the thirty-six most powerful men in the entire Soviet Union: in 1952, Stalin appointed him an alternate member of the Central Committee's Presidium. Immediately after Stalin died, Puzanov was dismissed from the Presidium and further demotions followed. In five years, he was reduced from being a top decision-maker to an ambassador to North Korea.

7. 'Dnevnik ... A.M. Puzanova', 5 July 1957, pp. 131–45.

8. Ibid., 3 Sept. 1957, pp. 275–300.

9. Ibid., 4 Sept. 1957, pp. 275–300.

10. Ibid., 9 Sept. 1957, pp. 275–300.

11. It was never reported in the press that Choe had been stripped of his rank, but after 20 Sept. 1957 he never appeared in public in a uniform and all subsequent publications about him, including his 1976 obituary, fail to mention him ever holding this rank. See 'Ch'oe Yong-gŏn tongji-ŭi sŏgŏ-e taehan pugo' [Obituary on the passing of Comrade Choe Yong-gon], *Chosŏn Inmin'gun*, 21 Sept. 1976, p. 1.

12. 'Kim Il-sŏng tongji-ege sae naegak chojik-ŭl wiim' [New cabinet of Comrade Kim Il-sung is appointed], *Rodong Shinmun*, 20 Sept. 1957, p. 1.

13. 'K besede s partiyno-pravitel'stvennoy delegatsiyey KNDR' [Notes for talks with the party and government delegation of the DPRK], Archive of the Foreign Policy of the Russian Federation, collection 0102, folder 13, file 72, item 11.

14. Lee Dong-hun, 'Puk "P'uebŭllo-ho" sagŏn ku-Soryŏn oegyo munsŏ kŭkpi haeje' [Soviet documents of the North Korean *Pueblo* incident were declassified], *Chugan Chosŏn*, 22 Sept. 2019, http://news.chosun.com/site/data/html_dir/2019/09/20/2019092002511.html (accessed 22 Sept. 2023); E. Titorenko, 'Zapis' besedy s Nam Mariyey Avksent'yevnoy,

zhenoy Nam Ira, chlena Politbyuro TsK TPK' [Record of conversation with Mariya Nam, wife of Nam Il, member of the Politburo of the WPK's Central Committee], Russian State Archive of Contemporary History, collection 5, inventory 49, folder 640, p. 204.

15. Andrei Lankov's interview with Kang Sang-ho, 7 Mar. 1990, Leningrad.

16. 'Iz dnevnika Puzanova A.M. Zapis' besedy s tov. Kim Ir Senom' [From the diary of A.M. Puzanov: Record of conversation with Comrade Kim Il-sung], 13 Nov. 1957, Archive of the Foreign Policy of the Russian Federation, collection 0102, inventory 13, item 5; 'Iz dnevnika 1-go sekretarya Posol'stva SSSR v KNDR Pimenova B. K. Zapis' besedy s zaveduyuschim 1-m otdelom MID KNDR Pak Kil' Yenom' [From the diary of the first secretary of the embassy of the USSR to the DPRK B.K. Pimenov: Record of conversation with Pak Kil-yong, chairman of the First Department of the Ministry of Foreign Affairs of the DPRK], 8 Dec. 1957, Archive of the Foreign Policy of the Russian Federation, collection 102, inventory 13, item 6, folder 72.

17. Lee Jong-sŏk, *Pukhan-Chungguk kwan'gye 1945–2000* [Sino-North Korean relations, 1945–2000], Seoul: Chungshim, 2000, p. 205.

18. *Pukhan ch'ongnam: '45–'68* [The comprehensive survey of North Korea: 1945–68], Seoul: Kongsan'gwŏn munje yŏn'guso, 1968, pp. 199–200. This is an excellent piece of research on the North, based, among other things, on the interrogation protocols South Korean intelligence conducted with people who had fled from the North; the book remains unsurpassed when it comes to research into the DPRK of the 1960s.

19. This three-strata system outlived Kim Il-sung, as North Korea adjusted the system in the late 1990s. At the time of writing, North Koreans are divided into five categories instead of three: special, nucleus, basic, wavering and hostile classes.

20. *Pukhan ch'ongnam: '45–'68* (1968), p. 200.

21. *Kim Il-sŏng-gwa Pukhan* [Kim Il-sung and North Korea], Seoul: Naeoe munje yŏn'guso, 1978, p. 75.

22. Peter Ward's article is the most detailed study of this conference in English. See Peter Ward, 'Purging "Factionalist" Opposition to Kim Il Sung: The First Party Conference of the Korean Workers' Party in 1958', *European Journal of Korean Studies*, 18, no. 2, 2019, pp. 105–25, https://www.researchgate.net/publication/332165615_Purging_'Factionalist'_Opposition_to_Kim_Il_Sung_-_The_First_Party_Conference_of_the_

Korean_Worker's_Party_in_1958/link/60952362299bf1ad8d81f444/ download (accessed 22 Sept. 2023).

23. *Chosŏn Rodongdang che 1 taep'yoja hoeŭi hoeŭirok* [Minutes of the first conference of the Workers' Party of Korea], Pyongyang: Chosŏn Rodongdang Chungang Wiwŏnhoe, 1958, pp. 491–2.

24. 'Kaein sungbae sasang' [The ideology of the personality cult], in *Taejung chŏngch'i yongŏ sajŏn* [Dictionary of political terminology for a mass audience], Pyongyang: Chosŏn Rodongdang ch'ulp'ansa, 1957, p. 47.

25. *Taejung chŏngch'i yongŏ sajŏn (chŭngbop'an)* [Dictionary of political terminology for a mass audience (revised edition)], Pyongyang: Chosŏn Rodongdang ch'ulp'ansa, 1959.

26. 'Ivan Afanasyeich ...' (1991), pp. 25–7.

27. Andrei Lankov's interview with Pak Il-san, son of Pak Ch'ang-ok, 4 Feb. 2001, Saint Petersburg.

28. Ryŏ Jŏng, *Pulgke muldŭn Taedonggang* (1991). Ryŏ Jŏng is Kang Su-bong's pseudonym.

29. V. Bakulin, 'Itogi dovyborov v Verhovnoye Narodnoye Sobraniye KNDR' [Results of the by-elections to the Supreme People's Assembly of the DPRK], 11 Aug. 1959. Document from the author's collection.

30. 'Kabinet Ministrov KNDR. Postanovleniye № 7 ot 22 yanvarya 1959 goda' [The Cabinet of Ministers of the DPRK: Decision 7, 22 Jan. 1959], Archive of the Foreign Policy of the Russian Federation, collection 0102, inventory 15, folder 83, item 32, pp. 8–10.

31. For one of the testimonies of people who experienced the system, see Ri Chun-ha, *Kyohwaso iyagi* [A story about the re-education camp], Seoul: Shidae chŏngshin, 2008. The most detailed study of these camps in English is David Hawk, 'The Parallel GULAG', Washington, DC: Committee for Human Rights in North Korea, 2017, https://www. hrnk.org/uploads/pdfs/Hawk_The_Parallel_Gulag_Web.pdf (accessed 22 Sept. 2023).

32. On the Soviet prototype, see Viktor Berdinskih, Ivan Berdinskih and Vladimir Veremeyev, *Sistema spetsposeleniy v Sovetskom Soyuze v 1930–1950-h godah* [System of special settlements in the Soviet Union of the 1930s–1950s], Moscow: ROSSPEN, 2017.

33. On the Security Committees, see *Pukhan ch'ongnam:'45–'68.* (1968), p. 158.

34. The following book, published in Aug. 1958, already features these

changes: Pak Ch'oe-wŏl, Yang Ri-jip and Ri Chi-hol, *Chosŏn Minjujuŭi Inmin Konghwaguk* [Democratic People's Republic of Korea], Pyongyang: Kungnip misul ch'ulp'ansa, 1958.

10. PREPARATIONS FOR A SECOND KOREAN WAR

1. 'Hanggari Naegag-esŏ kogŭp maekpun paegŭpche p'yeji shinch'ŏng' [Hungarian Cabinet of Ministers requested for public distribution system of high-quality wheat flour to be abolished], *Rodong Shinmun*, 6 Apr. 1950, p. 4; 'Pulgaria-esŏ kongŏp chep'um-ŭi paegŭpche ch'ŏlp'ye' [In Bulgaria, they abolish the public distribution system of industrial goods], *Rodong Shinmun*, 27 Apr. 1951, p. 4; 'Togil Minjujuŭi Konghwagug-esŏ paegŭpche p'ejiwa mulga inha' [The German Democratic Republic abolishes the public distribution system and decreases prices], *Rodong Shinmun*, 4 Apr. 1952, p. 4; 'P'aran-esŏ paegŭpche p'yeji' [Poland abolishes public distribution system], *Rodong Shinmun*, 11 Jan. 1953, p. 1.

2. 'Dnevnik vremennogo poverennogo v delah SSSR v KNDR Kryukova M.E.' [Journal of the *chargé d'affaires* of the USSR to the DPRK M.E. Kryukov], 19 Nov. 1957. Document from the author's collection.

3. 'Zapis' besedy s zamestitelem zaveduyuschego mezhdunarodnym otdelom, chlenom TsK TPK Kim Yun Sonom' [Record of conversation with deputy chief of the International Department Kim Yun-son, a member of the WPK's Central Committee], 26 Nov. 1970, Russian State Archive of Contemporary History, collection 5, inventory 62, item 456, pp. 327–32.

4. Natalia Matveeva, 'Building a New World: The Economic Development Strategies of the Two Koreas in the Cold War, 1957–1966', PhD thesis, University of London, School of Oriental and African Studies, 2021, pp. 34–5. Based on a large number of previously unknown sources, this thesis is a breakthrough in studies of the formation of the economic system of Kim Il-sung's North Korea, especially given that this system has persisted for decades and is responsible for the sorry state of the DPRK's economy.

5. Natalia Matveeva, 'Dizzy with Success: North Korea's Ambitious, and Troubled, First Five-Year Plan', NK News, 27 May 2019, https://www.nknews.org/2019/05/dizzy-with-success-north-koreas-ambitious-and-troubled-first-five-year-plan/ (accessed 22 Sept. 2023).

6. Natalia Matveeva, 'The Historical Roots of North Korea's Notoriously-Unreliable Statistics', NK News, 28 June 2019, https://www.nknews. org/2019/06/the-historical-roots-of-north-koreas-notoriously-unreliable-statistics/ (accessed 22 Sept. 2023).

7. For more on this, see the memoirs of Kim Jŏng-gi, a former employee of the bureau: *Milp'a* [Secret envoy], Seoul: Taeyŏngsa, 1967, p. 120.

8. Kim Il-sung conducted his first such visit in June 1957. See 'Tang tanch'e-dŭr-ŭi saenghwar-esŏ: Nongŏp hyŏptong chohap chido pangjo kŭruppa-dŭl hyŏnji chido saŏb-e ch'aksu' [From the daily life of party organisations: Guidance and assistance groups of collective farms start to participate in the on-the-spot guidance], *Rodong Shinmun*, 2 Dec. 1955, p. 2; 'Kim Il-sŏng tongji Namp'o chigu kongjang, kiŏpso-dŭr-ŭl hyŏnjijido-che1ch'a 5kaenyŏn kyehoek chaksŏng-esŏ tŏ manŭn yebi-rŭl tongwŏnhal kŏs-ŭl kangjo' [Comrade Kim Il-sung conducts on-the-spot guidance in factories and enterprises in Nampho, stresses the need for more reserves for the first five-year plan], *Rodong Shinmun*, 15 June 1957, p. 1.

9. Han Chae-dŏk, *Kim Il-sŏng-ŭl kobalha-nda: Chosŏn Nodongdang ch'iha-ŭi Pukhan hoegorok* [I accuse Kim Il-sung: Memoirs on North Korea under the rule of the WPK], Seoul: Naeoe munhwasa, 1965, p. 164.

10. 'Hyŏnji chido-nŭn kot pan'gwallyojuŭi t'ujaeng-ida' [On-the-spot guidance is the very struggle against bureaucratism], *Rodong Shinmun*, 20 Oct. 1956, p. 1.

11. One of Kim's speeches mentioning this doctrine is Kim Il-sŏng [Kim Il-sung], 'Hyŏn chŏngse-wa uri tang-ŭi kwaŏp' [Current situation and the tasks of our party], *Rodong Shinmun*, 6 Oct. 1966, pp. 2–7.

12. Kim Jŏng-nam, *4.19 hyŏngmyŏng* [The April Revolution], Seoul: Minjuhwa undong kinyŏm saŏp'oe, 2004. The author of this book is not Kim Il-sung's grandson Kim Jong-nam but rather his namesake.

13. Chŏn Yŏng-gi, '"Chang Do-yŏng ŏnhaeng hyŏngmyŏng panghae" JP, Pak sojang-ege pogo ank'o kisŭp ch'ep'o ... Pak Chŏng-hŭi "hyŏngmyŏng-edo ŭiri-ga? ..." JP "konoe·ap'ŭm ŏpsŭl su ŏpsŏtta"' [Kim Jong-pil said 'Chang Do-yong's words and actions obstruct the revolution.' He had Chang arrested without reporting to Major-General Park in advance. Park Chung-hee: 'Should not loyalty exist even during revolution?' Kim Jong-pil: 'It was a painful torment and could not be otherwise'], *Chungang*

Ilbo, 6 Apr. 2015, https://web.archive.org/web/20190808102748/https://news.joins.com/article/17520151 (accessed 1 Oct. 2020).

14. 'Incoming Telegram from Seoul to the Secretary of State', 26 May 1955, National Archives and Records Administration, Record Group 59, Central File 795.00/5–2655. I am grateful to Natalia Matveeva for sharing this document with me.

15. A North Korean concept according to which KPA personnel are theoretically qualified to command a unit above their regular qualification. For example, a company commander should be qualified to command a battalion, a regiment commander should be qualified to lead a division, etc.

16. 'Iz dnevnika Okonnikova O.V., Putivtsa A.D. O poyezdke v Chondin' [From the diary of O.V. Okonnikov and A.D. Putivets: On a trip to the Chongjin city], 8–12 Apr. 1963, Archive of the Foreign Policy of the Russian Federation, collection 0102, inventory 19, folder 99, item 26, p. 64. I am grateful to Natalia Matveeva for bringing this document to my attention.

17. The BBC report on one of the key battles can be found here: BBC On This Day, '1955: US Evacuates Pacific Islands', http://news.bbc.co.uk/onthisday/hi/dates/stories/february/10/newsid_2538000/2538891.stm (accessed 22 Sept. 2023).

18. 'Sahoejuǔi chinyǒng-ǔl onghohaja' [Let us defend the Socialist camp], *Chosǒn Nyǒsǒng*, Nov. 1963, pp. 1–22.

19. 'Zhu Chaoxian dashi Hao Deqing cixing baihui Jin Richeng Shouxiang tanhua qingkuang' [Hao Deqing, ambassador to the DPRK, paid a farewell visit on Premier Kim Il-sung and discussed with him the current events], Foreign Ministry of the PRC, declassified document 06–01480–07. Quoted from Cheng Xiaohe, '"Zhuyi" yu "anquan" zhi zheng: Liushinian dai Chaoxian yuzhong, suguanxi de yanbian' [The struggle between 'ideological principles' and 'security': The evolution of North Korea's relations with China and the Soviet Union in the 1960s], *Waijiao pinglun*, Feb. 2009, pp. 21–35.

11. CHARTING OUR OWN PATH

1. Jung Chang and Jon Halliday, *Mao: The Unknown Story*, New York: Random House, 2005, pp. 503–14.

2. 'Chajusŏng-ŭl onghohaja' [Let us protect independence], *Rodong Shinmun*, 12 Aug. 1966, pp. 1–3.

3. V. Tribunskiy, 'Informatsiya o poyezdke v provintsiyu Ryangan' [Information letter on a visit to the Ryanggang province], 27 Aug. 1969, Russian State Archive for Contemporary History, collection 5, inventory 64, folder 420, pp. 84–6.

4. Author's interview with An Chan-il, July 2018, Seoul.

5. Kádas István [István Kádas], 'Információ a kínai-koreai kapcsolatok alakulásáról' [Information about the development of Sino-Korean relations], Hungarian National Archives, box 59, 81–1, 002218/1. The document was kindly provided to the author by Balázs Szalontai.

6. The reported number of Chinese citizens in North Korea in 1958 was 14,351. See Yang Zhaoquan and Sun Yumei, *Chaoxian Huaqiao shi* [History of Chinese people in Korea], Beijing: Zhongguo Huaqiao chuban gongsi, 1981, p. 303.

7. Liang Senpei, 'Lishi huigu: Pingrang Zhongguoren gaozhong "tingke jiesan" shijian (wen, tu)' [Historical review: Case of suspension of classes in Pyongyang Secondary School for Chinese (text and pictures)], *Chaoxian Huaqiao*, https://web.archive.org/web/20181023044121/ http://www.cxhq.info/read.php?tid=1468 (accessed 22 Sept. 2023).

8. Author's interview with former North Koreans. See also Wang Yonggui, 'Chaoxian jiyi' [Reminiscences on North Korea], *Qiaoyuan*, vol. 160, Oct. 2013, pp. 68–9.

9. 'Perepiska s TsK KPSS (otchyot o poyezdke Sovetskoy Pravitel'stvennoy delegatsii na prazdnestva v Narodnuyu Koreyu i zapisi besed s Kim Ir Senom 12 i 13 sentyabrya 1968 g.)' [Correspondence with the Central Committee of the CPSU (report on the trip of the Soviet government delegation to the festivities in People's Korea and notes of conversations with Kim Il-sung on 12 and 13 Sept. 1968)], State Archive of Russian Federation, collection R-5446, folder 132, item 16, p. 5.

10. Ibid.

11. 'K'ambojya-nŭn chagug-e taehan konggyŏg-i kyesong toe-ndamyŏn pobo-gŭi kwŏlli-rŭl haengsaha-yŏ pan'gonggyŏk-ŭl kahal kŏsh-ida (K'ambojya Kukka Wŏnsu Shihanuk'ŭ-ga ŏnmyŏng)' [If attacks on Cambodia continue, it will exercise its right of vengeance and will counterattack: Proclamation of Sihanouk, the head of state of Cambodia], *Rodong Shinmun*, 5 Jan. 1966, p. 4.

12. Yu Wan-sik and Kim T'ae-sŏ, *Pukhan samsipnyŏnsa* [Thirty years of North Korean history], Seoul: Hyŏndae Kyŏngje Ilbo sa, 1975, p. 265.

13. Published between 1995 and 2001, the encyclopaedia remains the most authoritative source of officially recognised knowledge on North Korea.

14. 'Chuch'e sasang' [Juche Thought], in *Chosŏn Tae Paekkwa Sajŏn*, vol. 19 (2000), p. 342.

15. Bruce Cumings, a famous American historian of North Korea, has played a major role in contributing to this misconception by repeating the claims about the enigmatic nature of the word. See Bruce Cumings. 'Corporatism in North Korea', *The Journal of Korean Studies*, 4 (1982–3), pp. 269–94; Cumings, *Origins of the Korean War*, vol. 2, Princeton: Princeton University Press, 1990, p. 313; Cumings, 'The Corporate State in North Korea', in *State and Society in Contemporary Korea*, Ithaca: Cornell University Press, 1993, p. 214; Cumings, *North Korea: Another Country*, New York: The New Press, 2003, p. 159; and Cumings, *Korea's place in the Sun*, New York: W.W. Norton & Co., 2005, p. 414.

16. In 1965, a group of conspirators in Bulgaria tried to overthrow Todor Zhivkov, a moderate communist dictator who had ruled the country since 1956. One of the prominent members of the group was Tsolo Krastev, former ambassador to the DPRK, where he had been inspired by Kim Il-sung's policies. The group was planning to install their own version of national Stalinism in Bulgaria, allying themselves with Mao's China and Hoxha's Albania. Fortunately, the Bulgarian secret police apprehended the conspirators. The codename for the operation to capture them was 'Fools'. For more information, see Niko Yahiel, 'Preduprezhdenie na sedminata i zagovor na Ivan Todorov-Gorunya' [Warning of the week and plot of Ivan Todorov-Gorunya], in *Todor Zhivkov i lichnata vlast* [Todor Zhivkov and personal power], Sofia: M-8-M, 1997, pp. 344–54, http://prehod.omda.bg/public/knigi/t_zhivkov_lichnata_vlast_n_yahiel.pdf (accessed 22 Sept. 2023).

17. '1·21 Ch'ŏngwadae sŭpkyŏk sagŏn saengp'cja Kim Shin-jo chŏn'gyŏng chŭngŏn' [Shocking testimony of Kim Shin-jo, the survivor of the 21 Jan. raid on the Blue House], *Shindonga*, 29 Jan. 2004, http://shindonga.donga.com/3/all/13/103148/1 (accessed 22 Sept. 2023).

18. Kim Shin-jo, *Na-ŭi sŭlp'ŭn yŏksa-rŭl marhanda* [I speak about my sad history], Seoul: Tonga ch'ulp'ansa, 1994.

19. 'Kapitan Krasnoy Armii Kim byl horoshiy muzhik' [That Kim guy, the

captain of the Red Army, was a nice chap], *Kommersant Vlast'*, no. 38, 30 Sept. 2002, p. 72, https://www.kommersant.ru/doc/343387 (accessed 22 Sept. 2023).

20. It is a small miracle that this record exists. It was originally told to a Soviet diplomat, Dmitriy Kapustin, by Tatyana Lee, a Soviet Korean woman, one of a few dozen Soviet citizens in the DPRK, and Kapustin duly recorded her story. 'Iz dnevnika Kapustina D.T. Informatsiya o poseschenii goroda Vonsana' [From the diary of D.T. Kapustin: An information record on the visit to the city of Wonsan], 21 July 1969, Russian State Archive for Contemporary History, collection 5, inventory 61, folder 463, pp. 182–8.

21. For an excellent analysis of American sources relating to the incident, see Mitchell B. Lerner, *The Pueblo Incident: A Spy Ship and the Failure of American Foreign Policy*, Lawrence: University Press of Kansas, 2002.

22. The original report, later confirmed by the independent investigation, comes from '"Kongsandang-i shirŏyo" ŏrin hanggŏ ip tchijŏ' [They slice the mouth of the kid who said 'I hate the Communist Party'], *Chosŏn Ilbo*, 11 Dec. 1967, p. 4.

23. Cho Hyŏn-ho, '"I Sŭng-bok sagŏn" Kim Jong-bae mujoe·Kim Ju-ŏn chibyu hwakchŏng' [The sentence on the accused in the Lee Sung-bok case is confirmed: Kim Jong-bae is declared innocent, Kim Ju-on is out on probation], 24 Nov. 2006, http://www.mediatoday.co.kr/news/articleView.html?idxno=52102 (accessed 22 Sept. 2023).

24. 'Zapis' besedy s zamestitelem ministra inostrannyh del KNDR Ho Damom' [Record of conversation with Ho Dam, deputy minister of foreign affairs of the DPRK], 16 Apr. 1969, Russian State Archive for Contemporary History, collection 5, inventory 61, folder 462, pp. 71–4.

25. Andrei Lankov, 'Take to the Skies: North Korea's Role in the Mysterious Hijacking of KAL YS-11', NK News, 29 Mar. 2019, https://www.nknews.org/2019/03/take-to-the-skies-north-koreas-role-in-the-mysterious-hijacking-of-kal-ys-11/ (accessed 22 Sept. 2023).

26. 'Zapis' besedy s zamestitelem ministra inostrannyh del KNDR Kim Che Bomom' [Record of conversation with Kim Jae-bong, deputy minister of foreign affairs of the DPRK], 6 Jan. 1969, Russian State Archive for Contemporary History, collection 5, inventory 62, folder 461, pp. 23–4.

27. In later years, satellite imagery made it much easier to trace the villas of the North Korean leadership. The following article offers a list: 'Kim

Jŏng-il pyŏljang wich'i-wa t'ŭkching' [Location and features of Kim Jong-il's villas], *Chugan Tonga*, 582, 2007, pp. 16–17, https://weekly. donga.com/List/3/all/11/82177/1 (accessed 22 Sept. 2023).

28. Author's interview with Dmitriy Kapustin, Sept. 2019, online (Seoul–Moscow). Kapustin worked in the Soviet embassy in the late 1960s; his colleague, Vladimir Kekishev, the embassy's medic, visited Kim Il-sung's own clinic and was highly impressed by the standard of the equipment there.

29. 'Zapis' besedy ...', 6 Jan. 1969, pp. 23–4.

30. 'Zapis' besedy s chlenom Prezidiuma Politicheskogo Soveta TsK TPK, pervym zamestitelem Predsedatelya Soveta Ministrov KNDR Kim Irom' [Record of conversation with Kim Il, a member of the Standing Committee of the Political Committee of the CC WPK and deputy premier of the DPRK], 4 Jan. 1970, Russian State Archive for Contemporary History, collection 5, inventory 62, folder 456, pp. 16–19; 'Mao Zedong Zhuxi huijian Chaoxian junshi daibiaotuan tanhua jilu' [Transcript of Chairman Mao Zedong's meeting with the North Korean military delegation], 29 July 1970, in *Jimi dangan zhong xin faxian de Mao Zedong jianghua* [Mao Zedong's speeches recently discovered in restricted-access archives], New York: Guoshi chubanshe, 2018, p. 254.

31. 'Nambu Wennam chŏnyŏng wanjŏn haebang, koeroe todang mujokŏn hangbok' [The entire South Vietnam is completely liberated; The puppet clique has unconditionally surrendered], *Rodong Shinmun*, 1 May 1975, p. 1.

32. 'Widaehan Suryŏngnim-ŭi hyŏnmyŏngha-n ryŏngdo-rŭl pattŭrŏnaga-nŭn uri rodong kyegŭp-kwa inmin-ŭi hyŏngmyŏng wiŏb-ŭn p'ilsŭng pulp'ae-ida' [The revolutionary great deed of our working class and our people, who receive the wise leadership of the Great Leader, is ever victorious and never failing], *Rodong Shinmun*, 1 May 1975, p. 1.

33. 'Zapis' besedy s poslom SRV Le Chung Namom' [Record of conversation with Lê Trung Nam, the ambassador of the Socialist Republic of Vietnam], 3 Aug. 1976, Russian State Archive for Contemporary History, collection 5, inventory 69, folder 2427, pp. 78–81.

12. THE LONG NIGHT BEGINS

1. Kim Il-sŏng [Kim Il-sung], 'Tangsaŏb-ŭl kaesŏnhamyŏ tang taep'yojahoe kyŏljŏng-ŭl kwanch'ŏrha-lte taehayŏ' [On improvement of the party

work and on the fulfilment of the decisions of the party conference], 17–24 Mar. 1967, in *Kim Il-sŏng chŏjakchip*, vol. 21 (1983), pp. 135–258.

2. While South Korean intelligence eventually discovered that the plenum had occurred, as well as the nature of the decisions made there, the earliest South Korean publications incorrectly stated that it had taken place in Apr., not in May. Kongbobu [Department of Public Information], *Hyŏndaesa-wa kongsanjuŭi* [Modern history and communism], vol. 1, Seoul: Kongbobu [Department of Public Information], 1968, pp. 433–6.

3. *Paekkwa chŏnsŏ* [Complete encyclopaedia], vol. 4, Pyongyang: Kwahak, paekkwasajŏn ch'ulp'ansa, 1983, p. 491.

4. Kim Chin-gye, *Choguk: Ŏnŭ Puk Chosŏn inmin-ŭi sugi* [The motherland: Notes of one of the North Korean people], vol. 2, Seoul: Hyŏnjang munhaksa, 1990, p. 79.

5. Ibid., p. 80.

6. Sŏng Hye-rang, *Tŭngnamu chip* [A wisteria house], Seoul: Chisik Nara, 2000, pp. 312–17.

7. *Chosŏn minjok-ui Widaehan Ryŏngdoja* [The Great Chief of the Korean nation], Tokyo: Chosŏn sinbo sa, 1965, p. 138.

8. Kim Ju-wŏn, 'Ponmyŏng Kim Jŏng-ir-in Kim Jŏng-gi paksa-ŭi kaemyŏng' [Dr Kim Jong-gi's original name was 'Kim Jong-il', he changed it], Radio Free Asia, 19 July 2016, https://www.rfa.org/korean/weekly_program/ae40c528c77cac00c758-c228aca8c9c4-c9c4c2e4/hiddentruth-07192016100504.html (accessed 22 Sept. 2023).

9. 'Widaehan suryŏng Kim Il-sŏng tongji-ŭi purhuŭi kojŏnjŏk rojak-tŭr-ŭl yŏrŏ nara shinmun, chapchi, t'ongshin-dŭr-i kejae, pangsong-i podo' [The Great Leader Comrade Kim Il-sung's immortal classic works, newspapers, journals and media of several countries have published and broadcasts have aired], *Rodong Shinmun*, 26 Nov. 1977, p. 1. This is one of the thousands upon thousands of such examples.

10. 'P'yŏnjippu-robut'ŏ' [From the editorial department], in *Chosŏn Chungang Nyŏn'gam 1995 (t'ŭkpyŏlbon)* [Korean central yearbook, 1995 (special edition)], Pyongyang: Chosŏn Chungang T'ongshinsa, 1995, preface page.

11. *I kŏshi Pukhan-ida* [This is North Korea], Seoul: Naeoe t'ongshinsa, 1978, p. 8.

12. See, for example, Chang Se-jŏng, 'Kim Jŏng-ŭn ch'osanghwa ŏnje kŭrina ... yojŭm Pukhan 1ho hwaga-dŭl komin' ['When shall we start

drawing Kim Jong-un's portraits?' think the North Korean 'painters of the First One'], *Chungang Ilbo*, 30 June 2015, https://www.joongang. co.kr/article/18131576 (accessed 1 Oct. 2020).

13. A typical example of such a piece is 'K'ŭn mul p'ihae chiyŏg-esŏ nop'i parhwidoen suryŏng kyŏlsaongwi chŏngshin' [The spirit of defending the Leader at the cost of one's life is high in the places hit by floods], Korean Central News Agency, 8 Sept. 2007, http://kcna.co.jp/ calendar/2007/09/09-08/2007-0907-011.html (accessed 22 Sept. 2023).

14. Barbara Demick, *Nothing to Envy: Ordinary Lives in North Korea*, New York: Spiegel & Grau, 2009, p. 104.

15. Although it was clearly visible, the tumour does not seem to have caused Kim any physical discomfort. Author's interview with Kim Yŏng-hwan, 4 June 2019, Seoul.

16. 'Chosŏn Rodongdang Chungang Kunsa Wiwŏnhoe chishi, che 002 ho.' [Ordinance of the Central Military Commission of the Workers' Party of Korea no. 002], in 'Chŏnshi saŏp sech'ik'ŭl naeom-e taehayŏ' [On establishment of the 'Detailed regulations on the actions to be taken in case of a state of war'], 7 Apr. 2004. Document from the author's collection.

17. Ibid.

18. '[1 ho paeu] Kim Il-sŏng yŏk hanbŏn ha-myŏn p'yŏngsaeng tarŭn yŏk mot hae' [Actor no. 1: Once you play Kim Il-sung, you will never be able to play anyone else], *NK Chosŏn*, 20 Nov. 2001, http://nk.chosun.com/ news/articleView.html?idxno=12849 (accessed 22 Sept. 2023).

19. 'Chosŏn Minjujuŭi Inmin Konghwaguk Ch'oego Inmin Hoeŭi Sangim Wiwŏnhoe chŏngnyŏng' [Legislative order of the Presidium of the Supreme People's Assembly of the DPRK], 'Kim Il-sŏng hunjang-ŭl chejŏngha-m-ŭl taehayŏ' [On the establishment of the Kim Il-sung order], *Rodong Shinmun*, 21 Mar. 1972, p. 1.

20. *Pulgur-ŭi pan-Il hyŏngmyŏng t'usa Kim Hyŏng-jik sŏnsaeng* [Unyielding anti-Japanese revolutionary fighter, teacher Kim Hyong-jik], Pyongyang: Chosŏn Rodongdang ch'ulp'ansa, 1968.

21. *Kang Ban-sŏk nyŏsa-e ttara paeuja* [Let us learn from Lady Kang Ban-sok], Pyongyang: Chosŏn Minju Nyŏsŏng Tongmaeng Chungang Wiwŏnhoe, 1967.

22. One of the first books to narrate this discourse is Paek Pong, *Minjog-ŭi t'aeyang Kim Il-sŏng changgun* [Commander Kim Il-sung, the Sun of the Nation], vol. 1, Pyongyang: Inmin kwahaksa, 1968.

23. 'Tongbang-esŏ sosŭn t'aeyang' [The sun that rose from the East], *Rodong Shinmun*, 15 Aug. 2012, p. 2; '30daeŭi kŏn'guk suban-kke tŭrin kyŏngŭi' [Show of respect towards the founding head of state, who was in his thirties], *Rodong Shinmun*, 11 Sept. 2011, p. 4.

24. Han Man-gil, *T'ongil shidae Pukhan kyoyungnon* [Writings on North Korean education in the age of unification], Seoul: Kyoyuk kwahaksa, 1997, p. 162. While (undeservingly) not very well known, Han Man-gil's book is an excellent study of the history of North Korean education.

25. See Yuriy Vanin, 'Izucheniye istorii Korei' [Historical studies of Korea], in *Koreyevedeniye v Rossii: Istoriya i sovremennost'* [Korean studies in Russia: History and the current situation], Moscow: Pervoye Marta, 2004; *Dongbei kangri lianjun douzheng shi* [The history of the struggle of the North East United Anti-Japanese Army], Beijing: Renmin chubanshe, 1991.

26. Zhurin, 'Sdelan v SSSR' (2011).

27. Ibid.

28. Kim Ŭng-gyo, *Choguk* [Motherland], vol. 2, Seoul: P'ulbit, 1993, p. 91.

29. 'Chosŏn Minjujuŭi Inmin Konghwaguk ryŏgwŏn min sajŭng-e kwanhan kyujŏng' [Regulations on passports and visas of the DPRK], 8 Dec. 1960, in *Chosŏn Minjujuŭi Inmin Konghwaguk pŏpkyujip* (1961), pp. 668–75.

30. The name of the youth league has changed many times. Created as the 'Union of Democratic Youth of North Korea', it was subsequently renamed the 'Union of Socialist Workers Youth' in 1961, the 'Kimilsungist Union of Socialist Youth' in 1997, the 'Kimilsungist–Kimjongilist Union of the Youth' in 2016 and the 'Socialist Patriotic Youth League' in 2021.

31. Sŏ Dong-ik, 'Pukhan yŏsŏng-dŭr-ŭi kyŏrhon'gwan' [The things North Korean women value in marriage], *Wŏlgan Pukhan*, May 1988, pp. 96–103; Lankov, *KNDR vchera i segodnya* (2004), pp. 279–81; 'Ideologicheskaya rabota v KNDR v svyazi s podgotovkoy k 60-letiyu Kim Ir Sena' [Ideology-related activities in the DPRK in preparation for the celebration of Kim Il-sung's sixtieth birthday], 14 Feb. 1972, Russian State Archive for Contemporary History, collection 5, inventory 64, item 419, pp. 30–49.

32. See *Pukhan ch'ongnam* [The comprehensive survey of North Korea], Seoul: Pukhan yŏn'guso, 1983, p. 1505; 'Pukhan inmin'gun-ŭn 10 nyŏn pongmu' [Ten year-long service in the North Korean People's Army], DailyNK, 8 Jan. 2007, http://www.dailynk.com/korean/read.

php?cataId=nk09000&num=35446 (accessed 22 Sept. 2023); and Kim Gyun-t'ae, 'Yennal kundae, iraetsuda' [This is how the army was in the old times], in *An'gyŏng ŏmnŭn kundae iyagi* [A story about the army without glasses], Seoul: Ŭiam ch'ulp'an munhwasa, 1993, pp. 248–51.

33. Humphrey Hawksley, 'Lessons from the Death of North Korea's First Leader', BBC News, 19 Dec. 2011, http://www.bbc.com/news/world-asia-16252540 (accessed 22 Sept. 2023).

34. 'Amsŭt'ŭrong, Nel Alten' [Armstrong, Neil Alden], in *Chosŏn Tae Paekkwa Sajŏn*, vol. 26 (2001), p. 610.

35. L.V. Volkova, 'Zapis' besedy s grazhdankoy SSSR postoyanno prozhivayuschey v KNDR Li Tat'yanoy Ivanovnoy' [Record of conversation with Tatyana Lee, a USSR citizen permanently residing in the DPRK], 1 Dec. 1972, Russian State Archive for Contemporary History, collection 5, inventory 64, item 424, pp. 67–8.

36. Sŏng Hye-rang, *Tŭngnamu chip* (2000), p. 314.

37. The official message merely mentioned that all deputies were elected unanimously with a 100 per cent participation rate. See 'Widaehan suryŏng Kim Il-sŏng tongji-ŭi turi-e hana-ŭi sasang ŭiji-ro kutke mungch'in uri inmin-ŭi pulp'ae-ŭi t'ongil tan'gyŏl manse! Chŏnch'e sŏn'gŏja-dŭr-ŭi 100%ga t'up'yoe ch'amga chŏnch'e sŏn'gŏja-dŭr-ŭi 100%ga ch'ansŏng t'up'yo Ch'oego inmin hoeŭi taeŭiwŏn sŏn'gŏ sŏnggwajŏk-ŭro chinhaeng' [Glory to the invincible unity of our people, armed with one thought and will and united around the Great Leader Comrade Kim Il-sung! Elections to the Supreme People's Assembly have proceeded successfully, with 100 per cent of the voters participating and 100 per cent of them voting in support of the candidates], *Rodong Shinmun*, 13 Nov. 1977, p. 2. The country's military newspaper *Choson Inmingun* also failed to publish the list of deputies.

38. One of many contemporary observations is 'Vnutrenneye polozheniye i vneshnyaya politika Koreyskoy Narodno-Demokraticheskoy Respubliki' [The situation in the country and the foreign policy of the DPRK], 28 Mar. 1969, Russian State Archive for Contemporary History, collection 5, inventory 61, folder 466, pp. 71–81.

39. E. Velichko, 'O delenii naseleniya KNDR na kategorii' [About the division of the DPRK population into multiple categories], 4 Oct. 1974, Russian State Archive for Contemporary History, collection 5, inventory 67, folder 715, pp. 95–6.

40. The stratification system based on fifty-one categories was referenced for the first time in 'Home and Abroad Correspondence', an information bulletin published by South Korean intelligence from the 1970s up to the 1990s. See *Naeoe T'ongshin chonghapp'an* [Compendium of information from the Home and Abroad Correspondence], vol. 4, Seoul: Naeoe t'ongshinsa, 1978, pp. 482–9. Numerous studies have cited it as the prevailing system in North Korea for several decades. However, available data suggest that the 'fifty-one category' system was just one of the variations of North Korea's official stratification system and that it has since been replaced by another variation.

41. Kim Sang-sŏn and Lee Sŏng-hi, *Chumin tŭngnok saŏp ch'amgosŏ* [A reference book on the registration of citizens], Pyongyang: Sahoe Anjŏnbu Ch'ulp'ansa, 1993.

42. Ibid., p. 143.

43. Ibid., p. 149.

44. Ibid., pp. 157–8.

45. Ibid., p. 145.

46. Ibid., p. 149.

47. *I kŏshi Pukhan-ida* (1978), pp. 145–6.

48. Kim Sang-sŏn and Lee Sŏng-hi, *Chumin tŭngnok saŏp ch'amgosŏ* (1993), p. 118.

49. Velichko, 'O delenii naseleniya KNDR na kategorii' (1974), pp. 95–6.

50. Ibid.

51. However, marrying someone from a different stratum could also lead to tragedy: see Chŏng Sŏ-yŏng. 'Kanbu abŏji kyŏrhon pandae pudit'in oedongttal, moksumkkaji naenok'o' [Daughter of a high-ranking official killed herself after he opposed her choice of a spouse], DailyNK, 11 Mar. 2024, https://www.dailynk.com/20240311-2/ (accessed 26 Aug. 2024).

52. For the testimony of one of those who experienced this purge, see Hwang Min-yu, *Panyŏkcha-ŭi ttang* [Land of the traitor], Seoul: Samkwa kkum, 2002, p. 2.

53. 'Iz dnevnika Kapustina D.T. Informatsiya o poseschenii goroda Vonsana' [From the diary of D.T. Kapustin: An information record on the visit to the city of Wonsan], 21 July 1969, Russian State Archive for Contemporary History, collection 5, inventory 61, folder 463, pp. 182–8; L. Volkova, 'Zapis' besedy s grazhdankoy SSSR, postoyanno prozhivayuschey v KNDR, Ti Yekaterinoy' [Record of conversation with

Yekaterina Ti, a Soviet citizen permanently residing in the DPRK], 19 Apr. 1973, Russian State Archive for Contemporary History, collection 5, inventory 66, folder 682, pp. 81–3.

54. See Kim Dong-il and Lee T'ae-su, 'Pukhan-ŭi t'ŭksu kyoyuk kyoyuk kwajŏng-e kwanha-n t'amsaek-chŏk yŏn'gu' [Exploratory study on the curriculum of special education in North Korea], *T'ŭksu kyoyukhak yŏn'gu* [Studies of special education], 3, no. 42, 2007, pp. 149–65; Kang Ch'ang-sŏ, '[Changaein-ŭi nal]: "Changaein-dŭrŭn P'yŏngyang-e sal su ŏpsŏyo"' [[The day of the disabled]: 'Invalids cannot live in Pyongyang'], DailyNK, 20 Apr. 2005, https://www.dailynk.com/%5B%EC%9E%A5%EC%95%A0%EC%9D%B8%EC%9D%98%EB%82%A0%5D%EC%9E%A5%EC%95%A0%EC%9D%B8%EB%93%A4%EC%9D%80-%ED%8F%89%EC%96%91%EC%97%90-%EC%82%B4/ (accessed 22 Sept. 2023).

55. Kim Dŏk-hong, 'Pukhanŭi taehak ip'aksaeng sŏnbal mit taehak chorŏpsaeng paech'i shisŭt'em' [How they select students and assign jobs in North Korea], in *Nanŭn chayujuŭijaida* [I am a liberal], Seoul: Chipsajae, 2015, p. 60.

56. Kim Il-sŏng [Kim Il-sung], 'Inmin saenghwar-ŭl ch'aegim chigo tolbo-lte taehayŏ' [On the responsibility and care for people's lives], in *Kim Il-sŏng chŏnjip*, vol. 61 (2005), pp. 407–31; Kim Il-sŏng [Kim Il-sung], 'Inmin chŏnggwŏn kigwan ilkun-dŭr-ŭi yŏkhar-ŭl tŏuk nop'i-lte taehayŏ' [On making the role of people working in People's Committees even more important], in *Kim Il-sŏng chŏnjip*, vol. 66 (2006), pp. 504–28.

57. Lankov, *KNDR vchera i segodnya* (2004), p. 307.

58. 'Pukhan "sae sedae", chŏhang ŭishik itchiman ch'ulse wihan iptang wŏnhae' [The new generation in North Korea has a spirit of resistance but still wants to join the party for career purposes], VOA Korea, 16 Dec. 2014, https://www.voakorea.com/a/2559175.html (accessed 26 Aug. 2024). This material is based on an interview with Ch'oe Bong-dae, a leading specialist on daily life in North Korea.

59. 'Chosŏn Minjudang che6ch'a taehoe kaemak' [The opening session of the Sixth Congress of the Democratic Party of Korea], *Rodong Shinmun*, 29 Jan. 1981, pp. 2–3.

60. Multiple testimonies on this exist. See, for example, Volkova, 'Zapis' besedy', 19 Apr. 1973, pp. 81–3; 'Otdel TsK KPSS' [To a department of the Central Committee of the CPSU], Russian State Archive for

Contemporary History, collection 5, inventory 68, folder 1866, pp. 115–21; 'O vizite v KNDR delegatsii zhurnala TsK KPSS "Partiynaya zhizn"' [On the visit of the delegation of the journal "Partiynaya zhizn"' [Life in the party] to the DPRK], Russian State Archive for Contemporary History, collection 5, inventory 68, folder 1866, pp. 132–5.

61. 'Spravka o prebyvanii v Sovetskom Soyuze turistov iz Koreyskoy Narodno-Demokraticheskoy Respubliki' [Reference letter of the visit of tourists from the DPRK to the Soviet Union], 15 Sept. 1976, Russian State Archive for Contemporary History, collection 5, inventory 69, folder 2420, pp. 96–9.

62. E. Velichko, 'O nekotoryh politicheskih nastroyeniyah trudyaschihsya KNDR' [On tendencies in some political views of the labouring people of the DPRK], 6 Dec. 1976, Russian State Archive for Contemporary History, collection 5, inventory 64, folder 2422, pp. 240–6.

63. 'Zapis' besedy s poslom Rumynii v KNDR S. Popa' [Record of conversation with S. Popa, ambassador of Romania to the DPRK], 26 June 1969, Russian State Archive for Contemporary History, collection 5, inventory 61, folder 463, pp. 178–80; 'Vyderzhki iz 'Tezisov dlya izucheniya revolyutsionnoy istorii tovarischa Kim Ir Sena.' (Izdadel'stvo TPK, 1969 god)' [Excerpts from 'Theses for studying the revolutionary history of Comrade Kim Il-sung' (WPK Publishing House, 1969)], 23 Mar. 1970, Russian State Archive for Contemporary History, collection 5, inventory 62, folder 462, pp. 47–58 (this is an inner-track document obtained by the Bulgarian embassy to the North and partially provided to the Soviets); 'Zapis' besedy s chlenom Politicheskogo Soveta TsK TPK, pervym zamestitelem Predsedatelya Soveta Ministrov KNDR Pak Sen Cherom' [Record of conversation with Pak Song-chol, a member of the Political Committee of the CC WPK and deputy premier of the DPRK], 7 Nov. 1970, Russian State Archive for Contemporary History, collection 5, inventory 62, folder 456, pp. 333–6.

64. Kong T'ak-ho, *Pukkoe chŏngch'i powibu naemak* [The North Korean puppet regime's Department for Political Protection of the State: An insider's story], Seoul: Hongwŏnsa, 1976.

65. 'Ali Lameda: A Personal Account of the Experience of a Prisoner of Conscience in the Democratic People's Republic of Korea', Amnesty International, 1 Jan. 1979, https://www.amnesty.org/en/documents/ASA24/002/1979/en/ (accessed 22 Sept. 2023); 'Alí Lameda, tortura

terrible' [Ali Lameda, horrible torture], http://elestimulo.com/climax/
ali-lameda-tortura-terrible/ (accessed 22 Sept. 2023).

66. Amnesty International, 'Ali Lameda ...' (1979).

67. Kim Il-sung assumed the position of president when he imposed a new
    constitution on the country in late Dec. 1972. Before that, his state
    position was that of premier. One of the reasons for the change is likely
    that the previous constitution did not explicitly specify the position
    of the head of the state, which Kim Il-sung wanted to occupy. From
    1968, the DPRK also started to refer to him as 'the head of state of the
    Democratic People's Republic of Korea', and as time went by, this title
    became ever more frequent, until in 1972 the constitution was rectified
    to explicitly grant him that position.

68. This quote and those below come from the parts of the code that were
    stolen by South Korean intelligence and from North Korean books
    published in the 1980s, when the DPRK became less closed. See Kim
    Il-su, 'Ku Soryŏn hyŏngbŏb-i Pukhan hyŏngbŏb-ŭi pyŏnhwae mich'in
    yŏnghyang' [Role of the Soviet Criminal Code in the changes of the
    North Korean Criminal Code], Pukhan pŏmnyul haengjŏng nonjip
    [Papers on North Korean laws and administration], 9, Sept. 1992, pp.
    259–300. Parts of the code acquired by South Korean intelligence are
    also available in Pŏmmubu [Ministry of Justice], 'Chosŏn Minjujuŭi
    Inmin Konghwaguk hyŏngbŏp kakch'ik (1974nyŏn kaejŏng)' [Parts
    of the Criminal Code of the DPRK (1974 revision)], in Pukhan pŏb-
    ŭi ch'egye-jŏk koch'al [Systematic review of North Korean laws], vol. 2,
    Seoul: Ch'angshinsa, 1993, pp. 876–97.

69. Kim Il-su, 'Ku Soryŏn ...' (1992), pp. 259–300; Pŏmmubu, 'Chosŏn
    Minjujuŭi ...' (1993), pp. 876–97.

70. There are two versions of Kang Chol-hwan's memoirs. The first was
    published in French in co-authorship with French human rights activist
    Pierre Rigoulot: Kang Chol-hwan and Pierre Rigoulot, Les aquariums
    de Pyongyang [Aquariums of Pyongyang], Paris: Robert Laffont, 2000
    (for the English translation, see Kang Chol-hwan and Pierre Rigoulot,
    The Aquariums of Pyongyang (New York: The Perseus Press, 2001)). The
    book narrates the story of Kang's family, his life in the North including
    his years of imprisonment and his escape to South Korea. His Korean
    memoirs focus on his years in the Yodok camp and are written in a more

personal style: Kang Ch'ŏl-hwan [Kang Chol-hwan], *Suyongso-ŭi norae* [Song of the concentration camp], Seoul: Shidae chŏngshin, 2005.

71. An Myŏng-ch'ŏl [An Myong-chol], *Kŭ-dŭr-i ulgo itta* [They are crying], Seoul: Ch'ŏnji midiŏ, 1995; An Myŏng-ch'ŏl [An Myong-chol], *Wanjŏn t'ongje kuyŏk* [Total control zone], Seoul: Shidae chŏngshin, 2007. It is a pity that An's books, which are unique (both in terms of our knowledge of North Korea and of totalitarian states in general) in providing the testimony of a concentration camp guard, are not very well known.

13. HEIR TO THE GENERAL SECRETARY

1. 'Zhongguo Gongchandang zhangcheng' [Constitution of the Communist Party of China], http://cpc.people.com.cn/GB/64162/64168/64561/4429444.html (accessed 22 Sept. 2023).

2. Lee Jong-sŏk, *Pukhan-Chungguk kwan'gye 1945–2000* [Sino-North Korean relations, 1945–2000], Seoul: Chungshim, 2000, p. 252.

3. On North Korea's unpaid loans, see, for example, Kim Gwang-hyŏn, 'Oech'aeŭi nŭp'-e ppajin Pukhan kyŏngje' [North Korean economy in the swamp of foreign loans], *T'ongil Han'guk*, 46, Oct. 1987, pp. 12–13.

4. At the time of writing, the most detailed piece of research on the Kim–Brezhnev summit is I.V. Bezik, 'Sekretnaya vstrecha general'nogo sekretarya TsK KPSS L.I. Brezhneva s Kim Ir Senom vo Vladivostoke v maye 1966 goda' [A secret meeting in Vladivostok between Leonid Brezhnev, general secretary of the CPSU, and Kim Il-sung in May 1966], in *Rossiyskiy Dal'niy Vostok i integratsionnye protsessy v stranah ATR* [Russia's Far East and integration processes among Asian and Pacific countries], conference publication, n.p.: n.p., 2006, pp. 92–103.

5. 'P'ŭroret'aria tokchae-wa p'ŭroret'aria minjujuŭi-rŭl kosuhaja' [Let us adhere to proletarian dictatorship and proletarian democracy], *Rodong Shinmun*, 4 Feb. 1971, p. 1.

6. Wang Yonggui, 'Chaoxian jiyi' [Reminiscences on North Korea], *Qiaoyuan*, 160, Oct. 2013, pp. 68–9.

7. 'Chosŏn Rodongdang Chungang Wiwŏnhoe chŏnwŏnhoeŭi kyŏljŏngsŏ. Chosŏn Rodongdang che5ch'a taehoe sojib-e taehayŏ' [Decision of the plenum of the Central Committee of the WPK: On the convocation of the Fifth Congress of the WPK], *Rodong Shinmun*, 6 Dec. 1969, p. 1.

8. 'Perepiska s TsK KPSS (otchyot o poyezdke Sovetskoy Pravitel'stvennoy delegatsii na prazdnestva v Narodnuyu Koreyu i zapisi besed s Kim Ir Senom 12 i 13 sentyabrya 1968 g.)' [Correspondence with the Central Committee of the CPSU (report on the trip of the Soviet government delegation to the festivities in People's Korea and notes of conversations with Kim Il-sung on 12 and 13 Sept. 1968)], State Archive of Russian Federation, collection R-5446, folder 132, item 16, p. 18.

9. Chosŏn Chungang T'ongsin [Korean Central News Agency], 'Chusŏk-ui ch'osang hwijang' [Badges with the portrait of the president], 27 Oct. 1999, http://www.kcna.co.jp/item2/1999/9910/news10/27.htm#8 (accessed 22 Sept. 2023).

10. E. Velichko, 'O znachkah s izobrazheniyem Kim Ir Sena' [On the badges with Kim Il-sung's portrait], Oct. 1974, Russian State Archive for Contemporary History, collection 5, inventory 67, folder 720, pp. 147–8.

11. Roderick MacFarquhar and John K. Fairbank, *The Cambridge History of China*, vol. 15, Cambridge: Cambridge University Press, 1991, pp. 323–5.

12. Boris Solomatin, 'TsK KPSS' [To the Central Committee of the CPSU], 12 Feb. 1969, Russian State Archive for Contemporary History, collection 5, inventory 61, folder 462, pp. 7–9. Solomatin at the time occupied the position of the deputy director of the KGB—the First Main Department of the Committee for State Security.

13. Ibid.

14. 'Suryŏngnim-ŭi kangnyŏkchŏng kyoshi-rŭl nop'i pattŭlgo nyŏsŏng hyŏngmyŏnghwa-rŭl tŏuk ch'okchinha-myŏ hyŏngmyŏng-ŭi chŏn'gukchŏng sŭngni-wa sahoejuhŭi-ŭi wanjŏn sŭngni-rŭl wihayŏ himch'age chŏnjinha-ja!' [Let us uphold the powerful teaching of the Leader, expedite the revolutionisation of the women and advance forcefully towards the victory of the revolution in the entire country and the complete victory of socialism!], *Rodong Shinmun*, 11 Oct. 1971, p. 1.

15. Solomatin, 'TsK KPSS' (1969), pp. 7–9.

16. Since the rise of the Singular Thought System, North Korea has developed a tradition where individuals receive gifts from the state, which are officially considered to be given by the Great Leader himself. These range from candies to expensive home appliances. There are quite a few occasions when people receive them, the major one being Kim Il-sung's birthday.

17. Solomatin, 'TsK KPSS' (1969), pp. 7–9.
18. This Kim Jong-suk is a namesake of Kim Il-sung's second wife. She was granted permission to keep her name as she was a close relative of the Great Leader, even though other namesakes of the ruling family had to change theirs.
19. Solomatin, 'TsK KPSS' (1969), pp. 7–9.
20. This was testified by Mitov, a high-ranking Bulgarian diplomat. Mitov studied together with Kim Jong-il. See 'Kratkiye zapisi besed s poslami sotsialisticheskih stran, akkreditovannyh v KNDR' [Short records of talks with ambassadors of socialist nations accredited to the DPRK], Russian State Archive for Contemporary History, collection 5, inventory 67, folder 721, pp. 117–21.
21. V. Nemchinov, 'Zapis' besedy s vremennym poverennym v delah SRR I. Urianom i 2-m sekretaryom posol'stva D. Byodeke' [Record of conversation with *chargé d'affaires* of the Socialist Republic of Romania I. Urian and D. Bedeke, the second secretary of the embassy], 20 July 1969, Russian State Archive for Contemporary History, collection 5, inventory 61, folder 462, pp. 153–7.
22. Solomatin, 'TsK KPSS' (1969), pp. 7–9.
23. 'Sesŭp chedo' [System of hereditary succession], in *Chŏngch'i yongŏ sajŏn* [Dictionary of political terms], Pyongyang: Sahoe kwahak ch'ulp'ansa, 1970, pp. 414–15.
24. The document can be seen in the 2004 DPRK documentary *The 1970s, the Age of Great Changeover* (*Widaehan chŏnhwanŭi 1970nyŏndae*).
25. For one of many contemporary South Korean reports on it, see 'Nambuk Kongdong Sŏngmyŏng chŏnmun' [Full text of the Joint North–South Declaration], *Maeil Kyŏngje Shinmun*, 4 July 1974, p. 1.
26. The DPRK claims that both the 1972 constitution and its revised version of 1992 were entirely written by Kim Il-sung and are duly included in his collections of works. Kim Il-sŏng [Kim Il-sung], 'Chosŏn Minjujuŭi Inmin Konghwaguk sahoejuŭi hŏnbŏp' [Socialist constitution of the DPRK], in *Kim Il-sŏng chŏjakchip*, vol. 27 (1984), pp. 625–49; Kim Il-sŏng [Kim Il-sung], 'Chosŏn Minjujuŭi Inmin Konghwaguk sahoejuŭi hŏnbŏp' [Socialist sonstitution of the DPRK], in *Kim Il-sŏng chŏnjip*, vol. 43 (1996), pp. 312–41.
27. 'Inmin-ŭi taham ŏmnŭn ch'ingsong-ŭl pad-ŭshimyŏ' [He received constant praise from the people], in 'Uri minjok kangdang' [Auditorium

for our nation], http://ournation-school.com/process/download.php?
menu=lecture&id=361 (accessed 22 Sept. 2023).

28. 'Kim Sŏng-ae tongji-kkesŏ kakkŭp nyŏmaeng tanch'e-dŭrŭi saŏb-
    ŭl chidoha-shiyŏtta' [Comrade Kim Song-ae provided guidance to
    organisations of the Union of Democratic Women of multiple levels],
    Chosŏn Nyŏsŏng, May 1971, pp. 26–33.

29. 'Widaehan suryŏng Kim Il-sŏng tongjiŭi turi-e kutke mungch'in uri
    inmin-ŭi pulp'aeŭi t'ongil tan'gyŏl manse! Chŏnch'e sŏn'gŏja-dŭrŭi
    100%ga t'up'yo-e ch'amga chŏnch'e sŏn'gŏja-dŭrŭi 100%ga ch'ansŏng
    t'up'yo. Ch'oego Inmin Hoeŭi mit chibang kakkŭp Inminhoe-ŭi taeŭiwŏn
    sŏn'gŏ sŭngnijŏk-ŭro chinhaeng. Chungang Sŏnggŏ Wiwŏnhoe podo'
    [Glory to the invincible unity and solidarity of our people, united around
    the Great Leader Comrade Kim Il-sung! One hundred per cent of the
    voters participated and 100 per cent of them voted in support of the
    candidates: The elections to the Supreme People's Assembly and to the
    local People's Assemblies of various levels have proceeded victoriously;
    The Central Electoral Commission reports], *Rodong Shinmun*, 14 Dec.
    1972, p. 1.

30. The number '216' was used to signify a link to Kim as early as 1970. See
    Hwang Jang-yŏp, *Na-nŭn yŏksa-ŭi chilli-rŭl po-atta* [I saw the truth of
    the history], Seoul: Hanul, 1999, p. 239.

31. Author's interview with An Chan-il, July 2018, Seoul.

32. *Chŏngch'i sajŏn* [Political dictionary], Pyongyang: Sahoe kwahak
    ch'ulp'ansa, 1973.

33. A. Putivets, 'Zapis' besedy s pervym sekretaryom posol'stva SRR v
    KNDR Aurelio Lazerom' [Record of conversation with Aurelio Lazăr,
    the first secretary of the embassy of the Socialist Republic of Romania
    to the DPRK], 22 Sept. 1973, Russian State Archive for Contemporary
    History, collection 5, inventory 66, folder 682, p. 185; O. Chukanov,
    'Spravka k dokumentu № 33047 ot 27 sentyabrya 1973 g.' [Reference
    letter to the document no. 33047 from 27 Sept. 1973], 18 Feb. 1974,
    Russian State Archive for Contemporary History, collection 5, inventory
    66, folder 682, p. 186.

34. B.K. Pimenov, 'Zapis' besedy s sovetnikom posol'stva NRB v KNDR A.
    Apostolovym' [Record of conversation with A. Apostolov, a counsellor of
    the People's Republic of Bulgaria to the DPRK], 25 Feb. 1976, Russian

State Archive for Contemporary History, collection 5, inventory 69, folder 2428, pp. 20–1.

35. 'Chosŏn Rodongdang Chungang Wiwŏnhoe, Chosŏn Rodongdang Chungang Kunsa Wiwŏnhoe, Chosŏn Minjujuŭi Inmin Konghwaguk Kukpang Wiwŏnhoe-esŏ' [From the Central Committee of the Workers' Party of Korea, the Central Military Commission of the Workers' Party of Korea and the National Defence Commission of the Democratic People's Republic of Korea], *Rodong Shinmun*, 26 Feb. 1996, p. 1.

36. 'Chŏngnyŏng: Kim Yŏng-ju tongji-rŭl Chosŏn Minjujuŭi Inmin Konghwaguk Chŏngmuwŏn Puch'ongni-ro immyŏng-hame taehayŏ' [Ordinance: On the appointment of Comrade Kim Yong-ju to the position of deputy prime minister of the Administrative Council], *Rodong Shinmun*, 16 Feb. 1974, p. 1.

37. The concept of 'tracks' in North Korean propaganda was coined by an American scholar, Brian Myers. Myers suggests that the DPRK's official publications fall into one of three categories: 'inner track', solely for domestic audiences; 'export track', solely for foreign audiences; and 'outer track' for both.

38. The first mention of this sobriquet came just after Kim Jong-il's appointment on 14 Feb. 1974. 'Widaehan suryŏngnim-ŭi purŭshim-gwa tang chungang-ŭi hosor-ŭl pattŭl-go, chŏndang, chŏn'gun, chŏnmin-i sahoejuŭi taegŏnsŏl saŏb-e ch'ongdongwŏn toe-ja!' [Entire party, entire army and the entire people—answering the call of the Great Leader and of the Party Central, let us fully mobilise for the great socialist construction!], *Rodong Shinmun*, 14 Feb. 1974, p. 2.

39. 'Nam tarŭn kyŏmhŏsŏng' [Extraordinary modesty], Uri minjok kangdang [Auditorium for our nation], https://www.joongang.co.kr/article/22573872 (accessed 22 Sept. 2023).

40. Occasionally, it seems this term meant not just Kim Jong-il but also the inner circle of his advisors. See E. Krasnov, 'Otdel TsK KPSS' [To a department of the Central Committee of the CPSU], Russian State Archive for Contemporary History, collection 5, inventory 68, folder 1866, pp. 115–21.

41. 'Dorogomu rukovoditelyu tovarischu Kim Den Iru' [To Dear Leader Comrade Kim Jong-il], Russian State Archive for Contemporary History, collection 5, inventory 68, folder 1863, pp. 11–12. This document is a Russian translation of an article from a newspaper, which was obtained

by the Soviet embassy, of the Kim Chaek steel factory in Chongjin. The original's publication date is 1 Jan. 1975. See also 'Ch'inaeha-nǔn chidoja tongji-rǔl urǒrǒ tǔrinǔn ch'ungsǒng-ǔi norae' [Song of loyalty presented to Comrade Dear Leader whom we revere], *Chosǒn Inmin'gun*, 16 Feb. 1975, p. 5.

42. 'Che 5 chang: Chǒn'gunjuch'esasanghwaǔi kich'i nop'i tǔshigo' [Chapter 5: He hoisted high the banner of transforming the entire army with Juche ideas], in *Uri Minjok kkiri* [Our nation and no one else], 2006, https://web.archive.org/web/20170928143810/http://www.uriminzokkiri.com/index.php?ptype=book&no=2372&pn=7 (accessed 22 Sept. 2023).

43. 'Iz dnevnika Igerbayeva A.T. Zapis' besed s inostrannymi diplomatami, akkreditovannymi v Phen'yane' [From the diary of A.T. Igerbayev: Records of talks with foreign diplomats stationed in Pyongyang], Sept. 1974, Russian State Archive for Contemporary History, collection 5, inventory 67, folder 421, pp. 222–3.

44. 'Kim Jǒng-il saengil ch'uk'a Choch'ongyǒn chip'oe yǒrǒ' [Association of the North Korean Citizens in Japan held a rally to celebrate Kim Jong-il's birthday], *Tonga Ilbo*, 20 Feb. 1976, p. 1.

45. 'Nuri-e sosa pinna-nǔn Chǒng-il-bong-e kittǔ-n sayǒn' [Memorable story of the Jong-il Peak, which shines to the entire world], in *Uri Minjok kkiri* [Our nation and no one else], 16 Feb. 2015, http://uriminzokkiri.com/m/index.php?ptype=urigisa&categ=36&no=90738 (accessed 22 Sept. 2023).

46. 'Chǒng-il-bong-ǔn kohyang chib-esǒ 216m ... shinbisǔrǒwǒ' [The Jong-il Peak is located 216 metres from the house he was born in: How mysterious!]. DailyNK, 16 Feb. 2011, https://www.dailynk.com/%EC%A0%95%EC%9D%BC%EB%B4%89%EC%9D%80-%EA%B3%A0%ED%96%A5%EC%A7%91%EC%97%90%EC%84%9C-216m%EC%8B%A0%EB%B9%84%EC%8A%A4%EB%9F%AC%EC%9B%8C/ (accessed 22 Sept. 2023).

47. 'Ch'ǒnha cheil Chǒng-il-bong' [Jong-il Peak, the first in the universe], in *Uri Minjok kkiri* [Our nation and no one else], 26 Feb. 2017, http://www.uriminzokkiri.com/index.php?ptype=igisa2&no=124862 (accessed 22 Sept. 2023).

48. 'Zapis' besedy s prem'yerom Administrativnogo Soveta Kim Irom' [Record of conversation with Kim Il, the prime minister of the Administrative

Council], 11 May 1973, Russian State Archive for Contemporary History, collection 5, inventory 66, folder 682, pp. 133–4.

49. Lao Xiong, 'Jiemi Zhongguo yuanjian Pingrang ditie: zhen-de silehen duo gongren? Baisong lehen duo lieche ma?' [Demystifying China's aid to build the Pyongyang Metro: Did a lot of workers die? Did we send a lot of trains?], Read01, 4 May 2018, https://read01.com/J0Geg3d.html (accessed 26 Aug. 2024).

50. 'Widaehan suryŏng-nim-ŭi taehae kat'ŭn ŭndŏk kirigiri noraehari. Ryŏksa-e kiri pinnal Rodongdang shidae-ŭi kinyŏmbijŏkch'angjomul widaehan suryŏng Kim Il-sŏng tongjiŭi ch'amsŏk-ae P'yŏngyang chihach'ŏlto kaet'ongshig-i sŏngdaehi chinhaengdoeyŏtta' [O, sing forever on the Great Leader's grace, the one that is like the great sun! With the Great Leader Comrade Kim Il-sung present, an opening ceremony for the Pyongyang Underground Railway—the memorial, which will illuminate the history of the age of the Workers' Party—was solemnly held], Rodong Shinmun, 6 Sept. 1973, p. 1.

51. The abolition of taxes had already been stipulated in the 1972 constitution (article 33) and was ordered to be implemented at the same plenum that anointed Kim Jong-il as the successor to his father; it was eventually put into motion in Mar. 1974. See 'Segŭm chedorŭl wanjŏnhi ŏpsaelte taehayŏ' [On the complete abolition of the tax system], Rodong Shinmun, 22 Mar. 1974, p. 1.

52. Peter Ward, 'The Biggest Tax Cuts in North Korean History', NK News, 7 May 2018, https://www.nknews.org/2018/05/the-biggest-tax-cuts-in-north-korean-history/ (accessed 22 Sept. 2023).

53. Lee Ka-yŏng, 'Mun Jae-in Taet'ongnyŏng-gwa P'anmunjŏm-ŭi kwagŏ inyŏn "tokki manhaeng sagŏn"' [President Moon Jae-in and his relation to the Panmunjom 'axe murder incident' from the past], Chungang Ilbo, 27 Apr. 2018, https://news.joins.com/article/22573872 (accessed 1 Oct. 2020).

54. 'Chosŏn Inmin'gun ch'oego saryŏngbu-ŭi podo: Chosŏn Inmin'gun ch'oegosaryŏnggwan inmin'gun chŏnch'e pudaedŭl-gwa Ronong chŏgwidae, Pulgŭn ch'ŏngnyŏn kŭnwidae chŏnch'e taewŏn-dŭrege chŏnt'u t'aese-e tŭrŏga-lte taehan myŏngnyŏng hadal' [Announcement from the Supreme Command of the Korean People's Army: The supreme commander of the KPA has passed an order on the moving to the state of war readiness to personnel of all the units, of Corps of Workers or

the Farmers' Red Guards, and of the Young Red Guard Corps], *Chosŏn Inmin'gun*, 20 Aug. 1976, p. 1.

55. Richard A. Mobley, *Flash Point North Korea: The Pueblo and EC-121 Crises*, Annapolis: Naval Institute Press, 2003, p. 153.

56. South Korean KBS film *Kabong-ŭi Ponggo taet'ongnyŏng, kŭnŭn wae Han'guk ch'oegoŭi kukpin-i toeŏnna* [Why Gabon's President Bongo was received in South Korea with highest honours], broadcast on 7 June 2003, is an excellent portrayal of South Korea–Gabonese relations and of Seoul's policy towards Africa in general.

57. See Abiodun Alao, *Mugabe and the Politics of Security in Zimbabwe*, Montreal: McGill–Queen's University Press, 2012, pp. 42–4.

58. V. Volkov, 'O publikatsiyah za rubezhom statey i rechey Kim Ir Sena' [On the publications of Kim Il-sung's articles and speeches abroad], 14 Feb. 1972, Russian State Archive for Contemporary History, collection 5, inventory 64, folder 419, pp. 24–7.

59. *Inmin-dŭl sogesŏ* [Among the people], vol. 13, Tokyo: Kuwŏl sŏbang, 1977, front page.

60. O T'ae-sŏk, Paek Pong and Ri Sang-gyu, *Ŭnhyeroun t'aeyang* [Merciful sun], vol. 3, Tokyo: Inmin kwahaksa, 1977, p. 282.

61. Author's interview with An Chan-il, July 2018. An was a senior sergeant in the KPA until he fled to the South on 27 July 1979.

62. Author's interview with Adrian Buzo, April 2018.

63. Hungarian embassy in the DPRK, 'Celebration of Kim Jong Il's Birthday', 24 Feb. 1978, http://digitalarchive.wilsoncenter.org/document/116008 (accessed 22 Sept. 2023).

64. The above-mentioned An Chan-il fled the North on 27 July 1979. At that time, the campaign calling on North Koreans to praise Kim Jong-il was still suspended. However, on 29 July, at least one newspaper started hailing Kim Jong-il once again, showing that his promotion was back on track. 'Ch'inaehanŭn chidoja tongji-ŭi malssŭm-ŭl ch'ŏlchŏhi kwanch'ŏrha-ja' [Let us thoroughly carry out what the Dear Leader said], *Chosŏn Inmin'gun*, 29 July 1979, p. 5.

65. Ibid., p. 5.

66. See, for example, 'Yŏnggwangsŭrŏun Kim Il-sŏng-juŭi uri choguk Chosŏn Minjujuŭi Inmin Konghwaguk Ch'anggŏn 31tol manse! "Uri tang-gwa uri inmin-ŭi kyŏngae-hanŭn suryŏng Kim Il-sŏng wŏnsunim-kkewa ch'inaeha-nŭn chidoja Kim Jŏng-il tongji-kke tŭri-

nŭn ch'ungsŏng-ŭi norae moim' charyo'" [Praise to the thirty-first anniversary of our glorious Kim Il-sungist Fatherland—the Democratic People's Republic of Korea! Materials of 'meetings to sing the songs of loyalty to the Respected and Beloved Leader Marshal Kim Il-sung and to the Dear Leader Comrade Kim Jong-il'], *Chosŏn Inmin'gun*, 15 Aug. 1979, p. 6.

67. On Park's assassination, see Cho Gap-che, *Pak Chŏng-hŭi-ŭi majimak haru* [The last day of Park Chung-hee], Seoul: Wŏlgan Chosŏnsa, 2005.

68. 'Chosŏn Rodongdang Chungang Wiwŏnhoe chŏnwŏnhoeŭi kyŏljŏngsŏ' [Decision of the plenum of the WPK's Central Committee], *Rodong Shinmun*, 13 Dec. 1979, p. 1.

69. 'Pukkoe Cheneba taesa Kim Il-sŏng-ŭi hugyeja-ro Kim Jŏng-il 5nyŏn chŏn kyŏljŏng' [The North Korean puppet regime's ambassador to Geneva: It has been five years since it was decided that Kim Jong-il would be Kim Il-sung's successor], *Kyŏnghyang Shinmun*, 9 Oct. 1980, p. 1.

70. 'Chosŏn Rodongdang Chungang Wiwŏnhoe Che6ki Che1ch'a Chŏnwŏn hoee kwanhan kongbo' [Press release on the meeting of the first plenum of the Sixth Central Committee of the WPK], *Rodong Shinmun*, 15 Oct. 1980, p. 1.

71. 'Chosŏn Rodongdang Che6ch'a Taehoe kaemak' [The Sixth Congress of the WPK has started], *Rodong Shinmun*, 13 Dec. 1979, pp. 2, 15.

72. According to the *Grand Encyclopaedia of North Korean Terminology*, published by the South Korean Civil Counterintelligence Research Centre in 1976, in 1974 the DPRK conducted a campaign of sending Kim Jong-il congratulatory letters on the occasion of his thirty-third birthday. Thus, as of 1974, the heir was still officially considered to have been born in 1941. See Kungmin pangch'ŏp yŏn'guso [Civil Counterintelligence Research Centre], 'Kim Jŏng-il t'ansaeng 33chunyŏn ch'uk'amun' [Letters to congratulate Kim Jŏng-il on his thirty-third birthday], in *Pukhan yongŏ tae paekkwa* [Grand encyclopaedia of North Korean terminology], Seoul: Kungmin pangch'ŏp yŏn'guso, 1976, p. 311. A former North Korean diplomat also told this author that Kim Jong-il's birth year had been altered from 1941 to 1942.

73. Choe Un-hui, the wife of the above-mentioned Shin Sang-ok—a South Korean film director abducted by North Korea—carried a recording device with her during their conversations with Kim Il-sung and Kim Jong-il. Kim Il-sung's dreams about the South come from one such conversation.

See 'Kim Il-sŏng·Kim Jŏng-il yuksŏng nogŭm' [Voice recordings of Kim Il-sung and Kim Jong-il], in *Pukhan, kŭ ch'unggyŏg-ŭi shilsang* [Shocking reality of North Korea], Seoul: Wŏlgan Chosŏnsa, 1991, pp. 266–81.

74. 'Pŏma, Pukkoe-wa tan'gyo·sŭngin ch'wiso' [Burma severs diplomatic relations with the North Korean puppet regime, retracts recognition], *Kyŏnghyang Shinmun*, 5 Nov. 1983, p. 1.

75. '[Ilbonin Sŭwisŭ kijaŭi Syut'aji (STASI) charyo palgul] 5myŏng samang, 29myŏng pusang-han 1986nyŏn 9wŏl 14il Kimp'o konghang t'erŏ-ŭi chinshil "Puk'an ch'ŏngbu padŭn 'Abu Nidal' chojigi chŏjillŏ"' [(Findings of a Japanese journalist in Switzerland in Stasi archives) The 14 Sept. 1986 terrorist attack on Kimpo Airport that left five dead and twenty-nine wounded was perpetrated by Abu Nidal's group sponsored by North Korea], *Wŏlgan Chosŏn*, Mar. 2009, http://monthly.chosun.com/client/news/viw.asp?ctcd=&nNewsNumb=200903100019 (accessed 22 Sept. 2023).

76. See Kim Hyŏn-hŭi, *Ije yŏja-ga toe-go ship'-ŏyo* [Now I want to become a woman], Seoul: Koryŏwŏn, 1991; Kim Hyŏn-hŭi, *Sarang-ŭl nŭkkil ttae-myŏn nunmur-ŭl hŭlli-mnida* [Every time I feel love, I cry], Seoul: Koryŏwŏn, 1992.

77. Shin Sang-ok, 'Puk nyŏk hanŭr-e ttŭiu-n yŏnghwa-ŭi kkum' [Dream of the film flying to the northern sky], in *Nan, yŏnghwa-yŏtta* [I was a film], Seoul: Random House Korea, 2007, pp. 117–40.

78. Andrei Lankov's notes about his study in the DPRK in 1984. Unpublished draft kindly provided by Andrei to this author.

79. 'Chosŏn Minjujuŭi Inmin Konghwaguk hyŏngbŏp' [Criminal Code of the DPRK], n.p.: n.p., 1987.

80. One of the best books on this era is Ezra F. Vogel, *Deng Xiaoping and the Transformation of China*, Cambridge, MA: Harvard University Press, 2011.

81. Peter Ward, 'When North Korea Almost Backed China-Style Economic Reforms', NK News, 8 Jan. 2018, https://www.nknews.org/2018/01/when-north-korea-almost-backed-china-style-economic-reforms/ (accessed 22 Sept. 2023); 'Chŏngch'i nolliro mangch'in Pukhan nongŏp' [North Korean agriculture, botched for political reasons], *Shindonga*, 7 Mar. 2005, http://shindonga.donga.com/3/all/13/101347/1 (accessed 22 Sept. 2023).

82. See, for example, Kongdan Oh and Ralph C. Hassig, *North Korea through*

the Looking Glass, Washington, DC: Brookings Institution Press, 2000, p. 35, and Lee U-hong, *Kanan-ŭi konghwaguk* [Republic of poverty], Seoul: T'ongil Ilbosa, 1990. Lee U-hong, a Japanese Korean, was a scholar of agriculture who taught at Wonsan Agricultural College in the 1980s. Together with the sister book *Ŏdum-ŭi konghwaguk* [Republic of darkness], Lee U-hong's work provides a fascinating insight into life in North Korea during the late Kim Il-sung era.

83. O Jin-yong, *Kim Il-sŏng shidae-ŭi Chung So-wa Nam Pukhan* [China, the Soviet Union and both Koreas in the Kim Il-sung era], Seoul: Nanam, 2004, p. 83. At the time of writing, Mr O's work remains by far the most detailed study of Chinese and Soviet influence on North Korea in the late Cold War era.

84. 'Chumin-dŭre taehan sangp'um konggŭp saŏb-ŭl kaesŏnha-nŭndesŏ nasŏ-nŭn myŏt kaji munje-e taehayŏ' [On some issues of improving the supply of goods to the people], in *Kim Jŏng-il sŏnjip* [Selected works of Kim Jong-il], vol. 8, Pyongyang: Chosŏn Rodongdang ch'ulp'ansa, 1998, pp. 131–44.

85. 'Pukhan-ŭi "8.3pubu"rŭl a-shinayo?' [Have you heard about '3rd of August couples'?], *Ashia Kyŏngje*, 9 Oct. 2011, https://www.asiae.co.kr/article/2011100911513462162 (accessed 22 Sept. 2023).

86. 'Chosŏn Minjujuŭi Inmin Konghwaguk habyŏngbŏp' [Joint Enterprise Law of the DPRK], Chosŏn Muyŏk [Foreign trade of the DPRK], http://www.kftrade.com.kp/index.php/law/detail/99?lang=kp (accessed 26 Aug. 2024).

87. 'Habyŏngbŏp: Paegyŏng·naeyong' [Joint Enterprise Law: Background and contents], NK Chosŏn, 25 Oct. 2013, http://nk.chosun.com/bbs/list.html?table=bbs_24&idxno=2803&page=14&total=282 (accessed 22 Sept. 2023).

88. Dmitriy Volkogonov, *Sem' vozhdey* [The seven leaders], vol. 2, Moscow: AO Izdatel'stvo 'Novosti', 1995, p. 229.

89. Zhurin, 'Sdelan v SSSR' (2011).

90. 'Iz dnevnika Sudarikova N. G. Zapis' besedy s pervym zamestitelem ministra inostrannyh del KNDR Ho Damom' [From the diary of N.G. Sudarikov: Record of conversation with the First Deputy Minister of Foreign Affairs Ho Dam], 7 Feb. 1970, Russian State Archive for Contemporary History, collection 5, inventory 62, folder 461, pp. 42–4.

91. Sŏng Hye-rang, *Tŭngnamu chip* (2000), pp. 387–90.

92. Anna Fifield, *The Great Successor: The Divinely Perfect Destiny of Brilliant Comrade Kim Jong Un*, London: Hachette UK, 2019, pp. 217–18. Hye-rim's older sister, Hye-rang, fled the country and later detailed her life in the North in her memoirs, *Wisteria House*, which were published in 2000. Sŏng Hye-rang, *Tŭngnamu chip* (2000).

93. Ha Jun-su, '[T'ŭkp'awŏn rip'ot'ŭ] Piun-ŭi Sŏng Hye-rim, myo-majŏ ŏpsŏjilkka' [Correspondent's report: Will the grave of the unfortunate Song Hye-rim vanish too?], KBS News, 17 Feb. 2017, https://news.kbs.co.kr/news/view.do?ncd=3430825 (accessed 22 Sept. 2023).

94. 'Puk Kim Jŏng-ŭn "pisŏn shilse"nŭn ibok nuna Kim Sŏl-song?' [Kim Sol-song, Kim Jong-un's half-sister: A grey eminence of North Korea?], *Tonga Ilbo*, 29 Dec. 2016, http://www.donga.com/news/article/all/20161229/82084196/2 (accessed 22 Sept. 2023).

95. At the time of writing, Anna Fifield's *Great Successor* (2019) remains the most detailed biography of Kim Jong-un.

96. 'Yesurin-dŭrege Chosŏn Minjujuŭi Inmin Konghwaguk konghun paeu ch'ingho-rŭl suyŏha-me taehayŏ' [On the bestowing of the titles of merited actors upon artists], *Rodong Shinmun*, 31 Dec. 1972, p. 1.

97. Yun Go-ŭn, 'Kim Jŏng-il puin Kim Ok sukch'ŏng·Pukhan t'erŏjo p'agyŏn' [Kim Jong-il's wife Kim Ok gets purged, North Korea dispatches terror groups], 31 July 2016, https://www.yna.co.kr/view/AKR20160730027900033 (accessed 22 Sept. 2023).

98. Chŏn Du-hwan [Chun Doo-hwan], *Hoegorok* [Memoirs], vol. 2. P'aju: Chajak namusup, 2017, pp. 451–9.

99. 'Chaehoe hyŏryuk tashi "isan"' [Reunited families become divided once again], *Maeil Kyŏngje Shinmun*, 23 Sept. 1985, p. 1.

100. Alexandre Y. Mansourov, 'Inside North Korea's Black Box: Reversing the Optics', in 'North Korean Policy Elites', Institute for Defense Analyses, June 2004, pp. IV-8–IV-9.

101. Fyodor Tertitskiy, 'When Kim Il Sung Died in 1986', NK News, 29 Aug. 2017, https://www.nknews.org/2017/08/when-kim-il-sung-died-in-1986/ (accessed 22 Sept. 2023).

102. '6·29 minjuhwa sŏnŏn' [The 29 June proclamation on democratisation], National Institute of Korean History, http://contents.history.go.kr/front/hm/view.do?treeId=020108&tabId=01&levelId=hm_151_0050 (accessed 22 Sept. 2023).

103. 'Paegyŏk pannŭn pullyŏl, p'ogap, chŏnjaeng Ollimp'ik, nop'aga-nŭn pan-

Mi, pan-koeroe t'ujaeng' [Olympic games of division, oppression and war receive rejection, struggle against America and the puppets intensifies], *Rodong Shinmun*, 16 Sept. 1986, p. 5.

104. Kim Seok-hyang and Andrei Lankov, 'Unexpected Results of a Political Pilgrimage: Yim Su-gyong's 1989 Trip to North Korea and Changes in North Koreans' Worldview', *Asian Perspective*, 40 (2016), pp. 245–70.

105. 'Iz dnevnika Georgiya Kunadze: Zapis' besedy s Chrezvychaynym i polnomochnym poslom KNDR v SSSR Son Sen Phirom' [From the diary of Georgiy Kunadze: Record of conversation with the DPRK's ambassador extraordinary and plenipotentiary Son Sŏng-p'il], 20 Sept. 1991, State Archive of the Russian Federation, collection 10026, folder 4, item 2083, pp. 1–3.

106. Even official records of the time occasionally showed Kim Il-sung behaving like a capricious old man. In one revealing incident, he issued a directive to have a bear, gifted to him by Chong Chun-sil, one of his favoured cadres, brought to his palace so that he could see the animal more often. Kim Il-sŏng [Kim Il-sung], 'Ilkun-dŭrŭn tang-gwa suryŏng-ŭl wihayŏ choguk-kwa inmin-ŭl wihayŏ ch'ungshirhi irha-yŏya handa' [Labourers must carry their duties faithfully to the party, the Leader, to the fatherland and to the people], in *Kim Il-sŏng chŏjakchip*, vol. 43 (1996), pp. 212–18.

107. Author's interview with Kim Yŏng-hwan, 4 June 2019, Seoul.

108. For one of many testimonies about this, see Kim Dŏk-hong, 'Kim Il-sŏng-ŭi mallyŏn sŭt'ori myŏtkaji' [Several stories about Kim Il-sung's final year], in *Nanŭn chayujuŭijaida* (2015), p. 245.

109. Kim Il-sŏng [Kim Il-sung], 'Kim Jŏng-il tongji t'ansaeng 50tols-e chŭŭmhayŏ' [On the occasion of the fiftieth birthday of Comrade Kim Jong-il], in *Kim Il-sŏng chŏjakchip*, vol. 43 (1996), p. 288.

110. Aleksandr Zhebin, *Evolyutsiya politicheskoy sistemy KNDR v usloviyah global'nyh peremen* [The evolution of the political system of the DPRK in the time of worldwide changes], Moscow: Russkaya panorama, 2006, pp. 61–2; Kim Dŏk-hong, 'Kim Il-sŏng-ŭi mallyŏn sŭt'ori myŏtkaji' (2015), p. 250.

111. Zhebin, *Evolyutsiya politicheskoy sistemy KNDR* ... (2006), pp. 61–2.

112. 'Kto vy, marshal Kim Ir Sen?' [Who are you, Marshal Kim Il-sung?], *Habarovskiy ekspress*, 9–15 Oct. 1993, pp. 1, 5, http://debri-dv.com/article/5000 (accessed 22 Sept. 2023).

113. Kim Ch'an-jŏng, *Pigŭg-ŭi hangil ppalch'isan* [Tragic anti-Japanese partisans], Seoul: Tonga Ilbosa, 1992, pp. 56–7.
114. Kim Il-sŏng [Kim Il-sung], *Segi-wa tŏburŏ* [With the century], Pyongyang: Chosŏn Rodongdang Ch'ulp'ansa, 1992–8.
115. *Chosŏn Rodongdang Ryŏksa* [A history of the Workers' Party of Korea], Pyongyang: Chosŏn Rodongdang Ch'ulp'ansa, 1991, p. 157.
116. *Kim Il-sŏng tongji hoegorok Segi-wa tŏburŏ* (kyesŭngbon) (1998), p. 448.
117. Ibid., p. 450.
118. Ibid., p. 451.
119. Ibid., p. 453.
120. Ibid., p. 458.
121. Ibid., p. 459.

14. THE DEAD HAND OF THE GREAT LEADER

1. On Soviet–North Korean relations regarding the nuclear issue, see James Clay Moltz and Alexandre Y. Mansourov, eds, *The North Korean Nuclear Program: Security, Strategy, and New Perspectives from Russia*, Brighton: Psychology Press, 2000.
2. The North Korean nuclear programme is arguably the most-studied topic of all related to North Korea. For a detailed timeline of events surrounding the programme, see 'Chronology of U.S.–North Korean Nuclear and Missile Diplomacy', Arms Control Association, https://www.armscontrol.org/factsheets/dprkchron?c=1526528518057 (accessed 22 Sept. 2023).
3. 'Chŏn'guk, chŏn'gun, chŏnmin-e chunjŏnshi sangt'ae-rŭl sŏnp'oham-e taehayŏ' [Announcement of the state of pre-war readiness to the entire country, entire army and entire people], *Rodong Shinmun*, 9 Mar. 1993, p. 1.
4. 'Minjog-ŭi chajugwŏn-gwa nara-ŭi ch'oego riik-ŭl suhoha-gi wihayŏ chawijŏk choch'i-rŭl sŏnp'o' [Announcement of self-defence measures to preserve the sovereign rights of the nation and maximum benefit for the country], *Rodong Shinmun*, 13 Mar. 1993, p. 1.
5. 'Kyŏngaehanŭn Ch'oego Saryŏnggwan tongji-ŭi myŏngnyŏng-ŭl nop'i pattŭlgo chŏn'gun-i mandan-ŭi chŏnt'ut'aese-rŭl katch'uja' [Let us follow the order of the Respected and Beloved Comrade Supreme

Commander and do everything we can so that the entire armed forces would be ready for battle], *Chosŏn Inmin'gun*, 9 Mar. 1993, p. 1.

6. Francis Fukuyama, *The End of History and the Last Man*, New York: Free Press, 1992.

7. Paek Myŏng-gyu, 'Powisa-e millidŏn Kim Yŏng-nyong, ŭimunŭi chugŭm' [Suspicious death of Kim Yong-nyong, a man who was outsmarted by the Security Command], DailyNK, 25 Oct. 2005, https://www.dailynk.com/%EB%B3%B4%EC%9C%84%EC%8 2%AC%EC%97%90-%EB%B0%80%EB%A6%AC%EB%8D% 98-%EA%B9%80%EC%98%81%EB%A3%A1-%EC%9 D%98%EB%AC%B8%EC%9D%98-%EC%A3%BD% EC%9D%8C/ (accessed 22 Sept. 2023). The author of this column is a former serviceman of the DPRK's secret police. This column is part of a series where Paek Myong-gyu talks about the heads of the country's state security.

8. Pak Sŏng-gil, 'Pukhan kunsak'utet'a sakŏn chonghap' [Everything about military coup attempts in North Korea], in *Pukhangun-ŭi pulp'yŏnhan chinsil* [The inconvenient truth about the North Korean army], Seoul: Hanguk kunsa munje yŏnguwŏn, 2013, pp. 246–52. Some information about the planned coup can be obtained from Kang Myŏng-do, *P'yŏngyang-ŭn mangmyŏng-ŭl kkumkkunda* [Pyongyang dreams of exile], Seoul: Chungang Ilbosa, 1995, pp. 255–72. I have heard various reports from North Korea that also seem to corroborate the story.

9. Son Wŏn-t'ae, *Naega mannan Kim Sŏng-ju Kim Il-sŏng* [Kim Song-ju aka Kim Il-sung: The man I met], Seoul: Tongyŏn ch'ulp'ansa, 2020, p. 293.

10. '7wŏl 25ir-e P'yŏngyang-sŏ chŏngsanghoedam' [The summit is to be held in Pyongyang on 25 July], *Han'gyŏre*, 29 June 1994, p. 1.

11. Chu Sŏng-ha, '1994nyŏn 7wŏl 8il, Kim Il-sŏng chonghap taekagesŏ' [Kim Il-sung University, 8 July 1994], in *Sŏur-esŏ ssŭn P'yŏngyang iyagi [Stories about Pyongyang written in Seoul]*, Seoul: Kip'iring, 2010, pp. 118–25.

12. 'Kim Il-sŏng sumjin "Hyangsan pyŏljang" ch'ŏlgŏ twaetta' [Kim Il-sung's hidden villa in Myohyang mountains was demolished], Radio Free Asia, 29 Apr. 2014, https://www.rfa.org/korean/weekly_program/radio-world/radioworld-04292014151939.html (accessed 22 Sept. 2023).

13. Chu Sŏng-ha, '1994nyŏn 7wŏl 8il ...' (2010), pp. 118–25.

14. Ibid. In the 2000s, Kim Jong-il ordered this villa to be demolished. Satellite imagery, available through Google Earth and Planet.com services, shows that while the villa was still intact in Feb. 2004, by Apr. 2010 the building was gone. The villa's coordinates were N39°58'17.27 E126°19'13.88.

15. 'Widaehan Suryŏng Kim Il-sŏng tongji sŏgŏe taehayŏ' [On the passing of the Great Leader Comrade Kim Il-sung], *Rodong Shinmun*, 9 July 1994, p. 2.

16. 'Zhongguo Gongchandang Zhongyang Weiyuanhui, Zhonghua Renmin Gongheguo Quanguo Renmin Daibiao Dahui Changwu Weiyuanhui, Zhonghua Renmin Gongheguo Guowuyuan, Zhongguo Gongchandang Zhongyang Junshi Weiyuanhui, gao quandang quanjun quanguo gezu renmin shu' [Central Committee of the Communist Party of China, Standing Committee of the National People's Congress of the People's Republic of China, State Council of the People's Republic of China, Central Military Commission of the Communist Party of China's announcement to the whole party, the whole army, the people of all nationalities], *Renmin Ribao*, 10 Sept. 1976, p. 2.

17. 'Ot Tsentral'nogo Komiteta Kommunisticheskoy Partii Sovetskogo Soyuza, Soveta ministrov Soyuza SSR i Prezidiuma Verhovnogo Soveta SSSR' [From the Central Committee of the CPSU, the Council of Ministers of the USSR and the Presidium of the Supreme Soviet of the USSR], *Pravda*, 6 Mar. 1953, p. 1.

18. Chu Sŏng-ha, '1994nyŏn 7wŏl 8il ...' (2010), pp. 118–25; Barbara Demick has also collected some fascinating stories about common people's reactions to Kim's death: see Barbara Demick, 'Twilight of the God', in *Nothing to Envy* (2009), pp. 90–102.

19. 'Widaehan Suryŏng ...' (1994), p. 2.

20. Marcus Noland, 'The North Korean Famine', in *Routledge Handbook of Modern Korean History*, ed. Michael Seth, Abingdon: Routledge, 2016, pp. 234–45.

21. 'Uri tang-gwa inmin-ŭi widaehan suryŏng Kim Il-sŏng tongji-rŭl yŏngsaeng-ŭi mosŭb-ŭro moshin "Kŭmsusan kinyŏm kungjŏn" kaegwanshik ŏmsuk'i kŏhaeng' [Holding of the solemn opening ceremony of the Kumsusan memorial palace where the visage of eternal life of Comrade Kim Il-sung—the Great Leader of our party and of our people—is venerated], *Rodong Shinmun*, 9 July 1995, p. 1.

22. I am grateful to Anastasiya Korolyova, who confirmed this after visiting the mausoleum.

23. 'Chosŏn Rodongdang Chungang Wiwŏnhoe, Chosŏn Rodongdang Chungang Kunsa Wiwŏnhoe, Chosŏn Minjujuŭi Inmin Konghwaguk Kukpang Wiwŏnhoe, Chosŏn Minjujuŭi Inmin Konghwaguk Chungang Inmin Wiwŏnhoe, Chosŏn Minjujuŭi Inmin Konghwaguk Chŏngmuwŏn. Kyŏljŏngsŏ. Widaehan Suryŏng Kim Il-sŏng tongjiŭi hyŏngmyŏng saengae-wa pulmyŏ-rŭi ŏpchŏkŭl kiri pinnaeilte taehayŏ' [The Central Committee of the Workers' Party of Korea, the Central Military Commission of the Workers' Party of Korea, the National Defence Commission of the Democratic People's Republic of Korea, the Central People's Committee of the Democratic People's Republic of Korea and the Administrative Council of the Democratic People's Republic of Korea. Decision: On the long-time glorification of the life and immortal achievements of the Great Leader Comrade Kim Il-sung], *Rodong Shinmun*, 10 July 1997, p. 1.

24. 'Chuch'e nyŏnho-wa tŏburŏ Kim Il-sŏng Chosŏn-ŭn yŏngwŏnhi pinna-rira' [Kim Il-sung's Korea will forever shine together with the Juche calendar], *Rodong Shinmun*, 9 Sept. 1997, p. 2.

25. 'Widaehan Ryŏngdoja Kim Jŏng-il tongji-ŭi Kukka Chusŏk ch'udae chiji hwanyŏng mit Chosŏn Minjujuŭi Inmin Konghwaguk ch'anggŏn 50tol kyŏngch'uk chunbi Wiwŏnhoe kyŏlsŏng moim (yŏrŏ nara-esŏ chinhaeng)' [Meeting to support the veneration of the Great Chief Comrade Kim Jong-il as president of the republic and to prepare for the celebration of the fiftieth anniversary of the DPRK (held in various countries)], *Rodong Shinmun*, 11 Aug. 1998, p. 1.

26. 'Widaehan Suryŏng Kim Il-sŏng tongji-rŭl uri Konghwagug-ŭi Yŏngwŏnha-n Chusŏk-ŭro nop'i moshi-ja' [Let us forever venerate the Great Leader Comrade Kim Il-sung as the president of the republic], 11 and 19 July 1994, in *Kim Jŏng-il sŏnjip (chŭngbop'an)* [Selected works of Kim Jong-il (revised edition)], vol. 18, Pyongyang: Chosŏn Rodongdang ch'ulp'ansa, 2012, pp. 1–8. The two dates are given in the original, and it is unclear which one of these is correct. Given that in this speech Kim Jong-il declines to take the position of president of the DPRK and that North Korea had a campaign among its foreign supporters calling for him to accept the presidency as late as 1997, it is likely that both dates are wrong.

27. 'Konghwagug-ŭi Yŏngwŏnhan Chusŏk' [Eternal President of the Republic], *Rodong Shinmun*, 9 Oct. 1998, p. 1.

15. KIM IL-SUNG'S LEGACY

1. Komi Yoji [Gomi Yoji], *Annyŏnghaseyo, Kim Jŏng-nam-imnida* [Hello, my name is Kim Jong-nam], trans. Lee Yong-t'aek, Seoul: Chungang M&B, 2012, p. 67.

2. The first report on this appeared in the South Korean press about a week after it happened. See 'Kim Jŏng-il, 3nam Chŏng-un hugyeja chimyŏngsŏl' [There are rumours that Kim Jong-il appointed his third son Jong-un as his successor], NK Chosŏn, 16 Jan. 2009, http://nk.chosun.com/bbs/list. html?table=bbs_16&idxno=1993&page=84&total=3090&sc_area=&sc_ word= (accessed 22 Sept. 2023).

3. Author's interview with a former North Korean police officer, 6 Oct. 2023 (Seoul).

4. For more information on this, see Han Gi-bŏm, *Pukhan-ŭi kyŏngje kaehyŏk-kwa kwallyo chŏngch'i* [North Korea's economic reforms and bureaucratic politics], Seoul: Pukhan yŏn'guso, 2019.

5. By far the best research on the North Korean economy of the 2010s is Lee Sŏk-ki et al., *Kim Jŏng-ŭn shidae Pukhan kyŏngje kaehyŏk yŏn'gu: Urishik kyŏngje kwalli pangbŏb-ŭl chungshimŭro* [Economic reforms in North Korea of Kim Jong-un's era: Focusing on the 'our style method of administration'], Korea Institute for Industrial Economics and Trade, 2018, https://kdevelopedia.org/asset/99202104130160479/1618298659650.pdf (accessed 22 Sept. 2023).

6. Written by one of the deputy directors of the South Korean National Intelligence Service, Han Gi-bŏm's *Pukhan-ŭi kyŏngje kaehyŏk-kwa kwallyo chŏngch'i* [North Korean economic reforms and policy towards the bureaucracy], Seoul: Pukhan yŏn'guso, 2019, which is based on a large number of classified South Korean sources obtained by Seoul, is one of the best works on the post-famine economy of North Korea.

7. *Chosŏn Rodongdang Ryŏksa* [A history of the Workers' Party of Korea], vol. 1, Pyongyang: Chosŏn Rodongdang ch'ulp'ansa, 2017.

8. Kim Jŏng-il [Kim Jong-il], 'Orhae-rŭl kangsŏngtaeguk kŏnsŏr-ŭi widaehan chŏnhwan-ŭi hae-ro pinnaeija' [Let us illuminate this year as the year of the great breakthrough in the construction of the strong

and prosperous nation], 1 Jan. 1999, in *Kim Jŏng-il sŏnjip chŭngbop'an* [Selected works of Kim Jong-il: Extended edition], vol. 14, Pyongyang: Chosŏn Rodongdang ch'ulp'ansa, 2012, pp. 443–55. The quote can be found on page 449.

9. Ko Jae-hong, 'Pukhan'gun pongmu kigan-ŭi pyŏnhwa-wa hyanghu chŏnmang' [Changes and future perspectives in a term of conscription in North Korea], Institute for National Security Strategy, 2018, p. 9, https://www.inss.re.kr/common/viewer.do?atchFileId=F77523&fileSn=0 (accessed 22 Sept. 2023); Fyodor Tertitskiy, *The North Korean Army: History, Structure, Daily Life*, Abingdon: Routledge, 2022, pp. 32–3.

INDEX

Abe Nobuyuki, 49
Abu Nidal, 200
Adored Leader, 191–2, 195
Africa, 197
Agitation and Propaganda
  Department, 191, 193
agriculture, 64–5, 150, 202–3, 221,
  229
Albania, 220
Alia, Ramiz, 220
American-occupied Korea
  (1945–8), 41–2, 43, 50, 63, 73,
  76, 90
  border tensions, 81–2
  Communist Party in, 55, 59
  elections (1948), 83–4
  flag, 82, 84
  industry in, 73
  landlords in, 73
  Moscow Conference (1945),
    66–7, 68
  SPA elections (1948), 85
  unified Korea prospects, 51,
    56, 59, 67, 75–7, 82

Amnesty International, 184
An Chan-il, 197
An Kil, 28
An Myong-chol, 185
Andong, Manchuria, 44
Andropov, Yuri, 204
Antu, Fengtian, 18–20, 21
Apanasenko, Iosif, 31–2, 33
Apollo 11 mission (1969), 177
Armstrong, Neil, 177
Army of the World Fire, 17
Asahi Shimbun, 176
Association of North Korean
  Citizens in Japan (ANKCJ),
  115–16, 169, 197, 204
atheism, 74
Attlee, Clement, 223
August 3rd movement (1984), 203
August faction incident (1956),
  127–33, 135, 138, 140
Aung San, 200
Austria, 50
Autumn Eve, 45
axe murder incident (1976), 196

349

INDEX

INDEX

INDEX

INDEX

INDEX

INDEX